Web Application Architecture

Principles, Protocols and Practices

Second Edition

Leon Shklar and Rich Rosen

A John Wiley and Sons, Ltd., Publication

Other Wiley Editorial Offices

John Wiley & Sons Inc., 111 River Street, Hoboken, NJ 07030, USA

Jossey-Bass, 989 Market Street, San Francisco, CA 94103-1741, USA

Wiley-VCH Verlag GmbH, Boschstr. 12, D-69469 Weinheim, Germany

John Wiley & Sons Australia Ltd, 42 McDougall Street, Milton, Queensland 4064, Australia

John Wiley & Sons (Asia) Pte Ltd, 2 Clementi Loop #02-01, Jin Xing Distripark, Singapore 129809

John Wiley & Sons Canada Ltd, 6045 Freemont Blvd, Mississauga, Ontario, L5R 4J3, Canada

Wiley also publishes its books in a variety of electronic formats. Some content that appears
in print may not be available in electronic books.

Library of Congress Cataloging-in-Publication Data

Shklar, Leon
  Web application architecture : principles, protocols, and practices / Leon Shklar and Rich Rosen. – 2nd ed.
    p. cm.
  Includes bibliographical references and index.
  ISBN 978-0-470-51860-1 (pbk.)
  1. Web site development. 2. Application software–Development. 3. Web sites–Design. 4. Software architecture.
I. Rosen, Rich. II. Title.
  TK5105.888.S492 2009
  005.1'2–dc22

                                                                                          2008052051

British Library Cataloguing in Publication Data

A catalogue record for this book is available from the British Library

ISBN 978-0-470-51860-1

Typeset in 10/12.5 Times by Laserwords Private Limited, Chennai, India
Printed and bound in Great Britain by Bell and Bain, Glasgow

To my beautiful girls: my wife Rita and daughter Victoria.

To the memory of my parents, Hasya and Arcady Shklar, and my grandparents, Tasya and Boris Korkin.

Leon Shklar

To my parents, Arthur and Toby, and to Celia. Also, to the memory of my high school maths teacher, Jack Garfunkel, who instilled in his students the value of thinking things through logically, and the value of writing not for those who already know what you're talking about, but for those who don't.

Rich Rosen

Contents

About the Authors

Leon Shklar currently works for Thomson Reuters where he is the head of technology for Reuters Media. Previously, Leon headed up the development team for the online edition of the *Wall Street Journal* at Dow Jones. Prior to joining Dow Jones, he spent six years at Bell Communications Research and almost as long in the world of dot-coms and Internet software. Leon holds a Ph.D. in Computer Science from Rutgers University.

Rich Rosen is a senior developer in the Fixed Income Systems Group at Interactive Data Corporation. Previously, he was an Application Architect at Dow Jones. Rich began his career at Bell Labs, where his work with relational databases and the Internet prepared him for the world of Web application development. He is a co-author of *Mac OS X for Unix Geeks, 4th Edition (O'Reilly)*. Rich holds an M.S. in Computer Science from Stevens Institute of Technology.

Preface to the Second Edition

The expression "web time" connotes a world in which rapid change is the norm, where time is exponentially condensed. Technological advances that once upon a time might have taken years to transpire now occur in a matter of months or even days. What's more, these advances often result in radical paradigm shifts that change the way we interact with our technology, and with the world at large.

The first edition of this book was published in 2003. Since then, there have been many technological advances and paradigm shifts, causing some of what we wrote to become dated. New frameworks such as Ruby on Rails have arisen as a reaction to increasing complexity in the application development process. AJAX has taken client-side interactivity to a new level, blazing new frontiers in web application functionality. Search has become a fundamental part of our everyday web experience. Even the core protocols and markup languages representing the foundation of web technology have evolved since we first wrote about them over five years ago. Back then, who could have imagined the ascendance of today's most popular web applications, such as YouTube, Facebook, eBay, and Wikipedia, or the advances in real-time interactivity that are now commonplace?

For the second edition of this book, we provide new material covering these changes in the web technology landscape, while striving to bring existing content up-to-date. We have included new chapters on search technology and client-side interactivity (JavaScript, DHTML, and AJAX). We have added a second sample application implemented using Ruby on Rails as a complement to the original Struts application, which has been updated for the new edition. The chapters on Internet protocols, markup languages, server and browser architecture, and application development approaches have all been revised and enhanced. It is our hope that this updated edition will provide readers with deeper insights into the principles, protocols, and practices associated with the design and development of web applications.

Leon Shklar
Rich Rosen
October 31, 2008

Acknowledgments

I am grateful to my wife Rita for inspiration and music, and for still being around after all the work that went into the two editions of this book. My special thanks to our daughter Victoria for her insightful ideas throughout the project.

Leon Shklar

Ongoing and everlasting thanks to my wife, Celia, for the joy her singing brings into my life, and for enduring the continued insanity associated with the writing process. Thanks also to my parents and to Celia's parents for their love and support.

Rich Rosen

We would both like to thank the following people for their help:
- our editor, Jonathan Shipley, and his assistants, Georgia King and Claire Jardine, for their professionalism and flexibility throughout the project;
- our technical reviewers, Sue Fitzgerald, Ciarán O'Leary, Ilmi Yoon, Roger Beresford, Yuanzhu Peter Chen, Ray Cheung and Wei Ding, for taking the time to examine the text and provide us with valuable insights and advice;
- our colleagues, Otis Gospodnetich and Keith Kim, for their comments and suggestions for the search chapter, and Heow Eide-Goodman for his comments and suggestions for the chapters on development approaches and Rails application development.

Introduction

1.1 History and Pre-History of the Web

Back in 1989, at CERN (the scientific research laboratory near Geneva, Switzerland), Tim Berners-Lee presented a proposal for an information management system that would enable the sharing of knowledge and resources over a computer network. We now know this system as the *worldwide web* (the web). Building on the foundation of existing Internet protocols and services, it lives up to its name as a ubiquitous network providing information and communication services to hundreds of millions of people around the world.

From the very beginnings of Internet technology, many people shared the dream of using the Internet as a universal medium for exchanging information over computer networks. Internet file-sharing services (such as *FTP* and *Gopher*) and message forum services (such as *Netnews*) provided increasingly powerful mechanisms for information exchange and brought us closer to fulfilling those goals.

Ted Nelson's *Xanadu* project aspired to make that dream a reality, but the goals were lofty and never fully realized. Nelson coined the term "hypertext" as a way of describing "non-sequential writing – text that branches and allows choice to the reader." Unlike the static text of print media, hypertext was intended for use with an interactive computer screen. It is open, fluid and mutable, and can be connected to other pieces of hypertext by "links".

It took Tim Berners-Lee to "marry together" (in his words) the notion of hypertext with the power of the Internet, bringing those initial dreams to fruition in a way that the earliest developers of both hypertext and Internet technology might never have imagined. His vision was to connect literally *everything*, in a uniform and universal way. Berners-Lee originally promoted the web as a virtual library, a document control system for sharing information resources among researchers. On-line documents could be accessed via a unique document address, a *universal resource locator* (*URL*). These documents could be cross-referenced via *hypertext links*.

From its humble beginnings, the web has expanded exponentially to serve a wide variety of purposes for a wide variety of people:

- Given its origins, it seems natural that educational institutions and research laboratories were among the very first users of the web, employing it to share documents and other resources across the Internet.

- Popular adoption of the web by individuals followed gradually, originally through on-line services, such as America On-line (now AOL) that slowly but surely integrated with the web and the Internet. Initially, personal usage of the web was limited to e-mail and web surfing. Eventually, people began building their own web sites where they posted everything from on-line photo albums to personal journals that would become known as "blogs."

- Over time, businesses saw the potential of the web and began to employ it for *e-commerce*, providing an on-line medium for buying and selling goods interactively. As more and more people were connected to the web, the draw of a new source of revenue and the fear that competitors would get there first and undercut traditional revenue streams made e-commerce increasingly important to business. E-commerce applications are now being used for everything – from displaying catalogs of available merchandise to providing the means for customers to purchase goods and services securely on-line.

- As the impact of e-commerce grew, the back-end applications supporting e-commerce became increasingly important to the companies using it. The front-end, customer-facing web sites needed to be up to date, synchronized with inventory systems so that customers would know what items were or weren't immediately available. Automated fulfillment systems connected to the on-line ordering mechanisms became commonplace. With that, secure login and registration, including collection of credit card information and payment processing, became an absolute requirement for viable e-commerce sites.

- With the maturing of the web, a tug of war arose between sites offering free and paid content. Google was successful in tilting the balance in favor of free content supported by ads. Even the *Wall Street Journal*, which pioneered the notion of paid subscriptions for on-line content, has been opening up more and more of its content to non-subscribers. Critical technological challenges for free sites include tracking visitor behavior, providing adaptive personalization, and offering advanced community-building tools.

The web did not come into existence in a vacuum. It was built on top of core Internet protocols that had been in existence for many years prior to the inception of the web. Understanding the relationship between web technology and the underlying Internet protocols is fundamental to the design and implementation of true web applications. In fact, it is the exploitation of that relationship that distinguishes a web page or web site from a web application.

1.2   From Web Pages to Web Sites

The explosive growth of the web at least partially can be attributed to its grass-roots proliferation as a tool for *personal publishing*. The fundamental technology behind the web is relatively simple. A computer connected to the Internet running a *web server* was all that was necessary to serve documents. Both CERN and the *National Center for Supercomputer Applications* (*NCSA*) at the University of Illinois had developed freely available web server software. A small amount of *HTML* knowledge (and the proper computing resources) got you something that could be called a *web site*. Early web sites were just loosely connected sets of pages, branching hierarchically from a home page; now, a web site is much more than just a conglomeration of web pages.

When the web was in its infancy, academic institutions and technology companies owned the only computers that were connected to the Internet and could run server software. In those days, personal computers sitting on people's desks were still a rarity. If you wanted access to any sort of computing power, you used a *terminal* that let you "log in" to a large server or mainframe over a direct connection or dial-up phone line.

Still, creating and posting web pages quickly became popular among people that had access to scarce computing power. The original HTML language was simple enough that, even without the more sophisticated tools we have at our disposal today, it was an easy task for someone to create a web page. (Some would say *too* easy.) In the end, all that was needed to create first generation web pages was a simple text editor.

There is a big difference between a bunch of web *pages* and a web *site*. A web site is more than just a group of web pages that happen to be connected to each other through hypertext links:

- First, there are *content-related* concerns. Maintaining thematic consistency of content is important in giving a site some degree of identity.
- There are also *aesthetic* concerns. In addition to having thematically related content, a web site should also have a common look and feel across all of its pages, so that site visitors know what they are looking at. This means utilizing a common style: page layout, graphic design, and typographical elements.
- Then there are *architectural* concerns. As a site grows in size and becomes more complex, it is critically important to organize its content. This includes not just the layout of content on individual pages, but also the interconnections between the pages (site navigation). If the site becomes so complex that visitors cannot navigate their way through, even with the help of site maps and navigation bars, then it needs to be reorganized and restructured.

1.3   From Web Sites to Web Applications

Initially, what people shared over the Internet consisted mostly of static information found in files. They might edit those files, but there were few truly *dynamic* information services.

Granted, there were a few exceptions: search applications for finding files in on-line archives and services that provided information about the current weather, or the availability of cans from a soda-dispensing machine. (One of the first web applications that Tim Berners-Lee demonstrated at CERN was designed to look up numbers in an on-line phone book using a web browser.) However, for the most part, the information resources on the web were static documents.

The advent of the *dynamic web*, which resulted from the proliferation of dynamic information services, changed all that. The new services ranged from CGI scripts to search engines to packages that connected web applications to relational databases. No longer was it sufficient to build a web site (as opposed to a motley collection of web pages). It became necessary to design a *web application*.

What *is* a "web application?" It is a *client–server* application that uses a web browser as its client program. It delivers interactive services through web servers distributed over the Internet (or an intranet). A web site simply delivers content from static files. A web application can present dynamically tailored content based on request parameters, tracked user behaviors, and security considerations.

Web applications power information portals, retail sites, and corporate intranets. They not only provide information and interact with site visitors, but also collect and update information, maintain access controls, and support on-line transactions.

A prime example of a dynamic web application is an on-line shopping site. Site visitors browse on-line catalogs, search for items they want to purchase, add those items to an on-line shopping cart, and place their orders through a secure interface that encrypts personal information. To enable this functionality, the web application communicates with warehouses that maintain catalog and inventory information, storing this information in a database. Users can search the on-line database to obtain information about products. The application provides a way for users to select items to be added to their shopping carts, maintains shopping cart contents for the duration of the browser session, and records order information in the database. It communicates with outside financial institutions to verify credit card and address information, fulfills the order by directing warehouses to ship the purchased items, and sends confirmation e-mails to purchasers allowing them to track shipment of their orders.

1.4   Web 2.0: On-line Communities and Collaboration

Since 2000, another major trend has arisen in the on-line world, incorporating applications that support user-generated content, on-line communities, and collaborative mechanisms for updating on-line content. This trend is often referred to as *Web 2.0*, because it is closely tied to advances in web technology that herald a new generation of web applications.

In many respects, Web 2.0 is a harking back to the web as a network for presenting personal hyperlinked information. Information flow on the web is no longer one way, from the web site to the surfer. Site visitors contribute information of their own, ranging from reviews and ratings for movies, music, and books to personal journals, how-to information, and news for popular consumption. These journals go by the name *blogs* (short for "web logs") and the whole blogging movement has resurrected the idea of the personal web page and elevated its status.

Personal blogs and community web sites encouraging user input may bear a resemblance to the more personal web of old, but the technology behind them does not. Whereas individual owners could easily maintain the simple static web sites of old, this has become impractical given the enormous volume and increasingly malleable nature of content out there today. Blogs, user forums, and collaborative community sites may look like the simpler web sites of the past, but the underlying functionality supporting them is based on sophisticated web application technology incorporating user authentication, access control, and content management services.

1.5   The Brave New World of AJAX

Another radical change in the web application landscape was the advent of *AJAX* (an acronym that stands for Asynchronous JavaScript and XmlHttpRequest). While the technology advances behind it accumulated gradually, AJAX represents a paradigm shift that has changed the way web applications are conceived and developed.

Tim Berners-Lee's original concept of HTTP was that of a simple stateless request–response protocol. Such a protocol allows for independent processing of requests and responses, without requiring a persistent connection. This simplicity fostered wide acceptance of the HTTP protocol but imposed significant limitations. The only method available for updating page content was to replace the entire page. This limitation was unsatisfying to those who were used to client–server applications that communicated with their associated servers directly and continuously. For instance, in such an application, a server-side change to a value in a spreadsheet cell could immediately be reflected on the screen without refreshing the whole spreadsheet.

HTTP, and the web experience in general, have evolved in a number of ways since their inception, introducing elements that allow web transactions to transcend the limitations of a stateless request–response protocol (e.g., cookies and JavaScript). AJAX is the latest such element, essentially allowing what amounts to an "end-run" to communicate with a web server indirectly: instead of submitting a direct request to see a *new* page from the server, a subordinate background request is submitted (usually through a JavaScript object called *XmlHttpRequest*) and the response to that request is used to dynamically modify the content of the *current* page in lieu of replacing its content entirely.

The main impact of AJAX is that the web experience is brought closer to that of client–server applications, allowing for a more immediate dynamic interaction between the user and the web application.

1.6   Focus of This Book

The purpose of this book is to provide a guide for learning the underlying principles, protocols, and practices associated with designing flexible and efficient web applications. Our target audience is senior undergraduate or graduate students who have already learned the basics of web development and professional developers who have had some exposure to web application development and want to expand their knowledge.

We expect our readers to have *some* familiarity with HTML and JavaScript – not at the level of experienced web designers but enough to create web pages and embed simple JavaScript code to submit forms to a web server. We recommend at least some exposure to Internet protocols, such as

Telnet, FTP, SMTP, HTTP and SSL. We appreciate that many of our readers may not be familiar with Linux or Unix operating systems. However, it is helpful to have some understanding of the command-line interfaces provided by interactive shells, as some of our examples employ such an interface.

As we have said, there is a major difference between web *pages*, web *sites*, and web *applications*. There are excellent resources dedicated to web page and web site design, and the References section at the end of this chapter lists some of the best that we know. When we examined the current literature available on the subject of *web application development*, we found there were three main categories of book currently available.

- technical overviews
- reference books
- focused tutorials.

Technical overviews are usually very high level, describing technology and terminology in broad terms. They do not go into enough detail to enable the reader to design and build serious web applications. They are most often intended for managers who want a surface understanding of concepts and terminology without going too deeply into specific application development issues. Frequently, such overviews attempt to cover technology in broad brushstrokes; their subject may be Java, XML, e-commerce, or Web 2.0. Such books approach the spectrum of technology so broadly that the coverage of any specific area is too shallow for serious application developers.

Reference books are useful, naturally, as references, but not for the purpose of *learning* about the technology. They are great to keep on your desk to look things up once you are already deeply familiar with the technology, but they are not oriented toward elucidation and explanation.

The *focused tutorials* concentrate on the usage of specific platforms and products to develop web applications. Books in this category provide in-depth coverage of very narrow areas, concentrating on how to use a particular language or platform without necessarily explaining the underlying principles. Such books may be useful in teaching programmers to develop applications for a specific platform, but they do not provide enough information about the enabling technologies, focusing instead on the platform-specific implementation. Should a developer be called upon to rewrite an application for another platform, the knowledge acquired from these books is rarely transferable to the new platform.

Given the rate of change of the web technologies, today's platform of choice is tomorrow's outdated legacy system. When new development platforms emerge, developers without a fundamental understanding of the inner workings of web applications have to learn the new platforms from the ground up. The challenge is their lack of understanding of what the systems they implemented using specialized application programming interfaces (*APIs*) did behind the API calls. What is missing is the ability to use fundamental technological knowledge across platforms.

What was needed was a book that covered the basic *principles* of good application design, the underlying *protocols* associated with web technology, and the best *practices* for creating scalable, extensible, maintainable applications. With this in mind, we endeavored to write such a book.

The need for such a book is particularly apparent when interviewing job candidates for web application development positions. Too many programmers have detailed knowledge of particular languages and interfaces but they are lost when asked questions about the underlying technologies and how they relate to real problems (e.g., why is it necessary for a server to add a trailing slash to a URL and redirect the request back to itself?). Such knowledge is not purely academic – it is critical when designing and debugging complex systems.

Too often, developers with proficiency *only* within a specific application development platform (such as *Active Server Pages, Cold Fusion, PHP*, or *Perl* CGI scripting) are not capable of transferring that proficiency directly to another platform. The fundamental understanding of core technologies is critical to enable developers to grow with the rapid technological advances in web application development.

What do we have in mind when we refer to the *general principles* that need to be understood in order to properly design and develop web applications? We mean the core protocols and languages associated with web applications. This includes *HyperText Transfer Protocol (HTTP)* and *HyperText Markup Language (HTML)*, which are fundamental to the creation and transmission of web pages, but it also includes older Internet protocols such as *Telnet* and *FTP*, and the protocols used for message transfer such as *SMTP* and *IMAP*. A *web application architect* must also be familiar with JavaScript, XML, relational databases, graphic design and multimedia. Web application architects must be well-versed in application server technology and have a strong background in information architecture.

If you find people with all these qualifications, please let us know: we would love to hire them! Rare is the person who can not only design a web site but can also perform all the other tasks associated with web application development: working with graphic designers, creating database schemas, producing interactive multimedia programs, and configuring e-commerce transactions. More realistically, we can seek someone who is an expert in one particular area (e.g., e-commerce transactions or browser programming) but who also understands the wider issues associated with designing web applications.

We hope that, by reading this book, you can acquire the skills needed to design and build complex applications for the web. There is no "one easy lesson" for learning the ins and outs of application design. Hopefully, this book will enhance your ability to design and build sophisticated web applications that are scaleable, maintainable, and extensible.

We examine various approaches to the process of web application development, covering both client-side presentation technology and server-side application technology. On the client side, we look at both markup languages and programming languages, from *HTML* and *XML* to *CSS* and *JavaScript*. On the server side, we look at the full range of approaches, starting with *Server Side Includes (SSI)* and *CGI*, covering template languages such as *Cold Fusion* and *ASP*, examining the intricacies of *Java Platform, Enterprise Edition (Java EE)*, and finally looking at newer "rapid development" approaches such as *Ruby on Rails*. At each level, we concentrate not only on the particular development platform, but also on the underlying principles that span multiple platforms.

1.7   What Is Covered in This Book

The organization of this book is as follows:

- **Chapter 2: Core Internet Protocols** – This chapter offers an examination of the underlying Internet protocols that form the foundation of the web. It offers some perspectives on the history of TCP/IP, as well as some details about using several of these protocols in web applications.

- **Chapter 3: Birth of the Web: HTTP** – The HTTP protocol is covered in detail in this chapter, with explanations of how requests and responses are transmitted and processed.
- **Chapter 4: HTML and Its Roots** – In the first of two chapters about markup languages, we go back to SGML to learn more about the roots of HTML (and of XML). Rather than providing a tutorial on web design with HTML, the focus is on HTML as a markup language and its place in web application development.
- **Chapter 5: XML Languages and Applications** – This chapter covers XML and related specifications, including XML Schema, XPath, XSLT, and XSL FO, as well as XML applications such as XHTML and WML.
- **Chapter 6: Web Servers** – The operational intricacies of web servers is the topic of this chapter, with in-depth discussion of what web servers must do to support interactions with clients such as web browsers and HTTP proxies.
- **Chapter 7: Web Browsers** – As the previous chapter dug deep into the inner workings of web servers, this chapter provides similar coverage of the inner workings of web browsers.
- **Chapter 8: Active Browser Pages: From JavaScript to AJAX** – Here we cover the mechanisms for providing dynamic interactivity in web pages, including JavaScript, DHTML, and AJAX.
- **Chapter 9: Approaches to Web Application Development** – This chapter contains a survey of available web application approaches, including CGI, Servlets, PHP, Cold Fusion, ASP, JSP, and frameworks such as Struts. It classifies and compares these approaches to help readers make informed decisions when choosing an approach for their project, emphasizing the benefits of using the Model–View–Controller (MVC) design pattern in implementing applications.
- **Chapter 10: Web Application Primer: Virtual Realty Listing Services** – Having examined the landscape of available application development approaches, we decide on Struts along with the Java Standard Tag Library (JSTL). We give the reasons for our decisions and build a sample employing the principles we have been discussing in previous chapters. We then suggest enhancements to the application as exercises to be performed by the reader, including the introduction of an administrative interface component, using Hibernate for object-relational mapping, and using Java Server Faces for presentation.
- **Chapter 11: Web Application Primer: Ruby on Rails** – In this chapter, we revisit the *Virtual Realty Listing Services* application and implement its administrative interface using the Ruby on Rails framework. We describe the general structure of a Rails application, walk through the process of building an application in Rails, and compare the Java EE–Struts approach with Rails in terms of both ease of development and flexibility of deployment.
- **Chapter 12: Search Technologies** – Here we describe not only the process of indexing site content for internal search functionality, but also the mechanisms for structuring a site's content for optimal indexing by external search engines. Jakarta's Lucene and other tools are covered.
- **Chapter 13: Trends and Directions** – Finally, we look to the future, providing coverage of the most promising developments in web technology, as well as speculating about the evolution of web application frameworks.

Chapter 2 starts us off with a study of the core protocols supporting Internet technology, in general, and the web in particular. Although some might see this as review, it is a subject worth going over to gain both a historical and a technological perspective.

1.8 Bibliography

Berners-Lee, Tim, 2000. *Weaving the Web: The Original Design and Ultimate Destiny of the World Wide Web*. New York: HarperBusiness.

Gehtland, Justin, Galbraith, Ben and Almaer, Dion, 2006. *Pragmatic AJAX: A Web 2.0 Primer*. Raleigh (NC): Pragmatic Bookshelf.

Hadlock, Kris, 2007. *AJAX for Web Application Developers*. Indianapolis (IN): SAMS Publishing (Developer's Library).

Nelson, Theodor Holm, 1982. *Literary Machines 931*. Sausalito (CA): Mindful Press.

Rosenfeld, Louis and Morville, Peter, 2006. *Information Architecture for the World Wide Web*, 3rd Edition. Sebastopol (CA): O'Reilly & Associates.

Williams, Robin and Tollett, John, 2005. *The Non-Designer's Web Book*, 3rd Edition. Berkeley (CA): Peachpit Press.

CHAPTER 2

Core Internet Protocols

IN THIS CHAPTER

- TCP/IP
- Telnet
- Electronic mail
- Messaging
- Security and encryption
- FTP and file server protocols
- And then came the web . . .

OBJECTIVES

- Offer a historical perspective on TCP/IP.
- Explain the client–server paradigm.
- Provide an overview of key Internet protocols and application services that predate the web.
- Show how these protocols and services provided the foundation for HTTP and the web.

As we mentioned in the previous chapter, Tim Berners-Lee did not come up with the worldwide web in a vacuum. The web as we know it was built on top of core *Internet protocols* that had been in existence for many years. Understanding the ideas behind those underlying protocols is important for the discipline of building robust web applications.

In this chapter, we examine the core Internet protocols that make up the *TCP/IP protocol suite*, which is the foundation for the web protocols that are discussed in Chapter 3. We begin with a brief historical overview of the forces that led to the creation of TCP/IP. We then go over the layers of the TCP/IP stack, and show where various protocols fit into it. Our description of the client–server paradigm used by TCP/IP applications is followed by discussion of the various TCP/IP application services, including Telnet, electronic mail (e-mail), message forums, live messaging, and file servers. While some of these protocols and services may be deprecated, if not obsolete, knowledge of how they work and what they do provides critical insights into the present and future of web protocols and web applications.

2.1 Historical Perspective

The roots of web technology can be found in the original Internet protocols (known collectively as TCP/IP) developed in the 1980s. These protocols were an outgrowth of work to design a network called the *ARPANET*.

The ARPANET was named for the *Advanced Research Projects Agency* (ARPA) of the US Department of Defense (DoD). It came into being as a result of efforts in the 1970s to develop an open, common, distributed, and decentralized computer networking architecture. The DoD's goal was to resolve numerous problems with existing network architectures.

First and foremost among these problems was that the typical network topology was *centralized*. A computer network had a single point of control directing communication between all the systems belonging to that network. From a military perspective, such a topology had a critical flaw: destroy that central point of control and all possibility of communication was lost.

Another issue was the *proprietary* nature of existing network architectures. Most of them were developed and controlled by private corporations, who had a vested interest both in pushing their own products and in keeping their technology to themselves. Furthermore, the proprietary nature of the technology limited the interoperability between different systems. It was important, even then, to ensure that the mechanisms for communicating across computer networks were not proprietary or controlled in any way by private interests, lest the entire network become dependent on the whims of a single corporation.

Thus, the DoD funded an endeavor to design the protocols for the next generation of computer communications networking architectures. Establishing a *decentralized, distributed network topology* was foremost among the design goals for the new networking architecture. Such a topology would allow communications to continue without disruption, even if any one system was damaged or destroyed. In such a topology, the network "intelligence" would not reside in a single point of control. Instead, it would be distributed among many systems throughout the network.

To facilitate this (and to accommodate other network reliability considerations), ARPANET employed a *packet-switching* technology, whereby a network "message" could be split up into packets, each of which might take a different route over the network, arrive in completely mixed-up order, and still be reassembled and understood by the intended recipient.

To promote *interoperability*, the protocols needed to be *open*: readily available to anyone who wanted to connect their system to the network. An infrastructure was needed to design the set of agreed-upon protocols, and to formulate new protocols for new technologies that might be added to the network in the future. An *Internet Working Group* (INWG) was formed to examine the issues associated with connecting heterogeneous networks in an open, uniform manner. This group provided an open platform for proposing, debating, and approving protocols.

The Internet Working Group evolved over time into other bodies, such as the *Internet Activities Board* (IAB), later renamed the *Internet Architecture Board*, the *Internet Assigned Numbers Authority* (IANA), the *Internet Engineering Task Force* (IETF) and the *Internet Engineering Steering Group* (IESG). These bodies defined the standards that "govern" the Internet. They established the formal processes for proposing new protocols, discussing and debating the merits of these proposals, and ultimately approving them as accepted Internet standards.

Proposals for new protocols (or updated versions of existing protocols) are provided in the form of *Requests for Comments*, also known as *RFC*s. Once approved, the RFCs are treated as the standard documentation for the new or updated protocol.

2.2   TCP/IP Architecture

The original ARPANET was the first fruit borne of the DoD endeavor. The protocols behind the ARPANET evolved over time into the *TCP/IP Suite*, a layered taxonomy of data communications protocols. The name TCP/IP refers to two of the most important protocols within the suite, *Transmission Control Protocol* (TCP) and *Internet Protocol* (IP), but the suite is comprised of many other significant protocols and services.

2.2.1   Protocol layers

The protocol layers (above the "layer" of physical interconnection) associated with TCP/IP are:

- the Network Interface layer
- the Internet layer
- the Transport layer
- the Application layer.

Because this taxonomy contains layers, implementations of these protocols are often known as a *protocol stack*.

The *Network Interface layer* is responsible for the lowest level of data transmission within TCP/IP, facilitating communication with the underlying physical network.

The *Internet layer* provides the mechanisms for intersystem communications, controlling message routing, validity checking, and composition and decomposition of message headers. The protocol known as IP (which stands, oddly enough, for Internet Protocol) operates on this layer, as does the *Internet Control Message Protocol* (ICMP), which handles the transmission of control and error messages between systems. *Ping* is an Internet service that operates through ICMP.

The *Transport layer* provides message transport services between applications running on remote systems. This is the layer in which the *Transmission Control Protocol* (TCP) operates. TCP provides *reliable, connection-oriented message transport*. Most of the well-known Internet services make use of TCP as their foundation. However, some services that do not require the reliability (and overhead) associated with TCP make use of *User Datagram Protocol* (*UDP*). For instance, streaming audio and video services would gladly sacrifice a few lost packets to get faster performance out of their data streams, so these services often operate over UDP, which trades reliability for performance.

The *Application layer* is the highest level within the TCP/IP protocol stack. It is within this layer that most of the services we associate with the Internet operate.

2.2.2   Comparison with OSI model

During the period that TCP/IP was being developed, the International Standards Organization (ISO) was working on its own layered protocol scheme, called *Open Systems Interconnection (OSI)*. While the TCP/IP taxonomy consists of five layers (if you include the physical connectivity medium as a layer), OSI had seven layers: Physical, Data Link, Network, Transport, Session, Presentation, and Application.

There is some parallelism between the two models. TCP/IP's Network Interface layer is sometimes called the Data Link layer to mimic the OSI reference model, while the Internet layer corresponds to OSI's Network layer. Both models share the notion of a Transport layer, which serves roughly the same functions in each model. The Application layer in TCP/IP combines the functions of the Session, Presentation, and Application layers of OSI.

OSI never caught on and, while some people waited patiently for its adoption and propagation, it was TCP/IP that became the ubiquitous foundation of the Internet as we know it today.

2.2.3   The client–server paradigm

TCP/IP applications tend to operate according to the *client–server* paradigm. This simply means that, in these applications, *servers* (also called *services* and *daemons*, depending on the lingo of the underlying operating system) execute by waiting for requests from *client* programs to arrive and processing those requests.

Client programs can be applications used by human beings, or they could be servers that need to make their own requests that can only be fulfilled by other servers. More often than not, the client and the server run on separate machines, and communicate via a connection across a network.

Command line vs GUI

Over the years, user interfaces to client programs have evolved from *command-line interfaces* (CLI) to *graphical user interfaces* (GUI).

Command-line programs have their origins in the limitations of the oldest human interface to computer systems: the teletype keyboard. In the earliest days of computing, even simple text-based CRT terminals were not available – let alone today's monitors with advanced graphics capabilities. The only way to enter data interactively was through a teletypewriter interface, one character at a time. A command-line interface (CLI) prompts the user for the entry of a "command" (the name of a program) and its "arguments" (the parameters passed to the program). The original PC-DOS operating system and Unix *shells* use command-line interfaces.

Screen-mode programs allow users to manipulate the data on an entire CRT screen, rather than on one line. This means that arrow keys can be used to move a *cursor* around the screen or to scroll through pages of a text document. Screen-mode programs are still restricted to character-based interfaces.

GUI programs make use of a visual paradigm that offers users a plethora of choices. For most, this is a welcome alternative to manually typing in the names of files, programs, and command options. The graphics are not limited to just textual characters, as in screen-mode programs. The GUI paradigm relies on windows, icons, mouse, pointers, and scrollbars (*WIMPS*) to display graphically the set of available files and applications.

Whether command-line or GUI-based, client programs provide the interface by which end users communicate with servers to make use of TCP/IP services. Although debates rage as to whether GUIs or CLIs are "better", each has advantages and disadvantages for different types of users.

Client–server communications

Under the hood, communications between client and server programs take the form of request–response interactions. The imposition of this constraint on Internet communication protocols means that even the most primitive command-line interface can make use of TCP/IP services. More sophisticated GUI-based client programs often hide their command-line details from their users, employing point-and-click and drag-and-drop functionality to support underlying command-line directives.

After the server acknowledges the success of the connection, the client sends commands on a line-by-line basis. There are single-line and block commands. A single-line command, as the name implies, includes an atomic command directive on a single line. A block command begins with a line indicating the start of the command and terminates with a line indicating its end. For example, in the Simple Mail Transfer Protocol (SMTP), a line beginning with the word HELO initiates an SMTP session, while a line containing just the word DATA begins a block that ends with a line containing only a period. The server then responds to each command, usually beginning with a line containing a response code.

A *stateful* protocol allows a client to support a sequence of commands. The server is required to maintain the "state" of the connection throughout the transmission of successive commands, until the connection is terminated. The sequence of transmitted and executed commands is often called a session. Most Internet services (including SMTP) are session-based and make use of stateful protocols.

HTTP

HTTP is a stateless protocol (see Chapter 3). An HTTP request usually consists of a single command and a single response. There is no built-in ability to maintain state between transmitted commands.

Early implementations of client–server architectures did not make use of open protocols. This meant that client programs had to be as "heavy" as the server programs. A "lightweight" client (also called a *thin client*) could only exist in a framework where common protocols and application controls were associated with the client machine's operating system. Without such a framework, many of the connectivity features had to be included directly in the client program, adding to its "weight". One advantage of using TCP/IP for client–server applications was that the protocol stack was installed on the client machine as part of the operating system and the client program itself could be more of a thin client.

Web applications are a prime example of thin clients. Rather than building a custom program to perform desired application tasks, web applications use the web browser, a program that is already installed on most end-user systems. You cannot create a client much thinner than a program that users already have on their desktops!

How Do TCP/IP Clients and Servers Communicate with Each Other?

TCP/IP client programs open a socket, which is simply a TCP connection between the client machine and the server machine. Servers listen for connection requests that come in through specific ports. A port is not a physical interface between the computer and the network, but is simply a numeric reference within a request that indicates which server program is its intended recipient.

There are established conventions for matching port numbers with specific TCP/IP services. For example, Telnet services listen for connection requests on port 23, SMTP servers listen to port 25, and web servers (by default) listen to port 80.

2.3 TCP/IP Application Services

In this section, we discuss some of the common TCP/IP application services, including Telnet, e-mail, message forums, live messaging, and file servers. Where appropriate, we compare the original TCP/IP services with modern counterparts.

2.3.1 Telnet

The Telnet protocol operates within the Application layer. It was developed to support Network Virtual Terminal functionality, which means the ability to "log in" to a remote machine over the Internet. The latest specification for the Telnet protocol is defined in Internet RFC 854.

Before the advent of personal computers, access to computing power was limited to those who could connect to a larger server or mainframe computer, either through a dial-up phone line or through a direct local connection. Whether you phoned in remotely or sat down at a terminal connected directly to the server, you used a command-line interface to log in. You connected to a single system and your interactions were limited to that system.

With the arrival of Internet services, you could use the Telnet protocol to log in remotely to systems that were accessible over the Internet. As we mentioned earlier, Telnet clients are configured by default to connect to port 23 on the server machine, but the target port number can be overridden in most client programs. This means you can use a Telnet client program to connect and "talk" to *another* TCP-based service if you know its address and its port number, have proper authentication credentials, and understand the format of its transactions with the server.

Secure Shell

The Telnet protocol is now considered a poor mechanism for connecting to remote systems, because Telnet servers and clients transmit all their data (including passwords) unencrypted. Secure Shell (SSH) establishes connections and transfers data over secure channels, encrypting transmitted data and promoting security (see Section 2.3.5).

2.3.2 E-mail

Electronic mail, or *e-mail*, was probably the first "killer app" in what we now call cyberspace. Since the Internet had its roots in military interests, naturally the tone of e-mail started out being formal, rigid, and business-like. Once the body of people using e-mail expanded, and once these people realized what it could be used for, things lightened up.

Electronic *mailing lists* provided communities where people with like interests could exchange messages. These lists were closed systems, in the sense that only subscribers could post messages to the list or view messages posted by other subscribers. Obviously, lists grew and list managers had to maintain them. Over time, automated mechanisms were developed to allow people to subscribe (and, even more importantly, to unsubscribe) without human intervention. These mailing lists evolved into *message forums*, where people could publicly post messages on an *electronic bulletin board* for everyone to read.

These services certainly existed before the birth of the Internet. But in those days, users read and sent their e-mail by *logging in* to a system directly (usually via telephone dial-up or direct local connection) and running programs on that system (usually with a command-line interface). The methods for using these services varied greatly from system to system, and e-mail connectivity between disparate systems was hard to come by. With the advent of TCP/IP, the mechanisms for providing these services became more consistent, and e-mail became uniform and ubiquitous.

The transmission of e-mail is performed through the SMTP protocol. The reading of e-mail is usually performed through either POP or IMAP.

SMTP

As an application layer protocol, *Simple Mail Transfer Protocol* (SMTP) normally runs on top of TCP, though it can theoretically use any underlying transport protocol. The latest specification for the SMTP protocol is defined in Internet RFC 821 and the structure of SMTP messages is defined in Internet RFC 822. The application called "sendmail" is an implementation of the SMTP protocol for Unix systems.

SMTP, like other TCP/IP services, runs as a *server, service*, or *daemon*. In a TCP/IP environment, SMTP servers usually run on port 25. They wait for requests to send e-mail messages, which can come from local system users or from across the network. They are also responsible for evaluating the recipient addresses found in e-mail messages, determining whether they are valid, and whether their final destination is another recipient (e.g., a forwarding address or the set of individual recipients subscribed to a mailing list).

If the message embedded in the request is intended for a user with an account on the local system, then the SMTP server delivers the message to that user by appending it to their *mailbox*. Depending on the implementation, the mailbox can be anything from a simple text file to a complex database of e-mail messages. If the message is intended for a user on another system, then the server must figure out how to transmit the message to the appropriate system. This may involve direct connection to the remote system or it may involve connection to a *gateway* system. A gateway is responsible for passing a message on to other gateways or sending it directly to its ultimate destination.

Before the advent of SMTP, the underlying mechanisms for sending mail varied from system to system. Once SMTP became ubiquitous as the mechanism for e-mail transmission, these

```
220 mail.hoboken.mycompany.com ESMTP xxxx 3.21 #1 Fri, 22 Feb 2008 13:41:09 -0500
HELO ubizmo.com
250 mail.hoboken.mycompany.com Hello rosendesktop.mycompany.com [xxx.xxx.xxx.xxx]
MAIL FROM:<rich.rosen@mycompany.com>
250 <rich.rosen@mycompany.com> is syntactically correct
RCPT TO:<leon.shklar@myschool.edu>
250 <leon.shklar@myschool.edu> is syntactically correct
RCPT TO:<santos.l.halper@simpsons.org>
250 <santos.l.halper@simpsons.org> is syntactically correct
DATA
354 Enter message, ending with "." on a line by itself
From: Rich Rosen <rich.rosen@mycompany.com>
To: leon.shklar@myschool.edu
Cc: santos.l.halper@simpsons.org
Subject: Demonstrating SMTP

Leon,

Please ignore this note.  I am demonstrating the art of connecting to an SMTP server
for the book. :-)

Rich
.
250 OK id=xxxxxxxx
QUIT
221 mail.hoboken.mycompany.com closing connection
```

Figure 2.1   Command-line interaction with an SMTP server.

mechanisms became more uniform. Applications responsible for transmitting e-mail messages, such as SMTP servers, are known as *Mail Transfer Agents (MTAs)*. Likewise, the applications responsible for retrieving messages from a mailbox, including *POP* servers and *IMAP* servers, are known as *Mail Retrieval Agents (MRAs)*.

E-mail client programs are engineered to allow users to read and send mail. Such programs are known as *Mail User Agents (MUAs)*. MUAs talk to MRAs to read mail and to MTAs to send mail. In a typical e-mail client, once the user has composed and submitted a message, the client program directs it to the SMTP server. First, the client *connects* to the server by opening a TCP socket to port 25 (the SMTP port) of the server (even if the server is running on the user's machine). Figure 2.1 shows an example of an interaction between a client and an SMTP server.

The client program identifies itself (and the system on which it is running) to the server via the HELO command. The server decides (based on this identification information) whether to accept or reject the request. If the server accepts the request, it waits for the client to send further information. One line at a time, the client transmits commands to the server, sending information about the originator of the message (using the MAIL command) and each of the recipients (using a series of RCPT commands). Once all this is done, the client tells the server it is about to send the actual data: the message itself. It does this by sending a command line consisting of the word DATA. Every line that follows, until the server encounters a line containing only a period, is considered part of the message body. Once it has sent the body of the message, the client signals the server that it is done, and the server transmits the message to its destination (either directly or through gateways). Having received confirmation that the server has transmitted the message, the client closes the socket connection using the `QUIT` command.

Originally, SMTP servers executed in a very open fashion: anyone knowing the address of an SMTP server could connect to it and send messages. In an effort to discourage spamming (the sending of indiscriminate mass semi-anonymous e-mails), many SMTP server implementations allow the system administrator to configure the server so that it only accepts connections from a discrete set of systems, perhaps only those within their local domain. Additionally, SMTP servers can use an extension to the SMTP protocol called *SMTP-AUTH* to restrict the ability to send e-mail only to authenticated users.

When building web applications that include e-mail functionality (specifically the *sending* of e-mail), make sure your configuration includes the specification of a working SMTP server system, which will accept your requests to transmit messages. To maximize application flexibility, the address of the SMTP server should be a parameter that can be modified at run time by an application administrator.

MIME

Originally, e-mail systems transmitted messages in the form of standard ASCII text. If a user wanted to send a file in a non-text or "binary" format (e.g., an image or sound file), it had to be encoded before it could be placed into the body of the message. The sender had to communicate the nature of the binary data directly to the receiver, e.g., "The block of encoded binary text below is a GIF image."

Multimedia Internet Mail Extensions (MIME) provided a uniform mechanism for including encoded attachments within a multipart e-mail message. MIME supports the definition of boundaries separating the text portion of a message (the "body") from its attachments, as well as the designation of attachment encoding methods, including "Base64" and "quoted-printable." MIME was originally defined in Internet RFC 1341, but the most recent specifications can be found in Internet RFCs 2045 through 2049.

MIME also supports the notion of content typing for attachments (and for the body of a message). MIME-types are standard naming conventions for defining the type of data contained in an attachment. A MIME-type is constructed as a combination of a top-level data type and a subtype. There is a fixed set of top-level data types, including text, image, audio, video, and application. The subtypes describe the data in enough detail to select an appropriate processing program. For example, there are specific programs for processing `text/html`, `text/plain`, `image/jpeg`, and `audio/mp3` files.

POP

The *Post Office Protocol (POP)* gives users direct access to their e-mail messages stored on remote systems. *POP3* is the most recent version of the POP protocol, first defined in Internet RFC 1725 and revised in Internet RFC 1939. Most of the popular e-mail clients (including Microsoft Outlook and Mozilla Thunderbird) use POP3 to access user e-mail. (Even proprietary systems, such as Lotus Notes, offer administrators the option to configure remote e-mail access through POP.)

Before the Internet, people read and sent e-mail by logging in to a system and running command-line programs. User messages were usually stored locally in a mailbox file on that system. Even with the advent of Internet technology, many people continued to access e-mail by establishing a Telnet connection to the system containing their mailbox and running command-line programs (e.g., from a Unix shell) to read and send mail. (Some people who prefer command-line programs still do!)

Let us look at the process by which POP clients communicate with POP servers to provide user access to e-mail. First, the POP client must connect to the POP server (which usually runs on port 110), so it can identify and authenticate the user to the server. This is usually done by sending the user name (user id) and password one line at a time, using the USER and PASS commands. (Sophisticated POP servers may make use of the APOP command, which allows the secure transmission of the user name and password as a single encrypted entity across the network.)

Once connected and authenticated, the POP protocol offers the client a variety of commands it can execute. Among them is the UIDL command, which responds with an ordered list of message numbers, where each entry is followed by a unique message identifier. POP clients can use this list (and the unique identifiers it contains) to determine which messages in the list qualify as "new" (i.e., not yet seen by the user through this particular client). Having obtained this list, the client can execute the command to retrieve a message (RETR n). It can also execute commands to delete a message from the server (DELE n) or retrieve just the header of a message (TOP n 0).

Message headers contain *metadata* about a message, such as the addresses of its originator and recipients, its subject, etc. Each message contains a header block (see Figure 2.2) containing a series of lines, followed by a blank line indicating the end of that block.

The information that e-mail clients include in message lists (e.g., the From, To, and Subject of each message) comes from the message headers. As e-mail technology advanced, headers began representing more sophisticated information, including MIME-related data (e.g., content types) and attachment encoding schemes.

Figure 2.3 provides an example of a simple command-line interaction between a client and a POP server. GUI-based clients often hide the mundane command-line details from their users. The normal sequence of operation for most GUI-based POP clients today is as follows:

1. Get the user id and password (the client may already have this information or may need to prompt the user).
2. Connect the user and verify identity.
3. Obtain the UIDL list of messages.
4. Compare the identifiers in this list to a list that the client keeps locally, to determine which messages are "new".
5. Retrieve all the new messages and present them to the user in a selection list.
6. Delete the newly retrieved messages from the POP server (optional).

Although this approach is simple, it is inefficient. All the new messages are always downloaded to the client. This is inefficient because some of these messages may be quite long or have extremely large attachments. Users must wait for *all* of the messages (including large or unwanted messages) to

```
From: Rich Rosen <rich.rosen@mycompany.com>
To: Leon Shklar <leon.shklar@myschool.edu>
Subject: Here is a message...
Date: Fri, 22 Feb 2008 12:58:21 -0500
Message-ID: <G987W90B.D43@hoboken.mycompany.com>
```

Figure 2.2   Message header block.

```
+OK mail Server POP3 v1.8.22 server ready
user leon.shklar
+OK Name is a valid mailbox
pass xxxxxx
+OK Maildrop locked and ready
uidl
+OK unique-id listing follows
1 2412
2 2413
3 2414
4 2415
.
retr 1
+OK Message follows
From: Rich Rosen <rich.rosen@mycompany.com>
To: Leon Shklar <leon.shklar@myschool.edu>
Subject: Here is a message...
Date: Fri, 22 Feb 2008 12:58:21 -0500
Message-ID: <G987W90B.D43@hoboken.mycompany.com>

The medium is the message.
   --Marshall McLuhan, while standing behind a placard
     in a theater lobby in a Woody Allen movie.
.
```

Figure 2.3 Command-line interaction with a POP3 server.

download before viewing any of the messages they *want* to read. The current proliferation of spam makes this even more important today than it was in the past. It would be more efficient for the client to retrieve *only* message headers and display the information in a message list. It could then allow users the option to selectively download desired messages for viewing or to delete unwanted messages without downloading them. A web-based e-mail client helps remove some of this inefficiency.

IMAP

Some of the inefficiencies of the POP protocol can be alleviated by the *Internet Message Access Protocol (IMAP)*. IMAP was intended as a successor to POP, offering sophisticated services for managing messages in remote mailboxes. IMAP servers provide support for multiple remote *mailboxes* or *folders*, so that users can move messages from an incoming folder (the "inbox") into other folders kept on the server. In addition, they also provide support for saving sent messages in one of these remote folders and for multiple simultaneous operations on mailboxes. IMAP servers commonly listen on TCP port 143.

IMAP4, the most recent version of the IMAP protocol, was originally defined in Internet RFC 1730, but the most recent specification can be found in Internet RFC 2060. The approach used by IMAP differs in many ways from that of POP. POP clients download e-mail messages from the server. The default behavior for many POP clients is to delete messages from the server following the download; in practice, many users elect to leave viewed messages on the server, rather than deleting them after viewing. This is because many people who travel extensively want to check e-mail while on the road, but want to see *all* of their messages (even the ones they've seen) when they return to their "home machine." While the POP approach "tolerates" but does not encourage this sort of user behavior, the IMAP approach eagerly embraces it. IMAP was conceived with "nomadic" users in mind: users who might check e-mail from literally anywhere, who want access to all of their saved *and* sent messages wherever they happen to be. IMAP not only allows the user to leave messages on the server, it provides mechanisms for storing messages in user-defined folders for easier accessibility and better organization. Moreover, users can save sent messages in a designated remote folder on the IMAP server. While POP clients support saving of sent messages, they usually save those messages locally, on the client machine.

IMAP e-mail client programs work very similarly to POP e-mail clients. In fact, many e-mail client programs allow users to operate in either POP or IMAP mode. However, the automatic downloading of the content and attachments for incoming messages does not occur by default in IMAP clients. Instead, an IMAP client downloads only the header information associated with new messages, requesting the body of an individual message only when user expresses interest in seeing it.

POP vs IMAP

Although it is possible to write a POP client that downloads only the header information until the user expressly looks at a message, most do not. POP clients tend to operate in "burst" mode, getting all the messages on the server in one "shot." While this may be in some respects inefficient, it is useful for those whose on-line access is not persistent. By getting all the messages in one burst, users can work off-line with the complete set of downloaded messages, connecting to the Internet again only when they want to send responses and check for new mail.

IMAP clients assume the existence of a persistent Internet connection, allowing discrete actions to be performed on individual messages, while maintaining a connection to the IMAP server. Thus, for applications where Internet connectivity may not be persistent (e.g., a handheld device where Internet connectivity is paid for by the minute), POP might be a better choice than IMAP.

Because IMAP offers many more options than POP, the possibilities for what can go on in a user session are much richer. After connection and authentication, users can check new messages, recently seen messages, unanswered messages, flagged messages, and drafts of messages yet to go out. They can view messages either in their entirety or in part (e.g., header, body, attachment). They can delete or move messages to other folders. They can also respond to messages or forward them to others.

IMAP need not be used strictly for e-mail messages. Because security features allow mailbox folders to be designated as "read only", IMAP can be used for "message board" functionality as well. However, such functionality is usually reserved for message forum services.

Web-based e-mail services

Today, web-based e-mail systems, such as Hotmail, Yahoo! Mail, and Gmail, provide users with the means to access e-mail through a web browser, without requiring a specialized locally configured e-mail client program to access designated POP/IMAP and SMTP servers. This means users can read their e-mail from practically anywhere, without having to use their own computer. Users behind network firewalls, which block the ports required for POP3, IMAP, and SMTP access to outside e-mail servers, can read and send e-mail through web-based services.

Almost all web-based e-mail services employ standard Internet e-mail protocols to store and send e-mail. Many ISPs provide web-based e-mail services that use IMAP as the underlying storage and retrieval mechanism, but access to their SMTP and IMAP servers from the Internet is usually blocked. Blocked IMAP and SMTP servers can be accessed only through the web-based e-mail interfaces. Some services, including Gmail, expose their POP3 servers to allow e-mail clients retrieve messages (Yahoo! Mail does this only for paying customers). Open IMAP access is slowly becoming more commonplace, with both AOL and Gmail now providing this service. The vast majority of services tightly control access to SMTP servers for sending e-mail to prevent abuse by spammers.

2.3.3 Message forums

Message forums are on-line services that allow users to write messages to be posted on the equivalent of an electronic bulletin board and to read messages that others have posted. These messages are usually organized into categories so that people can find the kinds of messages they are looking for.

For years, on-line message forums existed in various forms. Perhaps the earliest form was the *electronic mailing list*. As we mentioned earlier, mailing lists are closed systems: only subscribers can view or post messages. In some situations, a closed private community may be exactly what the doctor ordered, but if the goal is to have open public participation, message forums are more appropriate.

Although message forums were originally localized, meaning that messages appeared only on the system where they were posted, the notion of distributed message forums took hold. Cooperative networks (e.g., FIDONET) allowed systems to share messages, by forwarding them to their network "neighbors." This enabled users to see all the messages posted by anyone on any member system.

The original Internet-based version of message forums was *Netnews*. Netnews organizes messages into *newsgroups*, which form a large hierarchy of topics and categories. Among the main divisions are comp (for computing-related newsgroups), sci (for scientific newsgroups), soc (for socially oriented newsgroups), talk (for newsgroups devoted to talk) and alt (an unregulated hierarchy for "alternative" newsgroups). The naming convention for newsgroups is reminiscent of domain names in reverse, e.g., comp.infosystems.www.

Usenet and UUCP

Netnews existed before the proliferation of the Internet. It grew out of *Usenet*, an interconnected network of Unix systems. Before the Internet took hold, Unix systems communicated with each other over *UUCP*, a protocol used to transmit mail and news over phone lines. It has been suggested, only half in jest, that the proliferation of Unix by Bell Laboratories in the 1980s was an effort by AT&T to increase long-distance phone traffic, since e-mail and Netnews were transmitted by long-distance calls between these Unix systems.

Today, Netnews is transmitted using an Internet protocol called *Network News Transfer Protocol (NNTP)*. The NNTP specification is defined in the Internet RFC 977. NNTP clients allow users to read (and post) messages in newsgroups by connecting to NNTP servers. These servers propagate the newsgroup messages throughout the world by regularly forwarding them to "neighboring" servers.

Netnews functionality is directly incorporated into browsers such as Mozilla, where it is included in the Thunderbird component. It is possible to create web applications that provide Netnews access through normal web browser interactions. Google Groups (originally called Deja News) provides an infrastructure for accessing current and archived newsgroup messages, using the Google search engine to find desired messages.

On-line forums continue to exist in a wide variety of formats. They are commonly implemented as database-driven services local to their related web sites. Today, the Netnews protocol is relegated to a niche role in the on-line forums world, but much can be learned from it when it comes to building collaborative technology for web applications. For the most part, Netnews functionality has been supplanted by web-based forums and blogging services.

2.3.4   Chat and messaging protocols

The *Instant Messaging (IM)* service of America On-line (now AOL) may be responsible for making the notion of IM-ing someone part of our collective vocabulary but, long before AOL, there was the *talk* protocol which enabled users who were logged in to network-connected Unix systems to talk to each other.

A talk server would run on a Unix machine, waiting for requests from other talk servers. (Since talk was a bi-directional service, servers had to run on the machines at both ends of a conversation.) A user would invoke a talk client program to communicate with a person on another machine somewhere else on the network, e.g., elvis@graceland.org. The talk client program would communicate with the local talk server, which would ask the talk server on the remote machine whether the other person is on-line. If so, and if that other person was accepting talk requests, the remote talk server would establish a connection and the two people would use a screen-mode interface to have an on-line conversation.

Today, the vast majority of Internet users eschew command-line interfaces and the notion of being logged in to a particular system to communicate with others (the way people used to connect to AOL or Compuserve) is alien to most people. A protocol such as talk would not work in its original form in today's diverse Internet world.

Efforts to create an open, interoperable Instant Messaging protocol have been unsuccessful thus far. Proprietary instant-messaging systems (such as those from AOL, Yahoo!, and Microsoft) are exclusive, and intense competition yields a lack of cooperation between instant messaging providers that further limits the degree of interoperability we can get from them. Many shareware or open-source client programs for instant messaging implement multiple protocols to provide access to multiple instant-messaging services. For now, the best solution would seem to be provided by tools that attempt to connect to the widest variety of services. The providers of these services make this difficult by keeping their specifications proprietary and updating them frequently, so it is a struggle to keep ahead of these changes. XMPP (formerly known as Jabber) is an open source instant-messaging protocol that is gaining traction but has not achieved the popularity of better-known commercial services.

2.3.5   Security and encryption

Virtually all the data we've discussed up to this point is transmitted "in the clear," meaning it is readable as plain text. A "packet sniffer" (a program that scans a TCP/IP network and collects transmitted data) can easily retrieve all this data. (Although the packet nature of TCP/IP would require observing programs to reorder and properly sequence all the gathered packets to make any sense of them, such a task is not difficult.) This means that all of your network traffic (e-mail, chat messages, Telnet connections, etc.) is available to anyone with the tools to scan that traffic. Securing your data transmissions means encrypting the data so that a hacker cannot easily decrypt it without knowing the specific "key" associated with the encryption process.

Secure Shell (*SSH*) serves as a secure replacement for Telnet, encrypting the traffic that would normally be exposed in a standard Telnet connection. SSH is more than just an alternative to Telnet. Using *public key authentication* and the capability called *tunneling*, SSH enables sophisticated mechanisms for secure data transmission.

Public key authentication requires a *key pair* consisting of a *private key* and a *public key*. The basic principle is that messages encrypted with the public key can only be decrypted with the corresponding private key and vice versa. The key pair is generated by its owner using a key generation utility that is usually included with SSH client programs. For an individual user, the private key is kept on the user's computer at a location known to the SSH client program. The public key is placed on the server machine at a location known to the SSH server program. Keys are complex (usually 1024 to 2048 bits in size) and breaking the encryption is sufficiently difficult to deter most attempts.

In practice, this exchange of keys is bidirectional. A server publishes its public key, often called a "host key." Clients connecting with that server download its host key and persist it locally. During subsequent connections, the server uses its private key to encrypt a message for the client. If the client can successfully decrypt this message using the downloaded host key, this confirms that the server is the machine it claims to be.

The SSH server tries to authenticate a user attempting to connect using public key authentication. The authentication process works as follows:

1. The user attempts to connect to a server using an SSH client.
2. The server sends its host key to the client. If this is the first time it connects to the server, the SSH client program asks the user whether the new host key should be accepted. If the user accepts, the host key is added to a local store on the client machine and is compared to the key sent down by the server the next time a connection is attempted. A disparity may be indicative of a "man-in-the-middle" attack, in which another machine tries to impersonate the target server.
3. The server sends a random message encrypted with the user's public key to the client.
4. The client attempts to decrypt the message using the user's private key.
5. The client then sends the decrypted contents of the message back to the server.
6. The server compares the contents of the returned message with the original content. If the contents match, this proves that the client knows the private key. This evidence is sufficient for the server to authenticate the user.

If the configuration is correct, connection is seamless. Note that no passwords are transmitted across the network if this mechanism is employed, although SSH *can* be configured to allow password access. Password access is less secure because the password must be transmitted in clear text over the network before the connection can be established.

A private key may be encrypted with a *passphrase*, meaning that SSH clients require entry of the passphrase to decrypt the private key before the connection is attempted. This is safer than password authentication because the passphrase is not transmitted across the network – the decryption process is local to the client machine.

SSH connections can provide secure access to a command-line login shell on a remote machine but other kinds of network traffic also need to be secured. Fortunately, SSH provides a way to do this by *tunneling* network traffic through an SSH connection using a technique called *port forwarding*. This means that TCP/IP requests bound for a particular port on the client machine are "tunneled" through the secure SSH connection to a port on the server.

Here is an example using IMAP. If you configure your e-mail client to access e-mail via IMAP on a remote server, it does not function if traffic to port 143 (the standard IMAP port) is blocked by a router or firewall. Using the port forwarding options of the SSH protocol, you can establish an SSH connection to the server that "tunnels" TCP/IP traffic directed to a port on your local client machine (e.g., port 9143) to port 143 on the remote machine. Instead of telling your IMAP client program that the IMAP server it wants to connect to has the address associated with the inaccessible remote server, you tell it that the IMAP server is located at `localhost` (your local machine) on port 9143. IMAP requests made by your e-mail client are then passed through from `localhost:9143` to port 143 on the remote server via the SSH tunnel.

SSH-tunneling approaches work well for securing individual user connections, but publicly accessible servers need to employ mechanisms that don't require users to build their own custom SSH tunnels to retrieve or send e-mail securely. Secure SMTP, POP, and IMAP services are provided over *Transport Layer Security (TLS)*, formerly known as *Secure Sockets Layer (SSL)*. More sophisticated e-mail providers offer these secure e-mail services, even as they continue to provide non-secure services for legacy clients. The secure protocols may be requested by clients through negotiation at connection time. Alternatively, a provider may elect to offer the secure version of the service on an alternate port (usually 995 for POP and 993 for IMAP).

2.3.6 File server protocols

E-mail and live messaging services represent fleeting, transitory communications over the Internet. Once an instant message or e-mail message has been read, it is usually discarded. Even forum-based messages, archived or not, lack a degree of permanence, and posters tend not to treat them as anything more than passing transient dialogs (or, in some unfortunate cases, monologs). Providing remote access to more persistent documents and files is a fundamental necessity to enable sharing of resources.

For years before the emergence of the Internet, files were shared using electronic *Bulletin Board Systems (BBS)*. People would dial into a BBS via a modem and gain access to directories of files to download (and, sometimes, "drop" directories into which their own files could be uploaded). Various file-transfer protocols (e.g., Kermit, Xmodem, and Zmodem) were used to enable this functionality over telephone dial-up lines.

To facilitate this functionality over the Internet, the *File Transfer Protocol* (*FTP*) was created. An FTP server operates in a manner similar to an e-mail server. Commands exist to authenticate the connecting user, provide information about available files, and allow the retrieval of selected files. While e-mail servers limit access to a preset collection of folders (e.g., the inbox) solely for purposes of downloading messages, FTP servers also allow users to traverse to different directories within the server's local file system and to download files from (and, if authorized, upload files into) those directories. The FTP specification has gone through a number of iterations over the years. The most recent version is Internet RFC 1579. It describes the process by which FTP servers make files available to FTP clients.

First, a user connects to an FTP server using an FTP client program. FTP interactions usually require *two* connections between the client and server: the *control connection* passes commands and status responses between the client and the server; the *data connection* is the connection over which the data transfers occur. User authentication occurs over the control connection. Once connected and authenticated, the user submits commands to set transfer modes, change directories, list the contents of directories, and transfer files. Whether or not the user can enter specific directories, view directory contents, and download or upload files depends on the access privileges associated with the user account on the server. Note that the root directory of the FTP server need not be the same as the root directory of the server machine's local file system. System administrators can configure FTP servers so that only a discrete directory subtree is accessible through the FTP server.

FTP servers can allow open access to files without requiring user authentication, through a service called *anonymous FTP*. When an FTP server is configured to support anonymous FTP, a user ID called "anonymous" is defined that accepts any password. Internet etiquette (often called *netiquette*) prescribes that users should provide their e-mail address as the password but this convention is rarely adhered to today. The system administrator can further restrict the file system subtree that is accessible to anonymous users, usually providing read-only access (although it is possible to configure a *drop folder* into which anonymous users can place files). Most of the FTP archives found on the Internet make use of anonymous FTP to provide open access to files.

Other file server protocols have come into being over the years, but none has achieved the popularity of FTP. FTP is still very popular, but its use over unsecured connections has fallen into disfavor. *Secure FTP (SFTP)*, which is nothing but FTP through an SSH tunnel, is the preferred mechanism. With the advent of next generation distributed *peer-to-peer* (P2P) file-sharing systems (e.g., LimeWire, BitTorrent), we can expect to see changes in the file server landscape over the next few years.

2.4   And Then Came the Web ...

While FTP provided interactive functionality for users seeking to transfer files across the Internet, it was not a very user-friendly service. FTP clients, especially the command-line variety, were tedious to use and provided limited interactivity. Once you traversed to the directory you wanted and downloaded or uploaded your files, your "user experience" was complete. Even GUI-based FTP clients did not appreciably enhance the interactivity of FTP.

Other services sought to make the on-line experience more interactive. *Gopher* was a service developed at the University of Minnesota (hence the name – Minnesota is the "gopher state") that served up *menus* to users. In Gopher, the items in menus were not necessarily file-system directories, as they were in FTP. They were logical lists of items grouped according to category, leading the user to other resources. These resources did not have to be on the same system as the Gopher menu. In fact, a Gopher menu could list both local resources and resources on other systems, including other Gopher menus, FTP archives, and (finally) files. Again, once you reached the level of a file, your traversal was complete. There was nowhere else to go, except to retrace your steps back along the path you just took.

Gopher only caught on as a mainstream Internet service in a limited capacity. Over time, for a variety of reasons, it faded into the woodwork, in part because a better and more flexible service came along right behind it. That system married the power of the Internet with the capabilities of *hypertext*, to offer a superior medium for user interactivity.

Of course, as you have already figured out, that system is the one promoted by Tim Berners-Lee in the late 1980s and early 1990s, known as the worldwide web. In the next chapter, we discuss the TCP/IP-based protocol underlying the web – HTTP.

QUESTIONS AND EXERCISES

1. Find and download the Internet RFCs associated with the POP3, SMTP and FTP protocols.

2. What kind of traffic is sent over ICMP?

3. What is the main difference between TCP and UDP? What kinds of traffic would be suitable for each? What kinds of traffic would be suitable for both? Provide examples.

4. If you get your e-mail from a provider that offers a POP3 service, use a "Telnet" client program to connect to your POP3 server. What POP3 commands would you use to connect, authenticate, and check for mail? What command would you use to read a message? To delete a message? To view message headers?

5. Assume you are implementing an e-mail client application (an MUA) for a handheld device that does not have a persistent connection to the Internet. Which protocol would you use for reading e-mail? For sending e-mail?

6. Which mode of FTP is used at public FTP sites? How does it differ from a "normal" FTP service?

2.5   Bibliography

Barrett, Daniel J. and Silverman, Richard E., 2001. *SSH, the Secure Shell: The Definitive Guide*. Sebastopol (CA): O'Reilly & Associates.

Comer, Douglas, 1991. *Internetworking with TCP/IP, Volume 1: Principles, Protocols, and Architecture*. Englewood Cliffs (NJ): Prentice-Hall.

Davidson, John 1988. *An Introduction to TCP/IP*. New York: Springer-Verlag.

Hafner, Katie and Lyon, Matthew, 1996. *Where Wizards Stay Up Late: The Origins of the Internet*. New York: Simon & Schuster.

Krol, Ed, 1994. *The Whole Internet User's Guide and Catalog*, 2nd Edition. Sebastopol (CA): O'Reilly & Associates.

Smith, Roderick W., 2002. *Advanced Linux Networking*. Boston (MA): Addison-Wesley Professional.

Stephenson, Neal, 1999. *In the Beginning Was the Command Line*. New York: Avon Books.

Wood, David, 1999. *Programming Internet E-mail*. Sebastopol (CA): O'Reilly & Associates.

CHAPTER 3

Birth of the Web: HTTP

IN THIS CHAPTER

- Historical perspective
- The Uniform Resource Locator
- Fundamentals of HTTP
- Better information through headers
- Evolution of the HTTP Protocol

OBJECTIVES

- Offer a historical perspective on the main building blocks of the web.
- Discuss fundamentals of the scheme for addressing web resources.
- Discuss fundamentals of the HTTP protocol.
- Set the stage for learning web technologies based on first principles.

3.1   Historical Perspective

3.1.1   CERN: birthplace of the web

For all practical purposes, the web started at CERN back in 1989. That is when Tim Berners-Lee wrote a proposal for a hypertext-based information management system and distributed it among the scientists at CERN. Although initially interest in the proposal was limited, it sparked the interest of someone else at CERN, Robert Cailliau, who helped Berners-Lee reformat and redistribute the proposal, referring to the system as a "World Wide Web."

By the end of 1990, Berners-Lee had implemented a server and a command-line browser using the initial version of the protocol (HTTP) that he designed for this system. By the middle of 1991, this server and browser were made available throughout CERN. Soon thereafter, the software was made available for anonymous FTP download on the Internet. Interest in HTTP and the web grew, and many people downloaded the software. A newsgroup, comp.infosystems.www, was created to support discussion of this new technology.

By the beginning of 1993, there were about 50 different sites running HTTP servers. This number grew to 200 by the autumn of that year. In addition, since the specification for the HTTP protocol was openly available, others were implementing their own server and browser software, including GUI-based browsers that supported typographic controls and display of images.

3.1.2 Building blocks of the web

There were three basic components devised by Tim Berners-Lee comprising the essence of web technology:

- a markup language for formatting hypertext documents;
- a uniform notation scheme for addressing accessible resources over the network;
- a protocol for transporting messages over the network.

The markup language that allowed cross-referencing of documents via hyperlinks was the *HyperText Markup Language*, or *HTML*, which we discuss in Chapter 4.

The uniform notation scheme is called the *Uniform Resource Identifier (URI)*. For historic reasons, it is most often referred to as the *Uniform Resource Locator (URL)*. We cover the fundamentals of the URL specification in Section 3.2.

The bulk of this chapter is devoted to the inner workings of the transport protocol: *HyperText Transfer Protocol*, also known as *HTTP*. Understanding HTTP is critical to designing efficient web applications. This will become apparent when we discuss the complex interactions between HTML, XML, and web server technologies such as the Common Gateway Interface (CGI) and the Servlet API. Understanding HTTP is also critical to maintaining those applications, as any effort to analyze problems in complex web applications will demonstrate. Understanding the HTTP messages passed between servers, proxies and browsers leads to necessary insights into the nature of underlying problems.

3.2 Uniform Resource Locator

Tim Berners-Lee knew that one piece of the web puzzle would be a notation scheme for referencing accessible resources anywhere on the Internet. He devised this notational scheme so that it would be flexible, so that it would be extensible, and so that it would support other protocols besides HTTP. This notational scheme is known as the *Uniform Resource Locator (URL)*.

I Am He As You Are He As URL as We Are All Together

Participants in the original World Wide Web Consortium (also known as the W3C) had reservations about Berners-Lee's nomenclature. There were concerns about his use of the word "universal" (originally, URL stood for Universal Resource Locator) and about the way a URL specified a resource's location (which could be subject to frequent change) rather than a fixed immutable name. The notion of a fixed name for a resource came to be known as the URN or Uniform Resource Name.

A URN would be a much nicer mechanism for addressing and accessing web resources than a URL. URLs utilize "locator" information that embeds both a server address and a file location. URNs utilize a simpler human-readable name that does not change even when the resource is moved to another location. The problem is that URNs have failed to materialize as a globally supported web standard, so for all practical purposes we are still stuck with URLs.

As a matter of convenience, W3C introduced the notion of the Uniform Resource Identifier (URI), which was defined as the union of URLs and URNs. "URL" is still the most commonly used term, though "URI" is what you should use if you are a stickler for formal correctness. Throughout this book, we favor the more widely accepted term "URL" for the strictly pragmatic reason of minimizing confusion.

The generalized notation associated with a URL is as follows:

```
scheme://host[:port]/path/.../[;url-params][?query-string][#anchor]
```

Here is an example of a URL:

```
http://www.mywebsite.com/sj/test;id=8079?name=bob&x=true#label
```

Let's break the URL down into its component parts:

- **scheme**: This portion of the URL designates the underlying protocol to be used (e.g., `http` or `ftp`); it is followed by a colon and two forward slashes. In the example URL, the scheme is `http`.
- **host**: This is the IP address (numeric or DNS-based) for the web server being accessed; it usually follows the colon and two forward slashes. In the example URL, the host is `www.mywebsite.com`.
- **port**: This is an optional portion of the URL designating the port number to which the target web server listens. (The default port number for HTTP servers is 80, but some configurations are set up to use an alternate port number. When they do, that number must be specified in the URL.) The port number, if it appears, is preceded by a colon.
- **path**: Logically speaking, this is the path through the file system from the "root" directory of the server to the desired document. (In practice, web servers may use aliasing to point to documents, gateways, and services that are not explicitly accessible from the server's root directory.) The path immediately follows the server and port number and, by definition, includes that first forward slash. In the example URL, the path is `/sj/test`.
- **url-params**: This portion of the URL includes optional name–value pairs ("URL parameters"). It was once rarely used but is now used commonly for session identifiers in application servers supporting the Java Servlet API. They are useful to protect against some browser actions. For example, when submitting HTML forms using the HTTP GET method, most browsers substitute query strings of action URLs with attribute–value pairs (see Section 3.3.4). URL parameters are preceded by a semi-colon immediately after the path information. In the example URL, the URL parameter is `id=8079`.

- **query-string**: This optional portion of the URL contains name–value pairs, which represent dynamic parameters associated with the request. These parameters are commonly included in links for tracking and context-setting purposes. They may also be produced from variables in HTML forms. If present, the query string is preceded by a question mark. Equals signs (=) separate names and values, and ampersands (&) mark the boundaries between name–value pairs. In the example URL, the query string is `name=bob&x=true`.
- **anchor**: This optional portion of the URL is a reference to a positional marker within the requested document, like a bookmark. If present, it is preceded by a hash mark or pound sign ("#"). In the example URL, the anchor is `label`.

The URL notation here applies to most protocols (e.g., `http`, `https`, and `ftp`). However, some protocols employ different notations (e.g., `mailto:rich.rosen@mycompany.com`).

3.3   Fundamentals of HTTP

HTTP is the foundation protocol of the web. The most current version of the HTTP protocol is HTTP/1.1, which is documented in Internet RFC 2616. Web servers and browsers exchange information using the HTTP protocol, which is why web servers are often called HTTP servers. Similarly, web browsers are sometimes referred to as HTTP clients, but their functionality goes beyond HTTP support.

It was Tim Berners-Lee's intent that web browsers should enable access to a wide variety of content, not just content accessible via HTTP. Thus, even the earliest web browsers were designed to support other protocols including FTP and Gopher. Today, web browsers support not only HTTP, FTP, and local file access, but e-mail and Netnews as well. When we refer to an HTTP client, the statements we make are applicable to browsers, proxies, and other custom HTTP client programs.

HTTP Proxies

HTTP proxies act as both servers and clients, making requests to web servers on behalf of other clients. Proxies enable HTTP transfers across firewalls. They also provide support for caching of HTTP messages and filtering of HTTP requests. They fill a variety of other interesting roles in complex environments.

HTTP is an application-level protocol in the TCP/IP protocol suite, using TCP as the underlying Transport Layer protocol for transmitting messages. The HTTP protocol uses the *request–response paradigm*, which basically means that an HTTP client program sends an HTTP request message to an HTTP server, which returns an HTTP response message. The structure of these request and response messages is similar to that of e-mail messages, in that they consist of a group of lines containing *message headers*, followed by a blank line, followed by a *message body*.

HTTP is a *stateless* protocol, which does not rely on a persistent connection for communication logic. An HTTP transaction consists of a single request from a client to a server, followed by a single response from the server back to the client.

Keep It Simple!

HTTP is a very simple protocol, which is both a limitation and a source of strength. Many people in the industry criticized HTTP because it was a simple stateless protocol with limited functionality, but it is HTTP that took the world by storm while more sophisticated protocols never found their momentum.

3.3.1   Request–response paradigm

First and foremost, HTTP is based on the *request–response paradigm*: browsers (and possibly proxies) send messages to HTTP servers, which generate messages that are sent back to the browsers. The messages sent to HTTP servers are called *requests* and the messages generated by the servers are called *responses*.

In practice, servers and browsers rarely communicate directly – there are one or more proxies in between. A connection is defined as a virtual circuit (see Figure 3.1) that is composed of HTTP agents, including the browser, the server, and intermediate proxies participating in the exchange.

3.3.2   Stateless protocol

HTTP is a *stateless* protocol, which contrasts with *stateful* protocols, such as FTP, SMTP, and POP. When a protocol is stateful, sequences of related commands are treated as a single interaction. The server must maintain the "state" of its interaction with the client throughout the transmission of successive commands, until the interaction is terminated. A sequence of transmitted and executed commands is often called a *session*.

Stateful Internet protocols manage their sessions within the scope of a single *persistent connection*. It is common to have multiple sessions during the course of a single connection. A session may be

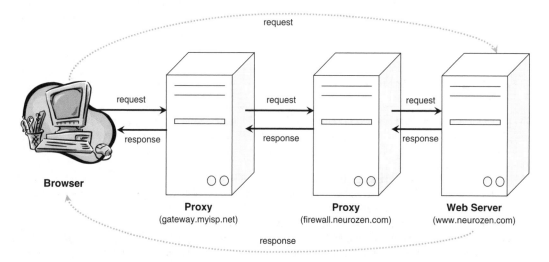

Figure 3.1   The request–response virtual circuit.

terminated without terminating the connection, but terminating the connection means all associated sessions are simultaneously terminated. Stateful protocols require persistent connections, but the use of persistent connections alone does not necessarily mean that a protocol is stateful.

In contrast, each HTTP exchange consists of a single request and a single response. Thus, HTTP clients and servers are not required to maintain state between transmitted commands.

Persistence and State

Defining HTTP as a stateless protocol makes things simpler, but it also imposes limitations on the capabilities of web applications. Prior to HTTP/1.1, the lifetime of a connection was limited to a single request–response exchange. This meant that there was no way to "batch" related requests together – for example, to retrieve an HTML page and all the embedded images in the course of a single connection. This also meant that there was no way to maintain persistent information about a "session" of successive interactions between a client and server.

HTTP/1.1 assumes that the connection remains in place until it is broken, or until HTTP servers or clients request that it be broken. This makes it possible to address the "batching" issue. However, the connection is maintained on a "best-effort" basis, which means that persistent connections cannot be used to maintain state across requests.

We come back to the technicalities of establishing and breaking HTTP connections in Section 3.5. In Section 3.4.4, we discuss the evolution of cookies as a mechanism for state and session management in web applications.

3.3.3 Structure of HTTP messages

HTTP messages (both requests and responses) have a structure similar to e-mail messages; that is, they consist of a block of lines comprising the *message headers*, followed by a blank line, followed by a *message body*. However, HTTP messages are not designed for human consumption and have to be expressive enough to control HTTP servers, browsers, and proxies. This requires quite a bit of sophistication.

E-mail Messages vs HTTP Messages

E-mail messages are intended to pass information directly between people. Thus, both the message headers and the body tend to be "human-readable." E-mail messages (originally, at least) had message bodies that consisted simply of readable plain text, while their message headers included readable information, such as the sender's address and the subject.

Over time, the structure of e-mail messages became more sophisticated, in part to provide support for MIME functionality. Headers were added to control decompression, decoding, and reformatting of message content. In addition, multi-part messages were introduced, allowing messages to have multiple independent sections (often corresponding to a body and a set of attachments).

When HTTP servers and browsers communicate with each other, they perform sophisticated interactions, based on headers as well as body content. Unlike e-mail messages, HTTP messages are not intended to be directly human-readable.

Another important difference is that HTTP request and response messages begin with a special line that does not follow the standard header format. For requests, this line is called the request line and for responses, it is called the status line.

Let us start with a very simple example: loading a static web page residing on a web server. A user may manually type a URL into a browser, click on a hyperlink found within the current page displayed in the browser, or select a bookmarked page to visit. In each of these cases, the desire to visit a particular URL is translated by the browser into an HTTP request with the following structure:

```
METHOD /path-to-resource HTTP/version-number
Header-Name-1: value
Header-Name-2: value

[optional request body]
```

The first, *request*, line contains a number of fields:

- METHOD represents one of several supported *request methods*, chief among them GET and POST.
- The /path-to-resource field represents the *path* portion of the requested URL.
- The version-number field specifies the version of HTTP used by the client.

After the first line we see a list of HTTP *headers*, followed by a blank line, often called a <CR><LF> (for "*carriage return and line feed*"). The blank line separates the request headers from the body of the request. The blank line is followed (optionally) by a *body*, which is in turn followed by another blank line indicating the end of the request.

If the requested URL is http://www.mywebsite.com/sj/index.html, the following code box shows a simplified version of the HTTP request that would be transmitted to the web server at www.mywebsite.com:

```
GET /sj/index.html HTTP/1.1
Host: www.mywebsite.com
```

Note that the request ends with a blank line. In the case of a GET request, there is no body, so the request simply ends with this blank line. Also, note the presence of a Host header. (We discuss headers in detail in Section 3.4.)

The server, upon receiving this request, attempts to generate a response. An HTTP response has the following structure:

```
HTTP/version-number status-code explanation
Header-Name-1: value
Header-Name-2: value

[response body]
```

The first, *status*, line contains the HTTP version, followed by a three-digit *status code* and a brief human-readable explanation of the status code. Here is a simplified version of the HTTP response that the example server would send back to the browser, assuming that the requested file exists and the requestor is authorized to access it:

```
HTTP/1.1 200 OK
Content-Type: text/html
Content-Length: 9934

...

<HTML>
<HEAD>
<TITLE>SJ's Web Page</TITLE>
</HEAD>
<BODY bgcolor="#ffffff">
<H2 align="center">Welcome to Sviergn Jiernsen's Home Page</H2>
...
</H2>
</BODY>
</HTML>
```

The request was processed successfully, so the status line shows the success code (200) and a rather brief explanation of this status (OK). Note the presence of header lines within the response, followed by a blank line, followed by a block of text. (We see later how a browser figures out that this text is to be rendered as HTML.)

The process of transmitting requests and responses between browsers and servers is rarely this simple. For instance, HTML pages may contain references to other accessible resources, such as images, Java applets, and multimedia objects (audio, video, Flash/Flex). Clients that support the rendering of images, the execution of applets, and the presentation of multimedia objects must parse the retrieved HTML page to determine what additional resources are needed to render the page, and then generate HTTP requests to retrieve these additional resources.

Consider a user who requests http://www.cs.rutgers.edu/~shklar/. In Figure 3.2a, the browser sends a GET request to the server, which sends back a response and the browser displays the results (Figure 3.2b). The response contains a reference to an image. The browser creates a GET request for the image and sends it to the server, which sends the image back (Figure 3.2c). The browser then displays the image to the user (Figure 3.2d).

3.3.4   Request methods

There are a variety of *request methods* specified in the HTTP protocol. The most basic ones defined in HTTP/1.1 are GET, HEAD, and POST. In addition, there are the less commonly used PUT, DELETE, TRACE, OPTIONS, and CONNECT.

Step 1: Initial User Request for `"http://www.cs.rutgers.edu/~shklar/"`

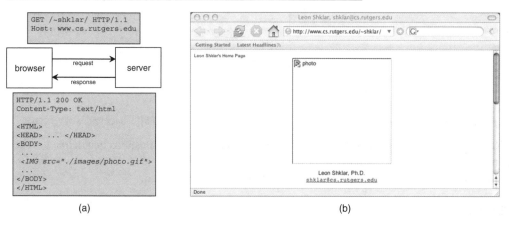

(a)   (b)

Step 2: Secondary Browser Request for `"http://www.cs.rutgers.edu/~shklar/images/photo.gif"`

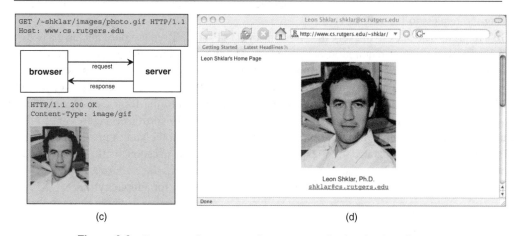

(c)   (d)

Figure 3.2   Sequence of requests and responses to load a simple web page.

Method to Their Madness

HTTP/1.1 servers are not obliged to implement all the request methods. At a minimum, any general-purpose server must support the methods `GET` and `HEAD`. All other methods are optional, though you'd be hard-pressed to find a server in common usage today that does not support `POST` requests. Most of the newer servers also support the `PUT` and `DELETE` methods.

Servers may implement custom methods and define constraints and processing behavior for them. This approach only makes sense for closed environments and is rarely used.

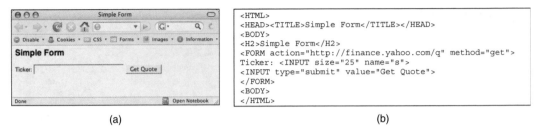

Figure 3.3   A web form (a) displayed in a browser and (b) the HTML that creates the form.

Request methods impose constraints on the message structure. Specifications that define how servers should process requests, including the *Common Gateway Interface* (*CGI*) and the *Java Servlet API*, include discussions of how different request methods should be treated.

GET method

GET is the simplest of the request methods. When you type a URL in your browser, follow a bookmark, or click on a hyperlink to visit another page, the browser uses the GET method when making the request to the web server.

GET requests date back to the very first versions of HTTP. A GET request does not have a body and, until version 1.1, was not required to have headers. (HTTP/1.1 requires that the Host header should be present in every request, in order to support *virtual hosting*, which we discuss in Section 3.5.1.)

Let's take a look at the request that is submitted by an HTTP/1.1 browser when you fill out a simple HTML form to request a stock quote. When we enter a value into the form (see Figure 3.3a), the browser constructs a URL comprised of the action field from the form (see Figure 3.3b) followed by a *query string* containing all of the form's input parameters and the values provided for them.

The query string is separated from the rest of the URL by a question mark. Thus, if the user enters "YHOO", the browser constructs the URL http://finance.yahoo.com/q?s=YHOO and the submitted request is as follows (some optional headers are omitted for simplicity):

```
GET /q?s=YHOO HTTP/1.1
Host: finance.yahoo.com
User-Agent: Mozilla/5.0 (Windows; U; Windows XP; en-US; rv:1.8.0.11)
```

The response that comes back from the server looks something like this:

```
HTTP/1.1 200 OK
Date: Tue, 08 Apr 2008 15:16:46 GMT
Connection: close
Content-Type: text/html

<HTML>
<HEAD>
<TITLE>YHOO: Summary for YAHOO INC - Yahoo! Finance</TITLE>
</HEAD>
<BODY>
. . .
```

```
</BODY>
</HTML>
```

POST method

The fundamental difference between GET and POST requests is that POST requests have a *body*: content that follows the block of headers, with a blank line separating the headers from the body. Going back to the sample form in Figure 3.3, let's change the request method to POST. Notice that the browser now puts form parameters into the body of the message, rather than appending them to the URL as part of the query string:

```
POST /q HTTP/1.1
Host: finance.yahoo.com
User-Agent: Mozilla/4.75 [en] (WinNT; U)
Content-Type: application/x-www-form-urlencoded
Content-Length: 6

s=YHOO
```

The response that arrives from `finance.yahoo.com` happens to be the same as when using the GET method, but only because the designers of the server application decided to support both request methods in the same way:

```
HTTP/1.1 200 OK
Date: Tue, 08 Apr 2008 15:33:04 GMT
Connection: close
Content-Type: text/html

<HTML>
<HEAD>
<TITLE>YHOO: Summary for YAHOO INC - Yahoo! Finance</TITLE>
</HEAD>
<BODY>
...
</BODY>
</HTML>
```

Note that we removed most of the optional headers in the GET and POST requests and the server responses to concentrate on the most essential communication parameters.

GET vs POST

Many web applications are sensitive to the request method employed when accessing a URL. Some applications may accept one request method but not another. Others may perform different functions depending on which request method is used.

For example, some JAVA EE application developers implement Java servlets that rely on the GET method to display an input form. The `action` field of the form references the same servlet through the same URL, but using the POST method. The application may be designed to display a form when it receives a request using the GET method and to process the form (and return the results of the processing) when it receives a request using the POST method.

HEAD method

Requests that use the HEAD method are processed similarly to requests that use the GET method, except that the server sends back only headers in the response. This means the *body* of the response is not sent back and only headers are available to the client. This may be sufficient to enable the client to make decisions about further processing and may reduce the overhead associated with future requests that return the actual content in the message body.

If we were to revisit the sample form in Figure 3.3 and change the request method to HEAD, we would notice that the request did not change (except for the word HEAD rather than GET), and the response contains the same headers as before but no body.

Historically, HEAD requests were often used to support caching. A browser can use a cached copy of a resource (rather than going back to the original source to re-request the content) if the cache entry was created after the date that the content was last modified. If the creation date for the cache entry is *earlier* than the content's last modification date, then the browser should retrieve a "fresh" copy of the content from the source.

Suppose we want to look at a page that we visit regularly in our browser (e.g., Leon's home page). If we have visited this page recently, the browser will have a copy of the page stored in its cache. The browser can determine whether it needs to re-retrieve the page by first submitting a HEAD request:

```
HEAD http://www.cs.rutgers.edu/~shklar/ HTTP/1.1
Host: www.cs.rutgers.edu
User-Agent: Mozilla/5.0 (Windows; U; Windows NT 5.1; en-US; rv:1.8.0.11)
```

The response comes back with a set of headers, including content modification information:

```
HTTP/1.1 200 OK
Date: Tue, 08 Apr 2008 15:55:04 GMT
Server: Apache/2.2.4 (Unix)
Last-Modified: Tue, 29 Oct 2002 04:22:52 GMT
Content-Length: 2111
Content-Type: text/html
```

As you can see from the response, this is a very old page. The browser (or some other HTTP client) can compare the content modification date with the creation date of the cache entry, and resubmit the same request with the GET method if the cache entry is obsolete. We save bandwidth when the content does not change by making a HEAD request. Since responses to HEAD requests do not include the message body, which contains the content, the data transfer overhead is smaller than with the GET request. On the flip side, when the content does change, it takes two requests instead of one to retrieve the content (a HEAD request to discover the change and a GET request to retrieve new content).

Today, more efficient ways to support caching are available (see Sections 3.4.2 and 3.5.2). The HEAD method is still very useful for implementing change-tracking systems, testing and debugging new applications, and discovering server capabilities.

3.3.5   Status codes

The first line of a response is the *status line*, consisting of the protocol and its version number, followed by a three-digit *status code* and a brief explanation of that status code. The status code tells an HTTP client (browser or proxy) either that the response was generated as expected, or that the client needs to perform a specific action, which may be further parameterized via information in the headers. The explanation portion of the line is for human consumption: changing it or omitting it does not cause a properly designed HTTP client to change its actions.

HTTP/1.1 defines five categories of response messages based on their first character:

- Status codes that start with "1" are classified as informational.
- Status codes that start with "2" indicate successful responses.
- Status codes that start with "3" tell the client to perform additional actions (e.g., redirection).
- Status codes that start with "4" represent client request errors or special conditions.
- Status codes that start with "5" represent server errors.

Informational status codes (1xx)

These status codes serve solely informational purposes. They do not denote success or failure of a request, but rather impart information about its further processing. Servers use the status code of 100 to notify clients that they may continue with a partially submitted request (e.g., submit a body after the initial submission of POST headers). Clients can indicate their intent to partially submit a request by including the `Expect: 100-continue` header. A server can examine such requests, determine whether it is capable of satisfying them, and send an appropriate response. If the server is capable of satisfying the request, the response contains a status code of 100:

```
HTTP/1.1 100 Continue
```

If the server cannot satisfy the request, it sends a response with a status code indicating a client request error (a code starting "4").

Successful response status codes (2xx)

The most common successful response status code is 200, which indicates that the request was successfully completed and that the requested resource is being sent back to the client:

```
HTTP/1.1 200 OK
Content-Type: text/html
Content-Length: 9934
...

<HTML>
<HEAD>
<TITLE>SJ's Web Page</TITLE>
</HEAD>
<BODY bgcolor="#ffffff">
<H2 align="center">Welcome to Sviergn Jiernsen's Home Page</H2>
...
</H2>
</BODY>
</HTML>
```

Status code 201 indicates that the request was satisfied and that a new resource was created on the server.

Redirection status codes (3xx)

Status codes starting with a "3" indicate that additional actions are required to satisfy the original request. Normally this involves a *redirection*: the browser is instructed to resubmit the request to another URL.

For example, 301 and 302 both instruct the HTTP client to look for the originally requested resource at the new location specified in the `Location` header of the response. The difference between the two is that 301 tells the client (and proxies) that the resource has moved permanently and that it should always look for that resource at the new location. 302 tells the client that the resource has moved temporarily, and to consider this relocation a one-time deal, just for purposes of this request. In either case, the client should, immediately upon receiving a 301 or 302 response, construct and transmit a new request "redirected" at the new location.

Redirections happen all the time, often unbeknownst to the user. Browsers are designed to respond silently to redirection status codes, so that users never see redirection happen. Some browsers either do not support redirection or allow users to disable the redirection temporarily for debugging and other purposes. To remain compatible with such browsers, web servers can include a message body that explicitly references a link to the new location. This affords the user an opportunity to follow the link manually.

An interesting example of redirection occurs when a user enters a URL specifying a directory, but leaves off the terminating slash. To visit Leon's web site at Rutgers University, you could enter `http://www.cs.rutgers.edu/~shklar` in your browser. This would result in the following HTTP request:

```
GET /~shklar HTTP/1.1
Host: www.cs.rutgers.edu
```

But `~shklar` is a directory on a Rutgers web server, not a file. Web servers are designed to treat a URL ending in a slash as a request for a directory. Such requests may, depending on the server configuration, return either a file with a default name, e.g., `index.html`, if it exists or a listing of the directory's contents. In either case, the web server must first redirect the request, from `http://www.cs.rutgers.edu/~shklar` to `http://www.cs.rutgers.edu/~shklar/`, in order to make the browser aware of the proper location:

```
HTTP/1.1 301 Moved Permanently
Location: http://www.cs.rutgers.edu/~shklar/
Content-Type: text/html
...

<HTML>
<HEAD><TITLE>301 Moved Permanently</TITLE></HEAD>
<BODY id="c03-body-0005">
<H1>301 Moved Permanently</H1>
The document has moved
<A href="http://www.cs.rutgers.edu/~shklar/">
here</A>.
</BODY>
</HTML>
```

Note that the body of the response would not be displayed by browsers that support redirection. Browsers that do not support redirection would display the HTML body leaving it up to the user to follow the link to the new location.

As we demonstrate in Chapter 7, pages that reference external objects through relative URLs may not render correctly, unless the browser knows the proper base URL. A missing slash would result in the browser omitting the trailing directory from the base URL, making it impossible to resolve relative URLs correctly within the body of the response.

Remember the Slash!

This example offers a valuable lesson: if you are trying to retrieve a directory listing (or the default page associated with a directory), don't forget the trailing "/". When manually visiting a URL representing a directory in your browser, you may not even notice the redirect and extra connection resulting from omitting the trailing slash. However, when your applications generate HTML pages containing links to directories, forgetting to add that trailing slash within these links may double the number of requests sent to your server.

Today's sophisticated proxies react to the 301 status by updating internal relocation tables, so that in the future they can submit the relocation response without contacting the destination server. This may sometimes lead to unexpected behavior when server applications are designed without proper regard for differences between 301 and 302 status codes. A typical example is redirecting users to the login page when they are trying to access a protected URL. It is common to include the original URL as a query string parameter. Applications can use this parameter to send users back to the original URL once their credentials are verified. Unfortunately, if the server uses 301 to redirect to the original page, the redirection may be cached. As a result, users may continue to be redirected to the login page every time they go to the original URL, even after they have obtained the credentials.

Imagine that you are a webmaster and you started getting complaints from some users that they cannot login. Neither you nor your quality assurance (QA) team can reproduce it. How long will it take you to figure out that the complainers access the Internet through a caching proxy that was upgraded and is now caching 301 redirections?

Client request error status codes (4xx)

Status codes that start with "4" indicate an abnormal condition with the client request. It can be a malformed request (`400 Bad Request`), an authorization challenge (`401 Not Authorized`), access denial (`403 Forbidden`), or the server's inability to find the requested resource (`404 Not Found`). Although 400, 401, 403, and 404 are the most common status codes in this category, other less common status codes are quite interesting. For example, if the server is not able to manage partially submitted requests using the `Expect: 100-continue` mechanism, it is supposed to respond with `417`:

```
HTTP/1.1 417 Expectation Failed
Date: Tue, 29 Apr 2008 22:26:59 GMT
Server: Apache/2.2.4
```

In another example, the client might use the `If-Unmodified-Since` header to request a resource only if it has not changed since a specific date:

```
GET /~shklar/ HTTP/1.1
Host: www.cs.rutgers.edu
If-Unmodified-Since: Fri, 11 Feb 2000 22:28:00 GMT
```

Since this resource has changed, the server sends back the `412 Precondition Failed` response:

```
HTTP/1.1 412 Precondition Failed
Date: Tue, 29 Apr 2008 22:28:31 GMT
Server: Apache/2.2.4
```

Server error status codes (5xx)

Status codes that start with "5" indicate a server problem that prevents it from satisfying an otherwise valid request (e.g., `500 Internal Server Error` or `501 Not Implemented`).

Status codes represent a powerful means of controlling browser and proxy behavior. There are a large number of different status codes representing different response conditions. Familiarity with status codes is critical when implementing HTTP servers, and it is just as critical when building advanced web applications.

3.4   Better Information Through Headers

As we already know, HTTP headers are a form of message metadata. Enlightened use of headers makes it possible to construct sophisticated applications that establish and maintain sessions, set caching policies, control authentication and authorization, and implement business logic. The HTTP protocol specification makes a clear distinction between *general headers, request headers, response headers*, and *entity headers*.

General headers apply to both request and response messages, but do not describe the body of the message, for example:

```
Date: Tue, 29 Apr 2008 22:28:31 GMT
Connection: close
Warning: Danger, Will Robinson!
```

- The `Date` header specifies the time and date that this message was created.
- The `Connection` header indicates whether the client or server that generated the message intends to keep the connection open. Note that `keep-alive` is the default setting for HTTP/1.1. It is often used for backward compatibility with HTTP/1.0 servers and proxies.
- The `Warning` header stores text for human consumption, something that would be useful when tracing a problem:

Request headers allow clients to pass additional information about themselves and about the request, for example:

```
User-Agent: Mozilla/5.0 (Windows; U; Windows XP; en-US; rv:1.8.0.11)
Host: www.neurozen.com
Referer: http://www.cs.rutgers.edu/~shklar/index.html
Authorization: Basic [encoded-credentials]
```

- The `User-Agent` header identifies the software (e.g., a web browser) responsible for making the request.
- The `Host` header was introduced to enable a single web server to service multiple domains (see Section 6.3.1).
- The `Referer` header provides the server with context information about the request. If the request came about because a user clicked on a link found on a web page, the header is set to the URL of that page.
- The `Authorization` header is transmitted with requests for resources that are restricted only to authorized users. Browsers include this header in follow-up requests after being notified of an *authorization challenge* via a response with a 401 status code and prompting the user for credentials (i.e., *userid* and *password*). Once the server accepts the credentials (as indicated by a successful status code), the browser continues to include them in all further requests that access resources within the same authorization realm. Note that the expiration of authorization credentials is browser-specific. For more information, see Section 3.4.3).

Response headers help the server to pass additional information about the response that cannot be inferred from the status code alone:

```
Location: http://www.mywebsite.com/relocatedPage.html

WWW-Authenticate: Basic realm="KremlinFiles"

Server: Apache/2.2.4
```

- The `Location` header specifies a URL toward which the client should redirect its original request. It always accompanies the 301 and 302 status codes that direct clients to the new location.
- The `WWW-Authenticate` header accompanies the 401 status code that indicates an authorization challenge. The value in this header specifies the protected realm for which proper authorization credentials must be provided before the request can be processed. In the case of a web browser, the combination of the 401 status code and the `WWW-Authenticate` header causes users to be prompted for authentication credentials (i.e., userid and password).
- The `Server` header is not tied to a particular status code. It is an optional header that identifies the server software.

Entity headers describe either message bodies or (in the case of request messages that have no body) target resources. Common entity headers include:

```
Content-Type: mime-type/mime-subtype
Content-Length: xxxx
Last-Modified: Tue, 29 Apr 2008 22:28:31 GMT
```

- The `Content-Type` header specifies the MIME type of the message body's content.
- The `Content-Length` header provides the length of the message body in bytes. It is optional for response messages and required for requests that have a body. When included in a response, it may be used by browsers to impart information about rendering progress. Without this header, the browser can only display how much data has been downloaded. When it is included, the browser can display the amount of data as a percentage of the total size of the message body.
- The `Last-Modified` header, when present in a response, provides the last modification date of the content that is transmitted in the body of the message. It is critical for the effective functioning of browser and proxy caching mechanisms.

3.4.1 Support for content types

So far we have concentrated on message metadata, and for a good reason: understanding metadata is critical to the process of building applications. Still, somewhere along the line, there'd better be some content. After all, without content, web applications would have nothing to present for end users to see and interact with.

You have probably noticed that, when it comes to content you view on the web, your browser might do one of several things. It might:

- render the content as a text page or an HTML page;
- present content inline (within the browser window) through a *plug-in*;

- launch a *helper application* capable of presenting non-HTML content;
- get confused into showing the content of an HTML file (or worse, a server-side script) as plain text without attempting to render or execute it.

What is going on? Obviously, browsers do *something* to determine the content type and to perform actions appropriate for that type.

HTTP borrows its content typing system from *Multipurpose Internet Mail Extensions* (*MIME*). MIME is the standard that was designed to help e-mail clients to display non-text content.

Extending MIME

HTTP has extended MIME and made use of it in ways that were never considered by its original designers. Still, the use of MIME means that web browsers and e-mail clients have much in common, which is why it was so natural to integrate the two.

As in MIME, the data type associated with the body of an HTTP message is defined via a two-layer ordered encoding model, using the `Content-Encoding` and `Content-Type` headers. In other words, for the body to be interpreted according to the type specified in the `Content-Type` header, it has to first be decoded according to the encoding method specified in the `Content-Encoding` header.

In HTTP/1.1, valid settings for the `Content-Encoding` header are `gzip`, for content encoded with the GNU zip program, `compress`, for content encoded with the Unix compress program, or `deflate`, for content encoded with the `zlib` format documented in Internet RFCs 1950 and 1951. (The HTTP/1.0 settings `x-gzip` and `x-compress` are equivalent to the HTTP/1.1 settings `gzip` and `compress`. HTTP/1.1 servers and browsers are required to support HTTP/1.0 settings for backward compatibility.)

Obviously, if web servers encode content using these encoding methods, web browsers (and other clients) must be able to perform the reverse operations on encoded message bodies prior to rendering or processing the content. When the web server includes the `Content-Encoding: gzip` header with the response, the browser knows to *decode* the encoded content prior to presentation. For example, a browser is intelligent enough to open a compressed document file (e.g., `test.doc.gz`) and automatically invoke Microsoft Word to let you view the original `test.doc` file.

The `Content-Type` header is set to a media type that is defined as a combination of a type, a subtype, and attribute−value pairs:

```
type "/" subtype [ ";" parameter-string ]
```

The most common example is:

```
Content-Type: text/html
```

The type is set to `text` and the subtype to `html`, which tells the browser to render the message body as an HTML page. Another example is:

```
Content-Type: text/plain; charset='us-ascii'
```

Here the subtype is plain. The parameter string is passed to whatever client program ends up processing the body whose content type is text/plain. The parameter may have some impact on how the client program processes the content. If the parameter is not known to the program, it is ignored. Some other examples of MIME types are text/xml and application/xml for XML content, application/pdf for Adobe Portable Data Format (PDF), and video/quicktime for QuickTime videos.

Since MIME was introduced to support multimedia transfers over e-mail, it is not surprising that it provides for the inclusion of multiple independent entities within a single message body. In the e-mail context, these *multipart messages* usually take the form of a textual message body plus attachments.

The multipart structure is very useful for HTTP transfers in both directions (client-to-server and server-to-client). In the client-to-server direction, form data entered through a browser can be accompanied by client-side file content that is transmitted to the server. We discuss multipart messages used for submitting HTTP requests via HTML forms in Chapter 6.

In the server-to-client direction, a web server can implement primitive image animation by feeding the browser a multipart sequence of images. Netscape used to provide an example of a primitive image animation technique that generates a stream of pictures of Mozilla (the Godzilla-like dragon that was the mascot of the original Netscape project). The original description and demonstration on the Netscape site are no longer available. We have reproduced them on our web site at http://www.webappbuilders.com/demo/pushpull. It is based on requesting a stream of images from a server application:

```
GET /demo/mozimation HTTP/1.1
Host: demo.webappbuilders.com
Date: Sun, 11 Jan 2009 12:22:19 GMT
```

The response is a multipart/x-mixed-replace message. This content type instructs the browser to render enclosed image bodies one at a time but within the same screen real estate. The individual images are encoded and separated by the *boundary* string specified in the header:

```
HTTP/1.1 200 OK
Date: Wed, 2 May 2001 12:22:31 GMT
Content-Type: multipart/x-mixed-replace; boundary=ThisRandomString
Connection: close

--ThisRandomString
Content-Type: image/gif

...

--ThisRandomString
Content-Type: image/gif

...
```

```
--ThisRandomString
Content-Type: image/gif


...

--ThisRandomString
```

Message typing is necessary to help both servers and browsers determine proper actions in process-ing requests and responses. Browsers use types and sub-types either to select a proper content-rendering module or to invoke a third-party tool (e.g., Microsoft Word). Multipart-rendering modules control recursive invocation of proper rendering modules for the body parts. In the example above, the browser's page-rendering module invokes the browser's image-rendering module once per image, passing it the same screen location for each image.

Server-side applications use type information to process requests. For example, consider a server-side application responsible for receiving files from a browser and storing them locally. This application requires type information in order to separate file content from accompanying form data that defines the file name and target location.

3.4.2 Caching control

HTTP caching is a set of mechanisms allowing HTTP responses to be held in some form of temporary storage medium, as a means of improving application performance. Instead of satisfying future requests by going back to the original data source, the saved copy of the data can be used. This eliminates the overhead of re-executing the original request and greatly improves server throughput.

Three types of caching are employed in web application environments: *server-side* caching, *browser-side* caching, and *proxy-side* caching. In this section, we deal with browser-side and proxy-side caching, leaving server-side caching for Chapter 6.

Take a Walk on the Proxy Side

In the real world, HTTP messages are rarely passed directly between servers and browsers. Most commonly, they pass through intermediate proxies. These proxies perform a variety of functions in the web application environment, including the relaying of HTTP messages through firewalls and supporting the use of server farms (conglomerations of server machines that look to the outside world as if they have the same IP address or host name).

Admittedly, proxies sit in the middle, between servers and browsers, so it may seem silly to talk about "proxy-side" caching. Even though the wording may seem strange, do not dismiss the notion of proxy-side caching as some sort of anomaly.

When is the use of a cached response appropriate? This is a decision usually made by the server or by web applications running on the server. Many requests arrive at a given URL, but the server may deliver different content for each request, as the underlying source of the content is constantly changing. If the server "knows" that the requested content is relatively static and is not likely to change, it can instruct browsers, proxies, and other clients to cache that particular response. If the content is so static that it is never expected to change, the server can tell its clients that the response can be cached for an arbitrarily long period. If the content has a limited lifetime, the server can still make use of caching by telling its clients to cache the response but only for that limited period. Even if the content is constantly changing, the server can make the decision that its clients can tolerate out-of-date content for a limited time.

Web servers and server-side applications are in the best position to judge whether clients should be allowed to cache their responses. There are two mechanisms for establishing caching rules, one for HTTP/1.0 and the other for HTTP/1.1. Because there are web servers and clients that still support only HTTP 1.0, any attempt to support caching must provide for both mechanisms in what is hopefully a backward-compatible fashion.

HTTP/1.1 provides a mechanism for enforcing caching rules based on the `Cache-Control` header, which can take the following values:

- The `public` setting removes all restrictions and authorizes both shared and user-localized caching mechanisms to store the response.
- The `private` setting indicates that the response is directed at a single user and should not be stored in a shared cache. For instance, if two authorized users both make a secure request to a particular URL to obtain information about their private accounts, obviously it would be a problem if an intermediate proxy decided it could improve performance for the second user by sending a cached copy of the first user's response.
- The `no-cache` setting indicates that neither browsers nor proxies are allowed to cache the response. However, there are a number of options associated with this setting that make it somewhat complicated. The header may list the names of specific HTTP headers that are not cached (i.e., that must be re-acquired from the server that originated the cached response). If such headers *are* listed, then the response may be cached, *excluding* those listed headers.

HTTP/1.0 browsers and proxies are not guaranteed to obey instructions in the `Cache-Control` header, which was first officially introduced in HTTP/1.1. For practical purposes, this means that the mechanism is only reliable in controlled environments where all the clients are compliant with HTTP/1.1. In the real world, there are still HTTP/1.0 browsers and proxies around.

A partial solution is to use the deprecated `Pragma` header, which has only one defined setting: no-cache. When used with the `Cache-Control` header, it prevents HTTP/1.0 browsers and proxies from caching the response. However, this alone may not have the desired effect on clients that are compliant with HTTP/1.1, since the `Pragma` header is deprecated and may not be properly supported in those clients. Thus, a more complete backward-compatible solution would be to include both `Pragma` and `Cache-Control` headers, as in the following example:

```
HTTP/1.1 200 OK
Date: Wed, 30 Apr 2008 03:26:18 GMT
Server: Apache/2.2.4
Last-Modified: Wed, 30 Apr 2008 03:25:36 GMT
Cache-Control: private
Pragma: no-cache
Content-Length: 2255
```

```
Content-Type: text/html

<HTML>
...
</HTML>
```

This response is guaranteed to prevent HTTP/1.0 agents from caching it altogether and to prevent HTTP/1.1 agents from storing it in a shared cache. HTTP/1.1 agents may or may not ignore the `Pragma: no-cache` header. If they don't ignore it, efficiency will suffer but at least we played it safe to ensure that we do not implement a potentially dangerous caching policy.

3.4.3 Security

Authentication is the process of verifying user identity; authorization is the process of checking whether the user has access to a particular resource. HTTP provides built-in support for *basic authentication*, where user credentials (userid and password) are transmitted via the `Authorization` header as a single encoded string. Since this string is simply encoded (not encrypted), this mechanism is only safe if performed over a secure connection. Many web applications implement their own authentication and authorization schemes that go beyond basic HTTP authentication.

HTTP authentication

It is very easy to tell whether an application is using built-in HTTP authentication or its own authentication scheme. When a web application is using built-in HTTP authentication, the browser displays its built-in, pop-up authentication dialog, prompting the user for the credentials, rather than requesting this information within the page-rendering window.

When built-in HTTP authentication is employed and a request for a restricted resource is sent to a server, the browser receives the 401 status code indicating that the request is not authorized, as in the following example:

```
HTTP/1.1 401 Authenticate
Date: Wed, 30 Apr 2008 03:41:23 GMT
Server: Apache/2.2.4
WWW-Authenticate: Basic realm="Chapter3"
```

Having received this response, the browser prompts the user for a userid and password associated with the realm specified in the `WWW-Authenticate` header (in this case, `Chapter3`). The realm name helps users to find their names and passwords, and serves as a logical organizing principle for access control – designating which resources require what types of authorization. Web masters can administer web servers to define realms, associate them with files and directories, and establish userids and passwords that limit access to these resources. (Note: Mechanisms for defining security realms are server-specific and can vary greatly between different servers and operating systems.)

In response to the browser prompt, the user specifies a name and password. After collecting this input from the user, the browser resubmits the original request with the `Authorization` header. The value of this header is a string composed of the word `Basic` (the only type of authentication that is officially supported) and the colon-separated, base64-encoded representations of the user name and password.

```
GET /book/chapter3/index.html
Date: Wed, 30 Apr 2008 03:41:24 GMT
Host: www.neurozen.com
Authorization: Basic eNCoDEd-uSErId:pASswORd
```

Insecurity

Note that the user name and password are encoded but not encrypted. Encryption is a secure form of encoding, wherein the content can only be decoded if a unique key is known. Simple encoding mechanisms, like the Base64 encoding used in basic HTTP authentication, can be decoded by anyone who knows the encoding scheme. Obviously, this is very dangerous when encoded (not encrypted) information is transmitted over an insecure connection.

Secure connections (using extensions to the HTTP protocol, such as Secure HTTP) encrypt all transmitted information; thus sensitive information (like passwords) is secure.

It is hard to believe that there are still a large number of web sites – even e-commerce sites – that transmit passwords over open connections and establish a secure connection only after the user has logged in!

As a user of the web, whenever you are prompted for your name and password, you should always check whether the connection is secure. With HTTP-based authentication, you should check that the URL of the page you are attempting to access uses `https` (Secure HTTP) for its protocol. With proprietary authentication schemes, you should check the URL that is supposed to process your user name and password. For example, with a form-based login, you should check the URL defined in the `action` attribute.

As a designer of applications for the web, you have to incorporate these safeguards into your applications to ensure the security of users' sensitive information.

The server, having received the request with the `Authorization` header, attempts to verify the user credentials. If the userid and password match the credentials for a valid user within that realm, the server serves the content. The browser associates the authorization credentials with the authorized URL, and uses them as the value of the `Authorization` header in future requests to *dependent URLs*. Since the browser does this automatically, users are not prompted again until they encounter a resource that belongs to a different security realm.

Dependent URLs

We say that a URL "depends" on a second URL, if the portion of the second URL up to and including the last slash is a prefix of the first URL. For example, the URL `http://www.cs.rutgers.edu/~shklar/classes/` depends on the URL `http://www.cs.rutgers.edu/~shklar/`. This means that, having submitted authorization credentials for `http://www.cs.rutgers.edu/~shklar/`, the browser would know to resubmit those same credentials within the `Authorization` header when requesting `http://www.cs.rutgers.edu/~shklar/classes/`.

If the server fails to verify the userid and password sent by the browser, it either resends the security challenge using the status code `401` or refuses outright to serve the requested resource, sending a response with the status code of 403 Forbidden. The latter happens when the server exceeds a defined limit of security challenges. This limit is normally configurable and is designed to prevent simple break-ins by trial and error.

We have described the so-called *basic* authentication that is supported by both HTTP/1.0 and HTTP/1.1. It is a bit simplistic but it does provide reasonable protection – as long as you are transmitting over a secure connection. Most commercial applications that deal with sensitive financial data use their own authorization and authentication mechanisms that are not built into HTTP. Commonly, user names and passwords are transmitted in the bodies of POST requests over secure connections. These bodies are interpreted by server applications that decide whether to send back content, repeat the password prompt or display an error message. These server applications don't use the 401 status code that triggers the built-in authentication mechanism, though they may choose to use the 403 status code indicating that access to the requested resource is forbidden.

3.4.4   Session support

We have mentioned several times now that HTTP is a stateless protocol. So what do we do if we need to implement a *stateful* application? The most obvious example of maintaining state in a web application is the on-line shopping cart. When you visit an e-commerce site, you view catalog pages describing items, then add them to your "cart" as you decide to purchase them. When the time comes to process your order, the site remembers what items you have placed in your cart. How does it know, if HTTP requests are atomic and disconnected from each other?

To maintain state between HTTP requests, it suffices to provide some mechanism for the communicating parties to establish agreements for transferring state information in HTTP messages. HTTP/1.1 establishes these agreements through Set-Cookie and Cookie headers. Set-Cookie is a response header sent by the server to the browser, setting state information or a *session* identifier that references a server-side state. Cookie is a request header transmitted by the browser in subsequent requests to the same (or a related) server. Either it consists of explicit elements of state information or it is set to a session identifier, which helps to associate requests with *sessions*.

Server applications can use the Set-Cookie header as follows:

```
Set-Cookie: <name>=<value>
            [; Comment=<value>] [; Max-Age=<value>]
            [; Expires=<date>] [; Path=<path>]
            [; Domain=<domain name>] [; Secure]
            [; Version=<version>]
```

An *attribute–value pair*, <name> = <value>, is sent back by the browser in qualifying subsequent requests. The Max-Age attribute defines the lifetime of the cookie in seconds (in other words, this attribute tells the browser how long to keep the cookie around). The Expires attribute represents a deprecated mechanism for defining the lifetime of the cookie by providing its expiration date. The Path and Domain attributes delimit which requests qualify, by specifying the server domains and URL paths to which this cookie applies. The Secure attribute tells the browser to forego submitting corresponding Cookie headers except over a secure connection. Finally, the Version attribute identifies the version of the state management specification. The absence of this attribute tells browsers to default to the original Netscape specification, which uses the Expires attribute to set an expiration date instead of the Max-Age attribute to set the time to live.

Servers may instead use the more recently defined Set-Cookie2 header, which is a slightly modified version of the Set-Cookie header:

```
Set-Cookie2: <name>=<value>
            [; Comment=<value>] [; CommentURL=<http_URL>]
            [; Max-Age=<value>] [; Path=<path>]
            [; Domain=<domain name>] [; Port=<portlist>]
            [; Secure] [; Version=<version>]
```

As you can see, the main difference is in making it possible to limit the applicability of the cookie further beyond the domain by adding an explicit list of ports.

Cookie2 Confusion

Browsers that support the Set-Cookie2 header use the advanced controls defined for this header in submitting follow-up Cookie headers. They are supposed to include Cookie2 headers in their requests to notify servers that they can include either Set-Cookie or Set-Cookie2 headers in their responses.

While the Set-Cookie2 header is a more advanced and flexible version of the Set-Cookie header, the Cookie and Cookie2 headers have nothing to do with one another. The Cookie2 header does not contain state information. Instead, it is set to the version of the state management specification supported by the browser.

Domains may be set to suffixes of the originating server's host name containing at least two periods (three, for domains other than com, org, edu, gov, mil, and int). The value of the domain attribute must match the server domain. For example, an application running on cs.rutgers.edu can set the domain to .rutgers.edu, but not to .mit.edu. A domain value of .rutgers.edu means that this cookie applies to requests destined for hosts with names of the form *.rutgers.edu. The value for the path attribute defaults to the path of the URL associated with the server application, but may be set to any path prefix beginning at "/", which stands for the server root.

For subsequent requests directed at URLs where the domain, path, and port match, the browser must include a Cookie header with the appropriate attribute–value pair.

Cookie Jars

Browsers and other HTTP clients must maintain a "registry" of cookies sent to them by servers. For cookies that are intended to last only for the duration of the current browser session, an in-memory table is sufficient. For cookies with a defined lifetime, persistent storage mechanisms are required.

In this example, a server application running on the cs.rutgers.edu server generates a Set-Cookie header of the following form:

```
HTTP/1.1 200 OK
Set-Cookie: Name="Leon"; Path="/test/"; Domain=".rutgers.edu";
            Version="1"
```

The domain is set to .rutgers.edu and the path is set to /test/. This instructs the browser to include a Cookie header with the value Name = Leon every time that a request is made for a resource on a Rutgers server where the URL path starts with /test/. The absence of the expiration date means that this cookie is maintained only for the duration of the current browser session.

Now let us consider a more complicated example for renting a movie. We start with submitting a registration by visiting a URL that lets us sign in to a secure movie rental web site. Let us assume we have been prompted for authorization credentials by the browser and have provided them so that the browser can construct the Authorization header:

```
GET /movies/register HTTP/1.1
Host: www.sample-movie-rental.com
Authorization: ...
```

Once the server has recognized and authenticated the user, it sends back a response containing a Set-Cookie header with a customer id:

```
HTTP/1.1 200 OK
Set-Cookie: CUSTOMER="Rich"; Path="/movies"; Secure; Version="1"
...
```

From this point on, every time the browser submits a request directed to https://www.sample-movie.rental.com/movies/*, it includes a Cookie header containing the customer id:

```
GET /movies/rent-recommended HTTP/1.1
Host: www.sample-movie-rental.com
Cookie: $Version="1"; CUSTOMER="Rich"; $Path="/movies"
```

In this case, we are visiting a page of recommended movies. The server response now contains a movie recommendation:

```
HTTP/1.1 200 OK
Set-Cookie: MOVIE="Matrix"; Path="/movies/"; Secure; Version="1"
...
```

Now we request access to the movie. Note that, given the URL, the browser has to include both the userid and the id of the recommended movie within the Cookie header:

```
GET /movies/access HTTP/1.1
Host: www.sample-movie-rental.com
Cookie: $Version="1"; CUSTOMER="Rich"; MOVIE="Matrix";
        $Path="/movies"
```

We get back the acknowledgment containing access information for the recommended movie:

```
HTTP/1.1 200 OK
Set-Cookie: CHANNEL="42"; PASSWD="123007";
            Path="/movies/action"; Secure; Version="1"
...
```

Note that the server sends back two new cookie values, CHANNEL and PASSWD, but they are associated with the URL path /movies/action/. Now, the browser has to include movie access information with action requests. Note that for such requests the Cookie headers contain values applicable both to /movies/ and to /movies/action/ paths:

```
GET /movies/action/check HTTP/1.1
Host: www.sample-movie-rental.com
Cookie: $Version="1"; CUSTOMER="Rich"; MOVIE="Matrix";
        $Path="/movies"
Cookie: $Version="1"; CHANNEL="42"; PASSWD="123007";
        $Path="/movies/action"
```

Requests directed at URLs matching only the /movies/ path do not include attribute–value pairs associated with the /movies/action/ path:

```
GET /movies/access HTTP/1.1
Host: www.sample-movie-rental.com
Cookie: $Version="1"; CUSTOMER="Rich"; MOVIE="Matrix";
        $Path="/movies"
```

Poisoned Cookies

Not all HTTP cookies are good for you – some are pure poison. Ill-behaved sites can use cookies not only to track your behavior, but also to collect and distribute personal information illicitly and to exploit browser security holes.

The Platform for Privacy Preferences (P3P) defines a self-policing mechanism designed to restrict browser acceptance of cookies based on declarations made by the originating sites about their purpose for collecting user information. These declarations are in plain English as well as XML. XML declarations are the input for generating HTTP headers that control browser acceptance of cookies. False XML declarations that do not match statements made in plain English can result in legal liability. (There is more about this in Chapter 7.)

Of course, rogue sites that do not abide by P3P policies are not especially concerned with legalities. They know they are toast if caught anyway – with or without P3P. So be safe – do not point your browser to sites that use numeric IP addresses instead of domain names or domain suffixes you do not recognize. Also, be careful about very long URLs with legitimate domains owned by ISPs – they can point to poorly controlled hosted environments.

3.5   Evolution of the HTTP Protocol

HTTP has evolved a good deal since its inception in the early 1990s. The more it evolves, the more care is needed to support backward compatibility. Many years have passed since the introduction of HTTP/1.1 but in the real world, there are still servers, browsers, and proxies that support HTTP/1.0.

What's more, not all HTTP/1.1-compliant programs properly fall back to the HTTP/1.0 specification when they receive an HTTP/1.0 message.

In this section, we discuss the reasoning behind some of the most important changes that were introduced with HTTP/1.1, the compatibility issues that affected protocol designers' decisions, and the challenges still facing web application developers in dealing with these issues.

3.5.1 Virtual hosting

One of the challenges facing HTTP/1.1 designers was to provide support for *virtual hosting*, which is the ability to map multiple host names to a single IP address. For example, a single server machine may host web sites associated with multiple domains. There must be a way for the server to determine the intended host. In addition, the introduction of proxies into the request stream creates additional problems in ensuring that a request reaches its host.

In HTTP/1.0, a request passing through a proxy has a slightly different format from the request ultimately received by the destination server. As we have seen, the request that reaches the host has the following form, including only the path portion of the URL in the first line of the request:

```
GET /q?s=YHOO HTTP/1.0
```

Requests that must pass through proxies need to include some reference to the destination server, otherwise that information would be lost and the proxy would have no idea which server should receive the request. For this reason, the full URL of the resource is included in the first line of the request, as shown below:

```
GET http://finance.yahoo.com/q?s=YHOO HTTP/1.0
```

Proxies that connect to the destination server are responsible for editing requests that pass through them, to remove server information from request lines.

HTTP/1.1 is designed to support virtual hosting. It requires that server information be retained for all requests because destination servers need to know which of the virtual hosts is responsible for processing the request. The obvious solution would have been to make HTTP/1.1 browsers and proxies always to include server information:

```
GET http://finance.yahoo.com/q?s=YHOO HTTP/1.1
```

This would have been fine except that there are still HTTP/1.0 proxies out there that are ready to cut server information from request URLs every time they see it. Obviously, HTTP/1.0 proxies do not know anything about HTTP/1.1 and have no way of making the distinction. Nonetheless, it makes sense to support this request format for both HTTP/1.1 servers and proxies. (There may come a day when we do not have to worry about HTTP/1.0 proxies any more. We can only hope . . . .)

For now, we need a redundant source of information that is not affected by HTTP/1.0 proxies. This is the reason for the Host header, which must be included with every HTTP/1.1 request:

```
GET http://finance.yahoo.com/q?s=YHOO HTTP/1.1
Host: finance.yahoo.com
```

Whether this request passes through an HTTP/1.0 proxy or an HTTP/1.1 proxy, information about the ultimate destination of the request is preserved. Obviously, requests with abbreviated URLs (only the path portion) must be supported as well:

```
GET /q?s=YHOO HTTP/1.1
Host: finance.yahoo.com
```

3.5.2   Caching support

In Section 3.4.2, we described mechanisms through which servers provide information about caching policies with responses to browsers, proxies, and other clients. If the supplied headers tell a client that caching is feasible for this particular response, the client must then make a decision as to whether it should use a cached version of the response that it already has available, rather than go back to the source location to access the data.

In HTTP/1.0, the main mechanism for supporting browser-side caching was based on HEAD requests. A request employing the HEAD method returns exactly the same response as its GET counterpart, but without the body. In other words, only the headers are present, providing the requestor with all of the response's metadata without the overhead of transmitting the entire content. If a client has a cached copy of a previously requested resource, it is sensible to submit a HEAD request for that resource, check the date provided in the Last-Modified header, and resubmit a GET request only if the date is later than that of the saved cache entry. This improves server throughput by eliminating the need for unnecessary retransmission of content. The only time the actual data has to be retrieved is when the cache entry is out of date. Unfortunately, for frequently changing data, most HEAD requests would require a follow-up GET request. In the worst-case scenario, we can double the number of requests without achieving savings on content transmission.

HTTP/1.1 implements a more efficient approach to this problem using two new headers: If-Modified-Since and If-Unmodified-Since. Going back to an earlier example:

```
GET /~shklar/ HTTP/1.1
Host: www.cs.rutgers.edu
If-Modified-Since: Sun, 27 Apr 2008 22:28:00 GMT
```

Assuming there is an expired cache entry for this resource that was last modified at 22:28 on April 27, 2008, the browser can send a request for this resource with the If-Modified-Since header set to that date and time. If the resource has *not* changed since that point in time, we get back the response with the 304 Not Modified status code and no body. Otherwise, we get back the body (which may then be placed in the cache, replacing any existing cache entry for the same resource).

On the flip side, let's examine the following request where we are attempting to retrieve a historic version of content, which does not include changes that occurred after 22:28 on April 27, 2008:

```
GET /~shklar/ HTTP/1.1
Host: www.cs.rutgers.edu
If-Unmodified-Since: Sun, 27 Apr 2008 22:28:00 GMT
```

For this request, we either get back the unchanged resource or an empty response (no body) with the `412 Precondition Failed` status code.

Both headers can be used in HTTP/1.1 requests to eliminate unnecessary data transmissions without the cost of extra requests.

3.5.3   Persistent connections

Since HTTP is a *stateless* protocol, it does not require persistent connections. A connection is supposed to last long enough for a browser to submit a request and receive a response. Originally, there was no support for extending the lifetime of a connection beyond a single request–response transaction.

Since the cost of connecting to a server across the network is considerable, there are mechanisms within existing network protocols for reducing or eliminating that overhead by creating persistent connections. To improve performance, we need to *allow* connections to persist across multiple requests, but we should not *depend* on persistent connections for application logic.

Early on, developers used workarounds involving multipart MIME messages to get connections to persist across multiple independent bodies of content. (We saw an example of this when we discussed image animation using server push via multipart messages.)

Late in the lifecycle of HTTP/1.0, developers of servers and browsers introduced the proprietary `Connection: keep-alive` header, as part of a somewhat desperate effort to support persistent connections in a protocol that was not designed for it. Not surprisingly, it did not work well. Considering all the intermediate proxies that might be involved in the transmission of a request, there are considerable difficulties in using this mechanism to keep connections open. Just one intermediate proxy that lacks support for the `keep-alive` extension is enough to cause the connection to be broken.

HTTP/1.1 connections are persistent, except when explicitly closed by a participating program via the `Connection: close` header. It is entirely legal for a server or a browser to be HTTP/1.1-compliant without supporting persistent connections as long as they include `Connection: close` with every message. Theoretically, including the `Connection: keep-alive` header in HTTP/1.1 messages makes no sense, since the *absence* of `Connection: close` means that the connection needs to be persistent.

However, there is no way to ensure that all proxies are HTTP/1.1-compliant and know to maintain a persistent connection. In practice, including `Connection: keep-alive` does provide a partial solution – it works for HTTP/1.0 proxies that support it as a proprietary extension. Once again, failure to maintain a persistent connection may degrade performance but does not have any impact on application behavior.

HTTP/1.1 support for persistent connections includes *pipelining* requests: browsers can queue request messages without waiting for responses. Servers are responsible for submitting responses to browser requests in the order of their arrival. Browsers that support persistent connections must maintain request queues, keep track of server responses, and resubmit requests that remain on queues if connections are dropped and reestablished. We discuss HTTP/1.1 support for persistent connections in further detail in Chapter 6.

3.6   Summary

In this chapter, we have discussed the fundamental facets of the HTTP protocol. We did not intend it as an exhaustive discussion of all the protocol's features, but rather as an overview of the main principles and a case study for understanding and working with current and future HTTP specifications from the World Wide Web Consortium. W3C specifications are the ultimate references that need to be consulted when architecting complex applications.

Understanding HTTP is critical to the design of advanced web applications. It is a prerequisite for utilizing the full power of Internet technologies that are discussed in this book. Knowledge of the inner workings of HTTP promotes reasoning from first principles, and simplifies the daunting task of learning the rich variety of protocols and APIs that depend on its features. We recommend that you return to this chapter as we proceed with our discussion of web application technologies.

In Chapter 4, we initiate our discussion of markup languages starting with HTML and its roots, moving on to XML and XML applications in Chapter 5.

QUESTIONS AND EXERCISES

1. Consider the following hyperlink:

   ```
   <a href="http://www.cs.rutgers.edu/~shklar/">
   ```

   What HTTP/1.0 request will be submitted by a browser?
   What HTTP/1.1 request will be submitted by a browser?

2. Consider the example in Question 1. Will these requests change if the browser is configured to contact an HTTP proxy? If yes, how?

3. What is the structure of a POST request? What headers have to be present in HTTP/1.0 and HTTP/1.1 requests?

4. Use a Telnet client program to submit a request to a web server. Start the Telnet client and connect to port 80 of the server machine. Build the request by manually typing it in line by line:

   (a) Start with a request method (e.g., GET or POST), a URL, and an HTTP version (e.g. HTTP/1.1).
   (b) Follow this line with the required Host header and a series of optional request headers (one header per line).
   (c) Enter an additional carriage return to end the request with a blank line.

   What do you see in the response that comes back from the server? Try adding and omitting headers, as well as changing the request method. Observe the changes in the response. What happens if you omit the Host header?
   Repeat the experiment with HTTP/1.0 in the request line.

5. Name two headers that, if present in an HTTP response, always have to be processed in a particular order. State the order and explain.

6. How can multipart MIME be used to implement "server push"? When is it appropriate? Construct a sample HTTP response implementing server push using Multipart MIME.

7. Suppose that a content provider puts up a "ring" of related sites:

```
www.site1.provider.hahaha.com
www.site2.provider.hahaha.com
www.site3.provider.hahaha.com
www.site4.provider.hahaha.com
www.site5.provider.hahaha.com
```

Suppose now this provider wants *unsophisticated* users to remain "sticky" to a particular site by preventing them from switching to a *different* site in the ring more frequently than once an hour. For example, after a user first accesses `www.site4.provider.hahaha.com`, she has to wait for at least an hour before being able to access another site in the ring but can keep accessing the same site as much as she wants.

Hints: Use cookies and look elsewhere if you need more than two or three lines to describe your solution.

8. Remember the example in which the server returns a redirect when a URL pointing to a directory does not contain the trailing slash? What would happen if the server did not return the redirect but returned an `index.html` file stored in that directory right away? Would that be a problem? If you are not sure about the answer, come back to this question after Chapter 7.

3.7 Bibliography

Gourley, David and Totty, Brian, 2002. *HTTP: The Definitive Guide*. Sebastopol (CA): O'Reilly & Associates.

Krishnamurthy, Balachander and Rexford, Jennifer, 2001. *Web Protocols and Practice*. Boston (MA): Addison-Wesley.

Loshin, Peter, 2000. *Big Book of World Wide Web RFCs*. San Francisco: Morgan Kaufmann.

Shiflett, Chris, 2003. *HTTP Developer's Handbook*. SAMS Publishing.

Thomas, Stephen, 2001. *HTTP Essentials*. Chichester: John Wiley and Sons Ltd.

Yeager, Nancy and McGrath, Robert, 1996. *Web Server Technology*. San Francisco: Morgan Kaufmann.

CHAPTER 4

HTML and Its Roots

IN THIS CHAPTER
- Standard Generalized Markup Language (SGML)
- Document Type Definitions (DTDs)
- Hypertext Markup Language (HTML)
- HTML rendering

OBJECTIVES
- Discuss SGML and its place in the history of markup languages.
- Discuss the evolution of HTML and prepare readers for XML.
- Discuss the structure of HTML documents.
- Discuss Cascading Style Sheets (CSS) and their role in separating markup from rendering.

One of the original cornerstones of the web is HTML – a simple markup language whose primary purpose is to enable cross-referencing of documents through hyperlinks. In this chapter, we discuss HTML and its origins as an SGML application. We cover SGML fundamentals and show how HTML is defined within the framework of SGML. We then cover selected HTML and CSS functionality. Dynamic presentation technologies (including DHTML, JavaScript, and AJAX) are covered in Chapter 8.

Our objective in this chapter is to discuss the capabilities of HTML and related technologies. In the course of our discussion we provide examples of HTML documents to illustrate selected facets of HTML as a language. We touch upon CSS and its relationship to HTML, with the goal of explaining

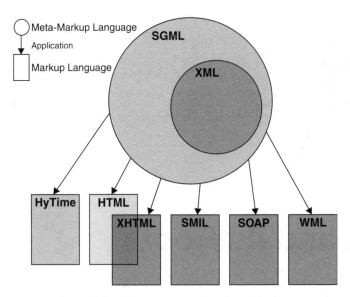

Figure 4.1   SGML, XML, and their applications.

the role of both languages in rendering documents. However, we do *not* intend this chapter to be an HTML tutorial nor are we aiming to convey the finer points of page design.

It is important to know HTML's origins in order to understand its place in the overall evolution of markup languages. Admittedly, SGML is a niche language, though it is certainly one with an extensive history. Thus, it may not be of interest to every reader. We believe that knowledge of SGML is useful both from a historical perspective and to better understand the advantages of XML and opportunities presented by XML and related technologies. However, readers who want to get through the material quickly can skip directly to Section 4.2, bypassing the details of our SGML discussion.

The eXtensible Markup Language (*XML*) is the cornerstone of a new generation of markup languages, which are covered in Chapter 5. Our immediate objective is to understand the relationship of SGML and HTML with XML, XHTML, and related technologies.

Both SGML and XML are meta-languages for defining specialized markup languages. Figure 4.1 illustrates that XML is a subset of SGML (at least, it was at the time of its initial introduction). As you can see, both HyTime and HTML are SGML applications, while XHTML, SMIL, SOAP, and WML are XML applications. Since XML was defined as a subset of SGML, it is theoretically possible to construct SGML specifications for these languages, but since they are much easier to define using XML, you are not likely to find SGML specifications for them. We come back to this discussion in Chapter 5.

4.1   Standard Generalized Markup Language

HTML did not just appear out of the void. It was defined as an application of the *Standard Generalized Markup Language* (SGML) – a language for defining markup languages. SGML was created long before the advent of the web. SGML's predecessor, GML, was introduced in 1969 in an IBM research project on integrated legal information systems. Its goal was to promote file sharing between editorial and information retrieval systems. Not by accident, GML stands not only for Generalized Markup Language, but also for the initials of the surnames of its inventors (Charles Goldfarb, Edward Mosher, and Raymond Lorie).

SGML was created by the *American National Standards Institute (ANSI)* in an effort to define a text description standard based on GML. The first working draft was published by ANSI in 1980. It took six drafts until it was declared an industry standard in 1983. Very soon after, it was adopted by the US Internal Revenue Service and the Department of Defense.

SGML was designed to define annotation and typing schemes that were jointly referred to as *markup*. Such markup schemes were originally intended to determine page layouts and fonts. Later, they were extended to cover all kinds of control sequences that are inserted into text to serve as instructions for formatting, printing, and other kinds of processing.

SGML was *not* the first attempt at digital typesetting – people had been using *LaTeX, troff*, and other programs that produced all kinds of incompatible proprietary formats. This caused tremendous pains and gave birth to a great number of conversion programs that never did the job correctly. SGML was the first attempt to create a language for creating different specialized but compatible markup schemes, which makes SGML a *meta-markup* language. As a result, it became quite easy to convert documents in LaTeX and other legacy formats to HTML and other SGML applications. In fact, as soon as it became clear that only a few converters were important and that converters to different SGML markups could share code, it became more practical to achieve decent results.

An SGML application (e.g., HTML) consists of four main parts that all have different roles in defining syntax and semantics of the documents:

- the SGML declaration, which specifies characters and delimiters that may legally appear in the application;
- the Document Type Definition (DTD), which defines valid markup constructs and may include additional definitions such as numeric and named character entities (e.g., `&#34;` or `&quot;`);
- a specification that describes the semantics to be ascribed to the markup and can impose additional syntax restrictions that cannot be expressed in the DTD;
- document instances containing content and markup that each contain a reference to the DTD that should be used to interpret it.

In this section, we discuss elements of sample SGML applications. Our examples center mainly on the HTML specification, setting the stage for the rest of the chapter.

DTDéjà Vu

Many among you may have encountered DTDs and other related constructs in the context of XML. Do not get confused – this chapter does not talk about XML. DTDs were first introduced in SGML and found their way into XML much later. We discuss the commonalities and differences between SGML and XML DTDs in Chapter 5. For now, keep an open mind and do not overreact when you see DTDs that look just a little different from what you may be used to.

4.1.1 SGML declaration

The role of the SGML declaration is to set the stage for understanding DTDs that define valid markup constructs for SGML applications. The declaration has to specify the character set, delimiters, and constraints on what may be specified in a DTD.

Document character set

The problem of defining a proper character set becomes apparent when you face a screen full of very odd characters that were perfectly readable when you composed your document on another system. That is when you realize that "A" is not always an "A" but something incomprehensible if interpreted by a program that has a different convention for representing characters. The two most commonly used conventions for representing text are American Standard for Coded Information Interchange (ASCII) and Extended Binary-Coded Decimal Interchange Code (EBCDIC). ASCII is the one you are probably most familiar with – it is used on most personal computers. EBCDIC is a format associated with older mainframe-based systems. Within both systems, there are many permutations, which depend on the country or the application domain.

What is needed is a way to associate the bit combination for a particular character used in the document with that character's meaning. It is too verbose to define character meanings directly, which is why SGML allows them to be defined as modifications to standard character sets. For example, the EBCDIC system represents capital letters C and D using bit combinations B′11000011′ (decimal 195) and B′11000100′ (decimal 196). Suppose that we need to represent these characters in the seven-bit character-encoding standard known as ISO 646. Characters "C" and "D" are encoded in this standard using bit combinations B′01000011′ (decimal 67) and B′01000100′ (decimal 68). The SGML declaration for this association looks like the example shown in Figure 4.2.

In this example, ISO 646 is the base character set. We define two additional characters that are mapped to characters "C" and "D" of the base set. In addition, we state that the EBCDIC capital letter "E" (decimal 197) does not occur in the document – a bit strange but it may make sense in some bizarre case.

Figure 4.3 contains the character set definition for HTML 4. As we can see, except for the unused characters, the HTML 4 character set maps directly into the ISO-defined base set. Characters that are mapped to "UNUSED" (e.g., two characters starting at decimal 11 and 18 characters starting at decimal 14) must not occur in HTML 4 documents.

```
CHARSET
BASESET "ISO 646:1983//CHARSET
          International Reference Version (IRV)//ESC 2/5 4/0"
DESCSET 195  2   67 -- Map 2 document characters starting at 195
                       (EBCDIC C and D) to base set characters 67
                       and 68 (ISO 646 C and D)
        197  1   UNUSED
```

Figure 4.2 An SGML character set definition for EBCDIC characters.

```
CHARSET
BASESET "ISO Registration Number 177//CHARSET
        ISO/IEC 10646-1:1993 UCS-4 with
        implementation level 3//ESC 2/5 2/15 4/6"
DESCSET 0       9        UNUSED
        9       2        9
        11      2        UNUSED
        13      1        13
        14      18       UNUSED
        32      95       32
        127     1        UNUSED
        128     32       UNUSED
        160     55136    160
        55296   2048     UNUSED
        57344   1056768  57344
```

Figure 4.3   SGML character set definition for HTML 4.

Concrete syntax

The SGML language is defined using "delimiter roles" rather than concrete characters. SGML always refers to delimiters by their role names. Once it comes to defining the concrete syntax for an application, roles are associated with character sequences. For example, even though most SGML applications use the </ character sequence as a delimiter, this sequence is not part of SGML. In practice, the SGML role "*etago*", indicating the start of the end tag is often associated with </ in syntax declarations but it could be associated with [*[/, <[!, or another bizarre sequence.

It is important to make a clear distinction between the SGML language and the *reference concrete syntax* that is also included in the SGML specification. For example, while SGML makes use of delimiter roles, the reference implementation associates these roles with commonly used character sequences (<, </, >, />, etc.). SGML applications can defer to definitions included in the reference concrete syntax for convenience. Syntax declarations also include the following components:

- characters that should not be used in documents ("shunned" characters);
- bit combinations that are mapped to the function characters (SPACE, record start);
- characters that can be used in names and other naming rules;
- reserved keywords that are used within SGML (e.g., PCDATA);
- additional constraints (e.g., the maximum name length).

Figure 4.4 contains the partial syntax definition for HTML 4. It starts with the enumeration of binary codes for characters that should be avoided in HTML documents. The format of the BASESET and DESCSET sections is the same as that used in defining character sets (see Figure 4.3) but here it applies to characters that may be used for syntax references. The FUNCTION section defines bit combinations for characters that denote *record start, record end, space*, and *tab* functions. The NAMING section does not provide for any additional name start characters (apart from the defined minimum set – lower and upper case letters), but defines additional characters (".", "-", "_", and ":") that may occur elsewhere in names. Finally, the DELIM section defines delimiters by deferring to the reference

```
SYNTAX
      SHUNCHAR CONTROLS 0 1 2 3 4 5 6 7 8 9 10 11 12 13 14 15 16
            17 18 19 20 21 22 23 24 25 26 27 28 29 30 31 127
      BASESET "ISO 646IRV:1991//CHARSET International Reference Version
            (IRV)//ESC 2/8 4/2"
      DESCSET 0 128 0

      FUNCTION
              RE            13
              RS            10
              SPACE         32
              TAB SEPCHAR    9

      NAMING LCNMSTRT ""
             UCNMSTRT ""
             LCNMCHAR ".-_:"
             UCNMCHAR ".-_:"
             NAMECASE GENERAL YES
                      ENTITY  NO

      DELIM GENERAL  SGMLREF
            HCRO     "&#38;#x" -- 38 is the number for ampersand
            SHORTREF SGMLREF
```

Figure 4.4 SGML syntax specification for HTML 4.

implementation with the only override, which is defined for the HCRO role. (The *Hex Character Reference Open* (HCRO) role is a delimiter used to open hex character references.)

Feature usage

SGML provides a lot of flexibility in defining markup minimization features. For example, the DATATAG feature of the declaration allows the DTD to specify character strings, which cause an end tag to be implied. In other words, it allows data to be treated both as data and as markup. This may arguably provide some convenience but complicates parsing and can introduce ambiguities. Other examples include SHORTTAG, which makes it possible to omit the tag's closing delimiters, and OMIT-TAG, which allows the omission of certain start or end tags. These features are the telling evidence of SGML's lineage with library sciences, which had priorities other than computational properties.

Later, we come back to these examples to illustrate differences in philosophy between SGML and XML.

4.1.2 Document Type Definition

The purpose of the Document Type Definition (DTD) is to define the syntax of markup constructs. It may also include additional definitions (e.g., numeric and named character entities). In this section, we discuss how to define elements, attributes and entities, and illustrate these discussions using HTML examples.

Entity definitions

The DTD for HTML 4 begins with *entity definitions*, which can be considered text macros. By now, we already have the concrete syntax, so we are not defining SGML entities. Rather, we are defining macros that may be expanded elsewhere in the DTD or in the target language (HTML 4). When macros are referenced, they are expanded into the strings that appeared in the entity definition.

In Figure 4.5, the following *parameter entities* are defined:

- `%head.misc` expands to the partial enumeration of elements (`SCRIPT|STYLE|META|LINK`) that may occur within the `HEAD` element.
- `%heading` expands to the enumeration of elements denoting section and block headings.
- `%attrs` expands to the sequence of other entities that are expanded recursively.

Notice the difference between the parameter entities, which are a matter of convenience for the DTD specification itself, and general entities (defined in the last line of Figure 4.5). General entities become part of the language that is being defined by a DTD and are referenced using the ampersand (e.g., `&attrs;`). General entities are not important for HTML, but remember them when we get to XML.

Element definitions

An SGML DTD defines *elements* that represent structures or behaviors. It is important to make the distinction between elements and tags. It is not uncommon for people to erroneously refer to elements as tags (e.g., "the P tag"). An element typically consists of three parts: a start tag, content, and an end tag (e.g., `<STRONG>test</STRONG>`). It is possible for an element to have no content and it is for such empty elements that notions of the element and the tag coincide (e.g., the HTML line break element, `<BR>`).

An element definition has to specify its name, the structure of its content (if any), and whether the end tag is optional or required. For example, the ordered list element is defined in Figure 4.6 to have the name `OL`, to require both the start tag and the end tag (the first and second dashes), and to contain at least one LI element as its content. The line break element is defined to have the name `BR` and it requires neither the end tag nor content.

```
<!ENTITY % head.misc "SCRIPT|STYLE|META|LINK">
<!ENTITY % heading "H1|H2|H3|H4|H5|H6">
<!ENTITY % attrs "%coreattrs %i18n %events">
<!ENTITY attrs "substitution text">
```

Figure 4.5   Entity definitions.

```
<!ELEMENT OL - - (LI)+>
<!ELEMENT BR - O EMPTY>
<!ELEMENT OPTION - O #PCDATA>
<!ELEMENT TABLE - - (CAPTION?, (COL*|COLGROUP*), THEAD?, TFOOT?, TBODY+)>
```

Figure 4.6   Element definitions.

The purpose of the DTD mechanism is to specify verifiable constraints on documents. To satisfy that purpose, it has to express relatively sophisticated relationships between different elements. Such relationships are expressed by defining content models. Very simple examples of such models are shown by the first three examples in Figure 4.6: the body composed of one or more LI elements, the empty body, and the body that can only contain document text (#PCDATA) but not other elements. More generally, content models make it possible either to specify forbidden elements or to enumerate allowed elements or text, their order, and number of occurrences.

An element definition uses *quantifiers* to determine how often an element must appear. The "?" *quantifier* indicates that an element may appear exactly 0 or 1 times, the "*" quantifier indicates that an element may appear any number of times or not at all, and the "+" quantifier requires that the element appears at least once. The last example in Figure 4.6 defines the TABLE element. As you can see, no text is allowed directly within TABLE, which is not to say that it cannot be specified within one of its contained elements; the CAPTION element may or may not be present; the COL and COLGROUP elements may appear any number of times; and there should be at least one TBODY element.

Another interesting observation relates to the grouping of COL* and COLGROUP* constructs using parentheses. The | operator indicates that the constructs may appear in any order and one of them may not appear at all. The & operator is similar except that both constructs have to appear. Of course, if the constructs themselves are defined using quantifiers that allow 0 occurrences (i.e., "?" or "*"), there is no practical difference between these operators (e.g., the COL*|COLGROUP* and COL*&COLGROUP* expressions are equivalent). The "," operator indicates a fixed order. In Figure 4.6, the CAPTION element may or may not occur within a TABLE (due to the "?" quantifier) but if it does, it has to occur first because expressions separated by the "," operator impose a fixed order. Figure 4.7 shows two valid HTML tables that match the TABLE definition in Figure 4.6 and Figure 4.8 shows an invalid table.

```
<TABLE>
        <THEAD>
            <TR>Table 1
        </THEAD>
        <TFOOT>
            <TR>December 2001</TR>
        </TFOOT>
        <TBODY>
            <TR><TD>1</TD><TD>2</TD><TD>3</TD>
            <TR><TD>6</TD><TD>8</TD><TD>5</TD>
        </TBODY>
        <TBODY>
            <TR><TD>23456</TD><TD>12345</TD>
        </TBODY>
</TABLE>
<TABLE>
        <THEAD><TR>Table 2
        <TBODY><TR><TD>1<TD>2<TD>3
            <TR><TD>6<TD>8<TD>5
        <TBODY><TR><TD>23456</TD><TD>12345</TD>
</TABLE>
```

Figure 4.7   Valid HTML tables.

```
<TABLE>
        <THEAD><TR>Table 2
        <TBODY><TR><TD>1<TD>2<TD>3
              <TR><TD>6<TD>8<TD>5
        <TFOOT><TR>December 2001</TR>
</TABLE>
```

Figure 4.8 Invalid HTML table (TFOOT occurs after TBODY).

Both HTML tables in Figure 4.7 are valid because close tags for THEAD, TFOOT, and TBODY elements are optional, and so is the entire TFOOT element. However, the table in Figure 4.8 is not valid because the order imposed by the , operator in the HTML DTD (Figure 4.6) is violated – the TFOOT element is present and occurs after the TBODY element.

The fact that the HTML fragment in Figure 4.8 is invalid does not necessarily mean that your browser will not display it correctly – desktop browsers are designed to be tolerant of bad HTML. However, writing invalid HTML is a bad habit that may cause problems when errors accumulate, or when your HTML is served by non-desktop browsers. Moreover, even the absence of optional closing tags may cause erratic rendering behavior with non-mainstream browsers. Such erratic behavior is becoming more common as newer browsers are designed to comply with XHTML syntax (see Chapter 5).

Attribute definitions

An element may allow one or more attributes that provide additional information to processing agents. For example, the src attribute of the HTML SCRIPT element instructs the browser to retrieve the script from the specified URL instead of the element body.

A list of attribute definitions begins with the keyword ATTLIST and is followed by the element name (e.g., TABLE and TH in the example in Figure 4.9) and the actual attribute definitions. An attribute definition starts with the name of the attribute (e.g., width or cols), and specifies its type and default value. Sample attribute types shown in Figure 4.9 include NUMBER, which represents integers, and CDATA, which represents document text. Other frequently used types include NAME and

```
<!ENTITY % TAlign "(left|center|right)">
...
<!ATTLIST TABLE           -- table element --
  width        CDATA      #IMPLIED  -- table width relative to window --
  cols         NUMBER     #IMPLIED  -- used for immediate display mode -
  align        %TAlign;   #IMPLIED  -- table position relative to window --
>
<!ATTLIST TH              -- th element --
  rowspan      NUMBER     1
  colspan      NUMBER     1
>
```

Figure 4.9 Attribute definitions for the TABLE and TH elements.

ID – both representing character sequences that start with a letter and may include letters, digits, hyphens, colons and periods; ID represents document-wide unique identifiers.

Notice the use of a DTD entity – TAlign – in defining the align attribute. This entity expands to (left|center|right); its use is simply a matter of convenience. Either way, the domain of the align attribute is defined as the enumeration of left, center, and right.

When an attribute is defined as #IMPLIED, its value is supplied by the processing agent (e.g., the browser). The keyword #REQUIRED indicates that the attribute should always be present with its element. Alternatively, an attribute may be set to a fixed value, as in the rowspan and colspan attributes for the table header element TH in Figure 4.9.

Making the Case

Notice that in our DTD and HTML examples, we use upper case characters for the element names and lower case characters for the attributes. This is consistent with the HTML 4.01 specification. You have probably noticed that desktop browsers have historically been very tolerant of pages that use lower case for element names or upper case for attribute names (even more so than they are with incorrect tag nesting and sequencing). However, these seemingly minor deviations from the specification accumulate very quickly and wreak havoc with the process of HTML validation, making it difficult to sift through warnings and errors when trying to clean up your documents in an effort to make them work consistently across different browsers.

4.2   HTML

Our SGML discussion does not attempt to teach you all the details of designing SGML applications. However, it is important that you understand the roots of HTML and its replacement, XHTML. In Chapter 5, we look back at SGML declarations and DTDs and think about how to make use of them in the XML world. Understanding this connection between SGML and XML is a critical prerequisite to understanding the relationship between HTML, XML, and XML applications.

For now, let us be concerned with HTML – both with the syntactic constraints imposed on HTML documents by HTML declarations and DTDs and with the semantics of HTML. This is why we used HTML examples throughout the SGML discussion. Speaking of which, you probably noticed that SGML declarations and DTDs do not assign semantics to HTML tags – that is done in HTML specifications using plain English. It is the responsibility of HTML agents (e.g., desktop or set-top box browsers) to read, understand, and follow the specification. By now, there are quite a few versions of such specifications around; we have to spend at least a little time sorting it all out. Once we do, we can discuss the more interesting HTML constructs, paying special attention to the relationship between these constructs and the HTTP protocol.

4.2.1   Evolution of HTML

As you should have noticed from our SGML discussion, HTML syntax is rather flexible. The syntax of HTML tags is set in stone, but the structure of HTML documents is relatively unconstrained. For example, many HTML elements have optional closing tags, which are commonly omitted. To make things worse, real HTML documents often violate even the liberal constraints imposed by the HTML specification because commercial browsers are tolerant of such violations. Nevertheless, bad HTML, even if it happens to be rendered properly, is likely to cause all kinds of problems over the lifetime of the document. A simple modification may add just enough insult to injury to break rendering through a forgiving browser. It is worse if it becomes important to re-purpose the same markup for non-desktop devices – non-desktop browsers are much less tolerant of bad HTML syntax.

Over the last ten years, the HTML specification has gone through a number of transformations. The common theme for all of these transformations is the tightening of the syntax. The current revision, HTML 4.01, was released in December 1999. It soon became apparent that future developments would be hard to achieve in the context of SGML. The major additional burden is the need to maintain backward compatibility. HTML 4.01 partially addresses this problem by providing both "strict" and "transitional" specifications. HTML 4.01 was supposed to be the final specification of the language, with all new development centering on its successor – XHTML. This intent died in 2004 with the initiative to define HTML 5, which would unify the HTML and XHTML specifications. The draft specification of HTML 5 is already available.

Rendering modules of early HTML browsers associated fixed behavior with every HTML element. The only way to modify such behavior was through settings global to the browser. Even at that time, the HTML 2 specification made early attempts at abstraction. For example, it was not recommended that designers use the `<B>` element to indicate bold text; instead, the `<STRONG>` element was recommended, leaving it up to the rendering engine to load a meaning for `<STRONG>` (which, by default, mapped to `<B>`). Unfortunately, very few web designers actually followed such recommendations.

By the time HTML 4 came out, this simple abstraction developed into a mechanism for style sheets that make it possible to control rendering of HTML elements. HTML 4 also includes mechanisms for scripting, frames and embedding objects. The new standard mechanism supports embedding generic media objects and applications in HTML documents. The `<OBJECT>` element (together with its predecessors `<IMG>` and `<APPLET>`) supports the inclusion of images, video, sound, mathematical expressions, and other objects. It finally provides document authors with a consistent way to define hierarchies of alternative renderings. This problem has been around since Mosaic and Lynx (early graphical and command-line browsers) that needed alternative ways to present images.

Another important development that was first introduced in HTML 4 is internationalization. With the expansion of the web, it became increasingly important to support different languages. HTML 4 bases its character set on the ISO/IEC:10646 standard (as you remember, SGML gives us the power to define the character set). ISO/IEC:10646 is an inclusive standard that supports the representation of international characters, text direction, and punctuation, which are all crucial in supporting the rich variety of world languages.

4.2.2 Structure and syntax

As we have already mentioned a few times, it is important not to be misled by the high tolerance to HTML syntax and structure violations that characterizes commercial desktop browsers. The HTML specification is the only common denominator for diverse commercial tools, and compliance to this specification is the best way to avoid problems over the lifetime of your documents.

```
<!DOCTYPE HTML PUBLIC "-//W3C//DTD HTML 4.01//EN"
   "http://www.w3.org/TR/html4/strict.dtd">
<HTML>
   <HEAD>
      <TITLE>Sample HTML Document</TITLE>
   </HEAD>
   <BODY>
      <P>I don't have to close the <P> tag.
   </BODY>
</HTML>
```

Figure 4.10 Document compliant with HTML 4.01.

According to the specification, an HTML 4 document must contain a reference to an HTML version, a *header* section containing document-wide declarations, and the *body* of the document. Figure 4.10 contains an example of a compliant HTML document.

As you see, the version declaration names the DTD that should be used to validate the document. HTML 4.01 defines three DTDs – one that is designed for strict compliance, another that supports the set of elements now considered deprecated, and a third that supports the same set of deprecated elements with the exception of frames.

HTML header

The optional header section starts with the <HEAD> element and includes document-wide declarations. The most commonly used header element is the <TITLE>, which dates back to early versions of HTML. Most browsers display the value of this element outside the body of the document. In a way, it is an early attempt to specify document metadata. It is widely used by search agents, which normally assign it greater weight than the rest of the document.

The more recent <META> element provides a lot more flexibility in defining document properties and providing input to browsers and other user agents. Figure 4.11 shows examples of defining the Author and Publisher properties using the <META> element.

The <META> element may also be used to specify HTTP headers. The last two lines in Figure 4.11 tell the browser to act as if the following two additional HTTP headers were present:

```
Expires: Sun, 17 Feb 2008 15:21:09 GMT
Date: Tue, 12 Feb 2008 08:05:22 GMT
```

```
<META name="Author" content="Leon Shklar">
<META name="Author" content="Rich Rosen">
<META name="Publisher" content="Wiley Computer Publishing">
<META http-equiv="Expires" content="Sun, 17 Feb 2008 15:21:09 GMT">
<META http-equiv="Date" content="Tue, 12 Feb 2008 08:05:22 GMT">
```

Figure 4.11 META elements.

You can use this syntax to define any HTTP header you want, but not all of them affect processing. No surprise here: certain headers have to be processed by the browser before the HTML document is parsed, and therefore those headers cannot be overridden using this method. For example, to start parsing the HTML document, the browser must have already established from the `Content-Type` header that the type of the body is `text/html`. Thus, the `Content-Type` cannot be modified using an instance of the `<META>` element in this way. The browser does not even recognize the `<META>` element until it has determined that the `Content-Type` is `text/html`. It follows that `Content-Type` headers defined through the HTML `<META>` tag, as well as `Content-Encoding` and `Transfer-Encoding` headers, are ignored. In short, any header that has to be interpreted and processed prior to parsing the HTML document is ignored if defined using this method.

There are advantages to embedding HTTP headers in HTML files. The main reason why we are discussing it in such detail is that it illustrates an important link between different web technologies. Embedding HTTP-based logic in HTML files may be invaluable in building applications that are very easy to install and distribute across different hardware and software platforms. Whenever you desire to employ this mechanism, you should consider the processing steps that occur prior to parsing the markup, to decide whether your `<META>` element would have any effect. This decision may depend on your processing agent – a browser or a specialized intelligent proxy. For example, a proxy may use the value of the `Content-Type` header defined in the `<META>` element to set the `Content-Type` of the response prior to forwarding it to the browser.

Other elements that are defined in the HTML header section include `<STYLE>` and `<SCRIPT>`. The `<STYLE>` element is designed to alter the default browser behavior when rendering the body of the markup. In Figure 4.12, we override the default rendering of the `<H1>` element, telling the browser to center its value in a box with a solid border.

The syntax of the style instructions complies with the *Cascading Style Sheets* (CSS) specification. It is not necessary to include the style specification in the header section. In fact, it is far more common to reference a standalone style document using the `src` attribute of the `<STYLE>` element. This way, it is possible to change the look and feel of HTML documents simply by changing the `src` attribute. We return to the CSS specification in Section 4.3.1 and again in Chapter 8.

```
<STYLE type="text/css">
H1 {border-width: 1; border: solid; text-align: center}
</STYLE>
```

Figure 4.12 STYLE element.

The `<SCRIPT>` element, in combination with event handlers that may be referenced from the body of the document, is designed to provide access to browser objects that are created when processing HTTP responses. Figure 4.13 illustrates using the `<SCRIPT>` element to define a sample JavaScript function (we discuss JavaScript in Chapter 8), which takes a Form object as an argument, sets the HTTP method to `GET` for Netscape 4.x and earlier browsers and to `POST` for other browsers, and submits the request.

```
<HTML>
<HEAD>
  ...
<SCRIPT type="text/javascript">
function setMethod(form) {
    if (navigator.appName == "Netscape" &&
        navigator.appVersion.match(/^\s*[1-4]/)) {
        form.method = "get";
    } else {
        form.method = "post";
    }
    form.submit();
}
</SCRIPT>
  ...
</HEAD>
<BODY>
  ...
<FORM action="http://www.neurozen.com/servlet/markupTest" name="testForm">
  ...
<INPUT type="button" value="Next" onClick="setMethod(testForm)">
</FORM>
</BODY>
</HTML>
```

Figure 4.13   SCRIPT element.

HTML body

The content of an HTML document is included within the <BODY> element. We refer you to the HTML specification and a rich selection of HTML textbooks for descriptions of different formatting elements. The most commonly used elements include <TABLE>, headings (<H1>, <H2>, etc.), ordered and unordered lists, and other elements designed to control screen layout.

Other important elements include anchors that reference documents or locations within documents and image elements (check out the <A href=...> and <IMG src=...> elements in Figure 4.14). The difference between these two elements is very important – the anchor represents a hyperlink that is evaluated only on request, while requests to load images are generated automatically when attempting to render the page, assuming the rendering agent is configured to support images.

Content accessibility

An interesting observation about the <IMG> element in Figure 4.14 has to do with the use of the ALT attribute and element content. The value of the alt attribute is displayed by browsers that support up-to-date HTML specifications but do not render images (for example, command-line browsers such as Lynx and browsers for text-based mobile devices).

This example conveys an important point that is applicable to many HTML elements that control rendering – it is important to design pages that render well in a wide variety of browsers, which differ in their level of compliance with HTML specifications.

```
<HTML>
<HEAD>
<TITLE>Leon Shklar, shklar@cs.rutgers.edu</TITLE>
<BASE href="http://www.cs.rutgers.edu/~shklar/">
</HEAD>
<BODY bgcolor="#ffffff">
<H3 align="center">Leon Shklar's Home Page</H3>
<P align="center">
<IMG src="images/photo_small.gif" align="absmiddle" alt="photo">
</P>
<P align="center">Leon Shklar, Ph.D.
<A href="mailto:shklar@cs.rutgers.edu">
<CODE>shklar@cs.rutgers.edu</CODE>
</A>
</P>
<P>
<EM>One of these days I will find time and make my pages look cool
</EM>
</P>
<P>
<A href="./classes/476">Here is a link to class notes ...</A>
</P>
</BODY>
</HTML>
```

Figure 4.14 Simple HTML page.

Forbidden Tags

Note that we cannot close the <IMG> tag because </IMG> is forbidden in HTML 4.01. For those of you who are familiar with the <.../> syntax and wonder why we did not use it in our examples, note that it is not well-formed HTML. It is XHTML syntax, which we discuss in Chapter 5.

HTTP requests

Most browsers provide a number of options for initiating HTTP requests. The most obvious options are by following a hyperlink or specifying a URL (by typing it in, selecting a bookmark or a history entry, etc.). A less obvious option is initiating requests through HTTP headers or HTTP-EQUIV constructs. In those cases, browsers use their own discretion in generating requests. We refer you to Chapter 7 for the gory details of request generation.

Let us take a quick look at the request generation controls that are available in HTML. The most simple and commonly used controls are available through HTML forms, which support selecting a URL and an HTTP method, as well as defining some HTTP headers including Content-Type. The example in Figure 4.15 illustrates using an HTML form for file transfer. Notice the use of the enctype attribute to set the Content-Type header of the request. This may not be necessary because major modern browsers default to multipart/form-data when transmitting files. Even so, it is a good practice, which helps keep your applications resilient as technologies change.

```
<FORM action="http://www.nobody.name/sendFile" method="post"
    enctype="multipart/form-data">
  <P>
  <LABEL for="localpath">Choose local file: </LABEL >
  <INPUT type="file" id="localpath"><BR>
  <LABEL for="filename">Target file name: </LABEL >
  <INPUT type="text" id="filename"><BR>
  <LABEL for="location">Target location: </LABEL >
  <INPUT type="text" id="location"><BR>
  <INPUT type="submit" value="Send"> <INPUT type="reset">
  </P>
</FORM>
```

Figure 4.15 File submission form.

In the example, the first `<INPUT>` element references a file – most browsers present it as a file selector dialog. The second and third `<INPUT>` elements represent attribute–value pairs for specifying the file name and location on the target system. The final `<INPUT>` element represents the submission button that, when pressed, initiates the request.

The browser uses multipart MIME messages to combine file content with information about the target location. A sample file transfer request is shown in Figure 4.16. It is a multipart message, the first part of which contains the body of the file, and the second part contains form information pertaining to the target location of the submitted file. It is assumed that `http://www.nobody.name/sendFile` is a server-side executable (e.g., a CGI script or servlet) that is capable of parsing the message to extract the file and its target location, and to save it at that location relative the document root.

This example illustrates HTML elements that control the formation of HTTP requests submitted by the browser. HTML provides many other controls, which are not discussed in this book – the

```
POST http://www.nobody.name/sendFile HTTP/1.1
Host: www.nobody.name
Content type: multipart/form-data; boundary=-----------------7d2202e1903de
User-Agent: Mozilla/4.0 (compatible; MSIE 6.0; Windows NT 5.0)
Locale: en_US

-----------------7d2202e1903de
Content-Type: text/plain
Content-Length: 1A

This is my test text file.
-----------------7d2202e1903de
Content-Type: application/x-www-form-urlencoded
Content-Length: 27

filename=mytestfile.txt&location=/leon/
-----------------7d2202e1903de
```

Figure 4.16 Sample file transfer request.

important part is to understand the idea of such controls and to know what to look for when searching for a solution.

4.3   HTML Rendering

As we mentioned in the previous section, the only way to modify rendering of HTML elements in older browsers was through global settings of the browser. However, early HTML specifications attempted to put stakes in the ground toward rendering abstractions to be achieved in the future (e.g., the distinction between <B> and <STRONG>). Very few HTML designers made such distinctions, since they had no immediate impact on the look and feel of their pages. Things changed when initial abstractions developed into style sheets that made it possible to exhibit fine-grained control over the rendering of HTML documents.

4.3.1   Cascading Style Sheets

Cascading Style Sheets (CSS) is a mechanism for controlling the style (e.g. fonts, colors, and spacing) for HTML rendering. A style sheet is made up of rules, each of which applies to an HTML element and controls a certain aspect of its rendering. There are various ways of associating these style rules with HTML documents, but the easiest is to use the HTML <STYLE> element, which is placed in the document header and contains style rules for the page (see Section 4.2.2).

Figure 4.17 demonstrates sample rules for rendering default fonts within a paragraph (the <P> element). In the first rule, font properties are defined through the font argument, while in the second and third rules they are defined through the more specific font-size argument. The font-size argument is limited to a subset of properties that could be defined through the font argument.

Another observation is that the same element property may be defined with a different level of abstraction. In the first rule, size is defined in absolute units that are independent of the browser properties. Such a setting means that you are willing to ignore the user's personal preferences, which is rarely a good idea. In the second rule, the font size is defined in terms that depend on browser properties but not the context of the element. In other words, medium may mean 10 point or 14 point depending on browser settings, but within the same page and the same browser window, the paragraph would always be rendered in exactly the same way. Similarly, the font color may be defined either by using absolute RGB (Red–Green–Blue) units (e.g., #0000F0 in the first rule) or by using symbolic names that might map to different RGB combinations.

Finally, in the third rule, the font size is defined relative to the context – larger may translate into different absolute sizes within the same page, depending on the default font size in the element context where the <P> element is included.

```
P { font: italic bold 12pt/14pt Times, serif; color: #0000F0  }
P { font-size: medium; color: blue }
P { font-size: larger }
```

Figure 4.17   CSS rules for the <P> element.

```
BODY { margin-top: 0 }
DT { margin-bottom: 2em }
A:visited { border: thin dotted #800080 }
P { display: list-item }
```

Figure 4.18 Sample *box* and *classification* properties.

As you can see from our example, CSS rules associate groups of properties with HTML elements. Properties that may be defined using style-sheet rules include font, color and text groups. Font properties include font family, weight, size, height, and style, while color properties describe fonts and backgrounds. Text properties are a bit more complex and control word and letter indentation, text decoration (e.g., underline) and alignment, and even simple transformations (e.g., to all lowercase or all uppercase letters).

Other interesting groups include *box* and *classification* properties. The first three rules in Figure 4.18 demonstrate the box properties. The first rule serves to eliminate the top margin of a page, the second rule sets the bottom margin of <DT> elements to two font heights, and the third describes the border for visited links. The fourth rule defines a sample classification property. According to this rule, paragraphs would be shown not only with preceding and trailing line breaks, but also with the list-item marker.

4.3.2 Associating styles with HTML documents

CSS makes it possible to achieve varying degrees of separation between markup and rendering. With this in mind, we consider alternatives for associating full style sheets and style elements with HTML pages and their fragments.

Linked style sheet

The approach that provides the highest degree of separation between HTML markup and style-based rendering is based on linking HTML documents with external style sheets, which do not contain any HTML markup, only style commands. The linking is accomplished through yet another HTML header element – <LINK>. Figure 4.19 contains examples of using this element to define the associations. The rel attribute defines the relationship with the associated file and the type attribute specifies the text/css MIME type for the style sheet. The href attribute references the location of the style sheet file. Finally, the media attribute defines the rendering media, which could be a regular desktop browser (screen), a speech synthesizer (aural), a printer (print), or other devices.

The media attribute can be specific enough to apply to just one kind of device: Apple's original iPhone development guidelines, for example, recommended the use of an iPhone-specific CSS style sheet by specifying the media attribute as "only screen and (max-device-width: 480px)".

The optional title attribute is only present when it is necessary to support alternative style sheets. Its absence, as in the first example, indicates that changing the style sheet is not supported. Style sheet alternation may have different forms, but normally involves user interaction. The second and third examples represent a default style sheet that is applied at rendering time and an alternative that can be explicitly selected by the user. The last example in Figure 4.19 is very similar to the first example except that the rendering device is a speech synthesizer.

```
<LINK rel="Stylesheet" href="mystyle.css"
      type="text/css" media="screen">

<LINK rel="Stylesheet" href="main.css" type="text/css"
         media="screen" title="Default Style">
<LINK rel="Alternative Stylesheet" href="alt.css"
         type="text/css" media="screen"
      title="Alternative Style">

<LINK rel="Stylesheet" href="audio.css"
         type="text/css" media="aural">
```

Figure 4.19   Using the HTML <LINK> element to associate styles.

Embedded style sheet

Figure 4.20 demonstrates the use of a style sheet embedded in an HTML document. It is similar to the example that we used to illustrate our discussion of HTML headers (Figure 4.12). One distinction is the use of the HTML comment syntax, which does not hinder browsers that support <STYLE> elements but helps older browsers to ignore the style instructions and avoid confusion. The second distinction is the use of the import statement. Use of the <STYLE> element in combination with the @import instruction is equivalent to the first example in Figure 4.19.

The embedded syntax makes it possible to override parts of imported styles with local definitions (e.g., the local definition of the <H1> element in Figure 4.20). This approach does violate the principle of separating markup and rendering but is borderline acceptable since the main style specification still comes from a separate file.

Inline style

Yet another alternative is to use the style attribute that may be applied to most body elements (including <BODY> but excluding <SCRIPT>, <PARAM>, and <FONT>). It allows for the definition of style attributes for a single instance of a tag within a page but it results in the mixing of style and markup (see Figure 4.21).

If you think that you have valid reasons to use an inline style, you are supposed to define a single style language for the entire document by including the proper header in the HTTP response (e.g., Content-Style-Type: text/css), even though most browsers default to using CSS when processing style attributes within tags. Alternatively, you can achieve the same result by using the HTML <META> element with the http-equiv attribute (see Section 4.2.2).

```
<STYLE type="text/css" media="screen">
<!--
@import url(mystyle.css);
H1 {border-width: 1; border: solid; text-align: center}
-->
</STYLE>
```

Figure 4.20   Embedded style sheet.

```
<H1 STYLE="border-width: 1; border: solid; text-align: center">Chapter 1 </H1>
```

Figure 4.21   Inline styles.

```
<SPAN style="color:#00DD45;">DRAFT</SPAN>
<DIV style="font-size: smaller">
    <TABLE><TR><TD>Column 1</TD><TD>Column 2</TD><TR>...</TABLE>
</DIV>
```

Figure 4.22   Associating styles with portions of HTML documents.

If you feel that there needs to be a middle ground between document-wide and inline styles, you are not alone. Such a middle ground can be achieved by using inline styles with <SPAN> and <DIV> elements, which were introduced for the express purpose of associating styles with arbitrarily delimited sections of HTML documents. While <SPAN> is an inline element, which is used in a manner similar to <STRONG> and <EM>, <DIV> may contain blocks that include paragraphs, tables, and, recursively, other <DIV> elements (Figure 4.22).

4.4   Summary

We have discussed HTML and related technologies; we have also established the necessary foundation for the upcoming discussion of XML in the next chapter. We discussed SGML, its DTD syntax, and using it to define HTML as an SGML application. We further discussed the HTML markup language, concentrating on the features that influence HTTP interactions, as well as features that enable the separation of presentation and rendering.

We stress that it is important to distinguish between the separation of presentation and rendering, and the separation of content and presentation. The former is accomplished through style sheets, while the latter is the function of proper application design. The CSS language discussed in this chapter is only the first step in style-sheet evolution. In Chapter 5, we refer to CSS as the starting point for our style-sheet discussion.

QUESTIONS AND EXERCISES

1. What is the relationship between HTML, XML, SGML, and XHTML? Explain.

2. Which kinds of HTTP headers would be ignored when specified using the HTTP-EQUIV mechanism? Which kinds of headers would not be ignored? Provide examples of each and explain.

3. Describe options for using HTML to generate HTTP requests. Can you control the Content-Type header for browser requests? What request settings can be imposed by the browser and under what circumstances?

4. Put together a simple HTML form for submitting desktop files to the server using POST requests. Remember to provide information about the target location of the file after transmission. What is the format of the request?

5. What is the purpose of introducing CSS? What are the alternatives for associating styles with HTML documents?

6. How difficult would it be to implement an HTML parser? Why? How would you represent semantics of HTML elements?

4.5 Bibliography

Maler, Eve and Andaloussi, Jeanne El, 1995. *Developing SGML DTDs*. Prentice Hall PTR.

Meyer, Eric, 2006. *Cascading Style Sheets: The Definitive Guide*, 3rd Edition. O'Reilly & Associates.

Musciano, Chuck and Kennedy, Bill, 2006. *HTML and XHTML: The Definitive Guide*, 6th Edition. O'Reilly & Associates.

CHAPTER 5

XML Languages and Applications

IN THIS CHAPTER

- Core XML
- XHTML
- Web services (SOAP and REST)
- Extensible Stylesheet Language (XSL)

OBJECTIVES

- Discuss core XML technologies setting the stage for the overview of XML applications and derivative technologies.
- Discuss XML DTDs, their limitations, and the advantages of XML Schemas.
- Consider XHTML as an XML application, discussing the differences and convergence between XHTML and HTML.
- Discuss XHTML Mobile Profile – a simplified version of XHTML for wireless applications.
- Provide insights about the advantages and drawbacks associated with competing web services strategies.
- Discuss XSL, showing how XSL Transformations and XSL Formatting Objects can be used to transform XML content and produce printable documents.

For all its power, SGML has remained a niche language. It originated in the 1970s and enjoyed a very strong following in the text representation community. However, the price for the power and flexibility of SGML was its complexity. Just as the simplicity of HTTP gave birth to the web, something a lot simpler than SGML was needed in the area of markup languages. The initial approach was to create a targeted SGML application, HTML, which worked relatively well during the early years of the web. However, it was neither sufficiently powerful and flexible, nor rigorous enough for the information-processing needs of sophisticated web applications.

The solution was to define a relatively simple subset of SGML that would retain the most critical features of the language. Such a subset, called the eXtensible Markup Language (XML), was designed to serve as the foundation for the new generation of markup languages. By giving up some of the flexibility (e.g., SGML's character set and concrete syntax declarations) and imposing additional structural constraints, it became possible to construct a language that is easy to learn and conducive to the creation of advanced authoring tools.

XML was originally designed as a subset of SGML, but its simplicity lent itself to an evolution that took it far beyond the confines of SGML. While XML document type definitions (DTDs) represent a subset of SGML DTDs, XML Schema is a new and more robust language for defining application-specific constraints. Moreover, entirely new mechanisms have emerged, such as XPath to address fragments of XML documents and XSL to define document transformations. XML is much more than a replacement for SGML-derived HTML. XML applications include specialized markup languages (e.g., MathML), communication protocols (e.g., SOAP), and configuration instructions (e.g., configuration files for HTTP servers and Java EE containers).

In this chapter, we discuss XML, covering both XML-related languages that stand on their own (e.g., XML DTD and XPath) and those that are defined as independent XML applications (e.g., XSL, XML Schema, and SOAP). We also discuss the relationship between SGML and HTML, on the one hand, and XML and XHTML on the other. Finally, we provide a brief overview of other specialized XML applications.

5.1 Core XML

As you may recall from Chapter 4, the first steps in defining SGML applications are to define the character set and the concrete syntax. XML syntax is relatively rigid – the character set is fixed and there is a limited number of tag delimiters (<, >, />, and </). Consequently, there is no need to define concrete syntax, since XML targets a much narrower set of applications than SGML and there cannot be an XML application without the familiar angle brackets.

The DTD that defines markup constructs is still required. However, XML DTD specifications have to be less expressive than SGML DTDs, to make it impossible to define element structures that violate constraints on element nesting.

XML Schemas are the next generation of DTDs: they provide more flexibility in defining document constraints. Unlike XML DTDs, the XML Schema language is defined as an XML application, so that developers do not have to use different syntaxes (and different tools) for creating documents and for defining document constraints.

Another very important notion is that of a namespace, which makes it possible to use qualified names to distinguish between elements that belong to different XML applications and may have different semantics. Interestingly enough, there is a close relationship between namespaces and XML schemas.

5.1.1 XML documents

XML documents are composed of declarations, elements, tags, comments, character references, and processing instructions. Every document has a single root element, for which neither its start tag nor its end tag are in the context of another element; all other elements have to be properly nested within each other. XML entities are syntactically very similar to HTML escape sequences; there are built-in entities (e.g., <, >, &, ', and ") but it is also possible to define new entities using either a DTD or an XML Schema. An XML document is well-formed if it includes a document declaration, satisfies element nesting and other syntactic constraints, and does not include undefined entities. A well-formed XML document is valid if it satisfies constraints specified in the associated DTD or a schema. Of course, only a well-formed document is valid.

The XML document in Figure 5.1 starts with an XML declaration, which is followed by a comment, the DTD reference, and a combination of tags and character sequences that satisfy constraints for well-formed XML documents.

XML comment syntax is similar to HTML comments. Comments can only appear after the XML declaration. They may not be placed within a tag, but may be used to surround and hide individual tags and XML fragments that do not contain comments (e.g., the second <book> element).

```
<?xml version="1.0" standalone="yes"?>
<!-- XML example for books in print -->
<!DOCTYPE books SYSTEM "books.dtd">
<books status="In Print">
  <book>
    <title>Web Application Architecture</title>
    <subtitle>Principles, protocols and practices</subtitle>
    <author firstName="Leon" lastName="Shklar"/>
    <author firstName="Rich" lastName="Rosen"/>
    <info>
      <pages count="500"/>
      <price usd="55" gbp="27.50"/>
      <publication year="2008" source="&jw;"/>
    </info>
    <summary>An in-depth examination of the basic concepts and general
             principles associated with web application development.
    </summary>
  </book>
  <!--
    <book>&lt;TBD&gt;</book>
  -->
  <notes><![CDATA[
    &lt;!-- This is our CDATA example that hides syntactically incorrect
    comments and XML fragments --><books><book>
    ]]>
  </notes>
</books>
```

Figure 5.1 Sample XML document.

In addition to comments, XML possesses an even stronger mechanism for hiding non-compliant fragments – CDATA sections. CDATA sections exclude enclosed text from XML parsing – all text is interpreted as character data. It is useful for hiding document fragments that contain comments, quotes, "&" characters, or simply any blocks of text that are invalid when interpreted as XML. For example, the CDATA section in Figure 5.1 hides the improperly formatted comment and two XML tags from the XML parser. The only character sequence that may not occur in a CDATA section is]]>, which indicates the closing of the section.

As you can see from Figure 5.1, XML elements can be represented with two kinds of tags. Non-empty elements use open and close tags that have the same syntax as HTML tags (e.g., <book>...</book> and <summary>...</summary>). Empty elements are represented by single tags that end with the />sequence (e.g., <pages.../> and <price.../>). An element may or may not have attributes, which, for non-empty elements, have to be included in open tags (for empty elements, there is only one tag, so there is not much choice).

The document in Figure 5.1 contains entities in the body of the second <book> element. Both < and > are references to built-in entities that are analogous to escape sequences in HTML. Since HTML is an SGML application, it already has a DTD, and we cannot change existing escape sequences or add new ones. XML is a subset of SGML, so it is possible to define new entities using an XML DTD. An example of a reference to a newly defined entity is &jw;. Since jw is not a built-in entity, it should be defined in the books.dtd file for the document to be considered well-formed. Note that the < character sequence that occurs within the CDATA section is not an entity reference – as we discussed, CDATA sections exclude the enclosed text from XML parsing.

Figure 5.2 is a graphic representation of the XML document in Figure 5.1. Here, internal nodes represent elements, solid edges represent the containment relationship, dashed edges represent the attribute relationship, and leaf nodes are either attributes or element content. For example, element <info> is represented as the combination of elements <pages>, <price> and <publication>, while elements <title> and <subtitle> are represented by their character content. Attribute names and values are shown in brackets, and attribute value edges are indicated by equal signs (e.g., [firstName="Leon"]).

Processing XML documents often involves traversing an element tree, which is commonly referred to as the Document Object Model (DOM) tree There is a special specification for the traversal paths, which is discussed in Section 5.4.1.

5.1.2 XML DTD

The meaning of XML tags is in the eye of the beholder. Even though you may be looking at the sample document and telling yourself that it makes sense, it is only because of the implied semantics associated with the English names of elements and attributes.

Language semantics are of course inaccessible to XML parsers. The immediate problem for XML parsers is validation. A person would most likely guess that the value of the usd attribute of the <price> element is the book price in dollars. It would come as a surprise if, for one of the books, the value of this attribute is the number 1000 or the word "table." Again, this surprise would be based on language semantics and not on any formal specification that can be used to perform automated validation.

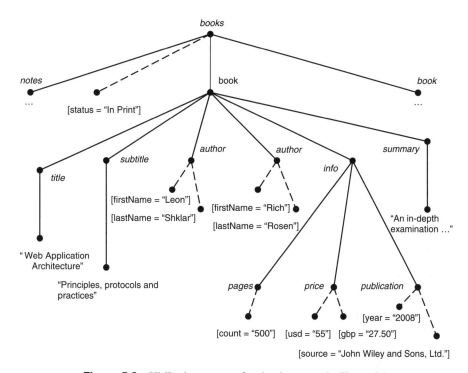

Figure 5.2 XML element tree for the document in Figure 5.1.

The second problem is even more complex. How do we make XML documents useful to target applications? It is easy with HTML – every tag has a well-defined meaning that is hard-coded into browser processing and rendering modules. XML elements do not have assigned meaning, though a particular XML application (e.g., XHTML) may have a predefined meaning for individual elements.

The XML DTD syntax for element definitions in Figure 5.3 is simpler than similar SGML syntax (see the SGML DTD fragment in Figure 5.4). If we were to add more element definitions to the example in Figure 5.4, all of them would have pairs of dashes indicating that both an open and a close tag are required. There is no reason to keep this part of the SGML DTD syntax – all XML elements always require both open and close tags.

Similarly to the SGML DTD examples in Chapter 4, the XML DTD specification in Figure 5.3 defines the nesting and recurrence of individual elements. The root element is defined to contain at least one `<book>`, which, in turn, contains exactly one `<title>`, at least one `<author>`, and may or may not contain `<subtitle>`, `<info>`, and `<summary>` elements.

XML DTDs provide simple mechanisms for defining new entities, which are very similar to those of SGML DTDs. In Figure 5.3, the entity `jw`, used in the sample document in Figure 5.1, is defined to expand to "John Wiley and Sons, Ltd.". An obvious reason for defining the name of a publisher as an entity is that it applies to multiple book entries. Another example in Figure 5.3 is the entity `JWCopyright`, which is defined as a reference to an HTTP resource.

```
<?xml version="1.0" encoding="UTF-8"?>
<!ELEMENT books (book+, notes)>
<!ATTLIST books
    status CDATA #IMPLIED
>
<!ELEMENT book (title, subtitle?, author+, info?, summary?)>
<!ELEMENT title (#PCDATA)>
<!ELEMENT subtitle (#PCDATA)>
<!ELEMENT author EMPTY>
<!ATTLIST author
    firstName NMTOKEN #REQUIRED
    lastName  NMTOKEN #REQUIRED
>
<!ELEMENT info (pages, price, publication)>
<!ELEMENT pages EMPTY>
<!ATTLIST pages
    count CDATA #REQUIRED
>
<!ELEMENT price EMPTY>
<!ATTLIST price
    usd   CDATA #REQUIRED
    gbp   CDATA #IMPLIED
    euro  CDATA #IMPLIED
>
<!ELEMENT publication EMPTY>
<!ATTLIST publication
    year   CDATA #REQUIRED
    source CDATA #REQUIRED
>
<!ELEMENT summary (#PCDATA)>
<!ELEMENT notes (#PCDATA)>
<!ENTITY  jw "John Wiley and Sons, Ltd.">
<!ENTITY  JWCopyright SYSTEM "http://www.wiley.com/xml/copyright.xml">
```

Figure 5.3 XML DTD for the document in Figure 5.1.

```
...
<!ELEMENT book  - - (title, subtitle?, author+, info?, summary?)>
<!ELEMENT title - - (#PCDATA)>
...
```

Figure 5.4 Fragment of an SGML DTD for the document in Figure 5.1.

DTDs do not provide an easy way of defining constraints that go beyond element nesting and recurrence. While it is easy to associate elements with attributes and to define basic constraints on attribute types (e.g., predefined tokens or enumeration), attempts to define more complex constraints are often an exercise in futility. And of course, DTDs are no help in defining semantics.

5.1.3 XML Schema

XML Schema is a specification from the World Wide Web Consortium (W3C). It was developed after the introduction of XML and does not have an analog in the SGML world. It was designed as an alternative to the DTD mechanism, providing stronger typing and utilizing XML syntax. It contains additional constructs that make it a lot easier to define sophisticated constraints.

XML Schema supports so-called "simple" and "complex" types. Simple types are defined by imposing additional constraints on built-in types, while complex types are composed recursively from other simple and complex types. Built-in types available in the XML Schema are much richer and more flexible than those available in the DTD context. This is very important because it means that the XML Schema makes it possible to express sophisticated constraints without resorting to application logic, which would need to be coded using a procedural language (e.g., Java) and would be much more expensive to maintain.

XML syntax for referencing schemas is shown in Figure 5.5. An XML schema specification does not provide for defining entities, so entity definitions have to use the DTD syntax.

In Figure 5.6, we demonstrate the brute force approach to defining an XML schema. This pattern is sometimes called the "Russian doll design", referring to the wooden dolls that are nested inside each other. Here, every type is defined in place, there is no reuse, and the resulting schema is relatively difficult to read. Nevertheless, it is a good starting point for our analysis.

We begin with defining the element <books> by associating it with the complex type that is defined using the sequence *compositor*. Sequence compositors impose a sequential order; they are equivalent to commas when defining constraints on element nesting in the DTD syntax. Other compositors include all, which does not impose an order as long as every enumerated element (or group of elements) is present in accordance with the occurrence constraints, and choice, which requires the presence of exactly one element or group of elements.

Here, the complex type for the <books> element is defined as the sequence of <book> and <notes> elements. In this design, types are defined in the depth-first manner, and it is often difficult to see all elements of the sequence when reading the schema. The <book> element is, in turn, associated with a complex type that is also defined as a sequence, etc.

The XML Schema syntax for defining element quantifiers (the number of occurrences of an element) differs from the DTD syntax, but both implement the same concepts. For example, the number of

```
<?xml version="1.0" encoding="UTF-8"?>
<!DOCTYPE books [
<!ENTITY jw "John Wiley and Sons, Ltd.">
<!ENTITY JWCopyright SYSTEM "http://www.wiley.com/xml/copyright.xml">
]>
<books xmlns:xsi="http://www.w3.org/2001/XMLSchema-instance"
       xsi:noNamespaceSchemaLocation="books1.xsd" status="In Print">
...
</books>
```

Figure 5.5 Schema-based validation for the XML document in Figure 5.1.

```
<?xml version="1.0" encoding="utf-8"?>
<xs:schema xmlns:xs="http://www.w3.org/2001/XMLSchema">
<xs:element name="books">
  <xs:complexType>
    <xs:sequence>
      <xs:element name="book" minOccurs="1" maxOccurs="unbounded">
        <xs:complexType>
          <xs:sequence>
            <xs:element name="title" type="xs:string"/>
            <xs:element name="subtitle" type="xs:string"
                       minOccurs="0" maxOccurs="1"/>
            <xs:element name="author" minOccurs="1" maxOccurs="unbounded">
              <xs:complexType>
                <xs:attribute name="firstName" type="xs:string"
                             use="required"/>
                <xs:attribute name="lastName" type="xs:string"
                             use="required"/>
              </xs:complexType>
            </xs:element>
            <xs:element name="info" minOccurs="0" maxOccurs="1">
              <xs:complexType>
                <xs:sequence>
                  <xs:element name="pages">
                    <xs:complexType>
                      <xs:attribute name="count" type="xs:integer"/>
                    </xs:complexType>
                  </xs:element>
                  <xs:element name="price">
                    <xs:complexType>
                      <xs:attribute name="usd" type="xs:decimal"
                                   use="required"/>
                      <xs:attribute name="gbp" type="xs:decimal"/>
                      <xs:attribute name="euro" type="xs:decimal"/>
                    </xs:complexType>
                  </xs:element>
                  <xs:element name="publication">
                    <xs:complexType>
                      <xs:attribute name="year" type="xs:integer"
                                   use="required"/>
                      <xs:attribute name="source" type="xs:string"
                                   use="required"/>
                    </xs:complexType>
                  </xs:element>
                </xs:sequence>
              </xs:complexType>
            </xs:element>
            <xs:element name="summary" type="xs:string"
                       minOccurs="0" maxOccurs="1"/>
          </xs:sequence>
```

Figure 5.6   XML Schema for the sample document in Figure 5.1.

```
          </xs:complexType>
        </xs:element>
        <xs:element name="notes" type="xs:string" minOccurs="0"
                    maxOccurs="1"/>
      </xs:sequence>
      <xs:attribute name="status" type="xs:string"/>
    </xs:complexType>
  </xs:element>
</xs:schema>
```

Figure 5.6   *(continued)*

occurrences for the element `<author>` is defined to be at least one, which is the same as "+" in the DTD syntax; the element `<subtitle>` is defined as optional (zero or one occurrences), which is the same as "?" in the DTD syntax. Just as in DTDs, the number of occurrences, if unspecified, defaults to exactly one.

Attributes can be defined only for complex types. It is quite a relief that schemas, unlike DTDs, support the same built-in types for attributes as they do for elements. By default, attributes are optional but they may be made required, as in the case of the `usd` attribute for the `<price>` element.

We can improve on the design in Figure 5.6. The new schema in Figure 5.7 uses named types to make the schema more readable and easy to maintain. Instead of defining complex types in place, as in Figure 5.6, we start by defining complex types that can be composed from simple types and attribute definitions, and proceed to define increasingly complex types.

For example, the complex types `authorType` and `infoType` are first defined and then referenced by name in the definition of `bookType`. The result is an XML schema composed of simple reusable definitions.

The primary purpose of the schema is to support document validation. It remains to be seen whether we can improve the validation by defining additional constraints. We have done our job in defining element quantifiers and nesting constraints. However, it would be very useful to impose custom constraints on simple types.

For example, we can assume that a name should not be longer than 32 characters, and that the price of a book should be in the range of 0.01 to 999.99, whether we are using dollars, pounds, or euros. In Figure 5.8, we define two new simple types – `nameBaseType` and `priceBaseType` – by imposing constraints on the base string type. In the first case, the new constraint is a maximum length, while in the second it is the pattern – one to three digits possibly followed by the decimal point and another two digits. Of course, we have to go back to the schema in Figure 5.7 and make changes to the type references in order to take advantage of these new constraints (see Figure 5.9).

XML schemas provide extensive capabilities for defining custom types and utilizing them in document validation. Moreover, XML schemas are themselves XML documents and may be validated, which serves as a good foundation for building advanced tools. However, advanced validation is not a solution for associating semantics with XML elements, which remains a very difficult problem. A partial solution to this problem is provided by XSL, which we discuss in Section 5.4.

```
<?xml version="1.0" encoding="utf-8"?>
<xs:schema xmlns:xs="http://www.w3.org/2001/XMLSchema">
<xs:complexType name="authorType">
   <xs:attribute name="firstName" type="xs:string" use="required"/>
   <xs:attribute name="lastName" type="xs:string" use="required"/>
</xs:complexType>
<xs:complexType name="priceType">
    <xs:attribute name="usd" type="xs:decimal" use="required"/>
    <xs:attribute name="gbp"  type="xs:decimal"/>
    <xs:attribute name="euro" type="xs:decimal"/>
</xs:complexType>
<xs:complexType name="pagesType">
    <xs:attribute name="count" type="xs:integer"/>
</xs:complexType>
<xs:complexType name="publicationType">
   <xs:attribute name="year" type="xs:integer" use="required"/>
   <xs:attribute name="source" type="xs:string" use="required"/>
</xs:complexType>
<xs:complexType name="infoType">
   <xs:sequence>
      <xs:element name="pages" type="pagesType"/>
      <xs:element name="price" type="priceType"/>
      <xs:element name="publication" type="publicationType"/>
   </xs:sequence>
</xs:complexType>
<xs:complexType name="bookType">
   <xs:sequence>
      <xs:element name="title" type="xs:string"/>
      <xs:element name="subtitle" type="xs:string"
                 minOccurs="0" maxOccurs="1"/>
      <xs:element name="author" type="authorType"
                 minOccurs="1" maxOccurs="unbounded"/>
      <xs:element name="info" type="infoType"/>
      <xs:element name="summary" type="xs:string"
                 minOccurs="0" maxOccurs="1"/>
   </xs:sequence>
</xs:complexType>
<xs:complexType name="booksType">
   <xs:sequence>
      <xs:element name="book" type="bookType"
                 minOccurs="1" maxOccurs="unbounded"/>
      <xs:element name="notes" type="xs:string"
                 minOccurs="0" maxOccurs="1"/>
   </xs:sequence>
```

Figure 5.7   Improved schema design for the sample document in Figure 5.1.

```
<xs:simpleType name="nameBaseType">
  <xs:restriction base="xs:string">
    <xs:maxLength value="32"/>
  </xs:restriction>
</xs:simpleType>

<xs:simpleType name="priceBaseType">
  <xs:restriction base="xs:string">
    <xs:pattern value="[0-9]{1,3}(\.[0-9]{2})?"/>
  </xs:restriction>
</xs:simpleType>
    <xs:attribute name="status" type="xs:string"/>
</xs:complexType>
<xs:element name="books" type="booksType"/>
</xs:schema>
```

Figure 5.8   Defining constraints on simple types.

```
<xs:complexType name="authorType">
   <xs:attribute name="firstName" type="nameBaseType" use="required"/>
   <xs:attribute name="lastName"  type="nameBaseType" use="required"/>
</xs:complexType>

<xs:complexType name="priceType">
   <xs:attribute name="usd"  type="priceBaseType" use="required"/>
   <xs:attribute name="gbp"  type="priceBaseType"/>
   <xs:attribute name="euro" type="priceBaseType"/>
</xs:complexType>
```

Figure 5.9   Using defined simple types in the XML schema from Figure 5.7.

5.2   XHTML

As we discussed in Chapter 4, the structure of HTML documents is defined rather loosely and is relatively unconstrained when compared to XML. For example, closing tags for many HTML elements are optional and are often omitted. Real-world HTML documents violate even the liberal constraints imposed by the HTML specification because commercial browsers are implemented to be tolerant of such violations. However, this is changing as it becomes more critical for newly authored HTML documents to comply with stricter XHTML constraints (e.g., closing tags and proper nesting).

XHTML 1.0 is a reformulation of HTML 4.01 (originally intended as the last HTML specification) as an XML application. Migration to XHTML makes it possible not only to impose strict structural

```
<?xml version="1.0" encoding="UTF-8"?>
<!DOCTYPE html
    PUBLIC "-//W3C//DTD XHTML 1.0 Strict//EN"
    "http://www.w3.org/TR/xhtml1/DTD/xhtml1-strict.dtd">
<html xmlns="http://www.w3.org/1999/xhtml" xml:lang="en" lang="en">
    <head>
        <title>Sample HTML Document</title>
    </head>
    <body>
        <p>I do have to close the &lt;p&gt; tag.</p>
    </body>
</html>
```

Figure 5.10 XHTML document.

constraints, but also to dispose of the legacy support for bad syntax. Even commercial browsers do not have to exhibit tolerance when validating documents that claim to implement the XHTML specification.

Differences between the sample HTML document in Figure 4.10 and the sample XHTML document in Figure 5.10 include the use of lower-case element names and the presence of the </p> tag. Apart from the document declaration, the document in Figure 5.10 is both valid XHTML and valid HTML. Many XHTML constraints, including the requirement to close tags and enclose attribute values within quotes, do not break HTML validation. Unfortunately, this is not true for all XHTML constructs that occur in real documents.

For example, adding the <br> tag after the words "I do have to close" would not affect HTML validation but would constitute a syntactic violation for XHTML. Replacing the <br> tag with the <br/> tag would produce the reverse effect. However, using the
</br> construct would not break either HTML or XHTML validation (Figure 5.11).

On the surface, there is no difference between HTML escape sequences and the XHTML use of references to pre-defined entities, but the real story is more complicated. The nature of XML processing is to recognize and process entity references in #PCDATA content. Elements that are defined to have #PCDATA content (e.g., <style> and <script>) are vulnerable to the presence of entity references. For example, < would be resolved to the < sign and considered the start of markup. To avoid this problem, in XHTML, bodies of <script> and <style> elements have to be included in CDATA sections (see Figure 5.12). Of course, the CDATA syntax breaks HTML validation and the only solution is to use external script and style documents (on those occasions when this problem arises).

As we already mentioned, XHTML is the reformulation of HTML as an XML application. XHTML elements have the same well-defined semantics as corresponding HTML elements. Element semantics

```
<p>I have to close the &lt;p&gt; tag.</p>         <!-- Valid HTML and XHTML -->
<p>I have to close<br> the &lt;p&gt; tag.</p>     <!-- Valid HTML -->
<p>I have to close<br/> the &lt;p&gt; tag.</p>    <!-- Valid XHTML -->
<p>I have to close<br></br> the &lt;p&gt; tag.</p> <!-- Valid HTML and  XHTML -->
```

Figure 5.11 Examples of valid HTML and XHTML.

```
<script type="text/javascript">
<![CDATA[
...
]]>
</script>
```

Figure 5.12   XHTML script syntax.

is an integral part of the XHTML specification and is hard-coded into presentation modules of browsers that support XHTML.

5.2.1   HTML 5

HTML 4.01 is a deprecated specification that was supposed to be the last version of HTML. With the release of new versions of XHTML, differences between HTML and XHTML were likely to accumulate. At some point, it would have become impossible to generate valid XHTML that is also valid according to the last HTML specification. With XHTML 2 failing to catch on, it became apparent that backward compatibility with HTML is far too important. This unhappy state of affairs gave rise to the HTML 5 effort, which aims to unify the HTML and XHTML specifications.

The HTML 5 specification aims to support both HTML and XHTML syntax. While both HTML and XHTML variations of HTML 5 documents are supposed to be well-formed XML documents, the error handling is quite different. XHTML error handling remains draconian but HTML error handling, while remaining pragmatic, is well-defined. This makes it possible to have consistent rendering of "tag soup" documents.

Historically, different browsers applied their own proprietary logic to infer DOM trees for ill-formed documents, resulting in inconsistent rendering across browsers. With HTML 5, ill-formed HTML documents still fail compliance tests, alerting users to problematic authoring tools. However, browsers can use the same well-defined logic to translate "tag soup" into compliant documents and use those compliant documents as the basis for rendering.

HTML 5 also defines incremental changes to HTML 4.01 and XHTML 1.0, including changes to existing elements and the introduction of new elements. Some of the new elements represent a significant step in evolving browser support from rendering documents to streaming applications. An example is the `<canvas>` element, which enables rendering of dynamic graphics on the fly.

It is very difficult to predict the future of any standard, particularly in the web space. Still, the very pragmatic nature of the HTML 5 specification makes its wide adoption very likely. Although it is often argued that silent error correction rewards bad coding practices, backward compatibility and consistent error correction go a long way toward achieving a better user experience.

5.2.2   XHTML MP

XHTML Mobile Profile (XHTML MP) is a simplified version of XHTML that was defined to support wireless applications. It is a replacement for WML, which was the previous markup language for mobile devices specified by the WAP Forum. WML contained page structures that were quite different from XHTML (e.g., "cards" which enabled traversal between different screens within the same WML file).

Devices that make use of XHTML MP are constrained by their limited memory, display size, and lower transmission bandwidth. It would be wasteful to require the device to make multiple requests for small chunks of data. Without special constructs, which were available in WML, XHTML MP developers have to use in-document anchor links to reference individual smaller screens within a single document. XHTML MP complies with the DTD maintained by the WAP Forum (see the DOCTYPE definition in Figure 5.13).

```
<?xml version="1.0" encoding="UTF-8"?>
<!DOCTYPE html PUBLIC "-//WAPFORUM//DTD XHTML Mobile 1.0//EN"
        "http://www.wapforum.org/DTD/xhtml-mobile10.dtd">
<html xmlns="http://www.w3.org/1999/xhtml">
<head>
    <title>Book Info</title>
</head>
<body>
    <h2>Books on Web Technology</h2>
    <hr/>
    <p><a id="subjects">Select one of the following subjects</a>:</p>
    <ul>
        <li><a accesskey="1" href="#webarch">
            Web Application Architecture</a></li>
        <li><a accesskey="2" href="#xmlcore">
            XML Core</a></li>
    </ul>
    <hr/><hr/>
    <p><a id="webarch">Web Application Architecture</a></p>
    <ol>
        <li>L. Shklar and R. Rosen. Web Application Architecture,
            2nd Edition. Wiley, 2008.</li>
        <li>M. Mahemoff. Ajax Design Patterns,
            O&apos;Reilly, 2006.</li>
    </ol>
    <hr/>
    <p><a id="xmlcore">Core XML Technologies</a></p>
    <ol>
        <li>Harold, Elliott Rusty. XML 1.1 Bible, 3d Edition.
            Wiley, 2004.</li>
        <li>Walmsley, Priscilla. Definitive XML Schema.
            Prentice Hall, 2001.</li>
    </ol>
    <a accesskey="5" href="#subjects">Go back to subjects</a>
</body>
</html>
```

Figure 5.13   XHTML MP document.

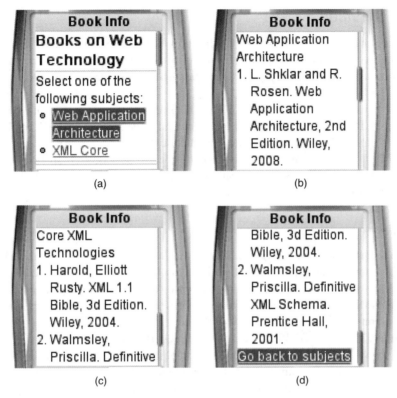

Figure 5.14   Screen captures for the XHTML MP document in Figure 5.13.

The sample XHTML MP document in Figure 5.13 contains three anchors, identified as `sub-jects`, `webarch`, and `xmlcore`, respectively. The first anchor references the list of subjects, the second points to books on web architecture, and the third to books on core XML technology (see Figure 5.14). Notice that the anchor id serves as the address within the document (e.g., `<a id = "subjects">`). Traversals within the document are executed by following links that reference in-document locations – either by selecting the links or by using key shortcuts if they are defined (e.g., `<a accesskey="5" href="#subjects">`).

Figure 5.14(a) shows the screen that is displayed when opening the sample document and selecting the first subject. The result of following the selection is shown in Figure 5.14(b). The screen in Figure 5.14(c) is displayed as the result of the user pressing the "2" key, which is defined as the shortcut for the second subject. Figure 5.14(d) is the result of scrolling down to the bottom of the document and selecting the link back to the subject list. It is not necessary to select this link to activate it – the alternative is to use the shortcut "5" key.

XHTML MP is a big departure from WML. There are no wireless-specific constructs – just a subset of the XHTML specification. WAP CSS (a simplified version of CSS) is the companion specification. The goal of XHTML MP is to bring together the technologies for mobile and for desktop Internet browsing, which is the traditional way of accessing the web.

5.3   Web Services

Web services are distributed web applications that provide discrete functionality and expose it in a well-defined manner over standard Internet protocols to other web applications. In other words, they are web applications that fit into the client–server paradigm, except that the clients are not people but other web applications.

In this section, we discuss SOAP and REST, which represent two implementation strategies for web services. SOAP is a highly formalized approach and is defined as an XML application. REST should be considered a design pattern rather than a formal specification. REST applications do not have to use XML but most of them do. It is good practice to provide web applications that support both SOAP and REST services. Such applications would naturally share the same XML schema for resource representations.

5.3.1   SOAP

The *Simple Object Access Protocol* (better known by the acronym *SOAP*) is an XML application that is different from the XML applications we have discussed so far. SOAP documents are not for rendering content – they invoke and pass information to and from web applications. SOAP is best described as an XML-based, application-layer protocol for constructing and processing web service requests and responses. It can use HTTP, SMTP, and a variety of other protocols (e.g., messaging protocols such as JMS and MQ/MSMQ) to transport requests and responses.

Figure 5.15 shows an example of a simple SOAP request with multiple parameters. In the example, the web service returns local weather information. The intent of the request is to retrieve information about New York. For that, you must provide the longitude and latitude of the region, as well as locale information (e.g., `en/us`), which determines not only the language but also the format for the temperature (Celsius or Fahrenheit) and wind velocity (mph or km/h).

Note the different namespaces, which provide the semantic context and the syntactic mechanism for separating elements. The namespaces are used to disambiguate elements of the SOAP envelope, references to XML data types, and service-specific elements. The SOAP envelope contains the `Body`

```
<?xml version="1.0" encoding="UTF-8" ?>
<soap:Envelope xmlns:xsi="http://www.w3.org/2001/XMLSchema-instance"
               xmlns:xsd="http://www.w3.org/2001/XMLSchema"
               xmlns:soap="http://schemas.xmlsoap.org/soap/envelope"
               xmlns:soapenc="http://schemas.xmlsoap.org/soap/encoding">
  <soap:Body>
    <w:getWeather xmlns:w="http://www.intlweather.com/services">
        <degreeslong xsi:type="xsd:float">-73.0</degreeslong>
        <degreeslat xsi:type="xsd:float">40.0</degreeslat>
        <locale xsi:type="xsd:string">en/us</locale>
    </w:getWeather>
  </soap:Body>
</soap:Envelope>
```

Figure 5.15   A SOAP request with multiple parameters.

```
POST /services HTTP/1.1
Host: www.intlweather.com
Content-Type: text/xml; charset="utf-8"
Content-Length: ...

<?xml version="1.0" encoding="UTF-8" ?>
<soap:Envelope xmlns:xsi="http://www.w3.org/2001/XMLSchema-instance"
               xmlns:xsd="http://www.w3.org/2001/XMLSchema"
               xmlns:soap="http://schemas.xmlsoap.org/soap/envelope"
               xmlns:soapenc="http://schemas.xmlsoap.org/soap/encoding">
  <soap:Body>
    <w:getWeather xmlns:w="http://www.intlweather.com/services">
        <degreeslong xsi:type="xsd:float">-73.0</degreeslong>
        <degreeslat xsi:type="xsd:float">40.0</degreeslat>
        <locale xsi:type="xsd:string">en/us</locale>
    </w:getWeather>
  </soap:Body>
</soap:Envelope>
```

Figure 5.16 The SOAP request from Figure 5.15 transmitted over HTTP.

element, which in turn contains a single element defining a remote procedure call, by specifying a method (getWeather) and its arguments (degreeslong, degreeslat, and locale).

The envelope is transported to a SOAP server over a protocol such as HTTP or SMTP. In the case of HTTP, the envelope comprises the body of the HTTP request, which follows the request line (i.e., "POST /services HTTP/1.1") and associated headers, as shown in Figure 5.16.

After receiving the request, the SOAP server invokes the specified method with the provided arguments and generates a response for transmission back to the requesting application. In Figure 5.17, the response contains values for pre-defined response elements, which inform the requestor that the temperature in New York is 25° (Fahrenheit), the conditions are partly cloudy, and the wind is from the southeast at 5 mph. Since the response is transmitted back to the requestor over HTTP, it includes the appropriate HTTP headers.

A SOAP client can translate this response into a human-readable format by using one of the available SOAP APIs or toolkits (e.g., Microsoft SOAP Toolkit, JAXM/SAAJ) or by transforming the body of the response using XSLT into XHTML, XHTML MP, or VoiceXML, as described in Section 5.4.

Web Services Definition Language (WSDL)

Defining a SOAP-based web service is only a partial step toward true interoperability. Constructing a SOAP request requires knowledge about the service – the name of the method to be invoked, its arguments, and their datatypes, as well as the response semantics. This knowledge could be available through human-readable documentation, but this falls short of the goal of true interoperability. Since web services are meant to be machine-understandable, their semantics (and even their existence) should be exposed to web applications, so that they can discover and make use of them without human intervention.

Web Services Definition Language (WSDL) and *Universal Description, Discovery, and Integration (UDDI)* are designed to close the interoperability gap. WSDL provides a common language for defining a web service and communication semantics. UDDI serves as a mechanism for registering and publishing web services.

Let us examine the web service definition in Figure 5.18 from the bottom up. The `<service>` element contains a `<documentation>` element (to give the service a human-readable description) and a `<port>` element.

The `<port>` element is linked to the `<binding>` element above it by the name WeatherServiceBinding, which, in turn, references the `<portType>` element with the name WeatherServicePortType. The `<port>` element also contains `<soap:address>` whose location attribute defines the URL that can be used to invoke the service.

The `<binding>` element defines the transport mechanism (SOAP over HTTP) and the names of operations that may be performed using the service. In this case, there is just one `<operation>` element, getWeather. Specifications for the encoding format for the input and output bodies are included here.

The `<portType>` element also lists the names of operations as `<operation>` elements. The sole `<operation>` element here contains `<input>` and `<output>` elements, which in turn refer to `<message>` elements (getWeatherInput and getWeatherOutput). The `<message>` elements specify references to complex data types, weatherRequest and weatherResponse. The definitions of complex types (which also make use of the XML schema data types that were covered in Section 5.1.3) specify components for both input messages (requests) and output messages (responses).

This may seem like overkill for a simple web service and, indeed, it is. There are a number of ways to simplify this definition. Our example avoids shortcuts to mention some of the more complex aspects of WSDL and demonstrate the available options.

```
HTTP/1.1 200 OK
Content-Type: text/xml; charset="utf-8"
Content-Length: ...

<?xml version="1.0" encoding="UTF-8" ?>
<soap:Envelope xmlns:xsi="http://www.w3.org/2001/XMLSchema-instance"
               xmlns:xsd="http://www.w3.org/2001/XMLSchema"
               xmlns:soap="http://schemas.xmlsoap.org/soap/envelope"
               xmlns:soapenc="http://schemas.xmlsoap.org/soap/encoding">
  <soap:Body>
    <w:getWeatherResponse xmlns:b="http://www.intlweather.com/services">
        <temperature xsi:type="xsd:int">25</temperature>
        <tempmode xsi:type="xsd:string">F</tempmode>
        <conditions xsi:type="xsd:string">partly cloudy</conditions>
        <windvelocity xsi:type="xsd:int">5</windvelocity>
        <windvelocityunits xsi:type="xsd:string">mph</windvelocityunits>
        <winddirection xsi:type="xsd:string">SE</winddirection>
    </w:getWeatherResponse>
  </soap:Body>
</soap:Envelope>
```

Figure 5.17 The response to the SOAP request in Figure 5.16.

```
<?xml version="1.0" ?>
<definitions name="InternationalWeather"
             targetNamespace="http://www.intlweather.com/weather.wsdl"
             xmlns:tns="http://www.intlweather.com/weather.wsdl"
             xmlns:xsd1="http://www.intlweather.com/weather.xsd"
             xmlns:soap="http://schemas.xmlsoap.org/wsdl/soap/"
             xmlns="http://schemas.xmlsoap.org/wsdl/">
  <types>
    <schema targetNamespace="http://www.intlweather.com/weather.xsd"
            xmlns="http://www.w3.org/2000/10/XMLSchema">
      <element name="weatherRequest">
        <complexType>
          <all>
            <element name="degreeslong" type="float" />
            <element name="degreeslat" type="float" />
            <element name="locale" type="string" />
          </all>
        </complexType>
      </element>
      <element name="weatherResponse">
        <complexType>
          <all>
            <element name="temperature" type="int" />
            <element name="tempmode" type="string">
            <element name="conditions" type="string">
            <element name="windvelocity" type="int">
            <element name="windvelocityunits" type="string">
            <element name="winddirection" type="string">
          </all>
        </complexType>
      </element>
    </schema>
  </types>

  <message name="getWeatherInput">
    <part name="body" element="xsd1:weatherRequest" />
  </message>
  <message name="getWeatherOutput">
    <part name="body" element="xsd1:weatherResponse"/>
  </message>

  <portType name="WeatherServicePortType">
    <operation name="getWeather">
      <input message="tns:getWeatherInput"/>
      <output message="tns:getWeatherOutput"/>
    </operation>
  </portType>

  <binding name="WeatherServiceBinding" type="tns:WeatherServicePortType">
```

Figure 5.18   A WSDL definition for the weather service in Figure 5.15. (*continued overleaf*)

```
                    <soap:binding style="document"
                         transport="http://schemas.xmlsoap.org/soap/http"/>
      <operation name="getWeather">
      <soap:operation soapAction="getWeather"/>
        <input>
          <soap:body use="literal"/>
        </input>
        <output>
          <soap:body use="literal"/>
        </output>
      </operation>
    </binding>
    <service name="InternationalWeatherService">
      <documentation>My first service</documentation>
      <port name="WeatherServicePort" binding="tns:WeatherServiceBinding">
        <soap:address location="http://www.intlweather.com/services"/>
      </port>
    </service>
  </definitions>
```

Figure 5.18   *(continued)*

Universal Description, Discovery, and Integration (UDDI)

While WSDL provides a common standard for defining web service semantics, UDDI provides the last piece of the interoperability puzzle through its mechanisms for registering and advertising web services.

UDDI servers provide two functions: inquiry and publishing. Inquiry allows users to look for web services that fit into specific categories (e.g., business name, service name, service type) and match specified search criteria. The inquiry request in Figure 5.19 is a query for businesses whose names contain the word "weather". You can see that this UDDI request is also a SOAP request (albeit somewhat simpler than the one found in our original web service example).

The results from such inquiries are (naturally) SOAP responses (as shown in Figure 5.20). SOAP clients can parse these responses to derive information about available web services that match the provided search criteria. The clients can choose a web service (from those located by the inquiry), access its WSDL definition, and invoke it. Note that, for simplicity, we have omitted the businessKey

```
<?xml version="1.0" encoding="UTF-8" ?>
<Envelope xmlns="http://schemas.xmlsoap.org/soap/envelope/">
  <Body>
    <find_business xmlns="urn:uddi-org:api" generic="1.0" maxRows="50">
      <findQualifiers />
      <name>weather</name>
    </find_business>
  </Body>
</Envelope>
```

Figure 5.19   A UDDI request from a SOAP client.

```
<?xml version="1.0" encoding="utf-8" ?>
<soap:Envelope xmlns:soap="http://schemas.xmlsoap.org/soap/envelope/"
               xmlns:xsi="http://www.w3.org/2001/XMLSchema-instance"
               xmlns:xsd="http://www.w3.org/2001/XMLSchema">
  <soap:Body>
    <businessList generic="1.0" operator="Microsoft Corporation"
                  truncated="false" xmlns="urn:uddi-org:api">
      <businessInfos>
        <businessInfo businessKey="...">
          <name>International Weather</name>
          <description xml:lang="en">Weather information</description>
          <serviceInfos>
            <serviceInfo serviceKey="..." businessKey="...">
              <name>InternationalWeatherService</name>
            </serviceInfo>
          </serviceInfos>
        </businessInfo>
        <businessInfo businessKey="...">
          <name>Weatherwax Dog Kennel</name>
          <serviceInfos />
        </businessInfo>
        ...
      </businessInfos>
    </businessList>
  </soap:Body>
</soap:Envelope>
```

Figure 5.20 A UDDI response to the request in Figure 5.19.

and `serviceKey` attributes. These are identifying keys assigned by a UDDI registrar when adding a business or service to the registry.

The publishing component of UDDI lets a web-service provider register their service in a UDDI registry (Figure 5.21). The publishing component accepts SOAP requests to add an entry to the registry, allowing the service provider to specify the service name, description, access point (i.e., the URL), and a reference to the service type (the *tModel*) associated with this service. Note that we have omitted various key attributes: `businessKey`, `serviceKey`, `bindingKey`, and `tModelKey`.

The importance of SOAP, WSDL and UDDI specifications is in providing formalized and rigorous definitions of web services, and methods for locating, accessing and utilizing them. This makes them structured, modular, and reusable for a wide variety of applications. Web services functionality provides a platform that promotes interoperability and helps many emerging technologies to flourish.

5.3.2   Representational State Transfer (REST)

For a time, the notion of web services was synonymous with SOAP. In the minds of developers, web services came to be identified with a well-defined but rather tedious mechanism. The overhead

```
<?xml version="1.0" encoding="utf-8" ?>
<soap:Envelope xmlns:soap="http://schemas.xmlsoap.org/soap/envelope/"
               xmlns:xsi="http://www.w3.org/2001/XMLSchema-instance"
               xmlns:xsd="http://www.w3.org/2001/XMLSchema">
  <soap:Body>
    <Service>
      <businessService serviceKey="..." businessKey="...">
        <name>International Weather</name>
        <bindingTemplates>
          <bindingTemplate bindingKey="..." serviceKey="..." >
            <description xml:lang="en">
              Weather information
            </description>
            <accessPoint URLType="http">
              http://www.internationalweather.com/services"
            </accessPoint>
            <tModelInstanceDetails>
              <tModelInstanceInfo tModelKey="..." />
            </tModelInstanceDetails>
          </bindingTemplate>
        </bindingTemplates>
      </businessService>
    </Service>
  </soap:Body>
</soap:Envelope>
```

Figure 5.21   A request to publish a web service in a UDDI registry.

associated with processing messages made SOAP impractical for use with high-traffic web sites. There was an expressed need for a more lightweight way to expose discrete application functionality on the Internet.

Representational State Transfer (REST) is an architectural pattern that gained popularity as an alternative to SOAP. It is based on considering items of interest on the web (identified by their URLs) as resources. An item is considered REST-compliant if it is uniquely identified by a URL that does not contain either a parameter string or a query string. REST is not tightly bound to XML, but XML is the common format for REST representations.

REST resources are not static pages, but calls to web applications. In Figure 5.22, a REST-compliant URL passes longitude and latitude information to the weather monitoring application. When accessed, such resources return their *representation*. A representation can be thought of as the browser *state*. Within this formalism, following a link would result in retrieving a different representation and can be considered a *state transition*. Note that all state information must be transmitted with the request, since REST service requests cannot take advantage of server-side context.

```
http://www.intlweather.com/services/-73.0/40.0
```

Figure 5.22   A REST-compliant URL.

```
<?xml version="1.0"?>
<w:WeatherReports xmlns:w="http://www.intlweather.com"
                  xmlns:xlink="http://www.w3.org/1999/xlink">
   <Report locale="en/us"
      xlink:href="http://www.intlweather.com/services/-73.0/40.0/en_us"/>
   <Report locale="fr"
      xlink:href="http://www.intlweather.com/services/-73.0/40.0/fr"/>
</w:WeatherReports>
```

Figure 5.23 A representation of a REST resource.

A critical aspect of SOAP was that requests should provide enough explicit information to receive a specific and detailed response. The SOAP request for a weather update in Figure 5.15 includes all information (longitude, latitude, and locale) needed to produce a weather report. The SOAP response contains detailed information in US English (the specified locale) about weather at the selected location. An equivalent REST representation may require multiple requests and state transitions. In contrast, the sample REST request shown in Figure 5.22 includes information about longitude and latitude but not the locale.

The response shown in Figure 5.23 is the representation of the requested resource. This representation contains links to more specific resources that correspond to the US English and French locales.

Selecting US English results in the state transition to the representation of the following resource:

```
http://www.intlweather.com/services/-73.0/40.0/en_us
```

The representation of this resource in Figure 5.24 contains details, in English, about the weather at the selected location. It is verifiably equivalent to the weather report contained in the SOAP response in Figure 5.17.

About XLink

The XLink specification[1] from W3C defines an XML markup language used for creating hyperlinks in XML documents. It defines methods for linking internal and external resources to XML documents. We have used XLink in Figure 5.23 to represent simple links pointing to a single resource. The specification also supports extended links for connecting multiple resources. So far, such extended links have limited use and do not enjoy consistent support by web agents.

The various HTTP request methods have different roles in the REST pattern, roughly analogous to create−read−update−delete (CRUD) functionality. We've already seen how the GET method is used to retrieve the REST representation of a resource. (Note that GET requests in this context should not produce side effects.) Similarly, the POST method is generally used to create new resources, the PUT method to modify existing resources, and the DELETE method to remove existing resources. For POST and PUT, the body of the request should contain a representation of a resource having the same format as a representation retrieved via a GET request.

```
<?xml version="1.0"?>
<w:WeatherReport xmlns:b="http://www.intlweather.com">
    <temperature xsi:type="xsd:int">25</temperature>
    <tempmode xsi:type="xsd:string">F</tempmode>
    <conditions xsi:type="xsd:string">partly cloudy</conditions>
    <windvelocity xsi:type="xsd:int">5</windvelocity>
    <windvelocityunits xsi:type="xsd:string">MPH</windvelocityunits>
    <winddirection xsi:type="xsd:string">SE</winddirection>
</w:WeatherReport>
```

Figure 5.24 Representation of the weather report.

It is not uncommon for applications to support both SOAP and REST services. Amazon.com, for example, provides both SOAP and REST versions of their web services API. SOAP services have a well-established infrastructure, provide greater flexibility in specifying parameters, and do not require multiple requests and state transitions. On the other hand, REST services avoid the processing overhead associated with parsing SOAP messages. Their simplicity and efficiency provides a major attraction for the users of these services. The nature of REST requests makes it easy to insert caching and authorization proxies to provide performance and security.

Just as WSDL provides a robust mechanism for defining SOAP services, *WADL*, which stands for *Web Application Description Language*, provides an XML vocabulary for describing REST-based Web Services. There is currently no real REST analog to the UDDI registry, which aids in the search and discovery of SOAP-based web services, but as the number of REST-based web services grows, something along the lines of UDDI is likely to emerge.

5.4 XSL

XHTML is an XML-based reformulation of an existing SGML application (HTML) with well-defined semantics. XHTML MP is, in turn, a reformulation of XHTML for mobile devices, also with well-defined semantics. What about other XML applications? DTDs and XML Schemas are great for document validation, but neither can bring meaning to XML elements. This is why there are so many different XML application standards. When related applications use the same XML elements, it becomes possible to encode element semantics in shared application libraries. This is similar to hard-coding XHTML semantics in browser-rendering modules.

It is not an attractive prospect having to change application logic every time we add, change, or delete XML elements. We need an abstraction to enable transformations between XML documents that comply with different schemas. This way, having implemented application logic for one set of elements, we can use the transformations and avoid having to re-implement the application logic for other related schemas.

The Extensible Stylesheet Language (XSL) serves the dual purpose of transforming XML documents and of exhibiting control over document rendering. Like XML schemas, XSL programs are well-formed and valid XML documents.

5.4.1 XSLT

The transformation component of XSL, called XSLT, makes it possible to select fragments of XML documents based on path patterns in the element hierarchy and to apply transformation operations to these fragments.

The sample XSLT style sheet in Figure 5.25 presents a particular view of the XML document in Figure 5.1. This view contains a simple table of book entries with only some of the properties defined in the original XML document (see Figure 5.26).

```
<?xml version="1.0" encoding="UTF-8"?>
<xsl:stylesheet version="1.0"
  xmlns:xsl="http://www.w3.org/1999/XSL/Transform"
  xmlns:fo="http://www.w3.org/1999/XSL/Format">

<xsl:template match="books">
<html xmlns="http://www.w3.org/1999/xhtml" xml:lang="en" lang="en">
<title>Book List</title>
<h2><xsl:text>Status: </xsl:text>
<xsl:value-of select="@status"/></h2>
<table border="1">
  <tbody>
    <tr>
      <th>Title</th>
      <th>Authors</th>
      <th>Publisher</th>
      <th>Year</th>
    </tr>
      <xsl:apply-templates select="book"/>
  </tbody>
</table>
</html>
</xsl:template>

<xsl:template match="book">
<tr>
  <td><xsl:value-of select="title"/></td>
  <td><xsl:apply-templates select="author"/></td>
  <td><xsl:value-of select="info/publication/@source"/></td>
  <td><xsl:value-of select="info/publication/@year"/></td>
</tr>
</xsl:template>

<xsl:template match="author">
  <xsl:value-of select="@firstName"/>
  <xsl:text> </xsl:text>
  <xsl:value-of select="@lastName"/>
  <br/>
</xsl:template>
</xsl:stylesheet>
```

Figure 5.25 XSLT style sheet.

```
<?xml version="1.0" encoding="UTF-8"?>
<html xmlns="http://www.w3.org/1999/xhtml" xml:lang="en" lang="en">
<h2>Status: In Print</h2>
<table xmlns:fo="http://www.w3.org/1999/XSL/Format" border="1">
  <tbody>
    <tr>
      <th>Title</th>
      <th>Authors</th>
      <th>Publisher</th>
      <th>Year</th>
    </tr>
    <tr>
      <td>Web Application Architecture</td>
      <td>Leon Shklar<br/>Rich Rosen<br/></td>
      <td>John Wiley and Sons, Ltd.</td>
      <td>2008</td>
    </tr>
  </tbody>
</table>
</html>
```

Figure 5.26   Result of applying the transformation in Figure 5.25 to the document in Figure 5.1.

You can see that the style sheet in Figure 5.25 is composed of three `<template>` elements. An XSL template is analogous to a function, though the invocation mechanism is quite different. The mechanism used in the example is based on matching patterns against elements in the document hierarchy. The first template is invoked when the XSL processor encounters the `<books>` element in the XML document in Figure 5.1. When applied, the template retains all elements except for those with the "`xsl:`" prefix. The latter are XSLT directives defined in the XSL schema.

XSL processing always occurs in the context of the current element node. On entering the first template, the current element node is `books`, so `<xsl:value-of select="@status"/>` returns the value of the `status` attribute of the `books` node. The `<xsl:apply-templates select="book"/>` directive instructs the XSL interpreter to locate the template defined to match the `book` pattern (the second template in Figure 5.25) and evaluate it repeatedly for every child `<book>` element. Since the XML document only contains one `<book>` element, the interpreter evaluates the second template only once.

The `<xsl:value-of select="title"/>` instruction in the second template is evaluated to the content of the `<title>` element of the XML document, which is the direct descendant of `<book>`. The evaluation of `<xsl:value-of select="info/publication/@source"/>` and `<xsl:value-of select="info/publication/@year"/>` is performed by traversing the element tree from the current element `<book>` down to `<info>`, then further down to `<publication>`, and, through attribute edges, to the attributes `source` and `year`.

Similarly, the `<xsl:apply-templates select="author"/>` directive instructs the interpreter to locate the template defined to match `author` (the third template in Figure 5.25) and evaluate it for every `<author>` element reachable via the child edge from the then-current `<book>` element.

Since there are two occurrences of `<author>`, the interpreter evaluates the third template twice and generates output for both authors (Figure 5.26).

Traversal expressions used in XSLT instructions (e.g., `title`, `info/publication/@year`) comply with the XPath specification – yet another XML-related standard. XPath is a simple query and traversal language for XML element trees. As you can infer from our examples, every "/" represents an edge (the first "/" is implied). By default, an edge leads to a child element with the specified name, but it may lead to other kinds of nodes. For example, the "@" sign in "`.../@year`" denotes the `year` attribute of the element node reached by traversing the preceding part of the XPath expression.

5.4.2 XSL Formatting Objects

XSL Formatting Objects (XSL-FO) is a markup language that describes the rendering vocabulary designed to support pagination. The XSL-FO specification is the descendant of the Cascading Style Sheets used by web browsers to control rendering. It defines generic rendering objects associated with elements of the XSL-FO vocabulary, including `<block>`, `<inline>`, `<page-sequence>`, and `<footnote>`, as well as style objects (e.g., `<font>`). XSL-FO style sheets tie the generic rendering objects to pagination and formatting.

XSL transformations are unique to XML and serve the purpose of transforming XML documents to an alternative representation. The common approach to rendering XML documents is to transform them to a target with well-defined presentation semantics (e.g., XHTML). The target XHTML document may contain a reference to a CSS style sheet to control browser rendering (Figure 5.27).

XSL-FO provides a superset of CSS functionality but, while the purpose of CSS is to support browser rendering, XSL-FO is designed to support print layouts. Semantically, controls for rendering individual components are very similar, but the variation in syntax is significant. As we discussed in the previous chapter, CSS has its own syntax:

```
P { font: italic bold 12pt/14pt Times, serif; color: #0000F0  }
```

while XSL-FO is an XML application:

```
<fo:block font-size="12pt" font-weight="bold">content</block>
```

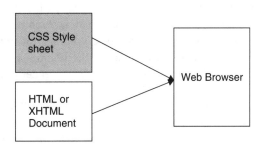

Figure 5.27   Using a CSS style sheet to render HTML and XHTML documents.

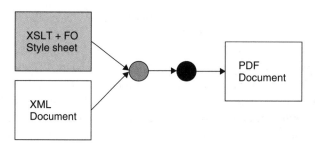

Figure 5.28   One way of using an XSL style sheet to print an XML document.

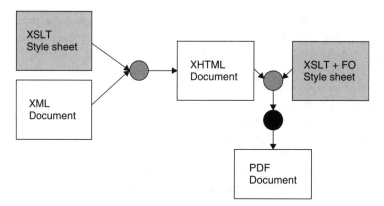

Figure 5.29   Another way of using XSL style sheets to print XML documents.

Apart from producing an alternative XML representation, XSLT processors can take advantage of styling and pagination information provided by the formatting objects to generate PDF, Postscript, or another form of print-oriented output. Figures 5.28 and 5.29 illustrate two different paths for creating print-friendly representations. Gray circles denote the XSLT processor and black circles denote the XSL-FO processor. Given that the target of the XSL transformation is the XSL-FO vocabulary, the output of the XSLT processor may serve as input to the XSL-FO processor.

The obvious solution for creating a printer-friendly presentation is to implement an XSL transformation from the desired XML format to the one based on the XSL-FO vocabulary. It is necessary to define formatting objects for the desired pagination, layout, and rendering (Figure 5.28). That it is quite a bit of work and we may already have a rich XSLT library for transforming our documents to XHTML. Since XHTML is ubiquitous, there already exist libraries of easy-to-parameterize XSL transformations from XHTML to PDF, which means that we can render to print with very little work (Figure 5.29).

Figure 5.30 is a variation on the XSL style sheet from Figure 5.25. It implements the direct transformation to the XSL-FO vocabulary and looks a lot more complicated than the original. The complexity is due to the use of XSL-FO as the target format. The template structure and the transformation instructions in the two style sheets are virtually identical, but `fo:` elements are used instead of XHTML constructs. Sometimes replacements are trivial (e.g., `<fo:table>` instead of `<table>`), but when

```
<?xml version="1.0" encoding="UTF-8" ?>
<xsl:stylesheet version="1.0" xmlns:fo="http://www.w3.org/1999/XSL/Format"
     xmlns:xsl="http://www.w3.org/1999/XSL/Transform">
<xsl:output method="xml" version="1.0" indent="yes" />
<xsl:include href="attributes.xsl"/>
<xsl:include href="pagelayout.xsl"/>
<xsl:template match="books">
  <fo:block xsl:use-attribute-sets="ablock">
      Status: <xsl:value-of select="@status"/></fo:block>
  <fo:block>
    <fo:table xsl:use-attribute-sets="table.info">
      <fo:table-column xsl:use-attribute-sets="table.info.td"
          column-width="27%"/>
      <fo:table-column xsl:use-attribute-sets="table.info.td"
          column-width="27%"/>
      <fo:table-column xsl:use-attribute-sets="table.info.td"
          column-width="27%"/>
      <fo:table-column xsl:use-attribute-sets="table.info.td"
          column-width="19%"/>
      <fo:table-header xsl:use-attribute-sets="table.info.th">
        <fo:table-row>
          <fo:table-cell xsl:use-attribute-sets="table.info.tc">
            <fo:block xsl:use-attribute-sets="cblock">Title</fo:block>
          </fo:table-cell>
          <fo:table-cell xsl:use-attribute-sets="table.info.tc">
            <fo:block xsl:use-attribute-sets="cblock">Authors</fo:block>
          </fo:table-cell>
          <fo:table-cell  xsl:use-attribute-sets="table.info.tc">
            <fo:block xsl:use-attribute-sets="cblock">Publisher</fo:block>
          </fo:table-cell>
          <fo:table-cell xsl:use-attribute-sets="table.info.tc">
            <fo:block xsl:use-attribute-sets="cblock">Year</fo:block>
          </fo:table-cell>
        </fo:table-row>
      </fo:table-header>
      <fo:table-body>
        <xsl:apply-templates select="book"/>
      </fo:table-body>
    </fo:table>
  </fo:block>
</xsl:template>
<xsl:template match="book">
  <fo:table-row>
    <fo:table-cell xsl:use-attribute-sets="table.info.tc">
      <fo:block xsl:use-attribute-sets="cblock">
        <xsl:value-of select="title"/>
      </fo:block></fo:table-cell>
      <fo:table-cell xsl:use-attribute-sets="table.info.tc">
        <xsl:apply-templates select="author"/>
      </fo:table-cell>
      <fo:table-cell  xsl:use-attribute-sets="table.info.tc">
```

Figure 5.30   XSL-FO version of the XSL style sheet from Figure 5.25. (*continued overleaf*)

```
      <fo:block xsl:use-attribute-sets="cblock">
        <xsl:value-of select="info/publication/@source"/>
        </fo:block>
    </fo:table-cell>
    <fo:table-cell xsl:use-attribute-sets="table.info.tc">
      <fo:block xsl:use-attribute-sets="cblock">
        <xsl:value-of select="info/publication/@year"/>
      </fo:block>
    </fo:table-cell>
  </fo:table-row>
</xsl:template>
<xsl:template match="author">
  <fo:block xsl:use-attribute-sets="cblock">
    <xsl:value-of select="@firstName"/>
    <xsl:text> </xsl:text>
    <xsl:value-of select="@lastName"/>
  </fo:block>
</xsl:template>
</xsl:stylesheet>
```

Figure 5.30 *(continued)*

```
<?xml version="1.0" encoding="UTF-8"?>
<xsl:stylesheet version="1.0"
    xmlns:xsl="http://www.w3.org/1999/XSL/Transform"
    xmlns:fo="http://www.w3.org/1999/XSL/Format">
<xsl:template match="/">
  <fo:root>
    <fo:layout-master-set>
      <fo:simple-page-master master-name="testMaster"
          page-height="29.7cm" page-width="21cm" margin-top="1cm"
          margin-bottom="2cm" margin-left="2.5cm"  margin-right="2.5cm">
      <fo:region-body margin-top="2cm"/>
        <fo:region-before extent="2cm"/>
        <fo:region-after extent="1.5cm"/>
      </fo:simple-page-master>
    </fo:layout-master-set>
    <fo:page-sequence master-reference="testMaster">
      <fo:flow flow-name="xsl-region-body">
        <xsl:apply-templates select="books" />
      </fo:flow>
    </fo:page-sequence>
  </fo:root>
</xsl:template>
</xsl:stylesheet>
```

Figure 5.31 The `pagelayout.xsl` file referenced from the style sheet in Figure 5.30.

it comes to table elements, the structure of the target markup is quite different – table columns are defined up front, so the XHTML's `<td>` is replaced with `<fo:table-cell>` and not with `<fo:table-column>`.

Notice that all textual components are encapsulated within `<fo:block>` elements. The XSL-FO block is one of the most basic constructs that controls text positioning – lines, fonts, etc.

You have probably noticed that we glossed over two very important constructs that are evident in the example – the `<xsl:include>` elements and `xsl:use-attribute-sets` attributes. The included elements are the pagination control file (shown in Figure 5.31) and the attribute set definitions (Figure 5.32) that parameterize document rendering. The `xsl:use-attribute-sets` attributes refer to attribute sets defined in the `attributes.xsl` file. This simple design pattern helps to separate the presentation and rendering logic. In fact, you may accumulate a rich library of attribute definitions and page layouts, reusable in different contexts.

```
<?xml version="1.0" encoding="UTF-8"?>
<xsl:stylesheet version="1.0"
     xmlns:xsl="http://www.w3.org/1999/XSL/Transform"
     xmlns:fo="http://www.w3.org/1999/XSL/Format">
  <xsl:attribute-set name="ablock">
    <xsl:attribute name="font-size">18pt</xsl:attribute>
    <xsl:attribute name="background-color">black</xsl:attribute>
    <xsl:attribute name="color">white</xsl:attribute>
    <xsl:attribute name="text-align">left</xsl:attribute>
  </xsl:attribute-set>
  <xsl:attribute-set name="cblock">
    <xsl:attribute name="font-size">14pt</xsl:attribute>
    <xsl:attribute name="text-align">center</xsl:attribute>
  </xsl:attribute-set>
  <xsl:attribute-set name="table.info">
    <xsl:attribute name="table-layout">fixed</xsl:attribute>
    <xsl:attribute name="width">100%</xsl:attribute>
    <xsl:attribute name="space-before">8pt</xsl:attribute>
    <xsl:attribute name="space-after">8pt</xsl:attribute>
    <xsl:attribute name="border-collapse">collapse</xsl:attribute>
  </xsl:attribute-set>
  <xsl:attribute-set name="table.info.th">
    <xsl:attribute name="background-color">#EEEEEE</xsl:attribute>
    <xsl:attribute name="font-family">sans-serif</xsl:attribute>
  </xsl:attribute-set>
  <xsl:attribute-set name="table.info.td">
    <xsl:attribute name="background-color">#EEEEEE</xsl:attribute>
  </xsl:attribute-set>
  <xsl:attribute-set name="table.info.tc">
    <xsl:attribute name="border-style">solid</xsl:attribute>
    <xsl:attribute name="border-width">1pt</xsl:attribute>
  </xsl:attribute-set>
</xsl:stylesheet>
```

Figure 5.32   The `attributes.xsl` file referenced from the XSL style sheet in Figure 5.30.

In combination with the approach shown in Figure 5.29, which assumes the conversion of original XML files to XHTML, this pattern is even more useful, making it possible to reduce XSL-FO programming to a configuration exercise in a properly organized development environment. Note however, that no solution is good for all cases, and conversion to XHTML may result in losing semantics, which are important, for example, for exhibiting control over pagination. Nevertheless, even if the intermediate format ends up being some XHTML+, the idea remains the same – define a simple intermediate format that allows for the best reuse of existing transformation and formatting libraries.

Getting back to our XSL-FO example, the pagination controls in Figure 5.31 define a single master page that is referenced by name (`testMaster`) in `<fo:page-sequence>`. Real applications are likely to require multiple different master pages used in different contexts. To further promote reuse, master pages may be defined in separate style sheets and included in page layout style sheets using `<xsl:include>`. The `<fo:flow>` element encapsulates rendering components that are generated by XSLT instructions in Figure 5.30 and invoked when the XSLT processor evaluates `<xsl:apply-templates name="books"/>` in Figure 5.31.

Target XSL-FO elements in Figure 5.30 make extensive use of the `xsl:use-attribute-sets` attribute. Named attribute sets are defined in the `attributes.xsl` file (Figure 5.32), to make it easier to parameterize the XSL style sheet in Figure 5.30. It is relatively easy to provide tools for editing simple style sheets, similar to `attributes.xsl`, for use by graphic designers with little or no knowledge of XSL.

As we showed in Figures 5.28 and 5.29, applying an XSL style sheet containing XSLT instructions and designed to target the XSL-FO vocabulary is a two-step process. The first step is performing the XSLT transformations. The output of the XSLT engine when applying the transformations in Figure 5.30 to the XML document in Figure 5.1 is shown in Figure 5.33. It is an XML document satisfying the XSL-FO schema. It contains XSL-FO elements, including pagination elements defined in the `pagelayout.xsl` file in Figure 5.31. As you can see, the style parameters originate in the `attributes.xsl` file.

The document in Figure 5.33 serves as input to the XSL-FO processor, which can produce a variety of outputs, including Postscript and PDF (Figure 5.34). It is not required to generate the intermediate representation in Figure 5.31. Most XSL-FO processors accept either the file in Figure 5.33 or the files in Figure 5.1 and Figure 5.30 as their input. In the latter case, the XSL-FO processor first invokes the XSLT engine and then processes the output to produce the final result (see Figure 5.34).

5.4.3   What is so important about XSL?

The XSL specification has had many twists and turns in its relatively short but eventful history. At this time, it is a combination of two well-defined components – XSLT and XSL-FO. The former is the transformation language that enables translations between XML documents that satisfy different schemas, and the latter is the style language that supports page layouts. There is a plethora of style languages compatible with XHTML (e.g., CSS and CSS2) but they are not integral parts of XSL even though XHTML *is* an XML application.

More twists and turns may still be ahead of us. It would be great for browsers to provide integrated support for XSL-FO, which may be sufficient to deprecate other style languages. Once it is practical to express XHTML semantics using the XSL-FO vocabulary, the former would become no more than

```
<?xml version="1.0" encoding="UTF-8"?>
<fo:root xmlns:fo="http://www.w3.org/1999/XSL/Format">
<fo:layout-master-set>
  <fo:simple-page-master master-name="testMaster" page-height="29.7cm"
      page-width="21cm" margin-top="1cm" margin-bottom="2cm"
      margin-left="2.5cm" margin-right="2.5cm">
    <fo:region-body margin-top="2cm"/>
    <fo:region-before extent="2cm"/>
    <fo:region-after extent="1.5cm"/>
  </fo:simple-page-master>
</fo:layout-master-set>
  <fo:page-sequence master-reference="testMaster">
  <fo:flow flow-name="xsl-region-body">
    <fo:block font-size="18pt" background-color="black" color="white"
        text-align="left">Status: In Print</fo:block>
    <fo:block>
      <fo:table table-layout="fixed" width="100%"
          space-before="10pt" border-collapse="collapse">
        <fo:table-column background-color="#EEEEEE" column-width="27%"/>
        <fo:table-column background-color="#EEEEEE" column-width="27%"/>
        <fo:table-column background-color="#EEEEEE" column-width="27%"/>
        <fo:table-column background-color="#EEEEEE" column-width="19%"/>
        <fo:table-header background-color="#EEEEEE"
              font-family="sans-serif">
          <fo:table-row>
            <fo:table-cell border-style="solid" border-width="1pt">
              <fo:block font-size="14pt" text-align="center">
                Title</fo:block>
            </fo:table-cell>
            <fo:table-cell border-style="solid" border-width="1pt">
              <fo:block font-size="14pt" text-align="center">
                Authors</fo:block>
            </fo:table-cell>
            <fo:table-cell border-style="solid" border-width="1pt">
              <fo:block font-size="14pt" text-align="center">
                Publisher</fo:block>
            </fo:table-cell>
            <fo:table-cell border-style="solid" border-width="1pt">
              <fo:block font-size="14pt" text-align="center">
                Year</fo:block>
            </fo:table-cell>
          </fo:table-row>
        </fo:table-header>
        <fo:table-body>
          <fo:table-row>
            <fo:table-cell border-style="solid" border-width="1pt">
              <fo:block font-size="14pt" text-align="center">
                Web Application Architecture</fo:block>
```

Figure 5.33 Output of the XSLT processor. (*continued overleaf*)

```
        </fo:table-cell>
        <fo:table-cell border-style="solid" border-width="1pt">
            <fo:block font-size="14pt" text-align="center">
                Leon Shklar</fo:block>
            <fo:block font-size="14pt" text-align="center">
                Rich Rosen</fo:block>
        </fo:table-cell>
          <fo:table-cell border-style="solid" border-width="1pt">
            <fo:block font-size="14pt" text-align="center">
                John Wiley and Sons, Ltd.</fo:block>
          </fo:table-cell>
        <fo:table-cell border-style="solid" border-width="1pt">
            <fo:block font-size="14pt" text-align="center">
                2008</fo:block>
        </fo:table-cell>
      </fo:table-row>
    </fo:table-body>
  </fo:table>
  </fo:block>
 </fo:flow>
 </fo:page-sequence>
</fo:root>
```

Figure 5.33 *(continued)*

Status : In Print			
Title	Authors	Publisher	Year
Web Application Architecture	Leon Shklar Rich Rosen	John Wiley and Sons, Ltd.	2008

Figure 5.34 PDF output of the XSL-FO processor.

a shortcut notation. Such a development can be very conducive to building advanced tools and simplifying presentation components.

XSLT is now the technology of choice for building applications that target multiple end-user devices and presentation formats. It allows for a "raw" XML representation of a document that can be personalized and transformed into various target formats (e.g., XHTML, WML, SMIL).

Historically, it was common for application developers to jump through many proprietary hoops to create print versions of legal documents, financial statements, etc. XSL-FO extends the list of devices and formats to include those that require pagination. This extension has the potential of streamlining application architecture and simplifying both the development and maintenance. XSL-FO continues to gain momentum since its initial release as a W3C recommendation in 2002.

5.5 Summary

In its speed of adoption and ever-growing momentum, XML rivals both the HTTP protocol and HTML. This is not surprising since XML applications transcend the world of desktop computers and even mobile devices. XML advanced from a markup language to an implementation platform. Not only do XML and XSL provide the basis for advanced browser applications, they are critical in large-scale application integration, including messaging and web services.

Core XML consists of a number of related technologies, including XML Schema, XSL, APIs for accessing XML parse trees, and a rich library of XML applications. Other critical technologies include the XML Linking Language (XLink) for linking resources and XML Query Language (XQuery) for querying XML documents. This chapter has barely scratched the surface – there is a lot more to these technologies. XML applications are as varied as the myriad tasks performed by architects, designers, developers, and users.

XML has become important at all stages of the application lifecycle. It is used at the application design stage as the representation medium for Universal Modeling Language (UML) diagrams, at implementation time to control and coordinate development, testing, and versioning tools, and at run time as the universal "glue" for application components.

XML is used to define presentation languages for a variety of target formats. In addition to XHTML and XHTML MP, there is also MathML for describing mathematics, Scalable Vector Graphics (SVG) for describing two-dimensional graphics, Synchronized Multimedia Integration Language (SMIL) used to control the sequencing and layout of multimedia presentations, and many other specialized languages.

You can find a large selection of XML books that cover the details of all aspects of XML and related technologies. The key to making the right choices and to understanding the details when you need them is the knowledge of underlying principles. The main objective of this chapter was to discuss the core technologies and to provide you with the understanding you need to choose and understand other resources.

QUESTIONS AND EXERCISES

1. What makes an XML document well-formed? Is every well-formed document valid? Why? Is every valid document well-formed? Why?

2. Are there documents that are both HTML and XHTML documents? Is every HTML document also an XHTML document? Is every XHTML document also an HTML document? Explain.

3. Are there constraints that can be expressed using XML Schema but not DTD? Provide examples.

4. What is XSL-FO? What is the relationship between XSL-FO and CSS? What is the relationship between XSL-FO and XSLT?

5. Name all XML *applications* that were mentioned in this chapter. Separately, name all XML *specifications* that were mentioned in this chapter.

6. Let us design our own CarML language. Define XML tags for describing your car and your friends' cars using these tags. Think about what properties should be defined as attributes and what properties are best described as elements. Make sure your documents are well-formed.

7. Define an XML DTD for CarML. You may want to revisit XML documents you defined in the previous exercise and rethink the element and attribute structure as you are defining the DTD. In the end, all your car specifications should be valid XML documents.

8. Define an XML Schema equivalent to the XML DTD from the previous exercise. Compare the two.

9. Strengthen the XML Schema to apply additional constraints. Discuss new simple types that would be introduced in this context. Are there any changes to the complex types as well? Why or why not?

10. What is SOAP? If SOAP is a protocol, what does it mean that SOAP is an XML application? What is the relationship between SOAP and HTTP? Is it possible to use SOAP with SMTP? Explain.

11. What is a web service? What specification is used to define formal web service semantics?

12. What is the role of WSDL and UDDI? Why do we need both specifications? How do WSDL, UDDI, and SOAP work together to support web services?

13. What is REST? What is the difference between a REST service and a SOAP service? What are the advantages and disadvantages of each kind of service?

14. Can you have the same application supporting SOAP and REST service paradigms? Why or why not? What are the challenges?

15. Implement an XSLT transformation to convert CarML documents to XHTML. Can your XHTML documents qualify as valid HTML documents as well? If not, can you make changes to your XSLT transformation to ensure that the output qualifies as both valid XHTML and valid HTML? Explain.

16. Implement an XSLT transformation to convert CarXML documents to WML. Re-factor your XSLT implementation from the previous exercise to share as many components as possible with the WML transformation.

17. Extend your XSLT implementation to support conversions of CarXML documents to WML, XHTML, or PDF documents.

5.6 Bibliography

Fielding, Roy Thomas, 2000. *Architectural Styles and the Design of Network-based Software Architectures*. Doctoral dissertation. Irvine: University of California.

Glass, Graham, 2001. *Web Services: Building Blocks for Distributed Systems*. Upper Saddle River (NJ): Prentice-Hall.

Harold, Elliott Rusty, 2004. *XML 1.1 Bible*, 3rd Edition. New York: John Wiley and Sons, Inc.

Lovell, Doug, 2002. *XSL Formatting Objects Developer's Handbook*. Indianapolis (IN): SAMS Publishing.

Mangano, Sal, 2005. *XSLT Cookbook*, 2nd Edition. Sebastopol, CA: O'Reilly Media.

Musciano, Chuck and Kennedy, Bill, 2006. *HTML and XHTML: The Definitive Guide*, 6th Edition. Sebastopol (CA): O'Reilly & Associates.

Richardson, Leonard and Ruby, Sam, 2007. *RESTful Web Services*. Sebastopol (CA): O'Reilly & Associates.

Tennison, Jeni, 2001. *XSLT and XPath: On The Edge*. New York: John Wiley and Sons, Inc.

Walmsley, Priscilla, 2001. *Definitive XML Schema*. Upper Saddle River (NJ): Prentice-Hall.

5.7 Web Links

W3C, 2001. *XML Linking Language (XLink), Version 1.0*. Available at http://www.w3.org/TR/xlink/.

5.8 Endnotes

1. http://www.w3.org/TR/xlink/

Web Servers

Web servers enable HTTP access to a collection of documents and other information organized into a tree structure, much like a computer's file system. In addition to providing access to static documents, modern web servers implement a variety of protocols for passing requests to custom software applications that provide access to dynamic content. This chapter begins by describing the process of serving static documents and goes on to explore the mechanisms used to serve dynamic data.

Dynamic content can come from a variety of sources. Search engines and databases can be queried to retrieve and present data that satisfies the selection criteria specified by a user. Measuring instruments can be probed to present their current readings (e.g., temperature or humidity). News feeds and wire services can provide access to up-to-the-minute headlines, stock quotes, and sports scores.

There are many methodologies for accessing dynamic data. There are approaches based on open standards, the most prominent of which is the *Common Gateway Interface* (*CGI*). While CGI is in widespread use throughout the web, it has significant limitations, which we discuss in Section 6.1.3. As a result, many alternatives to CGI have arisen. These include a number of open source and proprietary mechanisms, some of which have gained enough following to become de-facto standards. Among the more prominent alternatives are *PHP, Cold Fusion*, Microsoft's *Active Server Pages* (*ASP*), Sun's *Java Server Pages* (*JSP*) and *Servlet API*, and *Ruby on Rails*. We provide an overview of these and other mechanisms in Chapter 9.

In the final part of this chapter, we discuss how web servers process HTTP requests and how that processing is affected by server configuration. We also discuss methods for providing robust server security.

6.1   Basic Operation

Web servers, browsers, and proxies communicate by exchanging HTTP messages. Servers receive and interpret HTTP requests, locate and access requested resources, and generate responses, which they send back to the originators of the requests. The process of interpreting incoming requests and generating outgoing responses is the main subject of this section.

Figure 6.1 illustrates how a web server processes incoming requests, generates outgoing responses, and transmits those responses back to the appropriate requestors. The Networking module is responsible both for receiving requests and for transmitting responses over the network. When it receives a request, it must first pass it to the Address Resolution module, which is responsible for analyzing and "pre-processing" the request. This pre-processing includes:

- Virtual Hosting: If the web server is providing service for multiple domains, determine the target domain for this request and use the detected domain to select configuration parameters.
- Address Mapping: Determine whether this is a request for static or dynamic content, based on the URL path and selected server configuration parameters, and resolve the address into an actual location within the server's file system.
- Authentication: If the requested resource is protected, examine authorization credentials to see if the request is coming from an authorized user.

Once the pre-processing is complete, the request is passed to the Request Processing module, which invokes sub-modules to serve static or dynamic content as appropriate. When the selected sub-module completes its processing, it passes the results to the Response Generation module, which builds the response and directs it to the Networking module for transmission.

It is important to remember that, since the HTTP protocol is stateless, the only information available to the server about a request is contained within that request. State may be maintained in the form of

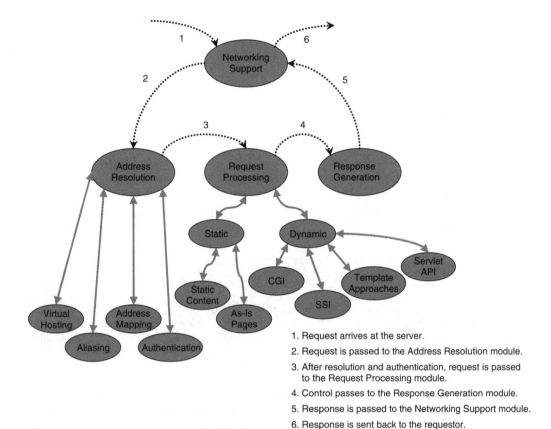

Figure 6.1 Server operation.

session information by server-side applications and application environments (e.g., servlet containers), but reference to this information must be contained within the request.

6.1.1 HTTP request processing

Let us take a step back and recollect what has to happen for an HTTP request to arrive at the server. For the purposes of this example, we examine a series of transactions in which an end user is visiting a friend's personal web site found at `http://mysite.org/`.

The process begins when the end user tells the browser to access the page found at the URL `http://mysite.org/pages/simple-page.html`. When the browser successfully receives and

```
GET http://mysite.org/pages/simple-page.html HTTP/1.1
Host: mysite.org
User-Agent: Mozilla/4.75 [en] (WinNT; U)
```

Figure 6.2 Browser request to load the page.

```
<HTML>
<HEAD><TITLE>Simple Page</TITLE></HEAD>
<BODY>
<H2>My Links</H2>
<UL>
<LI><A href="school.html">My school links</A></LI>
<LI><A href="home.html">My home links</A></LI>
</UL>
</BODY>
</HTML>
```

Figure 6.3   Simple HTML page returned to browser.

renders the page (Figure 6.2 and Figure 6.3), the user sees that it has links to two other pages, `school.html` and `home.html`. Suppose now that the end user follows the link to `school.html`.

You Say You Want a Resolution . . .

If the links found on a page are relative links (incomplete URLs meant to be interpreted relative to the URL of the current page), then they must be resolved so that the browser knows the complete URL referenced by the link. In Chapter 7, we discuss the steps that browsers take to resolve a relative link into an absolute URL in order to construct and submit the request.

Notice that the request in Figure 6.2 does not contain the `Connection: close` header. This means that, if possible, the connection to the server should be left open so that it may be used to transmit further requests and receive responses. However, there is no guarantee that the connection is still open at the time the user requests `school.html`. By that time, the server, a proxy, or even the browser itself might have broken it. Persistent connections are designed to improve performance but should never be relied upon in application logic.

If the connection is still open, the browser uses it to submit the request for the school links page (Figure 6.4). Otherwise, the browser must first re-establish the connection. Depending on the browser configuration, it may attempt either to establish a direct connection to the server or to connect via a proxy. Consequently, the server receives the request either directly from the browser or from the proxy.

For persistent connections, the server is responsible for maintaining a queue of requests and responses for each client. HTTP/1.1 specifies that, within the context of a single continuously open connection, a series of requests may be transmitted. It also specifies that responses to these requests must be sent back in the order of request arrival (FIFO).

```
GET http://mysite.org/pages/school.html HTTP/1.1
Host: mysite.org
User-Agent: Mozilla/4.75 [en] (WinNT; U)
```

Figure 6.4   Browser request to load the `school.html` page.

One common solution is for the server to maintain both an input and an output queue of requests. When a request is submitted for processing, it is removed from the input queue and inserted into the output queue. Once the processing is complete, the request is marked for release, but it remains on the output queue while at least one of its predecessors is still there. When all of its predecessors are gone from the output queue, it is released and its associated response is sent back to the browser either directly or through a proxy.

Once the server picks the request from the queue, it resolves the request URL to the physical file location and checks whether the requested resource requires authentication (Figure 6.1). If the authentication fails, the server aborts further processing and generates the response indicating an error condition (see Section 3.4.3). If authentication is not necessary or is successful, the server decides on the kind of processing required.

6.1.2   Delivery of static content

Web servers present both *static content* and *dynamic content*. Static content falls into two categories:

- *static content page*: static files containing HTML pages, XML pages, plain text, images, etc., for which HTTP responses (including headers) must be constructed;
- *as-is page*: static files containing complete HTTP responses (including headers).

For dynamic content, the server must take an explicit programmatic action to generate a response, such as the execution of an application program, the inclusion of information from an auxiliary file, or the interpretation of a template. This mode of processing includes *Common Gateway Interface* (*CGI*) programs, *Server-Side Includes* (*SSI*) pages, *Java Server Pages* (*JSP*), *Active Server Pages* (*ASP*), and Java servlets, among others.

We do not attempt to describe details of these and other server mechanisms (refer to Chapter 9 for a more detailed overview). Here, we concentrate on describing the common underlying principles that make it easier to learn new mechanisms and develop better mechanisms in the future.

Web servers use a combination of filename suffixes (extensions) and URL prefixes to determine which processing mechanism should be used to generate a response. By default, it is assumed that a URL should be processed as a request for a static content page. However, this is only one of a number of possibilities. A URL path beginning with `/servlet/` might indicate that the target is a Java servlet. A URL path beginning with `/cgi-bin/` and a URL where the target filename ends in `.cgi` might indicate that the target is a CGI script. A URL where the target filename ends in `.php` or `.cfm` might indicate that a template processing mechanism (e.g., PHP or Cold Fusion) should be invoked. We discuss address resolution in more detail in Section 6.4.

Static content pages

For a *static content page*, the server maps the URL to a file location relative to the server document root. In our example, the user visited a page on a personal web site found at `http://mysite.org/pages/school.html`. The path portion of this URL, `/pages/school.html`, is mapped to a specific filename within the server's local file system. For example, if the web server is configured so that the *document root* is `/www/doc`, then this URL is mapped to `/www/doc/pages/school.html` in the server file system.

```
HTTP/1.1 200 OK
Date: Tue, 29 May 2001 23:15:29 GMT
Last-Modified: Mon, 28 May 2001 15:11:01 GMT
Content-type: text/html
Content-length: 193
Server: Apache/1.2.5

<HTML>
<HEAD><TITLE>School Page</TITLE></HEAD>
<BODY>
<H2>My Links</H2>
<UL>
<LI><A href="classes.html">My classes</A></LI>
<LI><A href="friends.html">My friends</A></LI>
</UL>
</BODY>
</HTML>
```

Figure 6.5 Response to the request in Figure 6.4.

For static pages, the server must retrieve the file, construct the response, and transmit it back to the browser. For persistent connections, the response is placed in the output queue before transmission. Figure 6.5 shows a response generated for the HTTP request in Figure 6.4. As we discussed in Chapter 5, the first line of the response contains the status code that summarizes the result of the operation. The server controls browser-side rendering of the response content through the Content-Type header, set to a MIME type. Setting MIME types for static files is controlled through server configuration. In the simplest case, it is based on the mapping between file extensions and MIME types.

Even though desktop browsers have their own mappings between MIME types and file extensions, it is the server-side mapping that determines the Content-Type header of the response. This header – *not* the filename suffix or a browser heuristic based on content analysis – determines how the browser should render the body of the response.

An Experiment

If you have access to your own web server (and if not, you should install one), you can try experimenting with your browser and server to see how browser rendering is determined. Within the browser, map the file extension .html to text/plain instead of text/html, then visit an HTML page. You will notice that HTML pages are still rendered as hypertext.

Try changing the same mapping on the server: map the file extension .html to text/plain. Reload the page in your browser and you will see the HTML markup tags as plain text.

With all this in mind, it is important that the server sets the Content-Type header to the appropriate MIME type so that the browser can render the content properly. The server may also set the Content-Length header. This header is optional and may be missing for dynamic content because it is difficult to determine the size of the response before its generation is complete. Still, if it *is* possible to predict the size of the response, it is a good idea to include the `Content-Length` header. This allows the browser to report correctly on the content download progress.

We have already discussed HTTP support for caching. In Section 6.3.3, we come back to this example to discuss the `Last-Modified` header and its use by the browser logic in forming requests and reusing locally cached content. Even though `Last-Modified` is not a required header, the server is expected to make its best effort to determine the most recent modification date of requested content and use it to set the header.

As-is pages

Suppose that you do not want server logic to be involved in forming response headers and the status code. Maybe you are testing your browser or proxy, or maybe you want a quick and dirty fix by setting a special `Content-Type` for some pages. Then again, maybe you want an easy and convenient way to regularly change redirection targets for certain pages. It turns out there is a way to address all these situations – use *as-is pages*. The idea is that such pages contain a complete response and the server is supposed to send them back "as is", without adding status codes or headers. If we were to store a detailed response in a file that is recognized by the server as an as-is file, it should be guaranteed that, when the file is requested, the server returns its contents unchanged as the response.

The mechanism for recognizing as-is files is very similar to the mechanism for mapping static content to MIME types. It is common to configure the server to map the `.asis` file extension to as-is processing. The difference from static content is that, instead of generating the `Content-Type` header, the server defers to the `Content-Type` setting found in an as-is file.

Using the as-is mechanism, we can control server output by manually creating and modifying response messages. The word "manually" is of course the key here – whenever you want to change the response, you have to go in and edit it. This is convenient for very simple scenarios but does not provide an opportunity to implement even very basic processing logic.

6.1.3   Delivery of dynamic content

The original mechanisms for serving up dynamic content are CGI and SSI. Today's web servers use more sophisticated and more efficient mechanisms for serving up dynamic content, but CGI and SSI date back to the very beginnings of the web and it behooves us to understand these mechanisms before delving into the workings of the newer approaches.

CGI

CGI was the first consistent server-independent mechanism, dating back to the very early days of the web. The original CGI specification can be found at http://hoohoo.ncsa.uiuc.edu/cgi/interface.html.

The CGI mechanism assumes that, when a request to execute a CGI script arrives at the server, a new "process" is "spawned" to execute a particular application program, supplying that program with a set of parameters. (The terminology of "processes" and "spawning" is Unix-specific, but the analog of this functionality is available for non-Unix operating systems.)

The heart of the CGI specification is the designation of a fixed set of *environment variables* that all CGI applications know about and can access. The server is supposed to use request information to

Table 6.1 CGI environment variables

Environment variable	Description
SERVER_PROTOCOL	HTTP version as defined on the request line following HTTP method and URL
SERVER_PORT	Server port used for submitting the request; set by the server based on the connection parameters
REQUEST_METHOD	HTTP method as defined on the request line
PATH_INFO	Extra path information in the URL; if the URL is http://mysite.org/cgi-bin/zip.cgi/test.html and http://mysite.org/cgi-bin/zip.cgi is the location of a CGI script, then /test.html is the extra path information
PATH_TRANSLATED	Physical location of the CGI script on the server; in our example, if the server is configured to map the /cgi-bin path to the /www/cgi-bin directory, it would be /www/cgi-bin/zip.cgi
SCRIPT_NAME	The path portion of the URL, excluding the extra path information; in the example, it's /cgi-bin/zip.cgi
QUERY_STRING	Information that follows the "?" in the URL

populate the variables (see Table 6.1). Information used to populate these variables comes from the request line, connection parameters, URL, and other sources, but not from the HTTP headers.

The server is responsible for always setting the SERVER_SOFTWARE, SERVER_NAME, and GATE-WAY_INTERFACE environment variables, independent of information contained in the request. Other pre-defined variable names include CONTENT_TYPE and CONTENT_LENGTH, which are populated from the Content-Type and Content-Length headers. Additionally, every HTTP header is mapped to an environment variable by converting all letters in the name of the header to upper case, replacing the hyphen with an underscore, and pre-pending the "HTTP_ " prefix. For example, the value of the User-Agent header is stored in the HTTP_USER_AGENT environment variable, and the value of the Content-Type header is stored in both the CONTENT_TYPE and HTTP_CONTENT_TYPE environment variables.

It is important to remember that while names of HTTP headers do not depend on the mechanism (CGI, servlets, etc.), names of the environment variables are specific to the CGI mechanism. Some early servlet containers expected the CGI environment variables to retrieve header values because their implementers were CGI programmers and did not make the distinction. These servlet containers performed internal name transformations according to the rules defined for the CGI mechanism (e.g., Content-Type to CONTENT_TYPE), which was the wrong thing to do. These problems are long gone and you would be hard pressed to find a servlet container that does it now, but it is important to remember that the names of CGI environment variables have no meaning outside of the CGI context.

The CGI mechanism was defined as a set of rules, so that programs that abide by these rules would run the same way on different types of HTTP servers and operating systems. That works as long as these servers support the CGI specification, which evolved to a suite of related specifications for different operating systems.

CGI was originally introduced for servers running on Unix, where a CGI program always executes as a process with the body of the request available as standard input, and with HTTP headers,

URL parameters, and the HTTP method available as environment variables. For Windows servers, the CGI program runs as an *application process*. With these systems, there is no such thing as "standard input" (as there is in a Unix environment), so standard input is simulated using temporary files. Windows environment variables are similar to Unix environment variables. Information-passing details are different for other operating systems. For example, Macintosh computers pass system information through Apple Events. For simplicity, we refer to the CGI specification as it applies to Unix servers in the rest of this section. You would do well to consult your web server documentation for information-passing details.

Since the CGI mechanism assumes spawning a new process per request and terminating this process when the request processing is complete, the lifetime of a CGI process is always a single request. This means that even processing that is common for all requests has to be repeated every time. CGI applications may sometimes make use of persistent storage that survives individual requests but persistence is a non-standard additional service that is out of the scope of what is provided by HTTP servers.

Perl Before Swine

You have probably noticed that CGI programs are frequently called "CGI scripts." This is because they are often implemented using a scripting language, and most frequently this language is Perl. It is very common to see texts describing the mechanisms of "Perl/CGI programming."

While Perl is extremely popular, it is not the only language available for implementing CGI programs. There is no reason why you cannot use C or any other programming language, as long as that language provides access to the message body, headers, and other request information in a manner that conforms to the CGI specification. Nevertheless, Perl's popularity makes it the prime candidate for our examples.

The advantage of using Perl is that it is portable: scripts written in Perl can execute on any system with a Perl interpreter. Unfortunately, you pay the price in performance – Perl scripts run more slowly than programs written in a compiled language such as C.

Figure 6.6 shows a simple HTML page containing a form that lets users specify their names and zip codes. The `action` parameter of a `<FORM>` tag references the server application that can process form information. (It does not make sense to use forms if the `action` references a static page!)

```
<HTML>
<HEAD><TITLE>Simple Form</TITLE></HEAD>
<BODY>
<H2>Simple Form</H2>
<FORM action="http://mysite.org/cgi-bin/zip.cgi" method="post">
Zip Code: <INPUT size="5" name="zip">
Name: <INPUT size="30" name="name">
<INPUT type="submit" value="set zip">
</FORM>
<BODY>
</HTML>
```

Figure 6.6 Form for submitting user name and zip code.

```
POST http://mysite.org/cgi-bin/zip.cgi HTTP/1.1
Host: mysite.org
User-Agent: Mozilla/4.75 [en] (WinNT; U)
Content-Length: 26
Content-Type: application/www-form-urlencoded
Remote-Address: 127.0.0.1
Remote-Host: demo-portable

zip=08540&name=Leon+Shklar
```

Figure 6.7 HTTP request submitted by the browser for the form in Figure 6.6.

Figure 6.7 shows the HTTP request that is submitted to the server when the user fills out the form and clicks on the "submit" button. Notice that the entered information is *URL-encoded*: spaces are converted to plus signs, while other punctuation characters (e.g., equal signs and ampersands) are transformed to a percent sign (%) followed by the two-digit hexadecimal equivalent in the ASCII character set.

Also, notice that the Content-Type header is set to application/www-form-urlencoded, telling the server and server applications to expect form data. Do not confuse the Content-Type of the response that caused the browser to render this page (in this case, text/html) with the Content-Type of the form submission request. Form data submitted from an HTML page, WML page, or an applet would all have the same Content-Type: application/www-form-urlencoded.

The server, having received the request, performs the following steps:

1. Determines that /cgi-bin/zip.cgi is a CGI program. This decision may be based on a configuration parameter declaring /cgi-bin to be a CGI directory or on the .cgi file extension being mapped to the CGI processing module.
2. Translates /cgi-bin/zip.cgi, based on the server configuration, to a server file system location (e.g., /www/cgi-bin/zip.cgi).
3. Verifies that the computed file system location (/www/cgi-bin/) is legal for CGI executables.
4. Verifies that zip.cgi has *execute* permissions for the user id that is used to run the server. (This issue is relevant for Unix systems, where processes run under the auspices of a designated user id. It may not apply to non-Unix systems.)
5. Sets environment variables based on the request information.
6. Creates a child process responsible for executing the CGI program, passes it the body of the request in the standard input stream, and directs the standard output stream to the server module responsible for processing the response and sending it back to the browser.
7. On termination of the CGI program, the response processor parses the response and, if missing, adds the default status code, default Content-Type, and headers that identify the server and server software.

To avoid errors in processing request parameters that may be present either in the query string of the request URL (for GET requests) or in the body of the request (for POST requests), CGI applications must decompose the ampersand-separated parameter string into URL-encoded name–value pairs prior

```
sub ReadFormFields
{
  # set reference to the array passed into ReadFormFields
  my $fieldsRef = shift;
  my($key, $val, $buf_tmp, @buf_parm);

  #Read in form contents
  $buf_tmp = "";
  read(STDIN,$buf_tmp,$ENV{'CONTENT_LENGTH'});
  $buf_tmp = $ENV{QUERY_STRING} if (!$buf_tmp);

  @buf_parm = split(/&/,$buf_tmp);
  #Split form contents into tag/value associative array prior to decoding
  foreach $parm (@buf_parm) {
    # Split into key and value
    ($key, $val) = split(/=/,$parm);

    # Change + to space and restore all hex values
    $val = s/\+/ /g;
    $val = s/%([a-fA-F0-9][a-fA-F0-9])/pack("C",hex($1))/ge;

    # Use \0 to separate multiple entries per field name
    $$fieldsRef{$key} .= '\0' if (defined($$fieldsRef{$key}));
    $$fieldsRef{$key} .= $val;
  }
  return($fieldsRef);
}
```

Figure 6.8 Form and query string processing in CGI code.

to decoding them. Figure 6.8 shows a function found in a Perl script, which takes a reference to an associative array and populates it with name–value pairs either from the request URL's query string (for a GET request) or from the body of the HTTP request (for a POST request).

For forms found in HTML pages, the choice of request method (GET or POST) is determined by the method parameter in the <FORM> tag. In either case, the request parameters consist of ampersand-separated, URL-encoded name–value pairs. In our example, the browser composed the body of the request from information populated in the form in Figure 6.6: zip=08540&name=Leon+Shklar. The CGI script that invokes the ReadFormFields function would pass it the reference to an associative array. The read command is used to read the number of bytes defined by the Content-Length header from the body of the request. Note that read would be blocked when attempting to read more bytes than available from the body of the request, which will not happen if the Content-Length header is set properly. Real applications should take precautions to ensure proper timeouts, etc.

Having read the body of the request into the $buf_tmp variable, the next step is to split it into parts using the ampersand as the separator and using the foreach loop to split parts into keys and values at the = signs. Every value has to be URL-decoded which means that + signs need to be turned back into spaces and three-character control sequences (e.g., %27) need to be translated back into the original characters. It is very important that keys and values are separated prior to URL-decoding to avoid confusing the splitting operations with & and = signs that may be contained in the values. (For example, a parameter value may itself contain an encoded equal sign or ampersand, and URL-decoding before separation could cause a misinterpretation of the parameters.)

Figure 6.9 contains a sample CGI program that uses the ReadFormFields function to retrieve key–value pairs from the bodies of requests. The PrintFormFields function simply prints the Content-Type header and the HTML document with key–value pairs. The empty associative array, fields, is populated by ReadFormFields and then passed to the PrintFormFields function.

CGI programs may output status codes and HTTP headers but the HTTP server is responsible for augmenting the output to make them legitimate HTTP responses. In the example, the server has to add the status line and may include additional HTTP headers including Date and Server.

There are many commercial and open-source Perl packages that insulate CGI programmers from the HTTP protocol. There is nothing wrong with using convenience functions but it is important to understand the underlying data structures and protocols. Without that, finding and fixing problems may turn out to be very difficult. Moreover, understanding HTTP and mappings between the HTTP and CGI specifications simplifies learning other protocols and APIs for building Internet applications.

As we mentioned, Perl is not the only option. The CGI specification makes no assumptions about the implementation language and, as long as you access environment variables and standard input (or their equivalents for non-Unix operating systems), you can use any language you want. Nevertheless, the majority of CGI applications are implemented in Perl. It is no surprise since developers use the CGI mechanism for its simplicity, not for its performance characteristics. The additional overhead of interpreting a Perl program should not matter that much when balanced against the convenience of using an interpreted scripting language.

```perl
#!/usr/local/bin/perl

sub ReadFormFields { ... }

sub PrintFormFields
{
    my $fieldsRef = shift;
    my $key, $value;

    print "Content-Type: text/html\n\n";
    print "<html>\n<head><title>hello</title></head>\n";
    print "<body>\n";
    foreach $key (keys(%$fieldsRef)) {
        $value = $$fieldsRef{$key};
        print "<h3>$key: $value</h3>\n";
    }
    print "</body>\n</html>\n";
}

&ReadFormFields(\%fields);

&PrintFormFields(\%fields);

exit 0;
```

Figure 6.9   Printing parameters in CGI code.

As a server implementer, you are responsible for detecting CGI requests, starting a new child process for each CGI request, passing request information to the newly initiated process using environment variables and the input stream, and post-processing the response.

SSI

The *Server Side Includes* specification (SSI) dates back almost as far as the CGI specification. It provides mechanisms for including auxiliary files (or the results of the execution of CGI scripts) into an HTML page. The original specification for SSI still can be found at http://hoohoo. ncsa.uiuc.edu/docs/tutorials/includes.html.

Let us take another look at the sample CGI script in Figure 6.9. The PrintFormFields function outputs HTML tags; if you want to change the HTML, you have to go back and change the code. This is not at all desirable since it complicates maintenance. The most obvious solution is to create partially populated HTML pages, or templates, and fill in the blanks with the output of CGI scripts and, perhaps, other server-side operations. SSI is not a replacement for CGI, but it is an easy way to add dynamic content to pages without a lot of work.

SSI macros must have the following format:

```
<!--#command attr1="value1" attr2="value2" -->
```

The syntax is designed to place SSI commands within HTML comments ensuring that unprocessed commands are ignored when the page is sent to the browser. Valid commands include config for controlling the parsing, echo for outputting values of environment variables, include for inserting additional files, fsize for outputting file size information, and – the most dangerous – exec for executing server-side programs. The popular use of the exec command is to invoke CGI scripts as in exec cgi http://mysite.org/cgi-bin/zip.cgi but it may be used also to run other server-side programs.

Using the SSI mechanism to invoke the CGI script in Figure 6.9, we can simplify the script because we no longer need to print out the Content-Type header and the static part of the page. In the SSI example in Figure 6.10 and Figure 6.11, the shorter CGI script is invoked to fill blanks in the page, and the server uses the file extension of the page to set Content-Type. You can refer to the URL of an SSI page in the action attribute of the form tag (e.g., instead of the CGI URL in Figure 6.6), but only if you change the request method to GET. The server produces an error if you try to use POST – not at all surprising, since the CGI specification requires that bodies of POST requests be passed to CGI scripts as standard input. It is not clear what it means to pass the standard input stream to an SSI

```
<HTML>
<HEAD><TITLE>hello</TITLE></HEAD>
<BODY>
<!--#exec cgi http://mysite.org/cgi-bin/zip-ssi.cgi -->
</BODY>
</HTML>
```

Figure 6.10 Using SSI instead of the CGI program from Figure 6.9.

```
#!/usr/local/bin/perl

sub ReadFormFields { ... }

sub PrintFormFields
{
    my $fieldsRef = shift;
    my $key, $value;

    foreach $key (keys(%$fieldsRef)) {
        $value = $$fieldsRef{$key};
        print "<h3>$key: $value</h3>\n";
    }
}

&ReadFormFields(\%fields);
&PrintFormFields(\%fields);

exit 0;
```

Figure 6.11   Companion CGI program for the SSI instruction in Figure 6.10.

page. Making it a requirement for the server to pass bodies of POST requests to CGI scripts referenced in SSI pages would have complicated the implementation of the SSI mechanism. Moreover, SSI pages may include multiple exec cgi instructions, and it is unclear what it means to pass the same input stream to multiple CGI scripts.

As you no doubt remember, servers do not parse static pages – browsers are responsible for parsing pages and submitting additional requests for images and other embedded objects. This has to be different for SSI – the server cannot discover and execute SSI macros without parsing pages. Pages containing SSI macros are assigned different file extensions (e.g., .shtml) to indicate that special processing is required. In Section 6.4, we look at how different file extensions may be associated with different server-side processing modules.

CGI scripts that are invoked within SSI pages have access to additional context information that is not available in standalone mode. The context information is passed through environment variables; DOCUMENT_NAME, DOCUMENT_URI, and LAST_MODIFIED describe the SSI page and other environment variables (QUERY_STRING_UNESCAPED, DATE_LOCAL, DATE_GMT) are primarily the matter of convenience. The output of a standalone CGI script is sent to the browser after the server makes its final say in filling up the gaps – default values for required HTTP headers and the status code. When the CGI script is invoked from an SSI page, the server does not perform any error checking on the output. Responses that include the Location header are transformed into HTML anchors, but other response bodies are included in the page irrespective of the Content-Type of the response. You have to be careful or you can end up with GIF binaries mixed up with your HTML tags.

The SSI mechanism provides a simple and convenient way to add dynamic content to existing pages without having to generate the entire page. Nothing comes free, and the price of convenience in using SSI is both the additional load on the server and security worries since *fully* enabling SSI means allowing page owners to execute server-side programs. The security concerns lead server administrators to impose very serious limitations on the SSI mechanism, which limits the portability of SSI pages. Still, when used in a limited fashion (e.g., restricted to file includes), SSI may be a convenient and efficient way to implement applications that assemble pages dynamically from asynchronously modified static components.

6.2 Mechanisms for Dynamic Content Delivery

Even after you have built a web server that performs the basic tasks discussed in Section 6.1, there is still much to do. In this section, we discuss alternative mechanisms for building server-side applications. In the remaining sections, we discuss virtual hosting, other advanced server functionality, server configuration, and security.

6.2.1 Beyond CGI and SSI

CGI is a simple mechanism for implementing portable server-side applications. It is employed widely throughout the web. However, there are a number of problems associated with CGI processing. Its main deficiency is performance. Processing a request that invokes a CGI script requires the spawning of a child process to execute that script (plus another process if the script is written in an interpreted language such as Perl). Moreover, any initialization and other processing that might be common to all requests must be repeated for every single request.

SSI has similar deficiencies when its command processing employs CGI under the hood. It adds an additional performance penalty by requiring servers to parse SSI pages. Most importantly, SSI may represent a serious security risk, especially when not configured carefully by the server administrator. The SSI mechanism is not scalable and provides only limited opportunities for reuse.

With this in mind, a number of other approaches to dynamic content processing have arisen in the web server environment.

6.2.2 Native APIs (ISAPI and Apache Server API)

Efficiency concerns are sometimes addressed by using native server APIs. A *native server API* is a mechanism providing direct "hooks" into web server modules. Use of a native API implies the use of compiled code that is optimized for a specific web server environment. The Apache Server API and ISAPI are two approaches, employed by the Apache Web Server and Microsoft's IIS, respectively.

Unfortunately, there is no commonality or consistency amongst these native APIs. They are different from each other, and it is impossible to reuse code written for one API in another. This makes it impossible to implement portable applications. Additionally, applications that use native APIs are very intrusive and require extensive testing. For these reasons, the usage of native APIs remains limited.

6.2.3 FastCGI

FastCGI is an attempt to combine the portability of CGI applications with the efficiency of non-portable applications based on server APIs. The idea is simple: instead of requiring the spawning of a new process every time a CGI script is to be executed, FastCGI allows processes associated with CGI scripts to "stay alive" after a request has been satisfied. This means that new processes do not have to be spawned again and again, since the same process can be reused by multiple requests. These processes may be initialized once, rather than endlessly re-executing initialization code.

Server modules that enable FastCGI functionality talk to HTTP servers via their own APIs. These APIs attempt to hide the implementation and configuration details from FastCGI applications, but developers still need to be aware of the FastCGI implementation, as the various modules are not compatible with each other. Therein lies the problem: to ensure true portability, FastCGI functionality has to be supported across different HTTP servers in a consistent and compatible fashion.

The initial failure of FastCGI modules to proliferate to the main HTTP servers was the main cause for its temporary disappearance from the server-side application scene when *servlets* came along. Ironically, FastCGI has undergone a revival with the appearance of Ruby on Rails – a new and credible challenger for the Servlet API.

6.2.4   Template processing

Another approach used to serve dynamic content involves the use of template processors. Templates are essentially HTML files with additional "tags" that prescribe methods for inserting dynamically generated content from external sources. The template file contains HTML that provides general page layout parameters, with the additional tags placed so that content appears appropriately on the rendered page. Among the most popular template approaches are *PHP* (an open-source product), *Cold Fusion* (from Adobe), and *Active Server Pages* (*ASP*, from Microsoft).

SSI can be considered an early and rather trivial template-processing approach. While SSI directives can perform simple tasks, such as embedding external files and the output of CGI programs within a page, advanced template processors provide functionality that is more sophisticated. This functionality, which is available in most programming and scripting languages, includes:

- submitting database queries;
- iterative processing (analogous to repetitive "for-each" looping);
- conditional processing (analogous to "if" statements).

Figure 6.12 employs one of the popular template approaches, Adobe's *Cold Fusion*, and demonstrates each of these functions. (Note that Cold Fusion's special tags look like HTML tags, but begin with CF.) The <CFQUERY> block tag defines a database query. The <CFIF> block tag delimits a section that should only be included in the resulting page if the result set returned from the query is not empty (recordcount greater than zero). Within that block, the <CFOUTPUT> block tag specifies the contents of an HTML table row that should be repeated (with proper value substitution) for each row in the query's result set. (Note that text within Cold Fusion block tags that is delimited by # indicates a substitution parameter, e.g., #text#.)

The advantage of this approach is that templates can be created and maintained by *page designers*, who have background in HTML and web graphics but not in programming. Special tags that are "extensions" to HTML are considered similar enough to SSI tags to put their usage within the grasp of an average page designer. Employing these tags requires less expertise than writing code.

The problem is that the more sophisticated these template approaches get, the more they begin to resemble programming languages, and the more likely it becomes that this perceived advantage of simplicity will not be realized. Some template approaches provide advanced functionality by allowing

```
<CFQUERY name="query1" datasource="oracle" ...>
   SELECT id, columnX, columnY, columnZ
     FROM TABLE1
     WHERE id = #substitution-parameter#
</CFQUERY>

<CFIF query1.recordcount GT 0>
   <TABLE>
      <CFOUTPUT QUERY="query1">
         <TR>
            <TD>#columnX#</TD>
            <TD>#columnY#</TD>
            <TD>#columnZ#</TD>
         </TR>
      </CFOUTPUT>
   </TABLE>
</CFIF>
```

Figure 6.12 Template for Cold Fusion.

scripting within the template, but this only blurs the line between scripts and templates. It also means that, in all likelihood, two sets of people need to be responsible for building (and maintaining) the template: people with web design skills and people with programming skills.

6.2.5 Servlets

A better approach to serving dynamic content is the Servlet API – Java technology for implementing applications that are portable not only across different servers but also across different hardware platforms and operating systems. Like FastCGI, the Servlet API uses server application modules that remain resident and reusable, rather than requiring the spawning of a new process for every request. Unlike FastCGI, the Servlet API is portable across servers, operating systems, and hardware platforms. Servlets execute the same way in any environment that provides a compliant *servlet container*. The Servlet API has generated a very strong following; it is widely used in a variety of web server environments.

Implementers of Java servlets do not need to have any knowledge of the underlying servers and their APIs. Interfacing with server APIs is the responsibility of servlet containers, which include a Java Virtual Machine and are designed to communicate with host HTTP servers. Servlet containers do this by talking directly to server APIs through the Java Native Interface (JNI) or by running in a standalone mode and listening on an internal port for servlet requests that are redirected from general-purpose HTTP servers.

Servlets are Java programs that have access to information in HTTP requests. They generate HTTP responses that are sent back to browsers and proxies. Remember the CGI program in Figure 6.8 and Figure 6.9? Figure 6.13 shows what it looks like if implemented as a servlet.

As you see, methods defined on the `HttpServletRequest` class take care of extracting and decoding parameters and setting response headers. Notice that the `HttpServlet` class has different methods for different HTTP methods (`doGet()` and `doPost()`). In this example, we want to retrieve

```
import java.io.*;
import java.util.*;
import javax.servlet.*;
import javax.servlet.http.*;

public class FormServlet extends HttpServlet {
  public void doGet(HttpServletRequest request,
                    HttpServletResponse response)
      throws IOException, ServletException
  {
    response.setContentType("text/html");
    PrintWriter out = response.getWriter();
    out.println("<html\n<head><title>hello</title></head>");
    out.println("<body>");

    Enumeration e = request.getParameterNames();
    while (e.hasMoreElements()) {
      String name = (String)e.nextElement();
      String value = request.getParameter(name);
      out.println("<h3>" + name + &: & + value + "</h3>");
    }
    out.println("</body>\n</html>");
  }

  public void doPost(HttpServletRequest request,
                     HttpServletResponse response)
      throws IOException, ServletException
  {
    doGet(request, response);
  }
}
```

Figure 6.13   Parameter processing in servlets.

parameters passed in both GET and POST requests. We have the luxury of using exactly the same code in both cases – the `getParameterNames` and `getParameter` methods adjust their behavior depending on the type of request and protect programmers from having to know whether to retrieve parameters from the query string or the body of the request.

We revisit servlets in Chapters 9 and 10. It is worth noting that, unlike CGI scripts, servlets are capable of handling multiple requests concurrently. Servlets may forward requests to other servers and servlets. Of course, forwarding a request to another server results in an HTTP request even if programmers stick to method calls that are defined in the Servlet API.

6.2.6   Java Server Pages

The Java Server Pages (JSP) mechanism came about as Sun's response to Microsoft's template-processing approach, Active Server Pages. Originally, JSP was intended to relieve servlet programmers from the tedium of having to generate static HTML or XML markup through Java code. Today's JSP processors take static markup pages with embedded JSP instructions and translate them into servlets,

```
<HTML>
<HEAD><TITLE>hello!</TITLE></HEAD>
<BODY>
<%@ page import="java.util.*" %>
<% Enumeration e = request.getParameterNames();
   while (e.hasMoreElements()) {
       String name  = (String)e.nextElement();
       String value = request.getParameter(name);
%>
<H3><%=name%>:<%=value%></H3>
<% } %>
</BODY>
</HTML>
```

Figure 6.14 Parameter processing in JSP.

which are then compiled into Java byte code. More specifically, JSP processors generate Java classes, which extend the `HttpJspBase` class that implements the `Servlet` interface. What this means is that JSP serves as a pre-processor for servlet programmers. The resulting classes are compiled modules that execute faster than a processor that interprets templates at request time.

In contrast with earlier template approaches, most of which used proprietary tags, JSP instructions use XML syntax. Combined with Java code fragments, JSP tags express the logic for transforming JSP pages into the markup used to present the desired content.

It is not necessary for all application logic to be included in the page – the embedded code may reference other server-based resources. JSP's ability to reference server-based components is similar to SSI support for referencing CGI scripts. It helps to separate the page logic from its look and feel and supports a reusable component-based design.

Figure 6.14 illustrates that the task of displaying the parameters of an HTTP request is much simpler (compare with the servlet example in Figure 6.13). Notice, that we do not have to separately override the `doGet` and `doPost` methods since the `HttpJspBase` class is designed to override the `service` method (from which `doGet` and `doPost` are invoked).

Unlike servlets, the JSP technology is designed for a much wider audience since it does not require the same level of programming expertise. Even better, we do not have to pay as high a price as we did when using SSI technology instead of CGI scripts. As you remember, using SSI meant additional parsing overheads and issues with security. This is not a problem with JSP pages that are translated into servlets, which, in turn, are compiled into Java bytecode.

6.2.7 Future directions

The combination of servlets with JSPs does not, in itself, enforce or even encourage a truly modular approach to writing server-side applications. The example described in the previous section does not decouple data access logic from presentation logic, in fact it intermixes them excessively.

Still, this combination *can* be used effectively to implement the *Model–View–Controller* design pattern, which enforces the separation of content from presentation in a methodical modular way. Sun refers to this approach as *JSP Model 2*. It involves the use of a controlling "action" servlet (the

Controller component), which interfaces with JavaBeans that encapsulate access to data (the *Model* component), presenting the results of this processing through one or more Java Server Pages (the *View* component).

Strict application of this design pattern ensures that there is true separation of content and presentation. The controlling action servlet routes the request to ensure the execution of appropriate tasks. The JavaBeans (referred to in JSP "usebean" tags) encapsulate access to underlying data. JSPs refer to discrete data elements exposed in Java beans, presenting those data elements as desired.

Part of the elegance of this approach is the flexibility of the presentation. The same application can serve data to a wide variety of target devices, including desktop computers and handheld devices. Multiple view components for the same target platform could be used to enable personalized or customized presentations.

The *Struts Application Framework* (developed by the Apache Group as part of its Jakarta Project) provides a set of mechanisms to enable the development of web applications using this paradigm. Through a combination of Java classes, JSP tag libraries, and specifications for action mappings as XML configuration files, Struts provides a way to achieve the goal of truly modular and maintainable web applications.

The ultimate goal is a truly declarative framework, where it is enough to reference and configure necessary components and no coding is required. Although we are not there yet, existing mechanisms such as JSP Model 2 and Struts are moving us further along the path to that goal.

6.3   Advanced Functionality

Historically, server evolution went hand-in-hand with the evolution of the HTTP protocol. Some of the changes in the HTTP/1.1 specification were attempts to unify and legitimize proprietary extensions that were implemented in HTTP/1.0 servers, while others were genuinely new features that filled the need for extended functionality. For example, some HTTP/1.0 servers supported the `Connection: keep-alive` header even though it was never a part of the HTTP/1.0 specification. Unfortunately, for it to work properly it was necessary for every proxy between the server and the browser, and of course the browser itself, to support it as well. As we discussed in Chapter 3, servers, browsers, and proxies compliant with HTTP/1.1 have to assume that connections are persistent unless told otherwise via the `Connection: close` header. Examples of new features include virtual hosting, chunked transfers, and informational status codes.

6.3.1   Virtual hosting

As we covered in Section 3.5, virtual hosting is the ability to map multiple server and domain names to a single IP address. The lack of support for such a feature in HTTP/1.0 was a glaring problem for Internet Service Providers (ISPs). After all, you want your ISP to support your newly registered domain names!

HTTP/1.1 servers have a number of responsibilities with regard to virtual hosting:

- They use information in the `Host` header to identify the virtual host.
- They generate error responses with the proper status code (`400 Bad Request`) in the absence of the `Host` header.

- They support absolute URLs in requests, even though there is no requirement that the server identified in the absolute URL matches the `Host` header.
- They support isolation and independent configuration of document trees and server-side applications between different virtual hosts within the same server installation.

Most widely used HTTP/1.1 servers support virtual hosting. They make the important distinction between *physical* and *logical* configuration parameters. Physical configuration parameters are common for all virtual hosts: they control listening ports, server processes, limits on the number of simultaneously processed requests and the number of persistent connections, and other physical resources. Logical parameters may differ between virtual hosts: they include the location and configuration of the document tree and server-side applications, directory access options, and MIME type mappings.

6.3.2 Chunked transfers

You have probably experienced a number of occasions when you have spent long minutes sitting in front of your browser waiting for a particularly slow page. It could be because of a slow connection or it could be that the server application is slow. Either way you have to wait, even though all you need may be to take a quick peek at the content before you move on. The HTTP/1.1 specification introduced the notion of *transfer encoding* and an initial type of transfer encoding – *chunked* – that is designed to enable the processing of partially transmitted messages.

According to the HTTP/1.1 specification, servers must decode HTTP requests containing the `Transfer-Encoding: chunked` header prior to further processing. Similarly, browsers must decode HTTP responses containing this header (see Chapter 7). Chunked encoding is recommended for slow connections. It is most useful when servers (or browsers) can process individual chunks upon their decoding, without waiting for the entire content to arrive.

Figure 6.15 demonstrates a sample HTTP response – note the `Transfer-Encoding: chunked` header indicating the encoding of the body. The first line of the body starts with the hexadecimal number indicating the length of the first chunk (hexadecimal `1b` or decimal `27`) and is followed by an optional comment preceded by a semicolon. The next line contains exactly 27 bytes and is followed by another line containing the length of the second chunk (hexadecimal `10` or decimal `16`). The second chunk is followed by the line containing `0` as the length of the next chunk, which indicates the end

```
HTTP/1.1 200 OK
Content-Type: text/plain
Transfer-Encoding: chunked

1b; Ignore this
abcdefghijklmnopqrstuvwxyza
10
1234567890abcdef
0
a-footer: a-value
another-footer: another value
```

Figure 6.15 HTTP response for a chunked transfer.

of the body. The body may be followed by additional headers (called *footers*, since they follow the body). Their role is to provide information about the body that is impossible to obtain until the body generation is complete.

It may seem counter-intuitive that a browser request would be so huge as to merit separating it into chunks, but think about file transfer using PUT or POST requests. It gets a bit interesting with POST requests – try defining an HTML form with different input tags at least one of which refers to a file; upon submitting the form the browser creates the request with the Content-Type header set to multipart/form-data. Chunked encoding is not applicable across different body parts of a multipart message but the browser may apply it to any body part separately, e.g. the one containing the file.

Chunked encoding is a powerful feature but it is easy to misuse it without achieving any benefit. For example, suppose you are implementing a server application that generates a very large image file and zips it up. Even after being zipped up it is still huge, so you think that sending it in chunks may be helpful. Well, let us think about it – the browser receives the first chunk and retrieves the chunk content only to realize that it needs the rest of the chunks to unzip the file prior to attempting to render it. We just wasted all the time to encode and decode the body without obtaining any benefit.

6.3.3   Caching support

Caching is one of the most important mechanisms in building scalable applications. Server applications may cache intermediate results to increase efficiency when serving dynamic content, but such functionality is beyond the responsibility of HTTP servers. In this section, we concentrate our discussion on server obligations in support of browser caching as well as server controls with regard to browser caching behaviors.

Prior to HTTP/1.1, the majority of browsers implemented very simplistic caching policies – they cached only pages they recognized as static (e.g., only pages received in response to submitting requests initiated through anchor tags, as opposed to forms, and only those with certain file extensions). Once stored, the browser did not verify these cache entries for a fixed period (short of an explicit reload request).

There were, of course, problems with implementing more advanced caching strategies:

- On-request verification of cache entries meant doubling the number of requests for modified pages using HEAD requests. As you remember, HEAD requests result in response messages with empty bodies. On failed validation, such responses require follow-up GET requests.
- HTTP/1.0 servers, as a rule, did not include the Last-Modified header in response messages, making it much harder to check whether cache entries remained current. Verification had to rely on heuristics (e.g., changes in content length).
- There was no strict requirement for HTTP/1.0 servers to include the Date header in their responses (even though most did), making it harder to assign proper timestamps to cache entries.

HTTP/1.1 requires servers to comply with the following requirements in support of caching policies:

- Cache entries must be validated when receiving requests that include If-Modified-Since and If-Unmodified-Since headers set to a date in the GMT format (e.g., Date: Sun, 16 Sep

2007, 22:15:51 GMT). Invalid and future dates must be ignored. If the condition is satisfied (content has been modified, in the case of the If-Modified-Since header, or has not been modified, in the case of the If-Unmodified-Since header), the server should generate the same response as it would without cache validation. Servers are also responsible for generating proper status codes for failed conditions (304 Unmodified and 412 Precondition Failed, respectively).

- The Last-Modified header should be included in response messages whenever possible. Browsers use this value to compare against dates stored with cache entries.
- The Date header must be included with every response, which makes it possible to avoid errors that may happen when browsers rely on their own clocks.

It is not reasonable to expect servers to implement caching policies for dynamic content – this remains the responsibility of server applications. HTTP/1.1 provides applications with much finer controls than HTTP/1.0 (see Section 3.4.2). Depending on the processing mechanism (e.g. CGI or Servlet API), cache control headers may be generated directly by applications or by the enabling mechanism, but the headers are still the same. The key to understanding APIs is to examine the HTTP headers that are generated when you call a particular method and how these headers affect browser behavior. Such understanding is invaluable in designing good applications and troubleshooting problems.

6.3.4   Extensibility

Real HTTP servers vary in the availability of optional built-in components that support the execution of server-side applications. They also differ in the implementation of optional HTTP methods (all methods except GET and HEAD). Fortunately, servers provide system administrators with ways to extend the default functionality. As we discuss in Section 6.4.5, there are multiple ways to extend server functionality – from implementing optional HTTP methods to adding custom support mechanisms for building server applications.

6.4   Server Configuration

A web server's behavior is determined by its configuration. While the details of configuring a web server differ greatly between implementations, there are important common concepts that transcend these differences. For example, any HTTP server must map file extensions to MIME types, and any server must resolve URLs to addresses in the local file system. In this section, we use Apache configuration examples as a case study. We do not attempt to provide an Apache configuration manual, which is freely available from the Apache site; instead, we concentrate on the concepts, leaving it to our readers to utilize those concepts in the practical task of configuring their servers.

6.4.1   Directory structure

An HTTP server installation directory is commonly referred to as the *server root*. Most often, other directories (such as the document root, configuration directory, log directory, CGI and servlet root directories) are defined as subdirectories of the server root. An initial configuration file is normally loaded when the server comes up; it contains execution parameters, information about the location of other configuration files, and the location of the most important directories. Configuration file formats vary for different servers – from traditional attribute–value pairs to XML applications.

There exist situations when it is desirable to depart from the convention that calls for the most important directories to be defined as subdirectories of the server root. For example, you may have reasons to run different servers interchangeably on the same machine, which is particularly common in a development environment. In this case, you may want to use the same independently located document root for different servers. Similarly, you may need to be able to execute the same CGI scripts and servlets independent of which server is currently running. It is important to be particularly careful when sharing directories between different processes. If one of the processes is insecure, the integrity of your directory structure is in jeopardy.

6.4.2   Execution

An HTTP server is a set of processes or threads (for uniformity, we refer to them as *threads*), some of which listen on designated ports while others are dedicated to processing incoming requests. Depending on the load, it may be reasonable to keep a number of threads running at all times so that they do not have to be started and initialized with every request. Figure 6.16 contains a fragment of a sample configuration file for an Apache installation on a Windows machine.

The server type of `standalone` indicates that the server process is always running and, as follows from the value of the `Port` parameter, is listening on port 80. The server is configured to support persistent connections and every such connection is configured to persist for up to 100 requests. The keep-alive timeout setting dictates that the server should break the connection if 15 seconds go by without a new request. Many servers make it possible to impose a limit on the number of requests processed without restarting a child process. This limit was introduced for very pragmatic reasons – to avoid prolonged use that results in leaking memory or other resources. The nature of the HTTP protocol, with its independent requests and responses, makes it possible to avoid the problem simply by restarting the process. Finally, the timeout limits processing time for individual requests.

HTTP/1.1 is designed to support virtual hosting – the ability of a single server to accept requests targeted to different domains (which, of course, requires DNS aliases). This is useful when your favorite internet service provider hosts your site and is the reason for requiring the `Host` header in every request. Every virtual host may be configured separately. This does not apply to the operational parameters that have been discussed: different virtual hosts still share the same physical resources.

```
ServerName demo
ServerRoot "C:/Program Files/Apache Group/Apache"
ServerType standalone
Port 80
KeepAlive On
MaxKeepAliveRequests 100
KeepAliveTimeout 15
MaxRequestsPerChild 200
Timeout 300
```

Figure 6.16   Fragment of a configuration file.

6.4.3 Address resolution

An HTTP request is an instruction to the server to perform specified actions. In fact, you may think of HTTP as a language, an HTTP request as a program, and the server as a language interpreter. Requests are interpreted largely by specialized server modules and by server applications. For example, the servlet container is responsible for interpreting session identifiers in `Cookie` headers and mapping them to server-side session information. Application logic is responsible for interpreting URL parameters, request bodies, and additional header information (e.g., `Referer`).

The core server logic is responsible for the initial processing and routing of requests. The first and most important steps are to select the correct virtual host, to resolve aliases, to analyze the URL, and to choose the proper processing module. In Figure 6.17, `www.neurozen.com` is a virtual host. When a user accesses a URL containing this virtual host, the server has to locate configuration statements for it and use them to perform address translation.

Consider the following URL:

```
http://www.neurozen.com/test?a=1&b=2
```

In Figure 6.17, `/test` is defined to be an alias for `/servlet/test`. The server would first resolve the alias and then use module mappings to pass the URL to the servlet container which, in turn, invokes the *test* servlet.

Consider the following URL:

```
http://www.neurozen.com/images/news.gif
```

In Figure 6.17, `/images` is an alias for `/static/images`, which is not mapped to a module and is assumed to be a static file. Consequently, the server translates `/static/images` to the path starting at the document root and looks up the image with the path `/www/docs/neurozen/static/images/news.gif`.

The syntax of the configuration fragments in our examples is that of the Apache distribution. Do not get misled by the presence of angle brackets – this syntax only resembles XML. It may evolve to proper XML syntax in future versions. Note that almost all configuration instructions may occur within the `VirtualHost` tags. The exception is configuration instructions that control execution parameters (see Section 6.4.2). Instructions defined within the `VirtualHost` tag take precedence for respective host names over global instructions.

```
<VirtualHost www.neurozen.com>
   ServerAdmin    webmaster@neurozen.com
   Alias          /test      /servlet/test
   Alias          /images    /static/images
   DocumentRoot   /www/docs/neurozen
   ServerName     www.neurozen.com
   ErrorLog       logs/neurozen-error-log
   CustomLog      logs/neurozen-access-log common
</VirtualHost>
```

Figure 6.17 A configuration fragment.

6.4.4   MIME support

Successful HTTP responses (returning the code `200 OK`) are supposed to contain the `Content-Type` header instructing browsers how to render enclosed bodies. For dynamic processing, responsibility for setting the `Content-Type` header to a proper MIME type is deferred to the server application that produces the response.

For static processing, it remains the responsibility of the server. Servers set MIME types for static files based on file extensions. A server distribution normally contains a MIME configuration file that stores mappings between MIME types and file extensions.

In Figure 6.18, `text/html` is mapped to two file extensions (`.html` and `.htm`), `text/xml` is mapped to a single file extension (`.xml`), and `video/mpeg` is mapped to three extensions (`.mpeg`, `.mpg`, and `.mpe`).

There may be reasons for a particular installation to change or extend default mappings. Most servers provide for a way to do this without modifying the main MIME configuration file. For example, Apache supports special *add* and *update* directives that may be included with other global and virtual host-specific configuration instructions. The reason is to make it easy to replace default MIME mappings with newer versions without having to edit every new distribution. Such distributions are relatively frequent and are based on the work of standardization committees that are responsible for defining MIME types.

It is important to understand that MIME type mappings are not used exclusively for setting response headers. Another purpose is to aid the server in selecting an appropriate processing module. This is an alternative to path-based selections (see Section 6.4.3). For example, a mapping may be defined to associate the `.cgi` extension with CGI scripts; this means that the server would use the `.cgi` extension of the file name defined in the URL to select CGI as the processing module. This does not change server behavior in performing path-based selections when MIME-based preferences do not apply. Choosing CGI as the processing module for the incoming request is entirely independent from setting the `Content-Type` header in the response, which remains the responsibility of the CGI script.

6.4.5   Server extensions

HTTP servers are packaged to support the most common processing modules: As-Is, CGI, SSI, and servlet containers. Apache refers to these modules as *handlers*, and makes it possible not only to map built-in handlers to file extensions but also to define new handlers. In Figure 6.19, the `AddHandler` directive is used to associate file instructions with handlers. The `AddType` directive defines MIME types for the responses produced by these handlers through associating both types and handlers with

```
text/css       css
text/html      html htm
text/plain     asc txt
text/xml       xml
video/mpeg     mpeg mpg mpe
```

Figure 6.18   Fragment of the Apache MIME configuration file.

```
AddHandler send-as-is .asis

AddType text/html .shtml
AddHandler server-parsed .shtml

Action add-footer /cgi-bin/footer.pl
AddHandler add-footer .html

Script PUT /cgi-bin/my-put
```

Figure 6.19   Defining server extensions in Apache.

the same file extension. Further, the `Action` directive is designed to support new handlers. In the example, the `add-footer` handler is defined as a Perl script that is to be invoked for all `.html` files.

According to the HTTP 1.0 and 1.1 specifications, the only required server methods are `GET` and `HEAD`. You would be hard pressed to find a widely used server that does not implement `POST`, but many of them do not implement other optional methods: `PUT`, `DELETE`, `OPTIONS`, `TRACE`, and `CONNECT`. The set of optional methods for a server may be extended, but custom methods are bound to have proprietary semantics. The `Script` directive in Figure 6.19 extends the server to support the `PUT` method by invoking the CGI program `my-put`.

6.5   Server Security

The history of the human race has too many examples of the struggle between fear and greed. In Internet programming, this tug of war takes the form of the struggle between server security and the amount of inconvenience to server administrators and application developers. Server security is about 80:20 compromises – attempts to achieve 80% of the desired security for your servers at the cost of giving up 20% of the convenience in building and maintaining applications. Of course, there are always the degenerate cases when no security is enough, but that is a separate discussion.

This section is not intended as a security manual, but rather as an overview of the most common security problems in setting up and configuring HTTP servers. We do not attempt to provide all the answers, only to help you start looking for them. Where security is concerned, being aware of a problem takes you more than half way to finding a solution.

6.5.1   Securing the installation

HTTP servers are designed to respond to external requests. Some of the requests may be malicious and jeopardize the integrity not only of the server but of the entire network. Before we consider the steps necessary to minimize the effect of such malicious requests, we need to make sure that it is not possible to jeopardize the integrity of the server machine and corrupt the HTTP server installation.

The obvious precaution is to minimize remote login access to the server machine, up to and including disabling it entirely. (On Unix/Linux systems, this would mean disabling the telnet and login daemons.) If this is too drastic a precaution for what you need, at least make sure that all attempts to access the system are monitored and logged and all passwords are crack-resilient.

Every additional process running on a machine that serves outside requests adds to the risk – for example FTP and TFTP. In other words, it is better not to run any additional processes; if you have to, at least make sure that they are secure. Most problems are caused by a simple oversight. Do not neglect to check for obvious and trivial problems, such as file permissions on configuration and password files. There are free and commercial packages that can aid you in auditing the file system and checking for file corruption – a clear indication of danger. After all, if the machine itself can be compromised, it does not matter how secure is the HTTP server that is running on that machine.

The HTTP server itself is definitely a source of danger. Back in the early days, when the URL string was limited to a hundred characters, everyone's favorite way of getting through web server defenses was to specify a long URL and either achieve some sort of corruption or force the server to execute instructions hidden in the trailing portion of the URL. This is not likely to happen with newer HTTP servers but there are still gaping security holes that are occasionally exposed if server administrators are not careful.

As we discussed in Section 6.1.3, SSI is fraught with dangers. Primarily, this is due to its support for the execution of server-side programs. Commercial servers that allow the use of SSI commonly are configured to disable the invocation of server-side programs from SSI pages. Even so, subtler security holes occasionally are exposed because of buggy parsing mechanisms that get confused when encountering illegal syntax – a variation on the ancient problem with very long URLs, which caused buffer overflows. You may be asking for trouble if your server is configured to support SSI pages in user directories (particularly if the invocation of server-side programs is enabled). Similar precautions go for CGI scripts – enabling them in user directories is very dangerous. At the risk of repeating ourselves – it is simple security oversights that cause most problems.

6.5.2   Dangerous practices

Speaking of oversights, there are a few that seem obvious but are repeated over and over again. Quite a number of them have to do with the file system. We mentioned file permissions, but another problem has to do with symbolic links between files and directories. Following a symbolic link may take the server outside the intended directory structure, often with unexpected results. Fortunately, HTTP servers may be configured to ignore symbolic links when processing HTTP requests.

Of all the problems caused by lack of care in configuring the server, the one that stands out has to do with sharing the same file system between different processes. How often do you see people providing both FTP and HTTP access to the same files? You can spend as much effort as you want securing your HTTP server but it will not help if it is possible to establish an anonymous FTP connection to the host machine and post an executable in a CGI directory.

Now think of all the dangers of file and program corruption that may let outsiders execute their own programs on the server. It is bad enough that outside programs can be executed, but it is even worse if they can access critical system files. It stands to reason that an HTTP server should execute with permissions that don't give it access to files outside of the server directory structure. This is why, if you look at server configuration files, you may notice that the user id defaults to "nobody" – the name traditionally reserved for user ids assigned to HTTP servers. Unfortunately, not every operating system supports setting user ids when starting the server. Even less fortunately, system administrators, who log in with permissions that give them full access to system resources, are the ones to start servers.

As a result, the server process (and programs started through the server process), may have full access to system resources. You know the consequences.

6.5.3 Secure HTTP

Let us assume for the time being that the server is safe. This is still not enough to guard sensitive applications (e.g., credit card purchases). Even if the server is safe, HTTP messages containing sensitive information are still vulnerable. The most obvious solution for guarding this information is, of course, encryption. HTTPS is the secure version of the HTTP protocol. All HTTPS and HTTP messages are the same except that the former are transmitted over a Secure Sockets Layer (SSL) connection – messages are encrypted before the transmission and decrypted after being received by the server.

The SSL protocol supports the use of a variety of cryptographic algorithms to authenticate the server and the browser to each other, transmit certificates, and establish session encryption keys. The SSL handshake protocol determines how the server and the browser negotiate the encryption algorithm to use. Normally, the server and the browser select the strongest possible algorithm supported by both parties. Very secure servers may disable weaker algorithms (e.g., those based on 64-bit encryption). This can be a problem when a user tries to access a bank account and the server refuses the connection asking the user to install a browser that supports 128-bit encryption.

As always, you may spend a lot of effort and get bitten by a simple oversight. Even now, after so many years of Internet commerce, you can find applications that have the same problem – they secure the connection after authenticating a user but the authentication is not performed over a secure connection, which exposes user names and passwords. Next time, before you fill out a form to log in to a site that makes use of your sensitive information, check that the action attribute on the form references an HTTPS URL. If it does not, you should leave and never come back.

6.5.4 Firewall configurations

Today, more than a third of all Internet sites are protected by firewalls. The idea is to isolate machines on a Local Area Network (LAN) and expose them to the outside world via a specialized gateway that screens network traffic. This gateway is customarily referred to as a *firewall*. There are many different firewall configurations and they fall into two major categories: *dual-homed* gateways and *screened-host* gateways.

A dual-homed firewall is a computer with two interface cards, one of which is connected to the LAN and one to the outside world. With this architecture, there is no direct contact between the LAN and the world, so it is necessary to run a firewall proxy on the gateway machine and make this proxy responsible for filtering network packets and passing them between the interface cards. Passing every packet requires an explicit effort and no information is passed if the firewall proxy is down. Such a configuration is very restrictive and is used only in very secure installations.

Screened-host gateways are network routers that have the responsibility of filtering traffic between the LAN and the outside world. They may be configured to screen network packets based on source and destination addresses, ports, and other criteria. Normally, the router is configured to pass through only network packets that are bound for the firewall host and to stop packets that are bound for other machines on the LAN. The firewall host is responsible for running a configurable filtering proxy that selectively passes through the network traffic. The screened-host configuration is very flexible – it is easy to open temporary paths to selected ports and hosts. This comes in handy when you need to show a demonstration running on an internal machine.

6.5.5   HTTP proxies

It is all well and good to install a firewall but what do you do if you need to make your HTTP server visible to the outside world? The seemingly obvious answer – running it on the firewall machine – is not a good one. First, any serious load on the HTTP server that is running on the firewall machine may bring the LAN connection to the outside world to its knees. After all, the HTTP server and network traffic filters would share the same resources. Secondly, any security breach that exposes the HTTP server could also expose the firewall machine and, consequently, the entire LAN. Running the HTTP server on the firewall machine is a very bad idea altogether. Unfortunately, many installations do this anyway.

A better alternative is to take advantage of the flexibility of a screened-host gateway and allow network traffic to an internal machine when directed to a certain port (e.g., 80). It is much less dangerous than running the server on the firewall machine but still fraught with problems, since you are exposing an unprotected machine albeit in a very limited way. Additionally, this approach has functional limitations – how would you redirect the request to another server running on a different port or on a different machine?

It turns out there is another solution. Let us go back and think about the reasons why it is not a good idea to run an HTTP server on the firewall machine. The first reason is processing load and the second reason is security. What if we limited the functionality of the HTTP server that is running on the firewall machine and made it to defer processing to machines inside the firewall? This would solve the problem with processing load. How about security? Well, if the HTTP server is not performing any processing on the firewall machine and passes requests along to an internal machine on the LAN, it is hard to break into this server. The simpler the functionality, the harder it is for malicious outsiders to break in.

This sounds good, but what we are doing is simply passing requests along to another machine that still has to process these requests. Can malicious outsiders break into *that* machine? Well, it is not so easy – even if they manage to wreak havoc on the HTTP server machine, they cannot access that machine directly and use it as a staging ground for further penetration.

Our recommended solution is not to run a fully fledged HTTP server on the firewall machine but to replace it with an HTTP proxy that may be configured to screen HTTP requests and forward them to the proper internal hosts. Different proxy configurations may be selected depending on a wide range of circumstances but what is important is that no processing is performed on the firewall host and the internal machines are not exposed directly to the outside world.

6.6   Summary

By now, you should have enough information to build your own HTTP server or extend an existing open-source system. We attempted to make a clear distinction between the responsibilities of servers and those of server applications. Even if you do not implement your own server or server components, understanding server operation is invaluable when architecting, building, and debugging complex

Internet applications. Understanding server operation is also very important in making decisions about configuring a server and securing the server installation.

Implementing server applications was not the focus of this chapter. Instead, we concentrated on the comparative analysis of different application mechanisms and on passing request and response information to and from server applications. Chapters 9, 10, and 11 give an in-depth discussion of server-side applications.

QUESTIONS AND EXERCISES

1. Describe server processing of a POST request. In the case of CGI processing, how does the server pass information to a CGI program (request headers, body, URL parameters, etc.)?

2. What are the advantages and disadvantages of using the SSI mechanism?

3. What are the advantages of a Servlet API over the CGI mechanism?

4. How does the relationship between CGI and SSI mechanisms differ from the relationship between Servlets and JSP?

5. What was the reason for introducing `Transfer-Encoding: chunked` in HTTP/1.1?

6. Is it possible to use chunked transfer encoding with multipart HTTP messages? Explain.

7. Why was it necessary to introduce the `Host` header in HTTP/1.1? How is it used to support virtual hosting? Why was it not enough to require that request lines always contain a full URL (as in `GET http://www.cs.rutgers.edu/~shklar/ HTTP/1.1`)?

8. When (if ever) does it make sense to include HTTP/1.0 headers in HTTP/1.1 responses directed at HTTP/1.1 browsers?

9. HTTP/1.1 servers default to the `keep-alive` setting of the `Connection` header. Why then do most browsers include `Connection: keep-alive` in their requests even when they know that the target server supports HTTP/1.1?

10. Is it possible for an HTTP/1.1 server not to support persistent connections and still be HTTP-compliant?

11. Name *three* headers that, if present in an HTTP response, always have to be processed in a particular order. State the order and explain. Why did we ask you to name two headers in Chapter 3 but three headers in this exercise?

12. What is the difference between dual-homed gateways and screened-host gateways? Which is safer? Which is more flexible?

13. What functionality would be lost if servers did not know how to associate file extensions with MIME types?

14. Is it a good idea to run an HTTP server on a firewall machine? Explain.

15. Does your answer to question 14 depend on whether the HTTP server is running as a proxy?

16. Implement a mini-server that generates legal HTTP 1.0 responses to `GET`, `HEAD` and `POST` requests. Your program should be able to take the port number as its command-line parameter and listen on this port for incoming HTTP/1.0 requests (remember that a requirement for backward compatibility is part of HTTP/1.0 – this means support for HTTP/0.9). Upon receiving a request, the program should fork a thread to process the request and keep listening on the same port. The forked thread should generate the proper HTTP response, send it back to the browser, and terminate. The server should be capable of processing multiple requests in parallel. Pay attention to escape sequences and separators

between the key–value pairs in the bodies of POST requests and query strings of GET requests. Make sure that the necessary request headers are included in incoming requests (e.g., Content-Type and Content-Length in POST requests).

17. Your program has to generate legal HTTP headers according to HTTP 1.0 (including Content-Type). It should use a configuration file (mime-config) that will store mappings between file extensions and MIME types. It should use these mappings to determine the desired Content-Type, which is referenced by the URL (in your case, a file path) specified in the GET or POST request. You must support basic path translation – all static URLs will have to be defined relative to the document root. This also means that your server needs at least a basic general configuration file (see the Apache documentation). At a minimum, it should be possible to specify the server root, and the document root and the cgi-bin directory path relative to the server root.

18. Implement HTTP 1.1 support for the mini-server from Exercise 16. Your program should be able to take the port number as its command-line parameter and listen on this port for incoming HTTP/1.1 requests (remember that backward compatibility requirement is part of HTTP/1.1 – this means support for HTTP/1.0 and HTTP/0.9). Your server should support parallel processing of multiple requests. Upon receiving a request, your server should start a new thread to process that request and keep listening on the same port. The new thread should generate a proper HTTP response, send it back to the browser, and terminate. The server should be able to initiate processing of new requests while old requests are being processed.

You have to send HTTP/1.1 responses for HTTP/1.1 requests, HTTP/1.0 responses for HTTP/1.0 requests, and HTTP/0.9 responses for HTTP/0.9 requests. A minimal level of compliance is acceptable, which implies the following:

- HTTP/1.0 and HTTP/0.9 requests are processed as before.
- The server must check for presence of the Host header in HTTP/1.1 requests, and return 400 Bad Request if the header is not present; the server must accept both absolute and relative URL syntax.
- The server must either maintain a persistent connection or include Connection: close in every response.
- The server must include the Date header (with the date in GMT) in every response.
- The server must support the If-Modified-Since and If-Unmodified-Since headers.
- The following methods are defined in HTTP/1.1: GET, HEAD, POST, PUT, DELETE, OPTIONS, and TRACE. You must support GET, HEAD, and POST; return 501 Not Implemented for other defined methods; and return 400 Bad Request for undefined methods.

The result of this exercise should be a program that receives legal HTTP/1.1 requests and sends legal HTTP/1.1 responses back. It should function as an HTTP/1.0 server in response to HTTP/1.0 requests.

6.7   Bibliography

Castro, Elizabeth, 2001. *Perl and CGI for the Web*. Peachpit Press.

Hall, Marty, 2002. *More Servlets and Java Server Pages*. Prentice Hall.

Kopparapu, Chandra, 2002. *Load Balancing Servers, Firewalls and Caches*. John Wiley and Sons, Inc.

Luotonen, Ari, 1997. *Web Proxy Servers*. Prentice Hall.

Rajagopalan, Suresh et al., 2002. *Java Servlet Programming Bible*. John Wiley and Sons, Inc.

Thomas, Stephen, 2000. *SSL and TLS Essentials: Securing the Web*. John Wiley and Sons, Inc.

Yeager, Nancy and McGrath, Robert, 1996. *Web Server Technology*. Morgan Kaufmann.

Web Browsers

IN THIS CHAPTER

- Overview of browser functionality
- Architectural considerations
- Processing HTTP requests and responses
- Cookies, privacy, and P3P
- Complex HTTP interactions

OBJECTIVES

- Establish the set of tasks that web browsers must perform.
- Break down browser architecture into component modules, establishing the responsibilities of these modules and their interactions.
- Provide an in-depth analysis of the processing flow in a web browser.
- Examine how browsers create and transmit HTTP requests, receive and interpret HTTP responses, and interact with the user.
- Focus on browser support for cookies, caching, and authorization.
- Examine the page-rendering process, including generating requests for supporting data items and using plug-ins and helper applications to render multimedia content.

In this chapter, we go over the fundamental considerations in designing and building a web browser, and other sophisticated web clients. When discussing web browsers, our focus is not on the graphical aspects of browser functionality (i.e., the layout of pages or the rendering of images). Instead, we concentrate on the issues associated with the processing of HTTP requests and responses. The value of this knowledge will become apparent as we proceed to a discussion of sophisticated web applications in the following chapters.

It is not uncommon for the wisdom of studying web browser design to be questioned. After all, the task of designing a browser is a *fait accompli*, a known problem that already has a solution. Given the sophistication and proliferation of today's browsers, including Mozilla Firefox, Safari, Opera, and Internet Explorer, it may seem like a futile endeavor to "reinvent the wheel" by building a new browser application.

In reality, there is much benefit in learning the inner workings of modern web browsers:

- The browser is the most common example of a web client, but it is far from the only one. Other types of web clients include *agents*, which are responsible for submitting requests on behalf of a user to perform an automated function, and *proxies*, which act as gateways for passing requests and responses between servers and clients to enhance security and performance. These clients need to replicate much of the functionality found in browsers.
- Today's sophisticated mobile devices – including PDAs, smart phones, and wireless Internet appliances – offer web access and require browsers that are designed to work on devices with limited memory and screen space. The Opera Mini browser is a program that provides substantial functionality yet works well on a variety of mobile devices and understands the interface limitations associated with them. We should expect the introduction of many new devices in the years to come and they will need browsers customized and optimized to support their capabilities.
- Finally, today's browsers continue to evolve, and at least two of them are open-source efforts to which interested developers can contribute. While it would be difficult to develop and market a new desktop browser at this stage of the game, there are ample opportunities to enhance and augment the functionality of existing desktop browsers.

7.1   Overview of Browser Functionality

The main responsibilities of a browser are as follows:

- To generate and submit requests to web servers on the user's behalf, as a result of following hyper-links, explicit typing of URLs, submitting forms, and parsing HTML pages that require auxiliary resources (e.g., images, applets).
- To accept responses from web servers and interpret them to produce a visual representation for the user. At a bare minimum, this would involve examination of certain response headers such as `Content-Type` to determine what action needs to be taken and what sort of rendering is required.
- To render the results in the browser window or through a third-party tool, depending on the content type of the response.

This, of course, is an oversimplification of the complex tasks that real browsers perform. Depending on the status code and headers in the response, browsers have to perform other tasks, including:

- **Caching**: The browser must determine whether it needs to request data from the server. It may have a cached copy of the required data item. If so, and if this cached copy has not "expired," the browser can eliminate a superfluous request for the resource. In other cases, the server can be queried to determine if the resource has been modified since it was originally retrieved and placed in the cache. Caching can provide significant performance benefits.

- **Authentication and authorization**: A web server may require authorization for resources it has designated as secure. The browser must react to server requests for credentials by prompting the user for authentication credentials or by utilizing validated credentials from previous requests.

- **State maintenance**: In order to record and maintain state across requests and responses, web servers may request that the browser accept *cookies*, which are sets of name–value pairs included in response headers. The browser must store the transmitted cookie information and make it available to be included in appropriate requests. In addition, the browser should provide configuration options to let users choose whether or not to accept cookies.

- **Requesting supporting data items**: The typical web page contains images, Java applets, sounds, and a variety of other ancillary objects. The proper rendering of the page is dependent upon the browser retrieving those supporting data items for inclusion in the rendering process. This normally occurs without user intervention.

- **Taking actions in response to other headers and status codes**: The HTTP headers and the status code may provide additional processing instructions, which extend or supersede rendering information found elsewhere in the response. These instructions may indicate a problem in accessing the resource or may instruct the browser to *redirect* the request to another location. They may also indicate that the connection should be kept open, so that further requests can be sent over the same connection. Many of these functions are associated with advanced functionality that was introduced in HTTP/1.1.

- **Rendering complex objects**: Most web browsers inherently support content types such as `text/html`, `text/plain`, `image/gif`, and `image/jpeg`. This means that the browser provides native functionality to render objects with these contents within the browser window and without having to install additional software. To render or play back other more complex objects (e.g., audio, video, and multimedia), a browser must provide support for these content types. Mechanisms must exist for invoking external *helper applications* or internal *plug-ins* that are required to display and play back these objects.

- **Dealing with error conditions**: The browser must be equipped to deal with connection failures, invalid server responses, and other similar situations.

7.2 Architectural Considerations

Let us engage in an intellectual exercise: putting together requirements for the architecture of a web browser. What are those requirements? What functions must a web browser perform? And how should different functional components interact with each other?

The following list delineates the core functions of a web browser. Each function can be thought of as a distinct module within the browser. These modules must communicate with each other in order to allow the browser to function, but they should each be designed atomically. This module organization scheme is conceptual, for purposes of illustration, and may not be reflected literally in the codebase for a real-world browser (e.g., Mozilla's Firefox[1]).

- **User Interface**: This module is responsible for providing the interface through which users interact with the application. This includes presenting, displaying, and rendering the end result of the browser's processing of the response transmitted by the server.

- **Request Generation**: This module bears responsibility for the task of building HTTP requests to be submitted to HTTP servers. When asked by the User Interface module or the Content Interpretation module to construct requests based on relative links, it must first resolve those links into absolute URLs.

- **Response Processing**: This module must parse the response, interpret it, and pass the result to the User Interface module.

- **Networking**: This module is responsible for network communications. It takes requests passed to it by the Request Generation module and transmits them over the network to the appropriate web server or proxy. It also accepts responses that arrive over the network and passes them to the Response Processing module. In the course of performing these tasks, it takes responsibility for establishing network connections and dealing with proxy servers that may have been specified in the user's network configuration options.

- **Content Interpretation**: Having received the response, the Response Processing module needs help in parsing and deciphering the content. The content may be encoded; this module is responsible for decoding it. Initial responses often have their content types set to `text/html` but their bodies may contain references to images, multimedia objects, JavaScript code, applets, and style sheet information. The Content Interpretation module performs the additional processing necessary for browser applications to understand and process these references by telling the Request Generation module to construct additional requests for the retrieval of the auxiliary objects.

- **Caching**: Web browsers need a way to minimize the unnecessary retrieval of resources that are already available to them, "cached" away in local storage. Browsers can ask web servers whether a desired resource has changed since the last time that the browser retrieved it and stored it in the cache. This module must provide facilities for storing copies of retrieved resources for later use, for accessing those copies when viable, and for managing dedicated space (both memory and disk) allocated according to the browser's configuration parameters.

- **State Maintenance**: Since HTTP is a *stateless protocol*, some mechanism must be in place to maintain the browser *state* between related requests and responses. Cookies are the mechanism of choice for performing this task, and support for cookies is the responsibility of this module.

- **Authentication/Authorization**: This module takes care of providing authorization information when requested by the server. It must process response headers demanding authentication credentials by prompting the user to enter them (usually via a dialog). It also must store those credentials in case a request is made for another secured resource in the same security "realm". This absolves the user of the need to re-enter the credentials each time a request for such resources is made.

- **Configuration**: Finally, there are a number of configuration options that a browser application needs to support. Some of these are fixed, while others are user-defined. This module maintains the fixed and variable configuration options for the browser, and provides an interface for users to modify those options under their control.

Simplified diagrams providing a high-level illustration of different stages of request generation and response processing are presented in the next section. In addition, Section 7.9 provides a summary of the functionality associated with the browser modules.

Certain aspects of the browser's "state" should not be preserved beyond the end of the *browser session*. (A browser session is simply the series of interactions between a browser and the HTTP servers it communicates with, commencing with the first such interaction after the browser program starts and ending when the browser program terminates.) For example, cookies not designated as "persistent" should be preserved for the duration of the browser session, but not beyond it. Persistent cookies, on the other hand, should be stored on disk so that they can be accessed during subsequent browser sessions. Likewise, authentication credentials collected by the browser from user input should be retained for the duration of the browser session. This means that subsequent requests submitted to URLs within the same authentication realm reuse the credentials without re-prompting the user. These authentication credentials should be discarded when the browser program terminates.

Browser Sessions vs HTTP Sessions

Although browser sessions are often confused with HTTP sessions, they are not the same thing. HTTP sessions are maintained by the server, not by the browser. The browser, however, does maintain the HTTP session identifier as a cookie, providing a link between the browser session and the HTTP session. Because this cookie is not persistent, the HTTP session identifier is not available to subsequent browser sessions. This means that the browser cannot access information associated with previous HTTP sessions, even though those sessions may still exist on the server. Also, a browser session lasts for as long as the browser program is running, while HTTP sessions normally "time out" after a period of inactivity as configured on the server.

7.3   Overview of Processing Flow in a Browser

7.3.1   Transmitting a request

Figure 7.1 provides a high-level view of the processing flow for the creation and transmission of a request in a browser. It begins with a link that is followed by a user. Users can click on hyperlinks presented in the browser display window, choose links from lists of previously visited links (history or bookmarks), or enter a URL manually.

In each case, processing begins with the User Interface module, which is responsible for presenting the display window and providing the user with access to browser functions (e.g., through menus and shortcut keys). In general, an application using a Graphical User Interface (GUI) operates using an *event model*. User actions – such as clicking on a highlighted hyperlink – are considered *events* that must be interpreted properly by the User Interface module. Although this book does not concentrate on the user interfaces of HTTP browsers, it is important to note the events that are important for the User Interface module:

- *Entering URLs manually:* Usually, this is accomplished by providing a text entry box in which the user can enter a URL, as well as through a menu option that opens a dialog box for similar manual entry. The second option often interfaces with the operating system to support interactive selection of local files.
- *Selecting previously visited links:* This means that the User Interface module provides a mechanism for maintaining a history of visited links. The maximum amount of time that such links are maintained in this list, as well as the maximum size to which this list can grow, can be established as

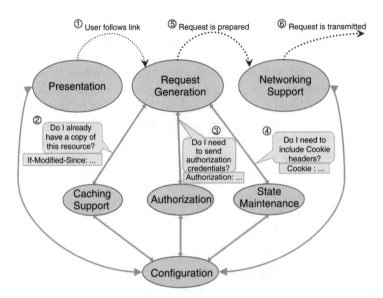

Figure 7.1 Browser request generation flow.

a user-definable parameter in the Configuration module. The Location or Address text area in the browser window can double as a *dropdown* field that allows users to select from recently visited links. The Back button allows users to go back to a previously visited page. In addition, users should be able to save links as "bookmarks" and access these links through the user interface at a later date.

- *Selecting displayed hyperlinks:* There are a number of ways for users to select links displayed on the current page. In a desktop computer browser, the mouse click is the most common mechanism for users to select a link, but there are other mechanisms as well. Accessibility guidelines dictate that alternative mechanisms should be provided for those unable to use a mouse or keyboard (e.g., using speech synthesis and recognition mechanisms for visually-impaired users). The User Interface module is responsible for rendering HTML pages according to the specification, which dictates the rendering not only of text but also of link highlighting. Most desktop browsers change the cursor shape when the mouse is "over" a hyperlink, indicating that this is a valid place for the user to click. Highlighting mechanisms vary for other platforms, but they always have to be present in some form.

Once the selected or entered link is passed on to the Request Generation module, it must be *resolved*. Links found on a displayed page can be either absolute or relative. Absolute URLs contain all the required URL components, i.e., <protocol>://<host>/<path> and do not need to be resolved; they can be processed without further intervention. The resolution of a relative URL is dependent on its href attribute (see Table 7.1):

- If it is set to a path that does not begin with a slash (e.g. <A href=some_directory/just_a_ file_name.html>), the relative URL specifies a location relative to the current location (i.e., the entire URL, up to and including the directory in which the current page resides).

Table 7.1 Resolution of Relative URLs

Current URL	`href` Attribute	Resolved URL

`http://www.server1.com/mydir/`
 	
 `(index.html is implied)`
	`dir2/page2.html`	`http://www.server1.com/mydir/` `dir2/page2.html`

	`/dir3/home.html`	`http://www.server1.com/dir3/` `home.html`
`http://www.server1.com/mydir/` `page3.html`	`dir2/page2.html`	`http://www.server1.com/mydir/` `dir2/page2.html`
	`/dir3/home.html`	`http://www.server1.com/dir3/` `home.html`
`http://www.server1.com/mydir/` `page3.html` **BASE href:** `http://www.server2.com/dir1/`	`dir2/page2.html`	`http://www.server2.com/dir1/` `dir2/page2.html`
	`/dir3/home.html`	`http://www.server2.com/dir3/` `home.html`

- If it is set to a path that *does* begin with a slash (e.g. `<A href=/root_level_directory/` `another_file_name.html>`), the relative URL specifies a location relative to the host portion of the current URL.

The process of resolution changes if the optional `<BASE href=...>` tag is present in the HEAD section of the page. The URL specified in this tag replaces the current location as the "base" from which URL resolution occurs (see the last example in Table 7.1).

Having resolved the URL, the Request Generation module builds the request, which is passed to the Networking module for transmission. To accomplish this task, the Request Generation module has to communicate with other browser components:

- It asks the Caching module *"Do I already have a copy of this resource?"* If so, it needs to determine whether it can simply use this copy or whether it needs to check with the server to see if a newer version of this resource is available.
- It asks the Authorization module *"Do I need to include authentication credentials in this request?"* If the credentials are required and the browser has not already stored them for the appropriate domain and path, it may need to contact the User Interface module to prompt the user for credentials.
- It asks the State Mechanism module *"Do I need to include Cookie headers in this request?"* to determine whether the requested URL matches domain and path patterns for saved cookies that have not yet expired.

The constructed request is passed to the Networking module so it can be transmitted over the network.

7.3.2 Receiving a response

Once a request is transmitted, the browser waits for a response. It may keep submitting requests while waiting. Requests may have to be resubmitted if the connection is closed before corresponding

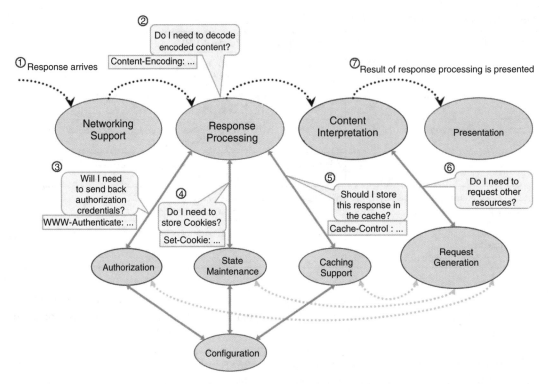

Figure 7.2 Browser response processing flow.

responses are received. It is the server's responsibility to transmit responses in the same order as the requests were received. However, the browser is responsible for dealing with servers that do not properly maintain this order, by delaying the processing of responses that arrive out of sequence. Figure 7.2 provides a high-level view of this processing flow.

A response is received by the Networking module, which passes it to the Response Processing module. This module must also cooperate and communicate with other modules to do its job. It examines response headers to determine the required actions:

- If the status code of the response is `401 Not Authorized`, the request lacked necessary authorization credentials. The Authorization module marks the response as requiring authorization credentials from the user. The User Interface module then prompts the user to enter their user name and password. Once they have been entered, the browser attempts to resubmit the original request – this time with the `Authorization` header containing the newly entered credentials.
- If the response contains `Set-Cookie` or `Set-Cookie2` headers, the State Maintenance module stores the cookie information using the browser's persistence mechanism.

The Content Interpretation module needs to *decode* the body of the response if the response contains `Content-Transfer-Encoding` or `Content-Encoding` headers. The Content Interpretation module also examines the `Cache-Control`, `Expires`, or `Pragma` headers (depending on the HTTP version of the response) to determine whether the browser needs to cache the decoded content of the response. If so, the Caching module is contacted, either to create a new cache entry and set its timestamp from the `Last-Modified` header or to update the existing entry and its timestamp.

The `Content-Type` header determines the MIME type of the body of the response. Different MIME types, naturally, require different kinds of content processing. Modern browsers support a variety of content types natively, including HTML (`text/html`), graphical images (`image/gif` and `image/jpeg`), and sounds (`audio/wav` and `audio/mpeg`). Native support means that processing of these content types is performed by built-in browser components. The Content Interpretation module must support such processing. Leading browsers provide support for additional content types, including vector graphics and XSL style sheets.

For MIME types that are not processed natively, browsers usually provide support mechanisms to associate MIME types with *helper applications* and *plug-ins*. Helper applications render content by invoking an external program that executes independently of the browser, while plug-ins render content within the browser window. The Content Interpretation module must communicate with the Configuration module to determine which plug-ins are installed and which helper application associations have been established, in order to take appropriate action when receiving content that is not natively supported by the browser.

Browsers also need a way to determine the MIME types associated with local files. A file's MIME type can be inferred from the local operating system's associations between filename extensions and MIME types. Alternatively, browsers can override (or even completely ignore) these settings, managing their own sets of associations through the Configuration module. These associations between filename extensions and MIME types may also be used when receiving responses that do not contain valid `Content-type` headers.

HTML pages support embedded references to additional resources, such as images, CSS style sheets, and JavaScript components. The Content Interpretation module must parse the content prior to passing it on to the User Interface module, determining if additional requests for embedded references are required. URLs associated with these requests are resolved when they are passed to the Request Generation module.

As each of the requested resources arrives, it is passed to the User Interface module so that it may be incorporated in the final presentation. The Networking module maintains its queue of requests and responses (per connection), ensuring that all requests have been satisfied and resubmitting any outstanding requests.

Along the way, various subordinate modules are asked questions to determine the course of processing (including whether or not particular tasks need to be performed at all). For example, the Content Interpretation module may say "*This page has IMG tags, so we must send HTTP requests to retrieve the associated images,*" but the Caching module may respond by saying "*We already have a usable copy of that resource, so don't bother sending a request to the network for it.*" (Alternatively, it may say "*We have a copy of that resource, but let's ask the server if its copy of the resource is more recent; if it's not, it doesn't need to send it back to us.*") Or the Configuration module may say "*No, don't send a request for the images on this page, this user has elected not to see images.*" Finally, the State Maintenance mechanism may jump in and say "*Wait, we've been to this site before, so send along this identifying cookie information with our requests.*"

The rest of this chapter is devoted to a more detailed explanation of the role each of these modules plays in the generation of requests and the processing of responses. As mentioned previously, we do not focus on the User Interface module's responsibility in rendering graphics, as this is an extensive subject, worthy of its own book. We concentrate on the interplay between browser modules and on how to design them to fulfill their obligations.

We begin by going over the basics of request generation and response processing, following that with details on the more sophisticated aspects of caching, authentication, and support for the advanced features of the HTTP protocol.

Not Just HTTP

Browsers should do more than just communicate via HTTP. They should provide support for Secure HTTP (over the Secure Sockets Layer). They should be able to send requests to FTP servers. And they should be able to access local files. These three types of requests correspond to URLs using the `https`, `ftp`, and `file` protocol schemes, respectively. Although we do not cover these protocols here, it is important to note that HTTP requests and responses are not the only kinds of transaction performed by browsers.

7.4   Processing HTTP Requests

The act of sending an HTTP request to a web server consists of three basic steps: constructing the HTTP request (Request Generation module), establishing a connection (Networking module) across the Internet to the target server or an intermediate proxy, and transmitting the request (Networking module) over the established connection.

Before the Request Generation module begins the process of building the request, it needs to ask a series of questions of the other modules:

1. *Do I already have a cached copy of this resource?* (Caching Support module)
   If an unexpired entry associated with the requested URL exists in the cache, no request is required. If the entry has expired, then the transmitted request should include an `If-Modified-Since` header, containing the last modification time associated with the stored cache entry. If the resource found on the server has *not* been modified since that time, the response will come back with a `304 Not Modified` status code and the cache entry can be passed directly to the User Interface module.
2. *Is there any additional information I need to send as part of this request?* (State Maintenance module)
   If this request is part of a series of requests made to a particular web server, or if the target web server has been visited previously, it may have sent "state" information (in the form of `Set-Cookie` headers) to the browser. The browser must set and maintain cookies according to the server instructions: either for a specified period of time or for the duration of the current session. Saved cookies must be examined prior to submitting a request to determine whether cookie information needs to be included in that request.
3. *Is there any other additional information I need to include as part of this request?* (Authentication/Authorization module)
   If this resource is part of an authorization realm for which the user has already supplied authentication credentials, those credentials should be stored by the browser for the duration of a session and should be supplied with requests for other resources within the same realm.

User preferences may modify the nature of the request, possibly even eliminating the need for one entirely. For example, users may set a preference via the Configuration module telling the browser not to request images found within an HTML page. They can turn off support for Java applets or JavaScript, meaning that requests for applets and scripts need not be created. They can also instruct the browser to reject cookies, meaning that the browser does not need to worry about including `Cookie` headers in generated requests.

In Chapter 3, we described the general structure of HTTP requests and provided some examples. To refresh our memories, here is the format of an HTTP request:

```
METHOD /path-to-resource HTTP/version-number
Header-Name-1: value
Header-Name-2: value

[ optional request body ]
```

An HTTP request contains a *request line*, followed by a series of *headers* (one per line) and a blank line that may serve as a separator, delimiting the headers from the optional *body* portion of the request. A typical example of an HTTP request might look something like this:

```
POST /update.cgi HTTP/1.0
Host: www.somewhere.com
Referer: http://www.somewhere.com/formentry.html

name=joe&type=info&amount=5
```

The process of constructing an HTTP request may begin when a web site visitor sees a link on a page and clicks on it, telling the browser to present the content associated with that link. There are other possibilities, such as entering a URL manually, or a browser connecting to a default home page when starting up, but this example is convenient for us to describe typical browser activity.

7.4.1 Constructing the request line

When a link is selected, the browser's User Interface module reacts to that *event*. The User Interface module determines and resolves the URL associated with that link and passes it to the Request Generation module, which begins to construct the request.

Filling Out a Form

In the case of a form, where the user has entered data into form fields and clicked a Submit button, it is more than just the URL that is passed to the Request Generation module. The entered data must be included as well. As we mentioned in Chapter 3, the data is converted into name–value pairs that are URL-encoded. The GET method includes the encoded data in the URL as a query string, while the POST method places the encoded data in the body of the request.

The first portion of the request that needs to be created is the *request line*, which contains a *request method* (e.g., GET, POST, or HEAD), a path to the resource (representing the *path* portion of the requested URL), and the version number of HTTP associated with the request.

Let us examine these in reverse order. The version number should be HTTP/1.1 or HTTP/1.0. A modern up-to-date client program should always seek to use the latest version of its chosen trans-mission protocol, unless the recipient of the request is not sophisticated enough to make use of that version. A contemporary browser should seek to communicate with a server using HTTP/1.1 and should only "fall back" to HTTP/1.0 if the server with which it is communicating does not support HTTP/1.1.

The path-to-resource parameter is a little more complicated. It depends on which version of HTTP is employed in the request.

- HTTP/1.0 requires the inclusion of the full URL for requests directed at proxy servers, but forbids the inclusion of domain information for requests that are sent directly to their target servers. This is because HTTP/1.0 *servers* do not understand requests where the full URL is specified in the request line. In contrast, HTTP/1.0 *proxies* expect that incoming requests contain the full URL. They have to, in order to identify target servers. When HTTP/1.0 proxies forward requests to their target servers, they remove the server portion of the request URL. When the requests are forwarded to other proxies, they remain unchanged.

- HTTP/1.1 is more flexible: it makes the inclusion of the entire URL on the request line acceptable in all situations, irrespective of whether a proxy is involved. To facilitate this flexibility, HTTP/1.1 requires that submitted requests include the Host header, specifying the name of the target server. This header was originally introduced to support virtual hosting, a feature that allows a web server to service more than one domain: a web server program could run on a single server machine, accepting requests associated with many different domains. The Host header identifies the domain, which may be associated with its own web server settings (location of the document root, redirect rules, etc.). This header also provides sufficient information to HTTP/1.1 proxies so that they can properly forward incoming requests. However, HTTP/1.1 still requires the inclusion of full URLs for requests that do not go directly to their target servers – to allow for the possible presence of HTTP/1.0 proxies.

In summary, HTTP/1.1 requests should contain the full URL in the request line as well as the required Host header. For HTTP/1.0, the presence or absence of the domain name in the request URL should depend on whether the request is being directed to an intermediate proxy.

The method portion of the request line is dependent on which request method is specified, implicitly or explicitly. When users follow a hyperlink (textual or image), they implicitly select the GET method. In the case of an HTML form, a particular request method may be specified in the <FORM> tag:

```
<FORM action="http://www.somewhere.com/update.cgi" method="POST">
    ...
</FORM>
```

As we mentioned in Chapter 3, the GET method represents the simplest format for HTTP requests: a request line, followed by headers, and no body. Other request methods (e.g., POST and PUT) use a request body, which follows the request line, the headers, and a blank line (the separator delimiting the headers from the body). The request body may contain parameters associated with an HTML form, a file to be uploaded, or a combination of both. Remember that in GET requests, parameters would be included in the query string or the path component of the URL.

The method defaults to GET for hyperlinks and for forms that do not explicitly specify a method. If a form does explicitly specify a method, that method is used instead.

7.4.2   Constructing the headers

Next, we come to the headers. Some of them are required and some are optional, but their inclusion has become common practice.

- Host is a required header, which was introduced in HTTP 1.1:

```
Host: www.neurozen.com
```

It enables web servers to service more than one domain. Without this header, web servers would not know which of their domains a request was intended for. In addition, this header provides information to proxies to facilitate proper routing of requests.

- User-Agent identifies the software (e.g., a web browser) responsible for making the request:

```
User-Agent: Mozilla/5.0 (Macintosh; U; Intel Mac OS X; en-US;
rv:1.8.1.7)
```

It is accepted practice for a browser (or for that matter *any* web client) to identify itself. The convention is to produce a header containing the name of the product, the version number, the language this particular copy of the software uses, and the platform it runs on.

- Referer should be set to the URL of the page containing the link that the user clicked:

```
Referer: http://www.cs.rutgers.edu/~shklar/index.html
```

- Date specifies the time and date that this message was created. All request and response messages should include this header:

```
Date: Sun, 14 Oct 2007 22:28:31 GMT
```

- The Accept headers list the MIME types, character sets, languages, and encoding schemes that the client can accept in a response from the server:

```
Accept: text/html, text/plain;q=0.5, type/subtype, ...
Accept-Charset: ISO-8859-1, character_set_identifier, ...
Accept-Language: en, language_identifier, ...
Accept-Encoding: compress, gzip, ...
```

The client's preferences with respect to these items can be prioritized by adding "quality" rankings in the form of q=*qvalue*, where *qvalue* can range from 0 to 1 (and defaults to 1). The quality value is a relative measure of the browser's ability to display different types of content. In the example above, the client states that it would do a fine job displaying text/html but would render text/plain with a 50% degradation in quality.

- The entity headers (see Section 3.4) provide information about the message body:

```
Content-Type: mime-type/mime-subtype
Content-Length: xxx
```

They are required for POST and PUT requests, because the server needs to know the MIME type of the content found in the body of the request, as well as the length of the body.
- Cookie contains cookie information that the browser has found in responses previously received from web servers.

```
Cookie: name=value
```

This information needs to be sent back to those same servers in subsequent requests, maintaining state by providing name–value combinations tied to server URLs. Interactions with the State Maintenance module determine the name–value combinations that need to be included.
- Authorization provides authentication credentials to the server in response to an authorization challenge received in an earlier response:

```
Authorization: scheme encoded-userid:password
```

The scheme (usually basic) is followed by a string composed of the user ID and password (separated by a colon), encoded using the Base-64 format.[2]   Interaction with the Authorization module determines what the content of this header should be.

7.4.3   Constructing the request body

This step of the request construction process applies only for methods, such as POST and PUT, that attach a message body to a request. The simplest example is that of including form parameters in the message body when using the POST method. They are URL-encoded to enable proper parsing by the server and the Content-Type header in the request is set to application/www-form-urlencoded.

There are more complex uses for the request body. File uploads can be performed through forms employing the POST method (using multipart MIME messages). It is possible to create or modify web resources using the PUT method (provided the server has been properly configured to support this). With the PUT method, the Content-Type of the request should be set to the MIME type of the content that is being uploaded. With the POST method, the Content-Type of the request should be set to multipart/form-data, while the Content-Type of the individual parts should be set to the MIME types of those parts.

With multipart requests, the Content-Type header requires the "boundary" parameter, which specifies a string of text that separates different parts of the body:

```
Content-Type: multipart/multipart_subtype; boundary="some-random-string"

--some-random-string
Content-Type: type/subtype of part 1
```

```
Content-Transfer-Encoding: encoding scheme for part 1

content of part 1
--some-random-string
Content-Type: type/subtype of part 2
Content-Transfer-Encoding: encoding scheme for part 2

content of part 2
```

Note that each part specifies its own `Content-Type` and `Content-Transfer-Encoding`. This means that one part can be textual, with no encoding, while another part can be binary (e.g., an image), encoded using the Base-64 format, as in the following example:

```
Content-Type: multipart/form-data; boundary="gc0p4Jq0M2Yt08jU534c0p"

--gc0p4Jq0M2Yt08jU534c0p
Content-Type: application/x-www-form-urlencoded

&filename=...&param=value
--gc0p4Jq0M2Yt08jU534c0p
Content-Type: image/gif
Content-Transfer-Encoding: base64

FsZCBoYWQgYSBmYXJtCkUgSST2xkIE1hY0Rvbm
GlzIGZhcm0gaGUgaGFkBFIEkgTwpBbmQgb24ga
IHKRSBJIEUgSSBPCldpdGggYSNvbWUgZHVja3M
BxdWjayBoZXJlLApFjayBxdWFhIHF1YWNrIHF1
XJlLApldmVyeSB3aGYWNrIHRoZVyZSBhIHF1YW
NrIHF1YWNrCEkgTwokUgSSBFI=
```

7.4.4   Transmitting the request

Once the request construction is complete, it is passed to the Networking module. This module must first determine the target of the request. The name of the target server is available in the `Host` header, which was originally constructed by parsing the URL. However, the Networking module must first contact the Configuration module to see whether the browser should use a proxy, which then becomes the immediate target of the request. Once this is done, the Networking module establishes a connection (unless one is already available) and transmits the request.

7.5   Processing HTTP Responses

In the request–response paradigm, the transmission of a request anticipates the receipt of a response. Hence, browsers and other web clients must be prepared to process HTTP responses. This task is the responsibility of the Response Processing module.

As we know, HTTP responses have the following format:

```
HTTP/version-number status-code message
Header-Name-1: value
Header-Name-2: value

[ response body ]
```

An HTTP response message consists of a *status line* (containing the HTTP version, a three-digit *status code*, and a brief human-readable explanation of the status code), a series of *headers* (one per line), a blank line, and finally the *body* of the response. The following is a sample HTTP response message:

```
HTTP/1.1 200 OK
Content-Type: text/html
Content-Length: 1234
   ...

<HTML>
<HEAD>
<TITLE>...</TITLE>
</HEAD>
<BODY BGCOLOR="#ffffff">
<H2 ALIGN="center">...</H2>
   ...
</BODY>
</HTML>
```

Here, we have a *successful* response: the server was able to satisfy the client's request and sent back the requested data. Now the requesting client must decide what to do with this data.

When the Networking module receives a response, it passes it to the Response Processing module. First, this module must examine the *status code* found in the first line of the response (the *status line*). In Chapter 3, we delineated the different classes of status code:

- informational status codes (1xx);
- successful-response status codes (2xx);
- redirection status codes (3xx);
- client-request error status codes (4xx);
- server error status codes (5xx).

Web clients have to take different actions depending on the status code. Since the successful response represents the simplest and most common case, we begin with status code 200.

7.5.1   Processing successful responses

The status code 200 represents a successful response, as illustrated by its associated message, OK. This status code indicates that the web client should process the associated content in accordance with the information in the headers:

- The `Content-Transfer-Encoding` and `Content-Encoding` headers indicate that the response content has been encoded and that, prior to doing anything with this content, it must be *de*-coded:

```
Content-Transfer-Encoding: chunked
Content-Encoding: compress | gzip
```

- `Content-Type` tells the browser the MIME type of the content in the body of the response:

```
Content-Type: mime-type/mime-subtype
```

- `Content-Length` defines the length of the message body in bytes:

```
Content-Length: xxx
```

Although it is optional, when it is provided a client may use it to impart information about the progress of a request (the browser can display the percentage of the total size of the message body received to date).

- `Set-Cookie` is included along with identifying information (name–value pairs) if the server wishes to establish and maintain state with the user's browser:

```
Set-Cookie: name=value; domain=domain.name; path=urlPath; [ secure ]
```

The browser is responsible for sending back this information in any follow-up requests it makes for resources within the same domain and path, using `Cookie` headers. The State Maintenance module stores cookie information found in the response's `Set-Cookie` and `Set-Cookie2` headers (see Chapter 3), so that the browser can later retrieve the information to build the `Cookie` headers. A response can contain multiple `Set-Cookie` headers.

- The following headers influence caching behavior:

```
Cache-Control: private | no-cache | ...
Pragma: no-cache
Expires: Sun, 10 Feb 2008 22:28:31 GMT
```

Depending on their presence or absence (and on the values they contain), the Caching Support module decides whether the content should be cached and, if so, for how long (e.g., for a specified period of time or only for the duration of the current browser session).

Once the content of a successful response has been decoded and cached, the cookie information stored, and the content type determined, then the response content is passed on to the Content Interpretation module. This module uses the content type to delegate processing to an appropriate component. For instance, images (`Content-Type: image/*`) are processed by code devoted to rendering images. HTML content (`Content-Type: text/html`) is passed to the HTML-rendering component, which in turn passes off processing to other components as it encounters embedded objects.

For instance, JavaScript – contained within `<SCRIPT>` block tags or requested via references to URLs in `<SCRIPT src=...>` tags – requires a dedicated processing component. CSS instructions embedded in the page must also be processed. (Style sheet and HTML processing are likely to be closely integrated.) After all this processing is complete, the resulting page is passed to the User Interface module to be displayed in the browser window. (Auxiliary requests for additional resources are discussed in Section 7.8.4.)

There are other status codes, in addition to "200 OK", that fit into the "successful response" category ("2xx") including:

- 201 Created: A new resource was created in response to the request and the Location header contains the URL of the new resource.
- 202 Accepted: The request was accepted but may or may not be processed by the server.
- 204 No Content: No body was included with the response so there is no content to present. This tells the browser not to refresh or update its current presentation as a result of processing this request.
- 205 Reset Content: This is usually a response to a form processed for data entry. It indicates that the server has processed the request, and that the browser should retain the current presentation, but that it should clear all form fields.

Although these status codes are used less often than the popular 200 OK, browsers should be capable of interpreting and processing them correctly.

7.5.2 Processing responses with other status codes

Aside from the successful status code of 200, the most common status codes are the ones associated with redirection (3xx) and client-request errors (4xx).

Client-request errors are usually relatively easy to process: either the browser has somehow provided an invalid request (400 Bad Request) or the URL the browser requested does not exist on the server (404 Not Found). In either of these cases, the browser simply presents a message indicating this state of affairs to the user.

Authorization challenges that are caused by the browser attempting to access protected resources (e.g., 401 Not Authorized) are also classified as "client error" conditions. Servers send responses with the 401 status code when authentication credentials required to access the requested resource are not available, causing the browser to prompt the user for those credentials. Responses with the 403 Forbidden status code are sent when the server will not provide access to the requestor at all. The latter situation may occur when the browser exceeds the server limit for unsuccessful authorization challenges. The methods for dealing with authorization challenges are discussed in Section 7.8.2).

Some web servers may be configured to provide custom HTML presentations when one of these conditions occurs. In those situations, the browser should render the HTML body included in the response instead of a built-in message:

```
HTTP/1.1 404 Not Found
Content-Type: text/html

<HTML>
<HEAD>
<TITLE>Whoops!</TITLE>
</HEAD>
```

```
<BODY bgcolor="#ffffff">
<H3>Look What You've Done!</H3>
You've broken the Internet!
<P>
(Just kidding, you simply requested an invalid address on this site.)
</P>
</BODY>
</HTML>
```

Redirection status codes are also relatively easy to process. They come in two varieties: `301 Moved Permanently` and `302 Moved Temporarily`. For responses associated with each of these status codes, there would be a `Location` header. The browser needs to submit a further request to the URL specified in this header to perform the desired redirection.

Some web servers may be configured to include custom HTML bodies when one of these conditions arises. This is for the benefit of browsers that do not support automatic redirection and default to rendering the body when they either do not recognize or do not support the status code. Browsers that support redirection can ignore this content and simply perform the redirection as specified in the header:

```
HTTP/1.1 301 Moved Permanently
Location: http://www.somewhere-else.com/davepage.html
Content-Type: text/html
<HTML>

<HEAD>
<TITLE>Dave's Not Here, Man!</TITLE>
</HEAD>
<BODY bgcolor="#ffffff">
<H3>Dave's Not Here, Man!</H3>
Dave is no longer at this URL. If you want to visit him,
click <A href="http://www.somewhere-else.com/davepage.html">here</A>.
</BODY>
</HTML>
```

This response should cause the browser to generate the following request:

```
GET http://www.somewhere-else.com/davepage.html HTTP/1.1
Host: www.somewhere-else.com
```

The difference between the 301 and 302 status codes is the notion of "moved permanently" versus "moved temporarily." The 301 status code informs the browser that the data at the requested URL is now *permanently* located at the new URL and thus the browser should always automatically go to the new location. In order to make this happen, browsers need to provide their own persistence mechanism for storing relocation URLs.

301 Forever: A True Tale of Mis-Redirection

A well-known subscription-based web site routinely used a status code of 301 for most of its redirects, including redirecting users to the login page when protected resources were accessed. If users tried to access a page restricted to subscribers, they were redirected to the login page. Once authenticated, users were taken to the original page they were attempting to access.

All was well until one day an ISP implemented a new proxy configuration that cached 301 redirects (which is allowed according to the HTTP specification). Consequently, users who received their Internet access services from that ISP started complaining that they could not log in. When attempting to view a protected page, they would be asked to log in, but instead of being sent to the original page after logging in, they would be redirected back to the login page again. Why was this happening? The redirect that took them from the page they wanted to view to the login page used a 301 status. It was cached by a proxy and subsequent requests for the original target page were automatically redirected back to the login page as a consequence of the cached redirect.

This problem affected only some users (those using this particular ISP) and thus was very difficult to diagnose. It was fixed by changing redirects to the login page so that they used 302 ("moved temporarily") instead of 301 ("moved permanently"). The ISP's proxies, appropriately, did not cache 302 redirects.

The moral is that response status codes must be understood and used with great care. Because of problems like this one, many browsers and proxies do not cache 301 redirects at all. Still, many do, and it is important to make sure that your applications work correctly with them. Using only 302 redirects would sacrifice efficiency because no redirects would be cached. Developers need to differentiate between 301 and 302 status codes and use them appropriately.

7.6   Cookie Coordination

As we have already mentioned many times, HTTP is a stateless protocol. Despite HTTP's stateless nature, it is meaningful (and quite useful) to consider the notion of a session, during which the state of the user's interactions with the server is preserved across multiple requests and responses.

Cookies are a mechanism for maintaining state within the browser across multiple HTTP interactions. The principle is simple: servers can include name–value pairs (cookies) in their responses and clients are responsible for remembering these name–value pairs. Every time the client sends a request back to a server for which it has received a cookie, it must include that cookie in the request (subject to additional conditions such as matching path and security constraints). This helps servers to *identify* specific browser instances, allowing them to associate sets of otherwise disjointed requests with user sessions. These requests, taken together, do not comprise an actual session in the traditional network connectivity sense, but rather a *logical* session.

Servers transmit cookies to browsers via the `Set-Cookie` response header. This header is set to name–value combinations that represent the cookies. In addition, this header contains information about the server domain and the URL path prefix with which the cookie is to be associated. It can also contain the `secure` keyword, which instructs the browser to limit the transmission of accompanied cookies to secure connections (e.g., by using HTTPS, which is no more than HTTP over SSL).

The *domain* parameter of the `Set-Cookie` header can be a fully qualified host name, such as `ecommerce.mysite.com`, or a pattern, such as `.mysite.com`, which corresponds to any fully qualified host name that *tail-matches* this string (e.g., for `domain=.mysite.com`, `ecommerce.mysite.com` and `toys.ecommerce.mysite.com` match, but `mysite.com` does not). The value of this parameter must match the domain that the server sending the cookie belongs to. In other words, `ecommerce.mysite.com` could set a cookie with a domain parameter set to `ecommerce.mysite.com`, or `.mysite.com`, but not to `.yahoo.com`.

The *path* parameter designates the highest level of a URL path for which the cookie applies. For instance, if a server includes the path parameter with a value of `/` in the `Set-Cookie` header, the browser should include the value of that cookie in the follow-up requests for *all* resources on the server. If the path parameter is set to `/cgi-bin/`, then the cookie need only be sent by the browser in requests for URLs with the `/cgi-bin/` prefix.

Browsers send identifying cookies back to appropriate servers by including the `Cookie` header in requests. The content of the `Cookie` header is a set of name–value pairs originally sent by the server, which the browser has stored for future reference:

```
Cookie: key1=value1; key2=value2; ...
```

The advent of the `Set-Cookie2` response header added a new layer of complexity. This header, as we mentioned in Chapter 3, is a slightly modified version of the `Set-Cookie` header, providing additional control over cookie processing. Browsers that support cookies sent via `Set-Cookie2` response headers must indicate this to the server by supplying a `Cookie2` request header that indicates the highest version of the cookie protocol supported by the browser.

```
Cookie2: $Version="1"
```

Details of what browsers must do to provide support for this feature are described in RFC 2965.

7.7 Privacy and P3P

Between the HTML forms you fill out and the cookies used to record your movements, web sites have access to a lot of your personal information. So-called *third-party cookies* are particularly dangerous in the way they can track user behavior. Third-party cookies are set in HTTP responses returning supporting data items served by third-party domains (i.e., any domain different from the one serving the page's primary content). Examples of supporting data items can include images, style sheets, and JavaScript fragments. (We discuss browser–server communication when requesting primary and supporting data items in Section 7.8.4.)

What servers do with collected information may be benign: they may use cookies solely for statistical purposes and never associate tracking data with personally identifiable information. On the other hand, they could tie that information together, associating your name and address with your web browsing behavior, and either sell that information or take advantage of it directly, in a number of legal and not-so-legal ways.

The *Platform for Privacy Preferences (P3P)* is a W3C effort to provide web users with a degree of control over which web sites are allowed to collect and use information about them. P3P is a way for companies and organizations with web presence to declare what they would and would not do with your information. This declaration is in the form of a "privacy policy", which is provided in both human-readable and machine-readable formats. User agents can examine the machine-readable version of the site's policy (or policies) to see whether these policies are in conflict with users' personal privacy preferences (set locally in the browser through the Configuration module). A site's policy is considered "weak" if it does not make any representations about use of collected user information. On the other hand, it is considered "strong" if it guarantees no usage or distribution of collected user-identifiable information.

Based on local settings, the user agent may block cookies or demote them (i.e., make them non-persistent) when they do not meet certain policy requirements (e.g., the policy is either not declared in the response containing the `Set-Cookie` header or is not sufficiently strong). It also may *leash* third-party cookies. Leashing is a mild form of blocking, in which the browser includes third-party cookies only when requesting supporting documents from a third party through the original first party. In other words, the cookie would only be included in requests for supporting data items from a third party if the page referencing those third-party data items comes from the same domain as the original page.

In a superficial sense, P3P relies on the honor system – an organization can say they follow a particular guideline in their privacy policy, while violating that guideline in practice. There is no easy way for a user agent to tell whether a web site is violating its presented policy. Nonetheless, disparities between the human-readable policy and the machine-readable policy – or between the human-readable policy and actual practice – are grounds for litigation, and investigation of web sites that appear to have such disparities between policy and practice has become a lucrative on-line business.

When a user first visits a web site, the browser must find the privacy policy on the site. There are several ways a site can supply browsers with privacy policy information:

- It can include a `<LINK>` tag containing a URL referencing the policy file within the `<HEAD>` portion of the returned HTML document.
- It can include a `P3P` response header that contains either a URL referencing the policy file or (more typically) a *compact policy declaration*.
- It can use the default location in the web site directory tree: `/w3c/p3p.xml`.

Organizations have the ability to provide different policy statements for different areas of their site. To make this work, the web application generating the response needs to supply different values in either the `P3P` response header or the `<LINK>` tag, depending on which privacy policy applies to each area on the web site. To be P3P-compliant, browsers need to interpret this information with each response they receive and take appropriate action (accept, leash, or block cookies).

Internet Explorer 7 provides native support for P3P. An optional extension exists to provide P3P support in the Mozilla family of browsers.

7.8 Complex HTTP Interactions

Now that we have covered the basics of request and response processing, let us move on to situations where the interplay of requests and responses yields more sophisticated functionality.

7.8.1 Caching

When we speak of *caching*, we are referring to persistence of generated and retrieved server resources to improve the performance of the response-generation process.

Server-side caching relieves the server of the responsibility for regenerating a response from scratch in appropriate situations. When resources (such as HTML responses or dynamically generated images) are stored in a server-side cache, the server does not need to go through the process of building these responses from the ground up. This can yield an enormous performance benefit, provided the stored response is still deemed usable (i.e., it has not *expired*). Such caching is application-specific and goes beyond the scope of HTTP specifications. (This is discussed further in Chapter 8.)

Client-side caching is more relevant to our concerns in designing a browser. Client-side caching can relieve the client of the responsibility for requesting a response from the server and can relieve the server of the responsibility for sending a response containing an unchanged resource. This can yield enormous savings in data transmission time. To support client-side caching, web clients must store retrieved resources in a local cache. Subsequent requests for the same resource (i.e., the response generated by a request to the same URL with the same parameters) should examine the cache to see if that resource is available in the cache and is still valid (i.e., has not expired). If it has expired, the client should ask the server to send back a copy of the resource only if it has changed since the last time it was requested.

Support for browser caching requires:

- a component for including appropriate headers in requests to support validation of existing cache entries (part of the Request Generation module);
- a component for examining response headers for directives regarding the caching of the response (part of the Response Generation module);
- a component for saving resources, as well as timestamps indicating their modification dates, in some persistent storage (in memory or on disk). This is carried out by the Caching module, which does the bulk of the decision making regarding how to construct requests to support caching and how to deal with potentially cacheable content found in the response.

Before an HTTP request is generated, the Request Generation module should query the Caching module to determine whether a saved copy of this resource exists and has not yet expired. If there is such a copy, it can be used to satisfy the request, rather than requiring the browser to transmit an explicit request to a server and wait for a response to be transmitted back. Even if the copy has "expired," the request for the resource can be sent with an If-Modified-Since header. If the resource has not changed since the time it was originally retrieved, the server should return the 304 Not Modified response, rather than returning a new copy of the resource.

If there is no copy stored in the local cache, the Request Generation module does not include the conditional header in the request. The content of the response should be considered as a candidate object to be stored in the cache. If there are no directives in the headers indicating that this item should *not* be cached, then the item should be stored in the cache, along with the associated expiration information. The Response Processing module must examine response headers and, if appropriate, pass the content of the response to the Caching module. The Caching module determines whether the content should be stored in the cache.

This HTTP response specifies that the content should not be cached:

```
HTTP/1.1 200 OK
Date: Thu, 10 Apr 2008 12:36:04 GMT
Content-Type: image/jpeg
Content-Length: 34567
    ...
Cache-Control: no-cache
Pragma: no-cache
```

Subsequent requests for the same resource would result in its repeated transmission from the server. This HTTP response has a defined expiration date (the entry expires one day after the original request):

```
HTTP/1.1 200 OK
Date: Thu, 10 Apr 2008 12:36:04 GMT
Content-Type: image/jpeg
Content-Length: 34567
Cache-Control: private
Expires: Fri, 11 Apr 2008 12:36:04 GMT
Last-Modified: Thu, 10 Apr 2008 12:36:04 GMT
```

The next time this particular resource is required, the cached copy may be used, at least until the specified expiration date.

When a copy of a resource is stored in the cache, the Caching module maintains other information (metadata) about the cache entry, namely its expiration date and its last modification date. This information is necessary in optimizing the use of cache entries to satisfy requests.

For example, let's say a full day passes from the point in time at which the resource above was cached. According to the expiration date specified in the Expires header, the cache entry has expired. At that point, the Request Generation module could simply submit a request for a fresh copy of the resource, telling the Caching Support module to dispose of the expired cache entry. However, this may not be necessary. If the content of the resource has not changed since it was retrieved, the stored copy is still usable. So, why not use it?

There are several ways to determine whether a resource has been modified since it was last accessed. Prior to HTTP/1.1, the most economical way to do this was to make use of the HEAD method. HEAD requests return the same results as GET requests, but without the response body. In other words, only the headers are sent in the response. The browser can check the Last-Modified header in the response and compare it to the last modification date associated with the cache entry. If the date specified in the header is not more recent than the date associated with the cache entry, the cache entry is used. Otherwise, the cache entry is deleted and a request is made for a new copy of the requested resource.

HTTP/1.1 provides a simpler and more efficient way to accomplish the same goal. Requests can include the If-Modified-Since header to specify the last modification date found in the cache entry. If the last modification date of the requested resource is *not* more recent than the date specified in the header, the server sends back a response with a status code of 304 Not Modified. This tells the browser that the cache entry can still be used. Otherwise, the server sends a new copy of the requested resource and the browser replaces the cache entry. With this new feature of HTTP/1.1, what used to take (potentially) two sets of HTTP requests and responses now can be accomplished in one.

The browser must choose between HTTP/1.0 and HTTP/1.1 prior to deciding which of the two cache validation mechanisms to use. By default, a browser should attempt to use HTTP/1.1, but if HTTP/1.1 requests are rejected by the server, it should fall back to HTTP/1.0. Cache validation exchanges are summarized in Figure 7.3.

Naturally, the cache cannot continue to grow indefinitely. There are physical limitations on how large it can become. To that end, there must be a mechanism that allows the browser to delete the

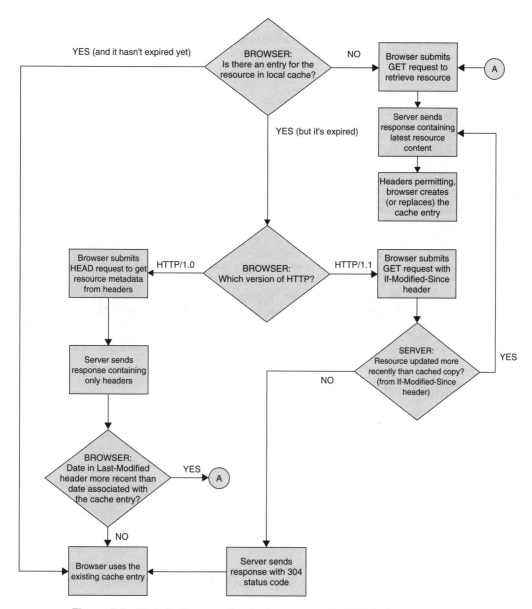

Figure 7.3   Optimized usage of cached resources with HTTP/1.0 and HTTP/1.1.

least useful cache entries when that limitation is reached, so that new entries can be created. The Caching module should search for and delete expired cache entries periodically, but this is not always sufficient. Typically, the *least-recently-used* algorithm is employed to select (as first candidates for deletion) those cache entries that have not been accessed for the longest time. Since most browsers use a combination of in-memory (RAM) cache and disk cache, coordination between these two caches is also needed. The browser may first move cache entries held in memory to disk rather than deleting them. The Configuration module controls maximum cache sizes and other caching behaviors, since these should be user-configurable settings that depend on the amount of RAM and disk space available on the user's computer.

History Repeats

An awkward situation that occurs in even the most sophisticated browsers is the history anomaly. Users can employ the Back button to see pages they already have visited. The browser history mechanism often stores not only a reference to links, but also the presentations associated with those links, regardless of any caching directives (e.g., `Cache-Control: no-cache`) that the server may have included in the original response headers! Browsers should treat the Back button event as a request for new content, making the decision to re-use the presentation only after examining caching directives associated with the original response.

When it comes to pages with form fields, even within the scope of this anomaly, browsers do not act consistently. Older browsers frequently left form fields filled in with whatever values had been entered on a previous visit to the page.

You may have noticed that some sites take precautions against this, explicitly taking action to clear form fields as the form is being submitted. To do this, they employ DHTML/JavaScript tricks, such as copying entered fields into another form with hidden fields, resetting the form with the visible fields, and submitting the hidden form.

7.8.2   Authorization: challenge and response

As with any sophisticated mechanism employed within HTTP requests and responses, the authorization mechanism associated with *basic HTTP authentication* is an ongoing interchange. If we start at the *very* beginning, it would be when a simple HTTP request is made for a resource that just happens to be "protected."

Mechanisms exist on virtually all web servers to "protect" selected resources. Usually this is accomplished through a combination of IP address security (ranges of addresses are explicitly allowed or denied access to the resources) and some form of *Access Control List* (*ACL*) delineating the identifiers and passwords for users that are allowed to access the resources. ACLs are generally associated with *realms*, which is an abstract classification that a webmaster can use to organize secure resources into discrete categories. Webmasters can associate groups of resources with specific realms (e.g., by configuring the web server to associate all files under a specific directory with a particular realm).

In Chapter 6, we discussed the design of services that implement both IP address security and ACL-based security. Here we cover the mechanisms that browsers and other web clients need to employ to interact with these services.

Let's start with a web client request for a protected resource. The request looks like (and is) a perfectly normal HTTP request, because the client may not even realize that this resource is protected:

```
GET /protected/index.html HTTP/1.1
Host: secret.resource.com
```

The web server, however, knows that the resource is protected (and is associated with a particular realm), and sends an appropriate response (the *authorization challenge*):

```
HTTP/1.1 401 Not Authorized
Date: Sun, 10 Feb 2008 22:28:31 GMT
WWW-Authenticate: Basic realm="Top Seekrit"
Content-type: text/html
```

The client must answer the challenge by providing *authentication credentials*.

Before it does anything else, the client should check whether it has provided credentials for this realm to this particular server during the current session. If it has, it does not need to obtain or derive these credentials again. It can simply retransmit the stored credentials in its response. But we're getting ahead of ourselves: let us go back to the *first* request for protected resources.

The web browser would obtain authorization credentials by prompting the user. Normally, this is accomplished by displaying a dialog box asking the user to enter a userid and password for the realm associated with the requested resource. Once the browser has obtained the credentials, it must include them in a resubmitted HTTP request for the same resource:

```
GET /protected/index.html HTTP/1.1
Host: secret.resource.com
Authorization: Basic encoded-userid:password
```

If the credentials do not match the userid and password in the ACL, the server returns another response with a `401 Not Authorized` status code, causing the browser to re-prompt for valid credentials. If the user elects to stop trying (e.g., by choosing the Cancel option), the browser presents an error message or the HTML content (if any) provided with the 401 response. Most servers give up after a fixed number of exchanges with the browser, changing the 401 status code to 403 (Forbidden).

If the credentials *do* match the userid and password in the ACL, the web server transmits the contents of the requested resource. The browser should mark credentials as validated so that it can reuse them for subsequent requests within the same realm.

7.8.3 Using common mechanisms for data persistence

Note that there are many similarities between the mechanisms provided for storing cached content, cookie information, and authorization credentials. They represent a form of *persistence* for similarly structured information that can be reused later. It may be a good idea to build a generalized persistence mechanism into your browser, and to use that mechanism for all of these purposes. This mechanism would need to support both in-memory persistence (saving persisted information only for the duration of the browser session and never permanently) and long-term persistence (where persisted information is placed in some form of permanent data storage so that it outlasts the browser session). Obviously, there *are* differences in using this mechanism for each of these functions, as summarized in Table 7.2.

For content, the decision to store the data in the cache is based on response headers that the Caching module must interpret. The *key* used for addressing a cache entry is the requested URL (including the query string, URL parameters and `POST` content associated with the request). Cache entries should be stored with an expiration date. If one is provided in an `Expires` header, then that should be used.

Table 7.2 Browser Mechanisms for Persistence

	Decision to Store	Access Key	When to Delete	Storage Mechanism
Cached Content	Depends on response headers	URL associated with request	Cache is full Replacing with a newer entry	Memory or disk
Cookies	Depends on user settings	Domain, path, and security parameters	At expiration date At end of session, if no date provided	Disk, for cookies with an expiration date Memory, for cookies that expire at end of session
Authorization Credentials	On validation	Server address and security realm	At end of session	Memory (never store on disk)

If the date provided is in the past, this indicates that the browser should cache the entry only for the duration of the current session and flush it when the session ends. There should be a mechanism in the Configuration module for establishing the maximum cache size. If that size is exceeded (or approached), the Caching module should flush the least recently used entries.

For cookies, the decision to store information found in a response's `Set-Cookie` header is based on two factors: whether or not the user has elected (via the interface to the Configuration module) to accept cookies, and whether or not the user's privacy preferences permit acceptance of cookies from the site sending the response, based on that site's declared privacy policy. The key for addressing a cookie is the domain and path information specified in the `Set-Cookie` header. Cookies also have an expiration date. If none is specified, the cookie information should be stored for the duration of the current browser session and flushed when the session ends. If the date specified is in the past, the cookie should be deleted. The browser can provide limits on the amount of space available to store cookies; it is not required that all cookies be stored indefinitely.

For authorization credentials, there is no decision to be made: this information should always be retained. However, authorization credentials are *always* flushed when the session ends and are *never* kept beyond the end of the browser session. Thus they should be kept in memory and never written to stable storage. The key for addressing authorization credentials is the IP address (or name) of the server and the name of the *realm* with which the server associates the requested resource.

Information that is required only for the duration of the browser session should be kept in memory, while information that must be persisted beyond the end of the session must be recorded using permanent data storage. This can be as simple as a text file (as Netscape did with cookies) or a directory subtree (as most browsers do for cached content), but more sophisticated mechanisms can be used as well.

7.8.4   Requesting supporting data items

Even the simplest web page is not "self-contained." Most pages, at the very least, contain references to images found at other URLs. In order to render graphics, apply externally defined CSS style sheets, or retrieve JavaScript code, a browser must make additional requests for supporting resources.

Step 1: Initial User Request for `"http://www.cs.rutgers.edu/~shklar/"`

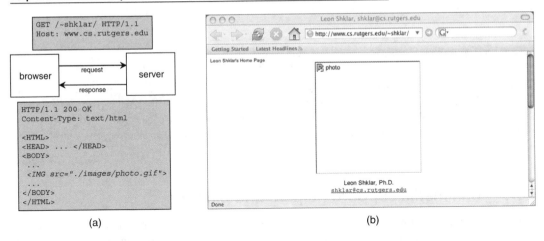

(a)   (b)

Step 2: Secondary Browser Request for `"http://www.cs.rutgers.edu/~shklar/images/photo.gif"`

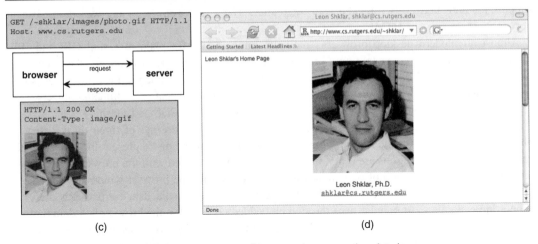

(c)   (d)

Figure 7.4 Browser steps for requesting supporting data items.

In order to issue secondary requests, the browser needs to parse HTML markup and find references to additional resources that are specified on the page. The Content Interpretation module is responsible for performing this analysis. Once it has determined which additional resources are desired, it must tell the Request Generation module to construct and transmit HTTP requests to obtain these resources.

Consider a user who requests `http://www.cs.rutgers.edu/~shklar/`. In Figure 7.4a, the browser sends a GET request to the server, which sends back a response containing a reference to an image. The browser creates a GET request for the image and sends it to the server, which sends back the image. The browser then displays the image to the user (Figure 7.4b).

Remember that caching comes into play when making supplemental requests. A well-organized site is likely to use the same images on many different pages. If the server indicates that these images can be cached and if a reasonable expiration date is specified, the browser may not need to make additional requests for some of these images: it may already have them in the cache!

Keep the Connection Open!

Resources (e.g., images) are often found on the same server as the HTML page itself. Prior to the advent of HTTP/1.1, a browser would repeatedly open and close connections to the same server to get all the resources it needed. Fortunately, HTTP/1.1 defaults to using persistent connections. Unless otherwise specified, the browser keeps the connection to a server open so that supplemental requests can be made without additional overhead.

7.8.5 Multimedia support: helpers and plug-ins

From the beginning, browsers have provided integrated support for many different types of data. Obviously, they rendered HTML (as well as plain text). When it came to graphics, support for GIF and JPEG images was practically ubiquitous with the early browsers (Mosaic and Netscape), and support for animated GIFs followed soon thereafter. The <IMG src=...> tag was defined in the very earliest versions of HTML.

Almost all modern desktop browsers "natively" support HTML, plain text, and GIF and JPEG images. There are exceptions: text-only browsers, such as Lynx, and browsers for handheld devices of limited bandwidth and screen size do not support images. Apart from images, there are other popular types of data presented via the web. The most prominent example is that of multimedia objects (audio and video), but there are also proprietary formats such as Adobe's PDF and Flash.

To enable the presentation of these data objects, browsers can do one of three things: they can provide native support for the format, they can invoke *helper* programs to present the object, or they can support *plug-ins*. Plug-ins are program modules closely integrated with the browser, which enable the rendering or presentation of particular kinds of object within the browser window.

The first option can be overwhelming. There are many multimedia data formats out there, and supporting even the most popular ones through embedded code within the browser is a daunting task. Furthermore, proprietary formats such as Flash and PDF are subject to frequent change, as vendors keep implementing new and more advanced versions of these formats. It seems a far better idea to offload support for these formats onto the people best capable of providing that support: the vendors themselves.

This leaves the choice between *helper* applications and *plug-ins*. Helper application support is relatively simple to implement. As we know, all of these different formats are associated with particular MIME types. Browsers can be configured to defer presentation of objects whose formats they do not support natively to programs that are specifically intended for presentation of such objects. A browser may create a mapping of MIME types to helper applications (and give users control over which applications should be invoked as helpers) or it can take the simpler route of using the operating system's native mapping of MIME types to associated helper applications.

The downside of this approach is that these objects are rendered or presented outside the browser window. A separate application is started to display the object, sometimes obscuring the browser window entirely, but at the very least abruptly shifting the user's focus from the browser to another application. This can be very confusing and detrimental to the user experience.

What's more, this approach is limited to usage with links pointing directly at the object, e.g., `<A href="flashmovies/mymovie.swf">`. In many cases, page designers want to embed an object directly into the current page, rather than forcing users to click on a link so that the object can be presented to them.

The plug-in mechanism is an alternative to helper applications for rendering proprietary formats. This mechanism can make use of the `<EMBED>` and `<OBJECT>` HTML tags to tell the browser to render content contained within the respective elements (between open and close tags) using a specialized plug-in module. The `<EMBED>` tag has been deprecated in favor of `<OBJECT>`. W3C sees `<OBJECT>` as a generalized approach to embedding multimedia objects. The `<EMBED>` tag is still predominant and is used by many DHTML widgets (see Chapter 8) to insert multimedia content into a web page.

Browsers that choose to enable plug-ins also need to support the registration of plug-ins through the browser's Configuration module, to make them available to the rendering mechanism invoked through `<EMBED>` and `<OBJECT>` tags. The browser needs a way to associate MIME types with built-in modules, plug-ins or helper applications. The Configuration module should provide ways for users to define and customize such associations. Omitted mappings should result in selecting the helper application mechanism and deferring the responsibility for choosing a helper application to the operating system.

The Configuration module must also associate MIME types with filename extensions (suffixes). These associations are needed when the browser attempts to present local files or responses that do not contain a properly formatted `Content-Type` header. Such responses violate HTTP protocol requirements, but a browser can use the table of associations to infer a MIME type from the filename suffix found in the URL.

Browsers should be designed not to be *too* clever in this regard: some versions of Internet Explorer tried to infer a response's MIME type by examining the content. If it "looked like" HTML, it would try to present it with a `Content-Type` of `text/html`. But webmasters sometimes want HTML content to be explicitly presented as `text/plain` (e.g., to show what the unprocessed HTML associated with a page fragment actually looks like). With this in mind, browsers should only engage in heuristic practices to infer the MIME type if all else fails (i.e., if there is no `Content-Type` and no known URL filename suffix).

Great Moments in MIME History

The notion of associating MIME types with designated applications dates back to the earliest uses of MIME. Remember that MIME was originally intended for use with e-mail attachments (you may recall that MIME stands for Multimedia Internet Mail Extensions). Unix systems made use of a `.mailcap` file, which was a table associating MIME types with application programs. From the earliest days of the web, browsers made use of this capability. Early browsers on Unix systems often used the `.mailcap` file directly, but as technology advanced and plug-ins got added into the mix, most browsers started to use their own MIME configuration tables.

7.9 Summary

In Chapters 6 and 7, we have examined design considerations for web servers and web browsers. We discussed their structure and operation, as well as the reasoning behind key design decisions. Given the proliferation of different devices, you just might end up having to implement your own server or browser. After all, web servers now run on everything from cable modems and network routers to home media appliances and web browsers run on everything from mobile phones to microwave ovens. Even if you don't go down this road, having a knowledge and understanding of web agents and their operation will give you an edge in building and troubleshooting sophisticated Internet applications.

This list provides a summary of the functionality associated with browser modules:

Table 7.3 Browser modules and their respective responsibilities

MODULE	FUNCTION	RESPONSIBILITIES

User Interface	Providing user interface. Rendering and presenting end results of browser processing.	1. Displays browser window for rendering the content received from **Content Interpretation** module.
		 2. Provides user access to browser functions through menus, shortcut keys, etc.
		 3. Responds to user-initiated events:
		   – selecting/entering URLs
		   – filling in forms
		   – using navigation buttons (e.g., "Back")
		   – viewing page source, resource info, etc.
		   – setting **Configuration** options
		 4. Passes request information to **Request Generation** module.

Request Generation	Constructing HTTP requests.	1. Receives request information from **User Interface** module or **Content Interpretation** module, resolves relative URLs.
		 2. Constructs request line and basic headers:
		   – `Content-Type:` / `Content-Length:`
		     (if body included in request)
		   – `Referer:`
		     (passed from **User Interface** module)
		   – `Host:`
		   – `Date:`
		   – `User-Agent:`
		   – `Accept-*:`
		 3. Asks **Caching** module if a usable cache entry exists:
		   – passes the entry to the **Content Interpretation** module if unexpired,
		   – or adds `If-Modified-Since` header to force the server to only send back newer content.
		 4. Asks **Authorization** module if this is a domain/path for which we have credentials:
		   – if so, adds `Authorization` header to provide credentials to server,
		   – if not, tells **User Interface** module to prompt the user.

		5. Asks **State Maintenance** module if this is a domain/path for which we have cookies? − if so, adds `Cookie` header to transmit cookies to server. 6. Passes fully constructed request to the **Networking** module.

Response Processing	Analyzing, parsing, & processing HTTP responses.	1. Receives responses from **Networking** module.
		2. Checks for 401 status code (Not Authorized):
		  − Asks **Authorization** module for credentials for realm named in `WWW-Authenticate` header:
		    yes - resubmit request with saved credentials,
		    no - prompt user for credentials and resubmit request.
		3. Checks for request redirection status codes (301/302/307):
		  − Resubmit request to URL specified in `Location` header.
		  − If 301, store new location in a lookup table (so browser relocates automatically when URL is visited again).
		4. Checks for `Set-Cookie`/`Set-Cookie2` headers:
		  − Stores cookies using browser's persistence mechanism.
		5. Passes result to **Content Interpretation** module.

Networking	Interfacing with operating system's network services, creating sockets to send requests and receive responses over the network, and maintaining queues of requests and responses.	1. Receives requests from **Request Generation** module and adds them to transmission queue.
		2. Opens connections to transmit queued requests to server (or proxy):
		  − Connection kept open as additional requests are created.
		  − Connection can be closed explicitly with last response.
		3. Waits for responses to queued requests, which are passed to **Response Processing** module.
		4. Queries **Configuration** module to determine proxy configuration and other network options.

Content Interpretation	Content-type specific processing (images, HTML, JavaScript, CSS, XML, applets, plug-ins, etc.)	1. Receives content from **Response Processing** module (in some cases, from the **Caching** module).
		2. Examines encoding headers (if present, decode content)
		  − `Content-Encoding:`
		  − `Content-Transfer-Encoding:`
		3. Passes decoded content to MIME-type-specific component based on `Content-Type` header.
		4. If content embeds other resources, passes URLs to **Request Generation** module to get auxiliary content.
		5. Passes each resource as it is processed to the **User Interface** module.

(continued overleaf)

Table 7.3   (*continued*)

MODULE	FUNCTION	RESPONSIBILITIES
Caching	Creating, keeping track of, and providing access to cached copies of Web resources.	1. **Request Generation** module asks whether appropriate cache entry exists: – If it does, either use it (not expired) or add `If-Modified-Since` header containing last modification date of cached entry to request. 2. **Response Processing** module requests caching of retrieved resource (when appropriate).
State Maintenance	Recording cookie information from response headers, and including cookie information in request headers when appropriate.	1. **Response Processing** module checks for `Set-Cookie` headers and requests recording of cookie information using browser's persistence mechanism. 2. **Request Generation** module examines stored cookie information and includes `Cookie` headers when appropriate.
Authorization	Providing mechanisms for submitting authorization credentials, and keeping track of supplied credentials so that users do not have to keep resubmitting them.	1. **Response Processing** module checks for responses with `"401 Not Authorized"` status code. – If browser has stored credentials for the realm defined in `WWW-Authenticate` header, add `Authorization` header containing credentials and pass to **Request Generation** module. – If not, **User Interface** module prompts user for credentials. (Credentials are stored for duration of browser session *only*, so that resources in same realm do not ask for credentials again.) 2. **Request Processing** module checks to see if any stored credentials match the domain/path of the request URL. If so, add `Authorization` header containing credentials.
Configuration	Providing persistence mechanism for browser settings. Providing interface for users to modify customizable settings.	1. Queried by all modules to determine user-specified preferences.

QUESTIONS AND EXERCISES

1. What main steps does a browser go through to submit an HTTP/1.1 request?

2. What main steps does a browser go through in processing an HTTP/1.1 response?

3. Is it possible for a browser not to support persistent connections and still be compliant with the HTTP/1.1 specification? Why or why not?

4. What is the structure of a POST request? How does it differ from a GET request?

5. What headers have to be present in HTTP/1.0 and HTTP/1.1 requests?

6. Revisit Exercise 4 from Chapter 3, in which a request–response interaction with a web server is emulated using a Telnet client. What aspects of the HTTP protocol make more sense now after examining what browsers have to do in order to submit requests and process responses?

7. What functionality would be lost if browsers did not know how to associate (a) file extensions with MIME types (b) MIME types with helper applications?

8. What is P3P? How does it affect your applications?

9. Consider an HTML document (such as, `http://www.cs.rutgers.edu/~shklar/`). How many connections would an HTTP/1.0 browser need to establish in order to render this document? What determines the number of connections? How about an HTTP/1.1 browser? What determines the number of connections in this case? What would be the answer for your own home page?

10. Describe a simple solution for using the HTTP protocol to upload files to the server through your browser. What about downloading files from the server? Use the POST method for transmitting files to the server and the GET method for transmitting files from the server. Make sure you describe the file transfer in both directions separately and take care of details (e.g., setting the correct MIME type and its implications). Do you need any server-side applications? Why or why not?

11. Take another look at Exercise 8 in Chapter 3. We asked what would happen if the server did not return a redirect when a URL pointing to a directory lacked a trailing slash. If the server were to return immediately an `index.html` file stored in the target directory, would it create a problem for browser operation? Why or why not?

12. Suppose we install a server application at this URL:

```
http://www.vrls.biz/servlet/xml
```

The servlet supports two ways of passing arguments: as a query string (e.g., `http://www.vrls.biz/servlet/xml?name=/test/my.xml`) and as path information (e.g., `http://www.vrls.biz/servlet/xml/test/my.xml`). It is designed to apply a default transformation to the referenced XML file that is located at the server, generate an HTML file, and send it back to the browser.

Suppose that the servlet generates exactly the same HTML in both scenarios, but the browser renders the response as HTML using the query string and as XML using the path information. When we compare HTTP responses (including status codes, headers, and bodies) in these two cases, it turns out that they are identical.

How is this possible? Is there a problem with the servlet? Why does the browser behave differently when the HTTP response is exactly the same? How do we fix this problem?

7.10 Bibliography

Berners-Lee, Tim, Fielding, R. and Frystyk, H., 1996. *RFC 1945: Hypertext Transfer Protocol – HTTP/1.0*.

Cranor, Lorrie Faith, 2002. *Web Privacy with P3P*. Sebastopol, California: O'Reilly Media.

Fielding, Roy, Gettys, J., Mogul, J., *et al*. 1999. *RFC 2616: Hypertext Transfer Protocol – HTTP/1.1*.

Franks, John, Hallam-Baker, P., Hostetler, J., Lawrence, S., *et al*. 1999. *RFC 2617: HTTP Authentication: Basic and Digest Access Authentication*.

Gourley, David and Totty, Brian, 2002. *HTTP: The Definitive Guide*. Sebastopol (CA): O'Reilly & Associates.

Kristol, David and Montulli, L., 2000. *RFC 2965: HTTP State Management Mechanism*.

Marchiori, Massimo and Cranor, L. *et al.*, 2002. *The Platform for Privacy Preferences 1.0 Specification (P3P 1.0)*. World Wide Web Consortium.

7.11   Web Links

Mozilla.org. *Module Owners*. Available at www.mozilla.org/owners.html.

Wikipedia. MIME type Base64. Available at en.wikipedia.org/wiki/Base64.

7.12   Endnotes

1. Mozilla.org *Module Owners*, http://www.mozilla.org/owners.html.
2. http://en.wikipedia.org/wiki/Base64

Active Browser Pages: From JavaScript to AJAX

IN THIS CHAPTER

- JavaScript
- Cascading Style Sheets (CSS)
- Dynamic HTML (DHTML)
- AJAX
- Case study: Five-star-rating widget

OBJECTIVES

- Review the evolution of dynamic page presentation techniques.
- Consider the limited options available for dynamic manipulation of page content before the advent of JavaScript.
- Illustrate how JavaScript is used to exercise programmatic control over web page presentation.
- Present an overview of CSS, with an emphasis on using it to facilitate dynamic presentation.
- Discuss DHTML, showing how it can be used to modify page content dynamically and to perform client-side validation.
- Introduce AJAX and discuss how it enhances the end-user experience.
- Show how remote content injection and validation are accomplished using AJAX-based techniques.
- Demonstrate the advantages of toolkits for enhancing productivity and eliminating cross-browser incompatibilities.
- Use a case study to illustrate the concepts.

Markup languages, while very powerful, have their limitations. They provide formatting instructions for the static rendering of content. HTML, especially in combination with CSS, makes it possible to control page layout, combine text with graphics, and support minimal interactive capabilities through links and forms. HTTP servers transmit responses whose bodies contain HTML documents, and browsers receive these responses and render the documents.

The problem is that the presentation is *static*: HTML does not provide a mechanism for modifying the page once it is rendered. The rendered page just stays there until the next request. Even a simple operation, such as the validation of a form entry, requires server-side processing, which means an extra connection to the server.

Static presentation is fine for fixed documents, but for the web it poses an artificial limitation. Why can't the layout of a page change over time, based on events triggered either by user interaction or simply by the passage of time? For that matter, why shouldn't the content of a page change similarly, without requiring the entire page to be reloaded and re-rendered?

The focus of this chapter is dynamic interactivity in presenting web pages. We start with history, discussing the "old-school" approaches for producing interactivity, and move on to programmatic interactivity through JavaScript, advances brought about by *CSS* and *Dynamic HTML (DHTML)*, and finally cover the latest approaches to dynamic interactivity, specifically *AJAX*.

This chapter is not an in-depth tutorial on JavaScript, CSS, DHTML, or AJAX. Our goal is to familiarize you with the concepts behind these technologies and how they support dynamic client-side interactivity in web applications. The chapter assumes a working knowledge of JavaScript. Readers who are not familiar with it should examine the JavaScript references and tutorials listed in Section 8.9 before proceeding further.

Active Browser Pages

We have coined the name "Active Browser Pages" to reflect the nature of the interactive client-side technologies discussed in this chapter. The techniques are reminiscent of server-side approaches, which allow content to be generated and presented dynamically based on information in user requests. This flexibility in determining content need not stop with the response. "Active Browser Pages" is our name for the collection of client-side methods that enable interactive presentation of content in the browser following the initial rendering step.

Making the Case

In previous chapters of this book, we have used HTML 4.01 notation for tags. This notation decrees that tag names should appear in upper case and attribute names should appear in lower case. Most modern tools that generate HTML use XHTML notation, where both tag and attribute names appear in lower case. While this is technically a violation of HTML 4.01, it is now common practice and the upcoming HTML 5 specification acknowledges this and makes it official. You will note that our examples from this point forward use the HTML 5/XHTML notation. We continue to use HTML 4.01 notation in discussions of past practices.

8.1   Pre-History

Since the early days of the web, there have been coarse approaches to changing page content and layout after the initial rendering. The "meta-refresh" technique uses the HTML <META> tag (see Section 4.2.2) to simulate the presence of an HTTP Refresh header that, after a specified timeout period, either reloads the page from its current URL (effectively refreshing it with new content) or redirects the browser to a new page.

```
<META http-equiv="Refresh" content="5;url=http://site.com/refreshme.cgi">
```

The directive above, when included in the <HEAD> portion of an HTML document, directs the browser to the specified URL after five seconds. Assuming this document was generated by a request to the URL http://site.com/refreshme.cgi, it would effectively reload the page generated from that URL every five seconds. This is a rather crude approach to dynamic content presentation. Take, for example, a static HTML page containing a *Server Side Includes* (SSI) call to a CGI script to produce dynamic content (e.g., the current temperature in a particular locale). In order to keep the temperature fragment of the page up to date, the entire page needs to be refreshed.

A more direct way to achieve the same result would be to have the web application that produces this page insert an HTTP Refresh header directly into the response:

```
Content-Type: text/html
Refresh: 5; url=http://site.com/refreshme.cgi
```

This option was not available with static content, even for pages that contained SSI instructions. It required fine-grained control over HTTP headers, which could be accomplished only through web application code. For flexibility, control over page refresh parameters had to be deferred to HTML using the meta-refresh technique.

8.2   JavaScript

The primitive meta-refresh technique described in the previous section can only take us so far. It is not a replacement for programmable behavior. More was needed to provide true programmatic functionality within the browser.

Over time, the HTML specification evolved to support *event handlers* – custom code that executes when a browser event occurs (e.g., when a user clicks on a link, when the mouse pointer hovers over an element, or when data is entered into a form field). Implementing these handlers required a programming language that would execute in the browser and interface with the page's document object model. The language that fulfilled this role was *JavaScript*.

JavaScript was developed initially for Netscape Navigator but is now supported by most desktop browsers, including Microsoft's Internet Explorer. Despite being perceived as a simple scripting language, it is actually a rather sophisticated object-oriented programming language. Its name was coined in the flurry of excitement surrounding Sun's introduction of Java. Although JavaScript bears some remote structural resemblance to Java, the languages are related in name only.

Unfortunately, many examples of JavaScript code you are likely to find on the web do not lend much credence to claims of its sophistication. The presence of disjointed, inconsistently formatted chunks of JavaScript scattered throughout HTML documents frequently makes pages completely unreadable (and impossible to maintain). This kind of jumbled JavaScript code is much too common even though the language is sophisticated enough to facilitate best practices in coding. We will step through some simple examples of JavaScript code with the goal of demonstrating how structured code can take advantage of JavaScript's object-oriented capabilities.

ECMAScript

Despite its origins as a proprietary language developed by Netscape for its browser (and, later, an equally proprietary variation by Microsoft for Internet Explorer), there is now an official specification (ECMA-262, from the European Computer Manufacturers Association) for the browser programming language, which is now officially called ECMAScript. There are some differences between the ECMAScript standard and the implementations of JavaScript found in web browsers, which is one reason why JavaScript is the name still used by most people involved in web development.

Browsers process JavaScript statements embedded in HTML documents, as they interpret the documents. This embedding can take one of two forms. Inline JavaScript code can be included in the page, in a block delimited by `<script>` and `</script>` tags:

```
<script type="text/javascript">
function populateElement(elementId, value) {
  document.getElementById(elementId).innerHTML = value;
}
</script>
```

JavaScript can be stored in a separate file and referenced through a `<script>` tag with the `src` attribute set to the URL denoting the location of the code:

```
<script type="text/javascript" src="http://site.com/script.js"></script>
```

(Although `application/javascript` is the designated Internet media type for JavaScript code, `text/javascript` is still the more commonly used value for the `type` parameter in the `<script>` tag, despite its being deprecated.)

Now, after years of consternation and anguish, there is some common ground, in the basic set of DOM-related JavaScript methods and properties that can be employed across most browsers:

- `getElementById` is perhaps the most commonly used method in modern JavaScript. Instead of sifting through collections of page elements to find the one you are looking for, you supply the value of its `id` attribute. Naturally, this requires that the page elements you plan to access and manipulate are assigned unique `id` values.

```
var node = document.getElementById("someElementId");
```

- The `innerHTML` property was first defined in Internet Explorer and was not supported for a long time in other browsers. Now it is supported much more widely. It provides a means of retrieving (or replacing) the content inside an element (i.e., between its opening and closing tags). If your needs are simple (e.g., if you are using a `<div>` as a container whose content is replaced or cleared programmatically), then `innerHTML` is a good choice.

```
node.innerHTML = "new text";
```

- Every node in the HTML DOM (except the document root) has the `parentNode` property.

```
var parent = node.parentNode;
```

- The `childNodes` property is an array containing all of a node's children (empty if it is a leaf node). In this example, the `parent.childNodes` property refers to the current node and all of its "siblings."

```
var siblings = parent.childNodes;
```

- The `style` property gives some degree of uniformity in referencing the "look" of a node. For a long time, the CSS style attributes of a page element were accessed inconsistently by different browsers. Cross-browser hacks were needed to retrieve or set style attributes such as background color, font, positions, and margins.

```
node.style.backgroundColor = "#ffffcc";
```

- The `getElementsByTagName` method returns an array of all the elements in a document with a particular tag name. In this example, all links in the document (those with tag `<a>`) are assigned to an array.

```
var allLinks = document.getElementsByTagName("a");
```

While it is also possible to retrieve links by referencing `document.links`, this generic method provides the ability to aggregate any elements with the same tag name, not just the ones found in pre-defined arrays. Similarly, the `document.getElementsByClassName` method makes it possible to retrieve all the elements assigned a particular CSS class name. These methods are useful if you want to change the status (e.g., visibility) of an entire group of elements on a page.

> **Toolkits**
>
> There are a number of JavaScript toolkits available to ease the pain of cross-browser incompatibilities by providing helper methods that work across all browsers supported by the toolkit or by extending JavaScript to provide common DOM-based methods, which are not supported directly by many browsers. We return to these toolkits and their benefits throughout this chapter.

8.2.2   Client-side form validation

One of the most common uses of JavaScript is to perform client-side validation of form entries. Without client-side logic to validate form field contents, it would be necessary to perform all validation on the server, requiring a request–response "roundtrip". For each validation, it would be necessary to:

- send a request to the server;
- allow the server-side application to perform validation;
- either continue processing based on the validated data in the submitted form or tell the browser to redisplay the original form (hopefully with detailed error messages) so that the user could re-enter fields whose content was deemed invalid.

Providing feedback for each form field as it is entered is ideal, but if validation must be performed on the server this becomes impractical. Performing form validation on the client side, using JavaScript, makes the user experience more immediately interactive, by obviating the need for communication with the server to perform validation and by making "field-by-field" validation more viable.

We begin with "classic" validation using JavaScript. Note that this is for historical purposes only. Better JavaScript validation techniques are supported today and we discuss them in Section 8.4.4.

In the past, validation was accomplished most frequently through the `<form>` tag's `onsubmit` event handler, which is executed prior to the submission of the form. If the code returned by the event handler evaluates to the Boolean value `true`, the HTML form has passed validation and an HTTP request is generated and submitted to the server. Otherwise, the code evaluates to `false` and no submission takes place. It is considered good practice for event handlers to display a JavaScript alert box describing validation errors.

Figure 8.1 provides a simple example of client-side form validation using JavaScript. The form contains two fields and the `<form>` tag calls for the execution of a JavaScript function, `validate()`, when the form is submitted. This function examines the values entered in the two form fields and determines whether they are valid. If either value is unacceptable, an appropriate error message is appended to the string variable `errors`. If the length of this variable is greater than zero after all the fields in the form have been checked, a JavaScript alert box is displayed containing the error messages, and the function returns `false`. Otherwise, the function returns `true`, causing the form to be submitted to the server.

```
<html>
<head>
<script type="text/javascript">
function validate(form) {
    var errors = "";
    if (form.firstname.value.length < 3) {
        errors += "\nFirst name must be at least 3 characters long.";
    }
    if (form.lastname.value.length < 2) {
        errors += "\nLast name must be at least 2 characters long.";
    }
    if (errors.length > 0) {
        alert("Please correct the following errors:" + errors);
        return false;
    }
    else {
        return true;
    }
}
</script>
</head>
<body bgcolor="#ffffff">
<form name="form1" method="post" action="..."
    onsubmit="return validate(this)">
<table cellpadding="5" border="0">
  <tr>
    <td align="right">First Name:</td>
    <td align="left">
      <input type="text" name="firstname">
    </td>
  </tr>
  <tr>
    <td align="right">Last Name:</td>
    <td align="left">
      <input type="text" name="lastname">
    </td>
  </tr>
  <tr>
    <td colspan="2" align="center">
      <input type="submit" value="Submit">
    </td>
  </tr>
</table>
</form>
</body>
</html>
```

Figure 8.1 Example of client-side form validation using JavaScript. (*continued overleaf*)

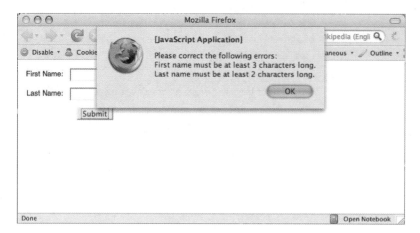

Figure 8.1   *(continued)*

With this approach, the validation process is initiated with the submission of the form. As we mentioned previously, it is possible to perform validation on a per-field basis, using the `onchange` or `onblur` JavaScript event handlers in the `<input>` tags associated with individual form fields. (These handlers are invoked when a field's value changes or when the focus of the browser moves away from that field.) The displaying of alert boxes as data is entered can become overwhelming and confusing to users. Depending on the application, the acceptability of entered field values may be dependent on other fields, in which case the "holistic" approach of validating on submission is preferable.

Naturally, validations that depend upon server-side calculations and comparisons still require communication with the server. This includes validations that require knowledge of stored authorization credentials and validations that require confirmation of user-supplied credit card information.

In practice, distinctions between the kinds of validation that can and cannot occur on the client are not so cut-and-dried. For example, even though confirmation of credit card information requires server-side information, it is possible to catch some errors (for example, credit card numbers that do not pass mod-10 checksum validation) on the client side. This preemptive validation weeds out simple typing errors before wasteful requests are sent to the server and, ultimately, to the credit-card validation service.

AJAX Validation

In the age of AJAX, the distinction between client-side and server-side validation becomes even more blurred. For example, it would be impractical for an on-line community web site to check requested user names for uniqueness using client-side validation, as that would require sending the entire list of current user names to the browser. AJAX requests can give the appearance of client-side validation by verifying whether or not a name exists in the database and flashing an error message without having to reload the page.

```
<a href="#"
   onmouseover="document.images['picture1'].src = 'images/pic1b.jpg';"
   onmouseout="document.images['picture1'].src = 'images/pic1a.jpg';">
   <img name="picture1" src="images/pic1a.jpg">
</a>
```

Figure 8.2 Simple implementation of `onmouseover` behavior.

8.2.3   Hovering behaviors: image rollover

JavaScript provides mechanisms to perform actions when the mouse pointer is hovering over a region specified as a hyperlink (e.g., presenting different images depending on the position of the mouse pointer). The `onmouseover` and `onmouseout` attributes in the HTML anchor tag (`<a>`) serve to define the respective handlers.

The *image rollover* technique, shown in Figure 8.2, is a simple illustration of `onmouseover` behavior. The `<img>` tag is identified through its `name` attribute, making it possible to reference the image directly, using the `document.images` object associated with the page. The `src` attribute of the `<img>` tag is set to the relative URL of the default image (`images/pic1a.jpg`). When the mouse pointer hovers over the image (`onmouseover`), JavaScript code is invoked to change the image's location (referenced by its `src` attribute) to a different URL, causing a different image (`images/pic1b.jpg`) to be displayed. Similar code is invoked when the mouse pointer leaves the area (`onmouseout`) to redisplay the original image.

Camel Case

Note that we are not using the expected "camel case" for the handler names. Although most browsers may accept the notations `onMouseOver` and `onMouseOut`, the name JavaScript expects for these handlers is strictly lowercase. This becomes important when we specify event handlers in inline JavaScript, rather than injecting handler code into HTML tags.

Let us consider incremental improvements to this basic example of image rollover functionality:

1. The `document.getElementById` method is now the more commonly used approach for selecting page elements, as it is least susceptible to cross-browser incompatibilities. This requires a change to the `<img>` tag to set the `id` attribute:

```
<a href="#"
   onmouseover="document.getElementById('picture1').src =
                                        'images/pic1b.jpg';"
   onmouseout="document.getElementById('picture1').src =
                                        'images/pic1a.jpg';">
   <img id="picture1" src="images/pic1a.jpg">
</a>
```

2. Rather than including JavaScript assignment statements in handler definitions within HTML tags, functions should be defined in the HEAD section of the document (either inline or via an externally referenced JavaScript source file). This way, the handler code embedded in the HTML tags is limited to a simple function call:

```
<html>
<head>
<script type="text/javascript">
var pix = [ "images/pic1a.jpg" , "images/pic1b.jpg" ];
function imageSwitch(elementId, mode) {
     document.getElementById(elementId).src = pix[mode];
     return true;
}
</script>
</head>
<body>
<a href="#"
   onmouseover="imageSwitch('picture1', 1)"
   onmouseout="imageSwitch('picture1', 0)">
   <img id="picture1" src="images/pic1a.jpg">
</a>
</body>
</html>
```

3. Instead of inserting handler code into HTML tags, the preferred approach is to tie event handlers with page elements declaratively:

```
<html>
<head>
<script type="text/javascript">
var pix = [ "images/pic1a.jpg" , "images/pic1b.jpg" ];
function imageSwitch(elementId, mode) {
    document.getElementById(elementId).src = pix[mode];
    return true;
}
</script>
</head>
<body>
<a href="#" id="link1">
   <img id="picture1" src="images/pic1.jpg">
</a>
<script type="text/javascript">
document.getElementById("link1").onmouseover =
       imageSwitch('picture1', 1);
document.getElementById("link1").onmouseout  =
       imageSwitch('picture1', 0);
</script>
</body>
</html>
```

Strictly Speaking: XHTML-Compliant Inline JavaScript

To make inline JavaScript blocks compliant with the XHTML specification, they must be marked as CDATA blocks, beginning with `<![CDATA[` and ending with `]]>`. To keep the CDATA start and end delimiters from being misconstrued as invalid JavaScript code by JavaScript interpreters, the lines containing those delimiters should begin with the JavaScript line comment notation, `//`.

```
<script type=text/javascript>
//<![CDATA[
  ...
//]]>
</script>
```

Although it has long been common practice to surround inline JavaScript blocks with HTML comment delimiters (`<!--` and `-->`), this is an archaic practice that is no longer required. It was necessary when the possibility existed that a browser might not understand the `<script>` tag and might try to render an inline JavaScript block as HTML. All modern browsers either support JavaScript or know to ignore content within `<script>` blocks.

8.2.4 JavaScript Object Notation

Before we wrap up our initial discussion of JavaScript, it is worthwhile to mention *JavaScript Object Notation (JSON)*. It is a native part of JavaScript that allows declaration of (and access to) complex variable content, using a simple lightweight notation (see Figure 8.3).

Brackets are used to wrap array constructs, while braces surround maps (whose key–value pairs are denoted as `key:value`). In the example, the JavaScript variable `complexThing` contains a variety of elements ranging from strings and a simple array of numbers to an array of maps. These elements are directly addressable with dotted or bracketed notation (Figure 8.4).

JSON is a common format for data transmitted from servers to browsers in AJAX responses. Although many presume that AJAX necessarily involves responses that are formatted as XML, XML is too complicated and heavyweight for many applications. Using JSON means that the data is already in a format that JavaScript understands natively. (Note the way the block of JSON is directly assigned

```
var complexThing = {
    id : "12345",
    name : "John Doe" ,
    simpleArray : [ 1, 2, 3 ],
    complexArrayOfAttributeLists : [
      { attributeX : "abc" ,    attributeY : "123" , attributeZ : "n/a" },
      { attributeX : "def" ,    attributeY : "45" ,  attributeZ : "junk" },
      { attributeX : "lmnop" ,  attributeY : "0" ,   attributeZ : "X" }
    ],
    countryCode : "US"
};
```

Figure 8.3 A complex JavaScript object defined using JSON.

```
alert(complexThing.id);        // displays the string "12345"
alert(complexThing["name"]);   // displays the string "John Doe"
var total = 0;
for (i = 0; i < complexThing.simpleArray.length; i++) {
    total += complexThing.simpleArray[i];
}
alert(total);                  //  displays 6 (calculated as 1 + 2 + 3)
alert(complexThing.complexArrayOfAttributeLists[1].attributeZ);
    // displays "junk" - the value of attributeZ from the second attribute
    // list in the complex array
```

Figure 8.4   Accessing attributes of the JavaScript object defined in Figure 8.3.

to the variable `complexThing` in Figure 8.3.) JSON bears a very close resemblance to *Yet Another Markup Language (YAML)*, which is used for configuration files in Ruby on Rails.

We come back to JSON in our discussions of DHTML toolkits and AJAX.

8.2.5   Summary

As we intimated, there are differences between JavaScript implementations used by different browsers, which range in effect from subtle to significant. In some extreme cases, there are major differences between the JavaScript implementations used by different versions of the same browser!

The result is code that exhibits serious cross-browser compatibility issues. It is possible to write JavaScript code that works consistently across different browsers, but it is not easy. Even when it comes to seemingly trivial functionality, there are enough quirks to make cross-browser JavaScript development a tedious trial-and-error process.

The best advice is to learn from those who have been through the mill of writing code that works consistently across most (if not all) browsers. It is very useful to study toolkits that do the tricky and complex tasks associated with reusable JavaScript components. In the rest of this chapter, as we demonstrate the capabilities associated with DHTML and AJAX, we also show the virtue in making use of these generic toolkits, to avoid reinventing the wheel over and over again.

JavaScript has acquired a bad reputation over the years as a poorly defined language that yields sloppy code that is very difficult to maintain. This reputation was borne out by the majority of examples of JavaScript code you were likely to find on the web. In the first edition of this book, we made the following statement about using JavaScript in web applications:

> *JavaScript is not the right language for implementing sophisticated logic. Apart from making your pages entirely unreadable, ... [it] is a little bit like an organic poison – it would kill you in large doses but may be an invaluable cure if you use it just right.*

To make this same statement today would be naïve. As we shall see, JavaScript has been "rehabilitated." It is the programming language associated with almost all AJAX code, making it the centerpiece of most Web 2.0 applications. When used properly, developers can avoid most of the negative characteristics commonly associated with the language in practice. From one perspective, JavaScript is a loosely defined language that gives developers more than enough rope to hang themselves. At the same time, it is a sophisticated object-oriented programming language, which makes it possible to produce well-organized, reusable code that runs correctly in the vast majority of web browsers.

8.3 Cascading Style Sheets

Cascading Style Sheets (CSS) is a mechanism for controlling style (e.g. fonts, colors, and spacing) in HTML. A style sheet is made up of rules that determine how elements should be rendered. Rules can apply to an individual element that has a unique `id` attribute, a group of elements that share the same `class` attribute, or elements represented by the same HTML tag. The word "cascading" is used because multiple rules may apply to the same sets and subsets of page elements, with those applied to the more specific subsets taking precedence. We provide examples of how this works later in this section.

There are numerous ways of associating style sheets with HTML documents. The simplest is to use inline CSS directives, placed within a `<style>` block in the `<head>` section of an HTML document:

```
<style type="text/css">
  P {
    display: block;
    font-family: times new roman;
    font-size: 11pt;
  }

  P.sidebar {
    font-size: smaller;
    font-family: arial;
  }
</style>
```

An alternative is to reference external files that contain CSS style sheet directives by using the `@import` directive inside a `<style>` block to specify the URL:

```
<style type="text/css">
  @import url("../css/main.css");
  @import url("../css/print.css") print;
</style>
```

The more proper approach to referencing external CSS style sheets is to use a `<link>` tag in the `<head>` section of the document:

```
<link rel="stylesheet" type="text/css" href="../css/main.css" />
<link rel="stylesheet" type="text/css" href="../css/print.css"
      media="print" />
```

The major benefit of maintaining style sheets separately from HTML documents is that this makes them available for reuse across multiple pages. Another benefit is that different style sheets can be associated with different modes of presentation (e.g., screen and print). In the examples above, two style sheets are imported, with one used for screen presentation (the default) and the other for print presentation. For additional reusability, an `@import` directive can be included in a style sheet externally referenced by a `<link>` tag.

8.3.1   Format of CSS rules

CSS rules follow the following format:

```
selector, ... {
   property1: value1;
   property2: value2;
   compositeProperty: property1Value property2Value ... ;
}
```

A selector within a rule can refer either to all elements in the document that use a particular HTML tag, to a particular named *class* of HTML element (e.g., `.authorName`), or to a single HTML element referenced by its *id*:

```
/* Applies to all <p> tags unless more specific rules override */
p {
  font-family: arial;
  font-size: 12pt;
}
/* Applies to all elements whose class is "authorName"
   e.g., <p class="authorName">written by Rich Rosen</p> */
.authorName {
  font-size: 11pt;
  font-family: verdana;
  color: blue;
}
/* Applies to the element whose id is "navbar"
   e.g., <div id="navbar"> ... </div> */
#navbar {
  font-size: 9pt;
  color: white;
  background-color: black;
}
```

A rule can have multiple selectors, separated by commas (e.g., a rule that applies to both `<pre>` elements and `<blockquote>` elements):

```
pre, blockquote {
  font-family: courier new;
  font-size: 10pt;
}
```

Rules contain declarations that specify properties and their values. A property can have a value that is a comma-separated list. The list represents alternatives that the browser should consider in order of preference:

```
.authorName {
   font-family: verdana, tahoma, georgia;
}
```

A composite property lists values for several subordinate properties in the same statement. Examples of this shorthand notation can be used for properties associated with padding (specifying the top, right, bottom and left padding for an element), borders (specifying the width, style, and color for a particular border), and fonts (specifying the style, variant, weight, size, and family for a font). The subordinate properties need to be listed in a specific order, separated by *spaces* and delimited with quotes if necessary (e.g., when individual values contain spaces):

```
.authorName {
   font: italic small-caps bold 11pt verdana, tahoma, "courier new";
}
```

Some properties associated with numeric values (such as font size) can be relative rather than absolute. For example, a rule for a particular class of element might specify a larger or smaller font than the one displayed in normal paragraphs. This can be done with a percentage value, a specification in em units (the size of the letter "m" in a font), or simply by providing an adjective that describes the relative size desired (e.g., "larger" or "smaller"):

```
p {
   font-family: arial;
   font-size: 12pt;
}
blockquote {
   font-family: courier new;
   font-size: 11pt;
}
p.emphasize, blockquote.bigger {
   font-size: 120%;
}
p#tiny {
   font-size: .5em;
}
```

As you may have surmised from the last example, this is where the "cascading" aspect of CSS comes into play. "Basic" rules apply to broad classifications of HTML elements, while more narrow rules are applicable to a specific element or set of elements. Paragraphs (<p> elements) in documents associated with the above style sheet fragment are in 12 point Arial. However, there is another more specific rule, which dictates that the font in all paragraphs given a class name of emphasize (as well as block quotes with the class name bigger) should be 20% larger. Similarly, there is a rule dictating that the paragraph with an ID attribute of tiny should have a much smaller font size. Notice that selectors that begin with a period refer to classes, and selectors that begin with # refer to unique element IDs.

The scoping of specific rules can get even more complex. Here, the specification p.bright a is a single selector, referring to <a> tags found within <p> elements of class bright:

```
p.bright a {
  background-color: #ffffee;
}
```

There is one more aspect to the "cascading" nature of CSS. Multiple style sheets can be associated with a document and they can have conflicting directives. Once again, rule specificity determines the resolution of the conflict. However, a rule can be specified as being "important" (meaning it should carry more weight in the conflict resolution process) by including the string !important in its declaration:

```
blockquote.quotation {
  background-color: #cccccc !important;
  border: 1px solid black !important;
}
```

Always Wear Your ID: Clearing up Confusion about CSS IDs and Classes

As we already mentioned, selectors that begin with a period refer to classes and selectors that begin with # refer to unique element IDs:

```
<style type="text/css">
    .group1 {
       font-family: funky font, comic sans ms, sans-serif;
    }
    #myUniqueElement {
       color: red; font-style: italic;
    }
</style>
```

The notion of a CSS class is useful to specify behavior for groups of elements that should behave similarly. Multiple elements can have the same class. An element's class is specified by including a class attribute in its opening tag:

```
<p class="group1">A paragraph of class group1.</p>
<p class="group1">Another paragraph of class group1.</p>
```

Notice that while the CSS rule defining a class begins with a period, class references in elements associated with the class do not.

An ID is something intended to be associated with one element only. Having more than one page element with the same ID should cause a validation error. An element's ID is specified by including an id attribute in its opening tag:

```
<p id="myUniqueElement">Some text.</p>
```

The id attribute is now preferable to the name attribute as a mechanism for uniquely identifying and accessing one particular element, and the JavaScript method document.getElementById() is now almost universally supported in modern browsers. Notice that while the CSS rule for an ID begins with a #, the id reference in the element does not.

It should be noted that IDs double as page anchors! Visiting this page with a URL that looks something like http://site.com/myPage.html#myUniqueElement causes the browser to position itself at this element within the page. This means there is no longer a need for <a name=anchor> tags that serve solely as page anchors.

Finally, a page element can have both an ID and a CSS class (or classes) associated with it:

```
<p id="myUniqueElement" class="group3">Some text.</p>
```

Since an ID is more specific than a class (it refers to only one element), the CSS specifications associated with the ID take precedence.

An element can be associated with more than one class, simply by appending more class names to the end of the class attribute, delimited by spaces:

```
<p class="group1 anotherGroup mySpecialClass"> ... </p>
```

What if the intent is to have a certain style apply to some fragment of the document that is not defined by HTML tag boundaries? The <span> and <div> elements were introduced for this express purpose: associating presentation styles with arbitrarily delimited portions of HTML documents. As we mentioned in Chapter 4, <span> is an inline element, used in a manner similar to <strong> and <em>, while <div> is a block element that may include paragraphs, tables, and, recursively, other <div> elements.

What if you want just one word to be displayed in green, bold, and italic but there's no greenBoldItalic class? Well, there are the old deprecated tags but, naturally, we would rather avoid using them: <FONT color="green">text</FONT>

It is much better to use <span> and <div> elements, which support inline CSS directives through the style attribute:

```
<span style="color: green;
             font-weight: bold;
             font-style: italic">text</span>
```

You can enclose the word you want to highlight within open and close tags of the <span> element.

The HTML specification now dictates that all tags should have a style attribute. However, using this attribute with elements other than <span> and <div> conflicts with the goal of separating out style directives from the document, to an even greater degree than embedding inline CSS in a <style> block. The style attribute within HTML elements should be used with utmost discretion, only when absolutely needed.

8.3.2 Hovering behaviors: the `a:hover` pseudo-class

A simple application of CSS for dynamic interactivity is the use of the `a:hover` *pseudo-class* to define rules for presenting links in their "normal" state and in a state where the mouse pointer is hovering over them. The following code block illustrates a common technique used on many web sites today:

```
<style type="text/css">
  a {
    color: #009900;
    text-decoration: none;
  }
  a:hover {
    background-color: #ffff99;
    color: #006600;
    text-decoration: underline;
  }
</style>
```

Hyperlinks are displayed as a shade of green (#009900) with no underlining. When the mouse pointer hovers over a link, it is underlined, its text color switches to a darker green (#006600), and its background color is transformed to a shade of pale yellow (#ffff99). All of this draws attention to the link as the mouse pointer hovers over it.

The `a:hover` pseudo-class can also be used to implement the kind of *image rollovers* we created in Section 8.2.3 with JavaScript. The text associated with a link could be defined not as an image tag (as in `<a href=...><img src=... /></a>`), but as an area with a specified background image defined via CSS rules. The width and height of the area can be specified in the CSS directive (along with `display: block`). One background image could be defined for the "normal" state, and another for the "rollover" state (see Figure 8.5).

Hover and Shift

One variation on the technique illustrated in Figure 8.5 employs a single background image that contains both the normal state image and the hover state image next to each other. Naturally, this image would be twice the size of the area associated with the link, so only half the image would be displayed initially. The CSS declaration for the `a:hover` state would specify, not a different background image, but a negative margin (coupled with the `overflow: hidden` property) that would offset the relative position of the image within the area in the hover state, causing the other half of the image to be displayed while the first half is hidden.

This trick is used in one interesting implementation of the "star-rating system" that we discuss in Section 8.6.[1] Instead of shifting between two halves of one image, this solution shifts between ten different image segments, one for each possible number of stars (one star through five stars) in two different colors. Although it works as an example of something that can be done using only CSS, some kind of JavaScript must ultimately be present to initiate action.

```
a#link1 {
    background-image: url("images/pic1a.jpg");
    text-decoration: none;
    width: ... ;
    height: ... ;
    display: block;
}
a:hover#link1 {
    background-image: url("images/pic1b.jpg");
}
```

Figure 8.5   Using the `a:hover` pseudo-class to implement image rollover.

The set of CSS directives in Figure 8.5 replicates the functionality we implemented in JavaScript, but in a declarative fashion. Of course, apart from certain built-in controls, the declarative nature of CSS limits what you can do without resorting to JavaScript. Behaviors that are more sophisticated can be configured by combining CSS with some JavaScript, and throwing in a little HTML DOM processing for good measure. This is the essence of DHTML, which we cover in Section 8.4.

8.3.3   Summary

In case you thought that CSS's pedigree as a rigorously defined specification agreed upon by a standards body meant that there would be no cross-browser compatibility issues, think again. Despite near universal acceptance of the standards in principle, some browsers (most specifically Internet Explorer) tend to interpret CSS rules slightly differently – enough to cause visible inconsistencies in layout. This means that cross-browser compatibility hacks to ensure consistent rendering across different browsers are not uncommon. Some browsers even employ "extensions" to CSS, defining their own CSS properties to take advantage of browser-specific features. This only adds to the confusion as browser-specific CSS directives pop up in style sheets.

In addition, there are several versions of CSS, with each succeeding version adding new capabilities to the specification. Most browsers claim to be compliant with CSS 2, though few if any achieve 100% compliance with that standard. Some browsers attempt to support advanced CSS 3 features without fully complying with the base CSS 2 specification. Finally, some browsers are stricter than others in interpreting supported CSS directives. (Apple's Safari browser, for example, fails to render pages properly if it finds style sheet syntax errors that other browsers blissfully ignore.)

There is much more to CSS than we can possibly convey in a brief section. Our goal was to illustrate the aspects of CSS that play a part in enhancing dynamic interactivity in page presentations.

8.4   DHTML

Dynamic HTML (usually called *DHTML*) is often talked about as if it were some new version of HTML, with advanced functionality above and beyond HTML itself. In reality, DHTML is just a catch-all name used to describe existing features in HTML, JavaScript and CSS that are combined to provide engaging forms of page presentation. While HTML provides a static presentation format, the coupling of HTML tags with JavaScript event handlers and CSS style specifications offers a degree of interactive control over page presentation. Where JavaScript, CSS, and HTML come together is the place where dynamic page interactivity really begins.

It is not our intention to provide a DHTML primer. Many good books are devoted to describing the intricacies of DHTML, but we believe it is worthwhile to understand the principles associated with DHTML presentation techniques.

8.4.1 Inner workings

The basic building block in DHTML is the *event handler*. Event handlers, as we have already discussed, are blocks of JavaScript code that are executed when triggered by browser events, be they user-initiated or time-driven. The association between a handler and an event is defined either by specifying in a page element the attribute associated with the event:

```
<a id="specialLink" href="#" onmouseover="doSpecialLinkMouseOver()">
```

or (preferably) by declaratively linking the name of a JavaScript function with a page element:

```
document.getElementById("specialLink").onclick = doSpecialLinkMouseOver;
```

So when does an event handler qualify as DHTML? Since DHTML is so loosely defined to begin with, there is no straight answer. In general, when a handler creates new page elements using HTML DOM processing in JavaScript or changes the style definitions associated with page elements to change their appearance in reaction to events, this is *Dynamic* HTML. Examples include (but are by no means limited to):

- Changing the visibility of an element: making a currently visible element invisible and vice versa.
- Changing aspects of an element's style so that it belongs to a different CSS class with different display characteristics. (Remember that a page element can be associated with more than one CSS class, which means that the set of classes an element belongs to can be appended or constricted.)
- Creating new list items (`<li>` elements) in existing ordered or unordered (`<ol>` or `<ul>`) lists. Note that the simplistic approach to creating new content within a page, using JavaScript `document.write()` statements, is strongly discouraged in favor of approaches that add elements to the DOM programmatically. (Note: The sidebar in Section 8.5.1 says more about the dangers of injecting "unsafe" requests for external content into your pages.)
- Moving elements from one position on a page to another as a result of user initiated dragging and dropping (e.g., to construct a custom portal page, such as My Yahoo!), provided the general layout and the style information for the target elements allow this.

8.4.2 Controlling content visibility

CSS positioning properties make it possible for more than one page element to occupy the same screen coordinates. Although sometimes it might make sense for two elements that occupy the same space to be visible at the same time (e.g., where the opacity setting of one makes it partially transparent), the usual application of this strategy calls for switching between the co-located page elements so that only one is visible at a time. This technique is often used to provide tabbed panes and collapsible menus.

```
<html>
<head>
<style type="text/css">
  #tab1 {
    position: absolute;
    visibility: visible;
    border: 1px solid black;
    margin: 5px;
    padding: 5px;
  }
  #tab2 {
    position: absolute;
    visibility: visible;
    border: 1px solid black;
    margin: 5px;
    padding: 5px;
  }
  #tab3 {
    position: absolute;
    visibility: visible;
    border: 1px solid black;
    margin: 5px;
    padding: 5px;
  }
</style>
<script type="text/javascript">
function show(objectID) {
    setVisibility(objectID,'visible');
}
function hide(objectID) {
    setVisibility(objectID,'hidden');
}
function setVisibility(objectID, state) {
    var obj = document.getElementById(objectID).style;
    obj.visibility = state;
}
</script>
</head>
<body bgcolor="#ffffff" onload="hide('tab1');hide('tab2');hide('tab3')">
<a href="javascript:show('tab1');hide('tab2');hide('tab3')">Show Tab 1</a>
<a href="javascript:show('tab2');hide('tab1');hide('tab3')">Show Tab 2</a>
<a href="javascript:show('tab3');hide('tab1');hide('tab2')">Show Tab 3</a>
<div id="container">
  <div id="tab1"> Text that appears when tab1 is visible</div>
  <div id="tab2"> Text that appears when tab2 is visible</div>
  <div id="tab3"> Text that appears when tab3 is visible</div>
</div>
</body>
</html>
```

Figure 8.6 Using CSS to create a tabbed interface.

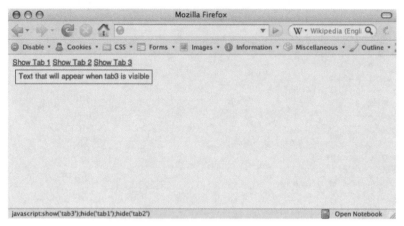

Figure 8.6   *(continued)*

In Figure 8.6, CSS styles are defined explicitly for `tab1`, `tab2`, and `tab3`. JavaScript functions are defined to change the visibility attribute of page elements. Hyperlinks give users the option to see `tab1` (which is visible when the page loads), `tab2` or `tab3` (which are initially hidden).

8.4.3   Leveraging toolkits

The `setVisibility()` JavaScript function in Figure 8.6 is somewhat simplified. Describing how to implement it in a manner that would be truly compatible across the majority of popular web browsers is too complex for a short overview. Suffice to say that cross-browser compatibility when using JavaScript and CSS (especially *positionable* elements) is difficult but by no means impossible. It is strongly advised that you make use of established DHTML toolkits, such as *Prototype* and *Dojo*, that do most of the complex browser-specific coding for you.

Do Try These at Home!

The examples in this chapter were tested with the latest stable versions of these toolkits: Prototype version 1.6.0.2, Scriptaculous version 1.8.1, and Dojo version 1.1.1.

The Prototype toolkit, for example, has `Element.show()` and `Element.hide()` methods that expose and hide page elements in a manner that is compatible across virtually all major web browsers. It also provides a very convenient shorthand, the `$()` method. Using a notation somewhat familiar to Unix/Linux users, this method addresses elements in the DOM by their `id` attribute, circumventing the need to use the `document.getElementById()` method, which does not work in some older browsers (Prototype takes this into account with its browser detection services and corrects for it).

Prototype also supplies a `document.getElementsByClassName()` method which returns the array of elements that are associated with a named CSS class.

Figure 8.7 shows how Prototype can be leveraged to simplify and modularize the show–hide functionality used to produce a tabbed interface. We replace our three JavaScript functions with one: the `showTab()` function, which is smart enough to show the desired tab after hiding all the tabs. This is accomplished using the `document.getElementsByClassName()` function. Notice that all of the tab `<div>` tags have been assigned a class name of `tab`. The function first uses Prototype's `Element.hide()` method to hide all elements of class `tab` and then uses the `Element.show()` method to reveal the tab passed in as an argument. The handler for each link that causes one of the tabs to be shown is established declaratively in the `<script>` block, rather than embedding it into the HTML code.

More dramatic effects can be achieved using the Scriptaculous toolkit, a companion package to Prototype, which provides methods for fading elements in and out, or making them appear and disappear with Venetian blind up and down effects.

Figure 8.8 replaces calls to Prototype's `Element.show()` method with calls to Scriptaculous's `Effect.Appear()` method, which gradually changes the opacity of an element over a specified period of time. The defaults for this method use the current opacity of the element as the starting point and complete opacity (represented as 1.0, or 100%) as the end point. In other words, the element is faded in over the period of time specified in the duration parameter.

This section is not a tutorial on using Prototype or Scriptaculous. It is an illustration of what such toolkits are good for. It is preferable to use the functions in these toolkits rather than attempting to implement all these functions from scratch. However, it is important to have an idea what is really going on when these toolkits are utilized.

Brace Yourself for JSON

You may notice an interesting but perhaps unfamiliar notation in the code example in Figure 8.8:

```
Effect.Appear(tabToShow, { duration: 0.5 } );
```

The notation here is JSON, which we discussed in Section 8.2.4. The code example shows how Scriptaculous effects use JSON in the argument lists for function calls. The supplied parameter surrounded by braces sets the duration for the effect to half a second. Some Scriptaculous effects and Prototype functions accept more complicated arguments in the form of attribute lists in JSON format:

```
Effect.Appear(tabToShow,
  { duration: 0.5,
    from: 0.3,
    to: 0.8,
    transition: Effect.Transitions.wobble
  } );
```

This statement causes the element to increase in opacity from 30% to 80% over the course of half a second but, instead of being linear, the transition from one opacity level to another wobbles.

```
<html>
<head>
<style type="text/css">
  #tab1 {
    position: absolute;
    border: 1px solid black;
    margin: 5px;
    padding: 5px;
  }
  #tab2 {
    position: absolute;
    border: 1px solid black;
    margin: 5px;
    padding: 5px;
  }
  #tab3 {
    position: absolute;
    border: 1px solid black;
    margin: 5px;
    padding: 5px;
  }
</style>
<script type="text/javascript" src="js/prototype.js"></script>
<script type="text/javascript">
function showTab(tabToShow) {
    var tabDivs = document.getElementsByClassName("tab");
    for (i = 0; i < tabDivs.length; i++) {
        Element.hide(tabDivs[i]);
    }
    Element.show($(tabToShow));
    return false;
}
window.onload = function() {
    $('linkTab1').onclick = function() { showTab('tab1'); };
    $('linkTab2').onclick = function() { showTab('tab2'); };
    $('linkTab3').onclick = function() { showTab('tab3'); };
    showTab('tab1');
};
</script>
</head>
<body bgcolor="#ffffff">
<a id="linkTab1" href="#">Show Tab 1</a>
<a id="linkTab2" href="#">Show Tab 2</a>
<a id="linkTab3" href="#">Show Tab 3</a>
<div id="container">
  <div id="tab1" class="tab"> Text that appears when tab1 is visible</div>
  <div id="tab2" class="tab"> Text that appears when tab2 is visible</div>
  <div id="tab3" class="tab"> Text that appears when tab3 is visible</div>
</div>
</body>
</html>
```

Figure 8.7   Creating a tabbed interface using the Prototype toolkit.

```
<html>
<head>
<style type="text/css">
   #tab1 {
    position: absolute;
    border: 1px solid black;
    margin: 5px;
    padding: 5px;    }
   #tab2 {
    position: absolute;
    border: 1px solid black;
    margin: 5px;
    padding: 5px;
   }
   #tab3 {
    position: absolute;
    border: 1px solid black;
    margin: 5px;
    padding: 5px;
   }
</style>
<script type="text/javascript" src="js/prototype.js"></script>
<script type="text/javascript" src="js/effects.js"></script>
<script type="text/javascript">
function showTab(tabToShow) {
    var tabDivs = document.getElementsByClassName("tab");
    for (i = 0; i < tabDivs.length; i++) {
        Element.hide(tabDivs[i]);
    }
    Effect.Appear(tabToShow, { duration: 1.0 } );
    return false;
}
window.onload = function () {
    $('linkTab1').onclick = function() { showTab('tab1'); };
    $('linkTab2').onclick = function() { showTab('tab2'); };
    $('linkTab3').onclick = function() { showTab('tab3'); };
showTab('tab1');
};
</script>
</head>
<body bgcolor="#ffffff">
<a id="linkTab1" href="#">Show Tab 1</a>
<a id="linkTab2" href="#">Show Tab 2</a>
<a id="linkTab3" href="#">Show Tab 3</a>
<div id="container">
  <div id="tab1" class="tab"> Text that appears when tab1 is visible</div>
  <div id="tab2" class="tab"> Text that appears when tab2 is visible</div>
  <div id="tab3" class="tab"> Text that appears when tab3 is visible</div>
</div>
</body>
</html>
```

Figure 8.8 Creating a tabbed interface using Scriptaculous effects.

8.4.4   Client-side validation using toolkits

We have already discussed how to accomplish client-side form validation using simple JavaScript. One elegant approach to client-side validation combines JavaScript with CSS to make the specification of validation rules more declarative.

With Dexagogo's `validation.js` package (which requires Prototype to function), you attach class names to each form element to indicate the types of validation rule to apply. Table 8.1 shows some of the validation classes.

There is an API for adding custom validation classes and attaching appropriate handler code to those classes. In the example below, a class name is defined to have certain textual validation characteristics, as well as requiring the field's content to match the value in another form field. Notice the use of JSON to supply validation parameters such as minimum and maximum length:

```
Validation.add(
  "validate-password-confirm-field",
  "message text to display when invalid", {
     pattern : new RegExp("^[a-zA-Z]+$","gi"),
     minLength : 6,
     maxLength : 8,
     notOneOf : ["password", "PASSWORD"], // not any of these
     equalToField : "password" // matches value in another form field
  }
);
```

Table 8.1   Validation Classes Defined in `validation.js`

Class name	Validation applied
`required`	The form element must be filled in.
`validate-digits`	The form element must only contain digits.
`validate-alpha`	The form element must only contain letters.
`validate-alphanum`	The form element must contain only letters or numbers.
`validate-date`	The form element must contain a valid date.
`validate-email`	The form element must contain a valid email address.
`validate-url`	The form element must contain a valid URL.

Validation is enabled by including appropriate JavaScript code in the page, coupled with associated class definitions for the form elements. This approach to form validation conforms to JavaScript best practices. The JavaScript code is separated from the HTML, and the only modifications to HTML page elements involve the insertion of appropriate CSS class names associated with the validation engine (see Figure 8.9).

8.4.5   Hovering behaviors using toolkits

We have revisited hovering behaviors a couple of times, each time injecting a new facet into the implementation that makes it more modular and reusable. In this example, we use Prototype's Event functions to watch for mouse-over events and process them accordingly:

```
<html>
<head>
<script type="text/javascript" src="js/prototype.js"></script>
<script type="text/javascript">
  function imageRollover(linkId, imageId, normalImageUrl,
                                          mouseOverImageUrl) {
    Event.observe($(linkId), "mouseover", function() {
      $(imageId).setAttribute("src", mouseOverImageUrl);
    });
    Event.observe($(linkId), "mouseout", function() {
      $(imageId).setAttribute("src", normalImageUrl);
    });
  }

    window.onload = function() {
      imageRollover("link1", "picture1",
                    "images/pic1a.jpg", "images/pic1b.jpg");
}
</script>
</head>
<body>
<a href="#" id="link1"><img id="picture1" src="images/pic1a.jpg" /></a>
</body>
</html>
```

This strategy applies to other applications beyond simple hovering behaviors and is included here for illustrative purposes.

```
<html>
<head>
  <script src="js/prototype.js" type="text/javascript"></script>
  <script src="js/effects.js" type="text/javascript"></script>
  <script type="text/javascript" src="js/dexagogo/validation.js"></script>
</head>
<body>
  <form id="form1" action="#" method="get">
    <div style="font-weight: bold">Name:</div>
    <div>
      <input id="username" class="required"
        title="Enter your name" /></div>
    <div style="font-weight: bold">Password:</div>
    <div>
      <input type="password" id="passwordField"
        class="required validate-password" />
    </div>
    <div style="font-weight: bold">Confirm Password:</div>
    <div>
      <input type="password" id="confirmPasswordField"
        class="required validate-password-confirm" /></div>
    <div style="font-weight: bold">Home Planet:</div>
    <div>
      <select id="planet" class="validate-selection">
        <option>Select one...</option>
        <option>Mercury</option>
        <option>Venus</option>
        <option>Earth</option>
        <option>Mars</option>
      </select>
    </div>
    <div style="font-weight: bold">Age:</div>
    <div><input id="age" class="validate-number" /></div>
    <div style="font-weight: bold">Sex:</div>
    <div>
      <input type="radio" name="sex" id="sex-male" value="Male" />
        Male<br />
      <input type="radio" name="sex" id="sex-female" value="Female"
        class="validate-one-required" />Female
    </div>
    <input type="submit" value="Submit" />
    <input type="button" value="Reset"
      onclick="valid.reset(); return false" />
  </form>
  <script type="text/javascript">
    var valid = new Validation('form1', { immediate : true });
    Validation.addAllThese([
      ['validate-password',
       'Password must be at least 7 chars and not your user name', {
         minLength : 7,
         notEqualToField : 'username'
```

Figure 8.9 Using Dexagogo's `validation.js` toolkit.

```
      }],
      ['validate-password-confirm',
       'Both entered password fields must be the same.', {
          equalToField : 'passwordField'
      }]
   ]);
  </script>
</body>
</html>
```

Figure 8.9 *(continued)*

8.4.6 Widgets

One prominent new category of dynamic presentation technology is *DHTML widgets*. They are simple mechanisms for adding "flair" to a page presentation by executing embedded JavaScript code that exercises DHTML functionality. The intent is for users who have limited technical knowledge to insert, with relative ease, JavaScript code fragments into their personal web sites, their MySpace pages, or their blog templates. The widgets are simple and brief enough to be used by users who are neither developers nor designers.

The widgets use server-side scripts or programs that generate JavaScript code to inject new content into a page, modify existing content, or provide some other add-on functionality. (Some may also employ the deprecated <iframe> tag as the container for newly injected content, while others simply require that you provide an empty <div> element with a predefined id attribute.) The code commonly traverses through the elements on the page (e.g., adding onmouseover handlers to certain links).

Widget providers usually require some sort of user registration and user identification information is embedded in the query string of the URL accessing the remote JavaScript code. To keep things simple for non-technical users, DHTML widget providers take shortcuts that deviate from established "best practice" for integrating JavaScript code into a page. For example, they advise that users put the inserted <script> blocks not in the <head> section of the page, but at the bottom of the page, just before the </body> tag. (This ensures that any page elements referenced by the widget have been rendered.) Also, the code they generate often employs document.write() statements (rather than using DOM-based techniques) to inject new content into the page. Despite these idiosyncrasies and issues, expect this technology to blossom in the coming years.

Google AdSense

If you register with Google and insert a block of code supplied by Google into your page or template, Google presents advertisements on your web site:

```
<script type="text/javascript">
  google_ad_client = "...";
  google_alternate_color = "404040";
```

```
    google_ad_width = 468;
    google_ad_height = 60;
    google_ad_format = "468x60_as";
    google_ad_type = "text_image";
    google_ad_channel = "...";
    google_color_border = "999990";
    google_color_bg = "E0E0D0";
    google_color_link = "808070";
    google_color_text = "000000";
    google_color_url = "AECCEB";
</script>
<script type="text/javascript"
  src="http://pagead2.googlesyndication.com/pagead/show_ads.js">
</script>
```

You are given options about the format and layout of the ads, but Google uses its well-known search capabilities to display ads that are related to the content presented on your site.

Amazon Associates

When you sign up as an Amazon affiliate, you get an affiliate ID that you can include in links on your pages to products offered on Amazon.com. In essence, this makes you an online bookseller, allowing you to sell books (or other products) on your web site. (Amazon gives you a "cut" from the sales arising from links on your site.)

The widget comes into play when you insert a <script> tag referencing a URL on Amazon's web site that dynamically generates JavaScript based on your affiliate ID (it must be included in the link defined in the src attribute of the <script> tag):

```
<script type="text/javascript"
  src="http://www.assoc-amazon.com/s/link-enhancer?tag=myAffiliateTag">
</script>
```

This code causes a DHTML popup to appear whenever site visitors hover over links on your pages that point to Amazon.com. The popup displays a thumbnail image of the book cover, CD, or other product, as well as other information about that product, including a link to allow visitors to purchase it using your affiliate ID.

Snap Shots

The Snap Shots service (from shots.snap.com) also enhances hovering behavior for links on a page. After you sign up, you receive a block of HTML code containing a <script> tag that you insert into your page:

```
<script type="text/javascript"
  src="http://shots.snap.com/snap_shots.js?ap=1&...&domain=mydomain.com">
</script>
```

This tag references a URL that produces dynamic JavaScript, which, in turn, causes a DHTML popup to appear whenever visitors to your page hover over links. The popup displays a thumbnail preview of the content found at the URL associated with the link. Since this behavior can be excessive if applied to *all* links on a page (including, for example, links to other pages on your site), the widget code can be configured to be more selective and page elements can be associated with specific CSS class names that selectively enable or disable this functionality.

8.4.7 Summary

Our examples barely scratch the surface in describing the capabilities of DHTML. Readers are invited to pursue the referenced sources and explore on their own the possibilities that arise from the interaction of JavaScript, CSS, and HTML. Our examples show how programmatic modifications to CSS attributes through JavaScript and insertion of new elements into the DOM offer great power to developers.

8.5 AJAX

AJAX is a name applied to a set of programmatic techniques that enable browsers to communicate asynchronously with web servers. Common uses of AJAX include retrieving content from the server to be inserted into the current page and transmitting new or updated information to be persisted on the server. AJAX techniques make it possible to achieve these results without causing a refresh or re-rendering of the current page.

What's in a Name?

AJAX is an acronym coined by Jesse James Garrett of Adaptive Path, a consulting firm that had been using the techniques described here without associating those techniques with an identifiable name. Garrett's blog post drew attention to these commonly used patterns and the AJAX label caught on. Depending on whom you talk to, AJAX stands for either **Asynchronous JavaScript And XML** or **Asynchronous JavaScript And X**MLHttpRequest. The word "asynchronous" is appropriate in that AJAX does make use of requests and responses processed in the background. AJAX does not necessarily make use of XML, but it almost always involves both JavaScript and the XMLHttpRequest object.

The functionality behind AJAX is made possible by an object called the XMLHttpRequest, which is the entity capable of transmitting an asynchronous HTTP request, waiting for a response, and using the contents of that response in some interactive fashion. The XMLHttpRequest object can be considered an independent background HTTP client executing within the browser's JavaScript-processing module. Originally an *ActiveX* object developed by Microsoft specifically for their Internet Explorer browser, it is now available in most modern browsers as a native JavaScript object with pretty much the same set of behaviors. Just as DHTML can be thought of as "JavaScript, CSS, and HTML DOM", AJAX can be summarized as "DHTML and XMLHttpRequest." (These trite descriptions, of course, do not accurately describe what either DHTML or AJAX can do.)

Beyond AJAX

The XMLHttpRequest object is not the only way to achieve the effects associated with AJAX.

Another technique uses a hidden frame (or IFRAME) as the vehicle for submitting background requests and accepting responses. This predates the creation of the XMLHttpRequest object by Microsoft. JavaScript code in the main content frame passes information to JavaScript code in the hidden frame, which submits an HTTP request. The response to this request refreshes the hidden frame, triggering additional JavaScript code that passes information (and control) back to the main content frame.

Adobe's Flex product is a descendant of Flash. It provides mechanisms for declaratively creating the equivalent of a Flash movie in MXML (an XML-based language tightly bound to Adobe's underlying APIs) and ActionScript (an ECMAScript-compliant scripting language). Flex employs interactive data services that populate and read data, analogous to the way AJAX uses the XMLHttpRequest object. Flex promises a world of "rich Internet applications" (RIAs) that do what AJAX does within a framework designed for instantaneous responses and live interactivity. Adobe plans to release as open source large portions of the Flex specification and code base, including the interface builder software.

Other similar approaches include OpenLaszlo (an open source framework also based on Flash but employing its own XML language, LZX) and Microsoft's Silverlight.

8.5.1   Content injection: manual approach

Content injection is one of the most common uses of AJAX. A background request is sent to the server to fetch content, which is used either to replace the content of an existing DOM element within the page or to create an entirely new element to hold the retrieved content.

Let us begin by understanding what is required to create an XMLHttpRequest object. As expected, the dual nature of the XMLHttpRequest object leads to cross-browser compatibility issues from the very start. Just the act of creating an instance of this object in JavaScript code is an exercise in tedium:

```
function getAjaxRequest() {
  var ajax = null;
  if (window.XMLHttpRequest) {
    ajax = new XMLHttpRequest();
  } else if (window.ActiveXObject) {
    ajax = new ActiveXObject("Microsoft.XMLHTTP");
  }
  return ajax;
}
```

This is just a sample JavaScript function for creating an XMLHttpRequest object in a compatible manner that works across different browsers. It checks to see if XMLHttpRequest is the name of a valid JavaScript entity and, if so, simply creates it; otherwise it attempts to create an XMLHttpRequest as an ActiveX object. As convoluted as this example looks, it is far from complete. More rigorous checks are needed to confirm which version of ActiveX (if any) is associated with the browser (so that an appropriate version of the XMLHttpRequest object can be created), and to fail gracefully if the browser lacks support for this object. (Be patient: there *are* easier ways to do this.)

Once you have an XMLHttpRequest object, what do you do with it? Obviously, you want to specify a URL that is the target of your request. After you have established the request URL and the associated request method, you attach a JavaScript callback function to the `XMLHttpRequest` object that is invoked when the response is received successfully. Then you submit the request by invoking the `send()` method.

In Figure 8.10, we use the `getAjaxRequest()` function to create an `XMLHttpRequest` object, point it at a URL, submit the request, wait for the response, and then replace the content of the named page element with the content retrieved from the server.

Notice the additional complexities in the callback function, `insertRetrievedContent()`. The `readyState` property of the `XMLHttpRequest` object indicates what it is currently doing: a readyState of 4 (or `complete` – another cross-browser incompatibility!) indicates that the response has arrived and is ready for consumption. This callback function is invoked, as the handler name implies, whenever the value of the `XMLHttpRequest` object's `readyState` changes. This happens several times over the lifetime of the request. When this value changes to the completed state, the code within the `if` block is executed, replacing the content of the page element named `divToReplace` with whatever was retrieved by the request.

```
<html>
<head>
<script type="text/javascript">
  function getAjaxRequest() {
    ...
  }
  var myAjax = getAjaxRequest();
  var divName = "divToReplace";
  var contentName = "xyz";
  var baseUrl = "/ajaxService/getContent";
  var fullUrl = baseUrl + "?name=" + contentName;
  // full URL is: /ajaxService/getContent?name=xyz
  function replaceDivContent() {
    myAjax.open("GET", fullUrl, true);
    myAjax.onreadystatechange = insertRetrievedContent;
    myAjax.send(null);
  }
  function insertRetrievedContent() {
    if (myAjax.readyState==4 || myAjax.readyState=="complete") {
      document.getElementById(divName).innerHTML = myAjax.responseText;
    }
  }
  window.onload = function() {
    document.getElementById("theLink").onclick = replaceDivContent;
  }
</script>
<body>
  <a href="#" id="theLink">Get content</a>
  <div id="divToReplace"></div>
</body>
</html>
```

Figure 8.10 Manual coding of AJAX functionality with custom callback function.

AJAX Response Data Formats

A common assumption is that the "X" in AJAX stands for XML, and that AJAX responses must contain XML. As we mentioned earlier, this is not necessarily the case. In fact, many server-side components used by AJAX applications do not return XML at all – they send back plain text or JSON instead because these are simpler to process.

To produce XML in AJAX responses, the `Content-Type` header in a server response must be set to `text/xml` or `application/xml`. In addition, the JavaScript function that interprets the content of the response must make use of the `responseXml` attribute of the `XmlHttpRequest` object, rather than the `responseText` attribute. The resulting content should be parsed as XML by the JavaScript code. This may require the use of additional JavaScript libraries for some browsers.

Plain text may be good enough if all you are trying to do is to insert retrieved text into an existing element (or insert a new element containing the retrieved text into the DOM). JSON may be useful if the data sent to the browser is more complicated.

JSON data is made available to JavaScript through the `eval()` function. The following fragment sets the `responseData` variable to the value of the JSON object included in the response:

```
function insertRetrievedContent() {
  if (xmlHttp.readyState==4 || xmlHttp.readyState==complete) {
    eval(var responseData = + myAjax.responseText);
  }
}
```

Simply assigning the response text to the variable does not work:

```
var responseData = myAjax.responseText;
```

That would set the variable to a string containing the content of the response, instead of building the complex data structure defined by the text.

There is a serious danger in using `eval()` with JSON-based responses. Rogue sites can engage in JavaScript hijacking[2] by sending responses that contain malicious executable code in place of (or hidden inside) JSON data. Care should be taken to exercise tight control over the use of JSON responses to prevent this from happening in your AJAX applications.

As complicated as the code in Figure 8.10 appears at first glance, it lacks proper error checking. What happens if the request fails? What happens if the named element does not exist? What happens if the request takes a long time and the user has to wait for a response with no indication of what is going on?

With this much conditional processing to account for differences between browsers and this much required error checking and event tracking to make the code robust, you would hope that there might be some sort of wrapper object that would encapsulate it all in a cross-browser compatible, abstract, and reusable fashion.

Hope springs eternal.

8.5.2   Content injection: using toolkits

Most of the better toolkits *do* abstract `XMLHttpRequest` functionality into wrapper objects that are much more usable, with a lot less need for the boilerplate code seen in the previous examples.

This is one of the reasons why using toolkits for JavaScript, DHTML, and AJAX has become a necessity.

One popular toolkit, Dojo, provides a nice wrapper mechanism through the `dojo.xhrGet` function (see Figure 8.11). Notice that we have eliminated our custom `getAjaxRequest` method (which was not robust enough any way) and simplified the callback function by making it unnecessary to test the value of `readyState`.

The Prototype framework provides an even simpler abstraction for this particular function, replacing text in a page element through the `Ajax.Updater` (see Figure 8.12).

8.5.3 Auto-completion

One of the most common uses of AJAX is to provide *auto-completion* functionality. Google made this popular with their experimental "Google Suggest" application. After entering a few characters into the search box, a list would appear under the box, containing ten entries, which begin with the characters you just entered. Google "suggests" one of these entries might be the one you are looking for, saving you the trouble of typing the entire search string. This is done by submitting an AJAX request as you enter each character. Each AJAX request queries Google's database for previously entered search strings that match the entered characters and returns the list of the ten most popular search strings.

```html
<html>
<head>
<script src="js/dojo.js" type="text/javascript"></script>
<script type="text/javascript">
  var divName = "divToReplace";
  var contentName = "xyz";
  var baseUrl = "/ajaxService/getContent";
  var fullUrl = baseUrl + "?name=" + contentName;
  function replaceDivContent() {
     dojo.xhrGet({
       url : fullUrl ,
       load : insertRetrievedContent ,
       handleAs : "text"
    });
  }
  function insertRetrievedContent(type, data, evt) {
    dojo.byId(divName).innerHTML = data;
  }
  window.onload = function() {
     document.getElementById("theLink").onclick = replaceDivContent;
   }
</script>
```

Figure 8.11   Content injection using the Dojo toolkit.

```
<body>
  <a href="#" id="theLink">Get content</a>
  <div id="divToReplace"></div>
</body>
</html>
```

Figure 8.11   *(continued)*

```
<html>
<head>
<script src="js/prototype.js" type="text/javascript"></script>
<script type="text/javascript">
  var divName = "divToReplace";
  var contentName = "xyz";
  var baseUrl = "/ajaxService/getContent";
  var fullUrl = baseUrl + "?name=" + contentName;
  function replaceDivContent() {
     new Ajax.Updater(divName, fullUrl, { method : "get" });
  }
  window.onload = function() {
     document.getElementById("theLink").onclick = replaceDivContent;
  }
</script>
</head>
<body>
  <a href="#" id="theLink">Get content</a>
  <div id="divToReplace"></div>
</body>
</html>
```

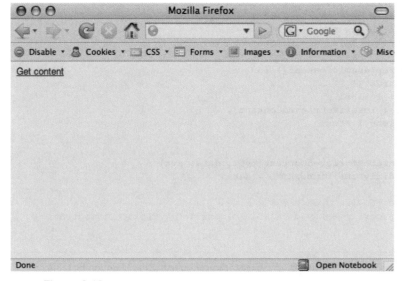

Figure 8.12   Content injection using Prototype's `Ajax.Updater`.

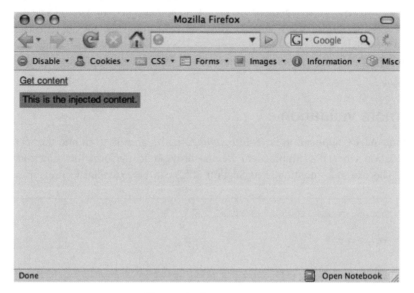

Figure 8.12   *(continued)*

This kind of function requires:

- a text field (the search box) whose `onchange` handler submits an AJAX request every time the content of the search box is modified;
- a page element (`<div>`) that contains the list of matches found by the AJAX request for the current content of the search box;
- a callback function that takes the AJAX response from the server and uses its content to populate the hidden element;
- a server-side script or program that produces an HTML unordered list (`<ul>`) containing the entries that begin with the characters currently in the search box.

As you might expect, the usual vagaries associated with cross-browser compatibility arise here as well. Browsers have their own native auto-complete functionality, which may interfere with this application. Other browser-specific issues may cause problems when an `onchange` handler is used. With this in mind, using toolkit functions to implement the AJAX auto-completion application is a very good idea.

Scriptaculous provides `Ajax.Autocompleter` to perform this function. It takes three required parameters:

- the ID of the text field whose content is being scanned;
- the ID of the `<div>` element (typically an HTML list) that will contain the results;
- the URL of the server-side program that determines which entries should be displayed in the list.

There are also optional parameters (in a JSON block) including the names of various callback functions (for example, after the content of the element has been updated). The target <div> is associated with CSS style directives to make the list stand out when presented (instead of looking like a normal unordered list). The Ajax.Autocompleter attaches the class name selected to the current list item. That class specifies a different background color to emphasize the selected item (see Figure 8.13).

8.5.4 Remote validation

Another common AJAX application is *remote validation*. Its goal is to mimic the responsiveness of client-side validation when it is impractical for the browser to perform this function with the data at its disposal. The example mentioned in Section 8.2.2 can be extended to prevent new registrants

```
<html xmlns="http://www.w3.org/1999/xhtml">
<head>
<style type="text/css">
  #searchResultList {
    width: 400px;
    border: 1px solid black;
    background-color: #cccccc;
  }
  #searchResultList ul {
    list-style-type: none;
    width: 100%;
    margin: 0px ;
    padding: 0px ;
  }
  #searchResultList ul li {
    list-style-type: none;
  }
  #searchResultList ul li.selected {
    background-color: #cccc99;
  }
</style>
<script src="js/prototype.js" type="text/javascript"></script>
<script src="js/effects.js" type="text/javascript"></script>
<script src="js/controls.js" type="text/javascript"></script>
<script type="text/javascript">
  window.onload = function() {
    new Ajax.Autocompleter("searchBox", "searchResultList",
                           "/ajax/autocomplete/demo", {});
  }
</script>
</head>
<body>
  <input id="searchBox" type="text" autocomplete="off" />
  <div id="searchResultList"></div>
</body>
</html>
```

Figure 8.13 Using Scriptaculous's Ajax.AutoCompleter.

from choosing user names that are already in use. Before AJAX, the alternatives would be either to download the entire list of user names so that the browser could perform the comparison locally or to use server-side validation.

The strategy for performing remote validation through AJAX is similar to that for auto-completion. An AJAX request is transmitted to the server containing the string to be validated (the requested user name). In this case, instead of a list, we are expecting a simple "yes" or "no" response: "yes" means that the user name already exists in the database and "no" means that the user name does not exist and can be claimed by a new user.

The example in Figure 8.14 shows a JavaScript function designated as the `onblur` handler for a text input field, `username`. When focus moves away from this field, the handler sends an AJAX request, examines the response to that request, and injects the content of the response into a `<div>`.

AJAX Limitations

AJAX has an important security limitation that we have not discussed up to this point. AJAX requests can be submitted only to servers in the same domain as their pages of origin.

While this may seem very restrictive, it is necessary to prevent malicious exploitations of AJAX technology by rogue sites. Legitimate web applications seeking to use AJAX to communicate with servers outside their domain have a simple mechanism for getting around this restriction. They can provide proxy services on their servers that forward AJAX HTTP requests to other domains, process the responses, and send them back to the requesting clients.

8.5.5   Where does DHTML end and AJAX begin?

The boundaries between DHTML and AJAX are somewhat blurry. Techniques that employ only DHTML functionality are often (erroneously) referred to as "AJAX." This is in part because many of the popular toolkits, such as Dojo and Prototype, include both DHTML and AJAX functions. Most of the visual effects in the Scriptaculous toolkit are DHTML, yet Scriptaculous is often referred to as an AJAX toolkit.

By definition, AJAX involves the transmission of a background request that causes discrete updates to the content displayed in the browser or updates to the data stored on the server. Applications with cool DHTML features that do not involve such requests are not AJAX. This includes Scriptaculous functions that make page elements appear and disappear, grow and shrink, and move around on the page. (In other words, just because it is cool does not mean it is AJAX.)

Not that these labels matter. DHTML was always a loosely defined term describing techniques that arose from the synergy between JavaScript, CSS, and the HTML DOM. AJAX is another loosely defined term describing techniques arising from the synergy between DHTML and the `XMLHttpRequest` functionality. As if all this wasn't confusing enough, the term "Web 2.0" (which refers to the features enabled by these technologies in collaborative community-driven web applications) is sometimes used erroneously to refer to the technologies themselves.

```
<html xmlns="http://www.w3.org/1999/xhtml">
<head>
<script src="prototype.js" type="text/javascript"></script>
<script type="text/javascript">
  window.onload = function() {
    $("userName").onblur = function() {
      new Ajax.Request("/ajax/checkUserName?name=" + $("userName").value,
        {
          onSuccess: function(transport) {
            if (transport.responseText == "present") {
              $("message").innerHTML = &Choose another name!";
            }
            // responseText == "absent"
            else {
              $("message").innerHTML = "User name accepted!";
            }
          }
        }
      )
    }
  };
</script>
</head>
<body>
  <form>
    <input id="userName" type="text" />
    <input type="submit" value="Enter Name" />
    <div id="message"></div>
  </form>
</body>
</html>
```

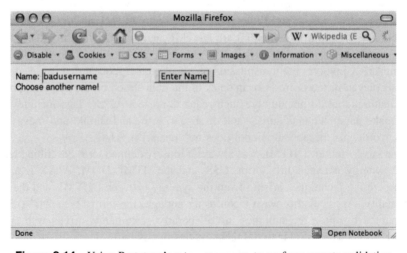

Figure 8.14 Using Prototype's `Ajax.Request` to perform remote validation.

8.5.6   Summary

In many ways, AJAX changed the landscape of the web, taking what was coming to be perceived as a stodgy mechanical request–response paradigm and turning it into a truly interactive application platform. Web applications were limited because of their dependency on request–response transactions that updated the entire presentation. Compared to the client–server applications prevalent in the 1990s, this was viewed as a step backward, to a world reminiscent of old-school, IBM-mainframe-terminal transactions. AJAX-based applications allowed user actions that modified the page (e.g., entering text into a form field) to be "instantaneously" reflected in some other aspect of the presentation (e.g., adding the analysis of entered text into some other page element).

The word "instantaneously" needs to be in quotes, because it reflects the perception, not the actual fact. When a server interaction is required, the application must wait for responses to one or more background requests in order to update the page. A slow network can make AJAX transactions slow. AJAX-heavy pages can bog down the browser as it attempts to process multiple background requests and responses.

The point is that AJAX needs to be used judiciously. Too much of it would be overwhelming, not just for the browser but also for the user who has to grasp and assimilate all that is happening on the page. While it is technically feasible to build applications that use empty HTML page skeletons that are filled via AJAX requests, this is rarely the best approach.

Above all, there is no reason to reinvent the wheel. Toolkits such as Dojo and Prototype can free you from the burden of coding routine support functions. On the flip side, do not treat these toolkits as magical black boxes, without any understanding of their underlying mechanisms; use them knowing what they do for you and what kind of work they are saving you from.

8.6   Case Study: 5-Star Rating

This technique (see Figure 8.15 – check our web site for full color image[3]) seems to have appeared everywhere on the web at once. One of its pioneers was the online DVD rental service, Netflix, but it is not clear whether they are the ones who originated it. In any case, the gist is as follows:

Figure 8.15   Star-rating images: unrated (gray), mouse-over highlighting (yellow) and recorded (red).

- An array of five images (usually stars) is displayed on a page associated with some item (e.g., a movie) that site visitors can "rate" as terrible (one star), excellent (five stars), or somewhere in between. The initial color of the stars is usually bland (gray, white, or transparent).
- As the mouse pointer hovers over a star, its color (and the color of all stars to the left of it) changes to something more vibrant. Moving the mouse away from the array of stars causes them to revert to their original color.
- Clicking on a particular star causes a background request to the server, recording the user's selection. For example, if the user clicks on the leftmost star, a rating of "one star" persists in the server database. If the user clicks on the star in the middle, a rating of "three stars" is recorded. If the user clicks on the rightmost star, the record indicates a rating of "five stars". The current page continues to be displayed after the mouse click (i.e., there is no page refresh).
- Once the server-side processing has succeeded, a confirmation message is displayed.

(A variation on this technique was mentioned in the sidebar toward the end of Section 8.3.2.)

8.6.1   Designing a star-rating component

Implementations of this functionality usually do more than persist individual user ratings; they often tally all the ratings submitted by site visitors and display an average rating. These added complexities make discussion of a real world example of this functionality impractical in this overview. For that reason, we concentrate on the mechanics of the star rating display. Our goal was to keep this example simple as an illustration for those who wish to use this functionality in their web pages:

- We use individual images for the stars, rather than using compound images with multiple segments.
- We want JavaScript to do as much of the work as possible, so that the required HTML is simple (no need for custom JavaScript code in script blocks or within the HTML).

We start with three star images, equal in size and orientation. One star is light gray (meaning unrated or unselected), one is yellow (actively hovering, highlighted), and one is red (rated).

We define a CSS class for each star type and for the enclosing list items. Links (<a> tags) within list items with a class of unratedStar-* should use the gray star as their background image, links with a class of highlightedStar-* should use the yellow star, and links with a class of ratedStar-* should use the red star (see Figure 8.16).

We then add code (see Figure 8.17) to change the CSS class of all the list items to the left of the selected list item. (The a:hover specification takes care of the hovered-over list item itself.) This would simulate the onmouseover handler for all affected star elements. Consequently, the image under the mouse pointer, plus the images to its left, would be highlighted.

We also need to add code to reverse this procedure and remove highlighting, as shown in Figure 8.18. This would serve as the onmouseout handler for the same set of elements. When the mouse pointer leaves the area, the stars return to their original state ("unrated").

We add code to submit an AJAX request to record the rating on the server and reset the handler definitions for all elements in the list once the rating has been recorded. This code (outlined in Figure 8.19) would serve as the onclick handler for the same set of elements. When a star is

```
ul.ratingBlock {
  list-style-type: none;
}
ul.ratingBlock li {
  float: left;
}
ul.ratingBlock li a {
  width: 25px;
  height: 25px;
  display: block;
}
ul.ratingBlock li.unratedStar-1,
ul.ratingBlock li.unratedStar-2,
ul.ratingBlock li.unratedStar-3,
ul.ratingBlock li.unratedStar-4,
ul.ratingBlock li.unratedStar-5 {
  background-image: url("unratedStar.jpg");
}
ul.ratingBlock li.highlightedStar-1 a,
ul.ratingBlock li.highlightedStar-2 a,
ul.ratingBlock li.highlightedStar-3 a,
ul.ratingBlock li.highlightedStar-4 a,
ul.ratingBlock li.highlightedStar-5 a,
ul.ratingBlock li.unratedStar-1 a:hover,
ul.ratingBlock li.unratedStar-2 a:hover,
ul.ratingBlock li.unratedStar-3 a:hover,
ul.ratingBlock li.unratedStar-4 a:hover,
ul.ratingBlock li.unratedStar-5 a:hover {
  background-image: url("highlightedStar.jpg");
}
ul.ratingBlock li.ratedStar-1 a,
ul.ratingBlock li.ratedStar-2 a,
ul.ratingBlock li.ratedStar-3 a,
ul.ratingBlock li.ratedStar-4 a,
ul.ratingBlock li.ratedStar-5 a {
  background-image: url("ratedStar.jpg");
}
```

Figure 8.16 CSS style sheet definitions for list items representing each star type.

clicked, that star and all stars to the left of it change permanently to the "rated" state. The resetting of event handlers means that subsequent hovering and clicking activity with the stars has no
effect.

Here is where the JavaScript code gets really interesting. Attach highlightAllToLeft, unHigh-
lightAll, and sendRating as onmouseover, onmouseout, and onclick handlers for all *children*
of elements that are associated with the class name ratingBlock. Remember that the <ul> element
is assigned the class name of ratingBlock, so its children are the list item (<li>) elements (see
Figure 8.20).

When building the HTML content for the page, we use an unordered list with the appropriate class
designation (ratingBlock) and give it a unique id attribute. Create list items (<li> tags) for each

```
var unratedPrefix = "unratedStar-";
var highlightedPrefix = "highlightedStar-";
var ratedPrefix = "ratedStar-";
var blankPrefix = "blankStar-";
function highlightAllToLeft(element) {
  // Change the class of all elements to the left of this one
  //   to "highlightedStar-*"
  var enclosingList = $(element).ancestors()[0];
  if (enclosingList.hasClassName("ratingBlock") &&
                    ! enclosingList.hasClassName("ratingSubmitted")) {
    var thisElementClass = $(element).classNames().find(function(s) {
      return (s.substring(0, unratedPrefix.length) == unratedPrefix)
    });
    var whichStarIsThis =
                    thisElementClass.substring(unratedPrefix.length);
    for (i = 1; i < whichStarIsThis; i++) {
      var star = (document.getElementsByClassName(unratedPrefix + i,
                                      enclosingList))[0];
      star.addClassName(highlightedPrefix + i);
      star.removeClassName(unratedPrefix + i);
    }
  }
}
```

Figure 8.17 Code fragment containing the `highlightAllToLeft` function.

```
function unHighlightAll(element) {
  // Change the class of all elements to the left of this one
  // back to "unratedStar-*"
  var enclosingList = $(element).ancestors()[0];
  if (enclosingList.hasClassName("ratingBlock") &&
                    ! enclosingList.hasClassName("ratingSubmitted")) {
    var kids = $(enclosingList).childElements();
    for (i = 0; i < kids.length; i++) {
      kids[i].addClassName(unratedPrefix + (i+1));
      kids[i].removeClassName(highlightedPrefix + (i+1));
    }
  }
}
```

Figure 8.18 Code fragment containing the `unhighlightAll` function.

star in the list, assigning each of them the appropriate class name. Assuming we are dealing with five stars, this means five list items:

```
<ul id="idOfThingToBeRated" class="ratingBlock">
  <li class="unratedStar-1"><a href="#" title="1 out of 5 stars"></a></li>
  <li class="unratedStar-2"><a href="#" title="2 out of 5 stars"></a></li>
  <li class="unratedStar-3"><a href="#" title="3 out of 5 stars"></a></li>
  <li class="unratedStar-4"><a href="#" title="4 out of 5 stars"></a></li>
  <li class="unratedStar-5"><a href="#" title="5 out of 5 stars"></a></li>
</ul>
```

```
function sendRating(element) {
  // Here is where an AJAX request would be submitted and processed.
  // Also, event handlers for the star elements would be reset here
  // after the request has been submitted since the rating has been sent.
  var enclosingList = $(element).ancestors()[0];
  if (enclosingList.hasClassName("ratingBlock") &&
                      ! enclosingList.hasClassName("ratingSubmitted")) {
    var thisElementClass = $(element).classNames().find(function(s) {
      return (s.substring(0, unratedPrefix.length) == unratedPrefix)
    });
    var whichStarIsThis =
                      thisElementClass.substring(unratedPrefix.length);
    // submit AJAX request here including star number
    // and enclosing class name in query string
    var url = "http://nowhere.com/saveRatings";
    alert(url + "?id=" + enclosingList.id + "&rating=" + whichStarIsThis);
    var id = $(element).id;
    var nameOfUpdateDiv = "updateDiv-" + id;
    if ($(nameOfUpdateDiv) == undefined) {
      nameOfUpdateDiv = "updateDiv";
    }
    new Ajax.Updater(nameOfUpdateDiv, &response.txt");
    $(element).removeClassName(unratedPrefix + whichStarIsThis);
    $(element).addClassName(ratedPrefix + whichStarIsThis);
    $(element).onmouseout = function() { };
    var kids = $(enclosingList).childElements();
    for (i = 0; i < kids.length; i++) {
      kids[i].removeClassName(unratedPrefix + (i+1));
      if (i+1 < whichStarIsThis) {
        kids[i].addClassName(ratedPrefix + (i+1));
      }
      else {
        kids[i].addClassName("blankStar-" + (i+1));
      }
      kids[i].onmouseover = function() { };
      kids[i].onmouseout = function() { };
      kids[i].onclick = function() { };
    }
    enclosingList.addClassName("ratingSubmitted");
  }
}
```

Figure 8.19 Code fragment containing the `unhighlightAll` function.

We can set up a similar list for any additional items to be rated on the page:

```
<ul id="idOfAnotherThingToBeRated" class="ratingBlock">
  <li class="unratedStar-1"><a href="#" title="1 out of 5 stars"></a></li>
  <li class="unratedStar-2"><a href="#" title="2 out of 5 stars"></a></li>
  <li class="unratedStar-3"><a href="#" title="3 out of 5 stars"></a></li>
  <li class="unratedStar-4"><a href="#" title="4 out of 5 stars"></a></li>
  <li class="unratedStar-5"><a href="#" title="5 out of 5 stars"></a></li>
</ul>
```

```
function raterSetup() {
  var allRatingBlocks = document.getElementsByClassName("ratingBlock");
  for (i = 0; i < allRatingBlocks.length; i++) {
    var kids = allRatingBlocks[i].childElements();
    for (j = 0; j < kids.length; j++) {
      $(kids[j]).onmouseover = function() {
        highlightAllToLeft(this);
      };
      $(kids[j]).onmouseout = function() {
        unHighlightAll(this);
      };
      $(kids[j]).onclick = function() {
        sendRating(this);
      };
    }
  }
};
window.onload = raterSetup;
```

Figure 8.20   Code fragment that sets up handlers for all rating blocks.

If the JavaScript code and the CSS style sheet are associated with the page, only the lists are necessary in the page itself.

8.6.2   When you click upon a star: what happens on the server?

Highlighting stars of different colors and clicking on them to change their presentation locally in the browser may be a nice visual effect, but something has to happen on the server in order for these ratings to be recorded for posterity. That is something we haven't covered yet, but be patient: when we provide examples of how web applications are designed and developed, you will get an idea what needs to happen.

Basically, the server-side code needs to register the fact that a rating (from 1 to 5 stars) has been submitted for a particular item (specified by the id attribute of the enclosing list). It would record that in the database as a new row in a ratings table.

The point is that all this browser-side magic requires supporting code on the server to record the events that transpire, or to fulfill the dynamic requests for data. Organizing your server-side code so that these operations can be performed atomically via AJAX requests makes your web applications more resilient and easier to test, extend, and maintain in the long run.

In essence, AJAX requests make use of discrete services to retrieve specific sets of data and to upload data that is persisted in a server-side database. Web applications that are organized around such services fit well into the AJAX paradigm. Using AJAX with applications that are not designed this way would require either duplication of code to perform the same operation in different ways, or major refactoring to make such code duplication unnecessary.

8.7   Summary

We entitled this chapter "Active Browser Pages" because we concentrated on technologies for producing dynamic interactive presentations in the browser: JavaScript, CSS, DHTML, and AJAX. AJAX produced a huge paradigm shift that changed the way web applications are conceived and designed. It also changed the way JavaScript, a language that grew to be scorned and dismissed over the years, was viewed. The gimmicks, snippets, and spaghetti code long associated with JavaScript have given way to a disciplined approach to building structured user interfaces. Combine JavaScript with CSS and the HTML DOM, and you get DHTML. Combine DHTML with the `XmlHttpRequest` object that allows communication with servers through background requests, and you get AJAX.

However, communicating with the web server will not be of much value unless applications running on the web server produce sophisticated dynamic content to be presented in the browser. Just as this chapter offered up a perspective on browser-side approaches to producing dynamic content, the next chapter will cover server-side approaches to web application development.

QUESTIONS AND EXERCISES

1. What is the purpose for introducing CSS? What are the alternatives for associating styles with HTML documents?

2. What is the relationship between HTML and JavaScript? What is the role of event handlers?

3. What is JSON? Name three ways that JSON can be used.

4. What is DHTML? Describe the most common DHTML usage patterns and the enabling technologies.

5. What is AJAX? What can AJAX do that previous technologies could not? How did the advent of AJAX change the structure of web applications?

6. Name three ways to create image rollover functionality.

7. Implement the "5-star rating" component described in Section 8.6, *Case Study: 5-Star Rating*. What functionality is missing from the finished product that is needed to make it usable in a real world web application environment?

8. What is the main advantage of using toolkits to perform sophisticated DHTML/AJAX functions? Name three popular toolkits and list some of the things they can do.

9. What would you expect to happen if the response to an AJAX request contained a redirection (301 or 302) status code? Investigate what actually happens in different browsers.

8.8 Bibliography

Angus, Chris, 2006. *Prototype and Scriptaculous: Taking the Pain Out of JavaScript* (O'Reilly Short Cuts Series). Sebastopol (CA): O'Reilly Media.

Goodman, Danny, 2006. *Dynamic HTML: The Definitive Guide*, 3rd Edition. Sebastopol (CA): O'Reilly Media.

Hadlock, Kris, 2006. *AJAX for Web Application Developers*. Indianapolis (IN): SAMS Publishing.

Meyer, Eric, 2006. *Cascading Style Sheets: The Definitive Guide*, 3rd Edition. Sebastopol (CA): O'Reilly & Associates.

Powers, Shelley, 2006. *Learning JavaScript*. Sebastopol (CA): O'Reilly Media.

Schutta, Nathaniel T. and Asleson, Ryan, 2006. *Pro Ajax and Java Frameworks*. New York: Apress.

Stephenson, Sam *et al*., 2007. *Prototype 1.5.1: The Complete API Reference*. Prototype Development Team.

Teague, Jason Cranford, 2006. *CSS, DHTML and AJAX for the World Wide Web: Visual Quickstart Guide*, 4th Edition. Berkeley (CA): Peachpit Press.

Zakas, Nicholas C., 2006. *Professional JavaScript for Web Developers*. Indianapolis (IN): Wrox Press/Wiley Publishing.

8.9 Web Links

Chess, Brian, O'Neil, Yekaterina Tsipenyuk and West, Jacob, 2007. *JavaScript Hijacking*. Available at http://www.fortifysoftware.com/servlet/downloads/public/JavaScript_Hijacking.pdf.

O'Brien, Paul, 2007. *CSS The Star Matrix Pre-loaded*. Available at http://www.search-this.com/2007/05/23/css-the-star-matrix-pre-loaded/.

8.10 Endnotes

1. `http://www.search-this.com/2007/05/23/css-the-star-matrix-pre-loaded/`
2. `http://www.fortifysoftware.com/servlet/downloads/public/JavaScript_Hijacking.pdf`
3. `http://www.webappbuilders.com/images/starrater.jpg`

CHAPTER **9**

Approaches to Web Application Development

IN THIS CHAPTER
- Taxonomy of web application approaches and frameworks
- Comparative survey of approaches and frameworks

OBJECTIVES
- Introduce the taxonomy of web application approaches and frameworks.
- Discuss the differences between programmatic, template, and hybrid approaches, and the compromises associated with these approaches.
- Clarify the distinction between frameworks and approaches.
- Offer a comparative survey of popular approaches and frameworks.
- Use examples to illustrate the advantages and drawbacks of individual approaches and frameworks.

It is neither desirable nor practical to design and develop every new web application from the ground up. We would have to keep building the same functional components that accept and interpret requests, authenticate and authorize users, access and transform requested data, and construct and transmit final responses. Many of these components would be identical across different applications. Web servers provide application developers with well-defined endpoints – the acceptance of requests and transmission of responses. Some servers lay the basic groundwork for building and deploying web applications (as discussed in Chapter 6). In practice, such groundwork is too basic to facilitate development and deployment of sophisticated applications.

In this chapter, we classify and analyze various strategies for building web applications, distinguishing between *approaches* and *frameworks*. We define *approaches* as libraries of functional components that take advantage of the web server foundation and can be reused across multiple applications. They usually revolve around a particular programming language, with supplementary APIs and packages providing the functionality needed by web applications.

Frameworks go beyond application development approaches. They provide a consistent infrastructure that includes a rich set of services, eliminating the need to write redundant "boilerplate" code for common application functions. They usually include integrated support for database access, authentication, and state or session management. Most importantly, frameworks strive to separate content from presentation, which is an elusive goal of good web application architecture. They aim to achieve this goal by making developers responsible for business logic and access to content, while giving creative designers control over page formatting. The best frameworks allow developers and designers to work on separate source modules, so that they do not interfere with each other as they go about their respective jobs.

In this chapter, we examine various approaches to web application development. We discuss the evolution of such approaches from the early years of the web through to the present day, with an eye toward the future.

9.1   Taxonomy of Web Application Approaches and Frameworks

We divide web application development solutions into four broad categories:

- scripting or programmatic approaches
- template approaches
- hybrid approaches
- frameworks.

Although there is overlap (as well as debate about where certain approaches fit into this categorization scheme), most established approaches are associated with one particular category. They differ in the types of object used as the "source" for generated pages and in the degree of support they provide for the development of advanced, scalable applications.

9.1.1   Programmatic approaches

In *scripting* or *programmatic* approaches, the source associated with the page object consists predominantly of code written in a scripting language (such as, Perl, Python, or Tcl) or in a high-level programming language, such as Java. The code may be interspersed with formatting constructs. Naturally, such approaches are oriented toward programmers. The bulk of the page source implements application logic, while the page formatting (e.g., HTML) is commonly produced using output statements written in the associated programming language. Among the approaches that fit into this category are CGI scripts and servlets (which were covered in Chapter 6).

The biggest issue with programmatic approaches to web application development is their *code-centric* nature. HTML and other formatting constructs are embedded within program logic.

This limits the creative input that web designers can have into the layout of the final page. A web designer can "mock up" a page, but a programmer must then translate it into code and integrate it into the script or program. Programmer intervention is required to modify practically any aspect of the generated page, whether it is a change in program logic or a change to the layout.

9.1.2   Template approaches

Template approaches utilize a source object (the template) that consists predominantly of formatting structures, with a limited set of embedded constructs that add programmatic power. The focus of the source object is on formatting, not programming logic. These approaches are friendlier toward web designers, whose expertise is in the area of layout and design rather than programming.

Template approaches revolve around the page structure and the formatting tags, not around the code. With this in mind, we call such approaches *page-centric*. The source objects are page templates, consisting mostly of HTML coupled with embedded constructs that support conditional processing, iterative result presentation, and parameter substitution.

Server-Side Includes (SSI) was an early mechanism for adding simple template functionality to web pages. Among other well-known template approaches are Adobe's *Cold Fusion* and Apache's *Velocity*.

Template Programming?

Some argue that the presence of programmatic constructs in templates means there is no real difference between the template and programmatic approaches. The argument is that the addition of programmatic constructs turns a template approach into a programming language, albeit less powerful than those commonly used to produce CGI scripts and other applications.

Comparing the two kinds of approach based solely on programming power, programmatic approaches appear to "win out." However, this is a flawed comparison: programmers have the background and skills to use the features of powerful programming languages, but most page designers do not. The purpose of template approaches is to put presentation objects in the hands of page designers. Introducing complex programming constructs subverts that purpose by forcing the designers to rely on programmers to implement design changes.

A page-centric approach that employs a minimal set of logic constructs provides unique value because it enables designers with limited programming skills to create presentation layouts without programmer intervention.

9.1.3   Hybrid approaches

Hybrid approaches employ source objects that combine formatting constructs with code. They have more programmatic power than template approaches because they allow embedded blocks containing "scripts". This would seem to combine the benefits of the template and programmatic approaches. Examples of hybrid approaches include *PHP*, Microsoft's *Active Server Pages (ASP)* and Sun's *Java Server Pages (JSP)*.

Most of these approaches translate hybrid source objects into code. The more sophisticated among them employ some form of pre-compilation, so that the translation and compilation process does not occur every time a page is requested.

Best of Both Worlds or a Web Developer's Worst Nightmare?

The intermixing of script blocks with page formatting is not just a violation of an important principle: separation of content from presentation. The worst part is that the issue of who "owns" the source object becomes muddled.

The frequent contention that page designers can easily learn to work around the embedded code constructs is not borne out by experience. When designers and developers work on the same source objects, this inevitably leads to problems when code changes break the HTML formatting, or when changes made by designers inadvertently introduce bugs into the embedded code.

A mechanism for separating application logic from presentation constructs would make a hybrid approach more viable. But as long as both content and presentation aspects of the application are contained in the same source objects, the problem remains. Separating out functions associated with application logic from page templates is necessary to minimize collisions and conflicts between developers and designers and to maximize productivity. This is what true frameworks aim to achieve.

9.1.4   Frameworks

Frameworks represent the next level of sophistication in web application development. Rather than combining layout and logic into a single module, frameworks follow the principle of *separating content from presentation*. The modules responsible for producing content (the *model*) are distinct from the modules that present that content in a particular format (the *view*).

Why is it so important to separate content from presentation? The answer has two components: increased application flexibility and the appropriate division of responsibility between designers and programmers.

Application flexibility

When people talk about "confusing the map and the territory," they are describing the problem that occurs when the distinct natures of content and presentation are confused. The map is not the territory; it is a representation of that territory in one of many possible ways. A map could be a street map, showing the highways and roads found in a region. It could be a topographical map, describing the surfaces and elevations of that region. A map might not even be graphical: a set of explicit verbal directions to get from one place to another is also a representation of the territory and thus a kind of map. We have the flexibility of representing the territory in a number of different ways, using a variety of different maps.

In web applications, the "territory" is the data or content. The "map" is the view – the organization and layout of the content in the desired form. The choice of presentation format should be separate from the choices made to access the data, so that any "territory" can be represented as any kind of "map" (HTML, XHTML MP, VoiceXML, etc.). The "map" can be personalized, co-branded, stylized, embedded, or otherwise customized in a variety of ways.

It terms of flexibility, it does not matter where your content comes from or how it is retrieved. What matters is that the data *model* is open enough so that the content can be transformed to multiple presentation formats (or *views*), and that there is a controlling mechanism (or *controller*)

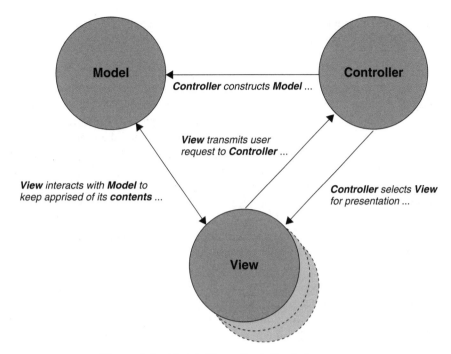

Figure 9.1   Model–View–Controller design pattern.

that can match up retrieved content with the appropriate view. That is, it should implement the *Model–View–Controller (MVC)* design pattern (see Figure 9.1).

The Controller receives a user request, accesses and modifies the Model that fulfills this request, and selects a View to present the results. The View communicates with the Model to determine its content, and presents that content to the user in the desired format. The View also serves as the interface for transmitting user requests to the Controller.

This pattern, designed to facilitate true separation of content from presentation, enables the development of applications that can dynamically tailor and customize presentations based on user preferences, device capabilities, business rules, and other constraints. The data model is not tied to a single presentation format that limits the flexibility of the application. View customization possibilities range from the simple (choosing a CSS style sheet) to the complex (choosing a target markup language).

Division of responsibility for processing modules

As we have already discussed, the people responsible for content and presentation have very different skills and agendas:

- Presentation experts are page designers whose skills focus on formatting languages, such as HTML and CSS, and on page design tools, such as Macromedia Dreamweaver and Microsoft FrontPage, with perhaps some exposure to XML with XSLT. They are not programmers, and their expertise is not in the area of coding and application logic.

- Content access and manipulation are the responsibility of application developers or database programmers. They may require elaborate conditional logic and complex queries to obtain the desired data.

Both sets of skills are very specialized; both require sophistication and are critical to the process of web application development. Just as you would not ask a page designer to code up your SQL stored procedures, you would not want an application developer to design and implement the layout of your pages. More often than not, applications in which developers designed the user interface have issues with usability. Similarly, applications which were fully conceived and built by page designers have problems with scalability and are difficult to maintain.

Many hybrid approaches, including Cold Fusion, ASP, and JSP, offer a great deal of power by combining presentation formatting with application and data access logic. Unfortunately, they do not clearly define who owns and is responsible for these hybrid page objects. What happens when the page designer's modifications break the application developer's embedded Java code? Conversely, what happens when a database programmer modifies an embedded query, inadvertently altering the HTML layout?

While some programmers like to believe they have the skills to perform *all* the tasks associated with dynamic page generation, experience teaches us that development of sophisticated web applications is a collaborative effort. To achieve maximum productivity, people with distinct skills should have the opportunity to work independently on components most suitable for their expertise.

There is always the temptation to turn a page into one contiguous block of code (like a CGI script). Anyone who has worked heavily with PHP, ASP, or JSP can attest to this challenge. Over time, the intermixing of code and formatting constructs gets ugly; the page modules become extremely difficult for both designers and developers to read – and to maintain. Because these hybrid page objects are so dense and complicated, even simple design changes are likely to require developer intervention.

An MVC-based approach makes it possible to combine application flexibility with the appropriate division of responsibility. Developers are responsible for the *controller*. This is often a lightweight module, which delegates processing to appropriate subordinate tasks, also created by developers. These tasks are responsible for retrieving data and making changes to the *model*. Designers are responsible for building the *views*. The *controller* determines dynamically which *view* should present the data associated with the *model*. Designers can implement changes to views without the need for developer intervention.

Good frameworks allow projects to come together naturally, like interlocking puzzle pieces, without force-fitting dissimilar functionality into a single component. With framework approaches, we no longer encapsulate both logic and formatting in a single module. Instead, they are relegated to different modules that interact with each other. The degree of complexity associated with these interactions requires that conventions and standards for them are well-defined and easily understood.

Rapid Application Development

In recent years, there has been a backlash over the degree of complexity inherent in modern web application frameworks. Frameworks, particularly those associated with Java EE, are viewed by many as being too cumbersome, making development and deployment of even simple applications an onerous task.

The rise of a new generation of Rapid Application Development (RAD) approaches to web application development is a reaction to this complexity. The hope is that an approach can be devised that eschews the complexities associated with advanced frameworks while retaining the advantages such frameworks provide (e.g., scalability, configurability, and the separation of roles). Later in this chapter, we examine one such framework, Ruby on Rails and, in Chapter 11, we build an application using it, to see how close it comes to achieving those goals.

9.2 Comparative Survey of Web Application Approaches and Frameworks

What follows is a historical survey describing the evolution of web application development approaches and frameworks. We offer a brief summary of how the approaches work and what they offer. These summaries are not intended as in-depth tutorials, nor should they be considered endorsements or dismissals of any particular approach. The goal is to provide observations about the evolution of these approaches.

9.2.1 CGI and FastCGI

We discussed the CGI approach in Chapter 6. To review briefly, web servers process requests to execute CGI programs by spawning new processes. A set of CGI environment variables that are derived from information in the HTTP request is supplied to the executing program, along with the body of the request.

Most approaches that employ CGI are historically code-centric, providing a structure for writing programs that generate dynamic web pages in C, Perl, or another programming language. Formatting and layout constructs are embedded within the code. The CGI mechanism gives programmers access to request context information, including headers and URL parameters. Support for state and session management, database access, and other functionality (all of which are important for web applications) is made available through specialized packages.

Historically, the major deficiency of the CGI mechanism has been the overhead in creating a new web server process for every request. Various server extensions have arisen to alleviate this problem, including embedded language interpreters, such as `mod_perl` and `mod_php` for the Apache Web Server.

One such extension was FastCGI, which uses a variation on the CGI protocol to reduce the process creation overhead. Although FastCGI provides the same services as the original CGI protocol (including the same set of environment variables passed to executing programs), the underlying architecture is different. To take advantage of the performance improvements afforded by FastCGI, developers must structure their code so that it employs a reentrant loop that executes for each request passed to the program. A FastCGI application continues to execute for as long as the web server is running. Theoretically, a failure of an individual FastCGI application should not bring down the web server. (In this sense, FastCGI has many things in common with *Java Servlets*, discussed in Section 9.2.4.)

FastCGI's popularity dissipated somewhat over the years, but it has undergone a revival. One reason for this revival is that FastCGI is seen by some as a better performer and a more flexible mechanism than language-specific embedded interpreters. Another reason is that FastCGI has served as the environmental underpinning for advanced approaches, such as Ruby on Rails.

Not all FastCGI applications are code-centric. Some web application development approaches that have used FastCGI (including Ruby on Rails) transcend the programmatic category by providing template processing and other advanced functionality (such as support for the MVC paradigm).

9.2.2 Server-Side Includes (SSI)

The *Server-Side Includes* (*SSI*) mechanism was a popular adjunct to CGI scripts in many early web applications. The simple syntax for SSI directives, which are embedded in HTML comments, allowed page designers to embed dynamic output in HTML pages:

```
<!--#include virtual="/common/include.html" -->
<!--#config timefmt="%B %e, %Y - %I:%M:%S" -->
It is currently <!--#echo var="DATE_LOCAL" -->
This page was last modified on <!--#echo var="LAST_MODIFIED"-->
```

The dynamic output could include:

- the results of executing various system commands;
- the results of executing a CGI script;
- CGI environment variables associated with the request;
- other environment variables associated with the file and the server;
- date and time.

The Apache implementation of the SSI mechanism added simple constructs for conditionally including portions of HTML pages depending on the values of environment variables.

The combination of CGI scripts with SSI offered additional power to web page designers, but not enough to support sophisticated pages, especially for database-driven applications. The problem with accessing the database from a CGI script and invoking that script from an SSI template is that the script itself is responsible for all formatting of query results, meaning that designers have little or no direct control over the look and feel of the results.

9.2.3 PHP

PHP is a recursive acronym that stands for "PHP Hypertext Preprocessor" (though it originally stood for "Personal Home Page"). It allows developers to embed code within HTML templates, using a language similar to Perl and Unix shells. The source object is structured as an HTML page, but dynamic content generation is programmatic. For example, the PHP fragment:

```
<b>
<?php if ($xyz >= 3) { print $myHeading; }
      else {
?>
      DEFAULT HEADING
<?php  }    ?>
</b>
```

is equivalent to the following:

```
print "<b>";
if ($xyz >= 3) { print $myHeading; }
else { print "DEFAULT HEADING"; }
print "</b>"
```

In other words, text embedded within "`<?php... ?>` " blocks is processed using PHP syntax, while text *outside* these blocks is treated as arguments passed to "print" statements. (We see this strategy again when we discuss Java Server Pages in Section 9.2.8.)

It is debatable whether PHP qualifies as a programmatic approach or a template approach. While other template-based approaches provide several distinct elements designed to perform specific tasks, in PHP there is one element – `<?php... ?>` – that serves as a "container" for PHP code. Although PHP scripts are often referred to as templates, they depend on code to perform most of the work associated with dynamic page generation. This makes PHP a hybrid approach, and one that is closer to a programmatic approach than a template one. Its reliance on code puts it beyond the reach of the average page designer as a tool for building dynamic web pages.

PHP Challenges

Many of the popular open source web applications, including MediaWiki (the software behind Wikipedia) and the blogging, or content-management, application WordPress, are implemented using PHP. They offer a degree of presentation customization in the form of "skins" and "themes", but creation and maintenance of these customizations requires knowledge not only of HTML and CSS, but of the PHP programming language as well.

Developers of these applications seem unconcerned about the barrier this poses for page designers who do not have a programming background. The common attitude in blogs and forums devoted to these applications is either that programmers should be the ones maintaining and configuring them, or that designers should just learn PHP.

The current popularity of these applications insulates them from pressure to change, but there is hope. Template extensions, such as Smarty, lower the barrier for non-programmers, even though the PHP community still looks down on them. Unfortunately, PHP approaches have not evolved to accommodate true separation of content and presentation.

9.2.4   Java Servlet API

The *Java Servlet API* implements the programmatic approach to dynamic page generation using Java. Like CGI, it provides access to request and response information. Unlike CGI programs, servlets are loaded and initialized either at server startup time or as initial requests for the servlets are processed. Requests are processed by threads, so there is no per-request overhead of process creation and initialization.

Servlet programmers have access to the *servlet context* (e.g., servlet initialization parameters, server information) as well as attributes associated with the incoming requests and with the session. The Servlet API provides support for state and session management, making it the responsibility of servlet containers to deal with the stateless nature of the HTTP protocol. The containers implement session

management based on server-side storage of state information, by employing cookies that contain
session identifiers or by embedding these identifiers in the request through URL rewriting.

This simple servlet makes use of selected aspects of servlet functionality:

```java
import javax.util.* ;
import javax.io.* ;
import javax.servlet.* ;
import javax.servlet.http.* ;

public class MyServlet extends HttpServlet {

  private Map _initParams = new HashMap() ;

  public void init() throws ServletException {

    Enumeration enum = getServletConfig().getInitParameterNames() ;
    while (enum.hasMoreElements()) {
      String initParamName = (String) enum.nextElement() ;
      _initParams.put(initParamName,
                  getServletConfig().getInitParameter(initParamName)) ;
    }
  }

  public void doGet(HttpServletRequest req, HttpServletResponse resp)
    throws ServletException, IOException {

      PrintWriter out = resp.getWriter() ;
      String browser = req.getHeader("User-Agent") ;

      HttpSession session = req.getSession() ;
      String title = (String) session.getAttribute("title") ;
      resp.setContentType("text/html") ;
      out.println("<html><head><title>") ;
      out.println(title) ;
      out.println("</title></head><body id="c09-body-0001">") ;
      out.println("<h1>" + title + "</h1>") ;
      out.println("Your browser: " + browser) ;
      out.println("<h3>Initialization Parameters:</h3>") ;
      Iterator i = _initParams.keySet().iterator() ;
      while (i.hasNext()) {
        String initParamName = (String) i.next() ;
        out.println(initParamName + " = " +
                                    _initParams.get(initParamName)) ;
      }
      out.println("</body></html>") ;
      out.close() ;
  }
}
```

When loaded, the servlet enumerates the set of initialization parameter names and stores them in a member variable as a `Map`. For each request, it gets the name of the "user agent" from request headers, and determines the value of the session attribute called "title." It then sets the MIME type of the response to `text/html` and outputs the collected information in HTML format via the "writer" associated with the response.

The Servlet API took dynamic page generation to another level. It transcended many of the inadequacies associated with CGI processing, but did not get us past our dependency on programmatic approaches for dynamic page generation. However, it did set the stage for important advancements toward eliminating this dependency. Just as FastCGI provided a foundation for more advanced platforms, the Servlet API was the foundation for a series of progressively advanced Java-based approaches to web development, discussed later in this chapter.

9.2.5 Cold Fusion

Cold Fusion represents one of the first commercial template approaches to dynamic server-side page generation, providing a set of tags that support the inclusion of external resources, conditional processing, iterative result presentation, and data access. Cold Fusion owes much of its success to two features:

- Queries are very simple to create and use.
- Every form of data access behaves just like a query and formats its results in the same way that a query does.

Database queries are constructed using the `<CFQUERY>` element, referencing an ODBC or JDBC data source with the SQL code embedded between the opening `<CFQUERY>` and the closing `</CFQUERY>` tags. It is possible to traverse the results using the `<CFOUTPUT>` element, with each column available for variable substitution (see Figure 9.2).

In addition to `<CFQUERY>` for talking to databases, Cold Fusion provides tags for accessing other sources of data, including POP3 e-mail servers, FTP servers, and the local file system. Each of these elements utilizes the same method for accessing and presenting iterative results through variable substitution:

```
<CFPOP USERNAME="userid" PASSWORD="*****"
       SERVER="pop3.email.com" NAME="email">
...
<table>
  <CFOUTPUT QUERY="email">
  <tr>
    <td>#MSGNUMBER#</td>
    <td>#FROM#</td>
    <td>#SUBJECT#</td>
  </tr>
  </CFOUTPUT>
</table>
```

Like the Servlet API, Cold Fusion provides access to scoped environment variables (e.g., query string parameters, HTTP headers, and session data). It also allows for the creation of custom tags (much like JSP custom tags that we discuss in Section 9.2.8).

As the Cold Fusion platform evolved, it succumbed to the pressure to provide scripting capabilities within templates. Although this capability gives programmers more power, it also makes it easy to create that clumsy mixture of code and formatting within the same source object.

Although Cold Fusion offers many of the features associated with a solid template approach to web application development, it is a proprietary software product, and the Cold Fusion Markup Language (CFML) is the intellectual property of Adobe Systems. The irony is that many of the tag specifications in Sun's *Java Standard Tag Library* (see Section 9.2.10) are semantically similar to Cold Fusion tags.

```
<CFQUERY DATASOURCE="oracle-prod" NAME="dbquery1">
  SELECT NAME, ADDRESS, PHONE
    FROM CUSTOMERS
    WHERE LAST_PURCHASE_DATE < '2001-01-01';
</CFQUERY>
  ...
<table>
<tr>
  <td align="center"><b>Name</b></td>
  <td align="center"><b>Address</b></td>
  <td align="center"><b>Phone</b></td>
</tr>
<CFOUTPUT QUERY="dbquery1">
<tr>
  <td>#NAME#</td>
  <td>#ADDRESS#</td>
  <td>#PHONE#</td>
</tr>
</CFOUTPUT>
</table>
```

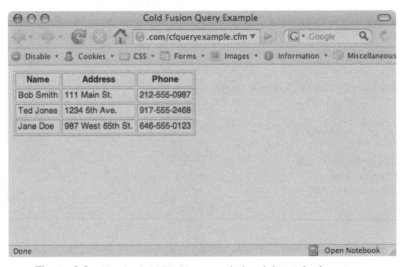

Figure 9.2 Simple Cold Fusion example involving a database query

This does not make Cold Fusion any less proprietary, but it is a sign that it may have been on the right track regarding tag functionality.

Over the years, Cold Fusion has evolved from a proprietary product that executed only on top of FastCGI or proprietary server plug-ins (such as ISAPI or NSAPI) into an application compliant with Java Platform, Enterprise Edition (Java EE) and compatible with the MVC paradigm. Despite its proprietary origins, Cold Fusion still maintains a stable share in the web application software market, serving as the underlying platform for a number of major web sites including myspace.com.

9.2.6 Velocity

Velocity is a true template-based approach to dynamic page generation. Using a small set of logic constructs to support iteration, conditional processing, and the inclusion of external resources, it provides the functionality needed to build dynamic web pages without scattering code fragments and related clutter throughout the page. Although by itself it is not MVC-compliant, it does function well as the *view* component in MVC frameworks that support inclusion of external technologies.

> **Jakarta Project**
>
> Velocity started out as an open-source implementation (by Apache's Jakarta Project) of another template approach for building web applications, WebMacro. Today both approaches co-exist as independent open-source projects. Their syntaxes and structure are similar but not equivalent.

The following code fragment is from a sample *Velocity Template Language* (VTL) template:

```
#set ($message = "Blah blah blah!")

#if ($x == $y)
Here is your message: $message
#end
...
#include filename.wm
...
<table>
  #foreach ($row in $dbquery.results)
  <tr>
    <td>$name</td>
    <td>$address</td>
    <td>$phone</td>
  </tr>
  #end
</table>
```

The VTL directives in this example include a conditional construct (a message that is only displayed if $x is equal to $y), the inclusion of an external file (filename.wm), and the iterative construct that maps the result set produced by the database query stored in a previously defined variable ($dbquery) to the HTML table.

Velocity templates depend on the request context that is established by a controlling Java servlet. This makes it possible to provide template designers with access to content that has been transformed into an appropriate data model by an MVC-compliant controller.

Notation, notation, notation!

Velocity employs Unix-style parameter substitution, with variables indicated by dollar signs (`$variable`). This notation is intuitive to Unix users and Perl programmers, but it may take some getting used to on the part of designers. The same variable-name boundary issues that arise in Unix shells come into play in Velocity templates as well. They are resolved by providing a more formal notation for variable names (e.g., `$variable`) to alleviate confusion, for example, clarifying whether `$correctness` means `${correctness}` or `${correct}ness`. (This notation is also employed in the expression language that is part of the JSP 2.0 specification.)

Velocity's notation is a major improvement over approaches that require program code to display variables and those that enclose variable names in < and > delimiters (which, as we explain in Section 9.2.8, create their own set of problems related to nested angle brackets).

9.2.7 Active Server Pages and .NET

By the late 1990s, many companies had developed their own proprietary server-side processing solutions. Netscape offered LiveWire (which evolved into Server-Side JavaScript), and other companies developed products to support their own approaches for building dynamic web applications, including NetDynamics, Dynamo, and Cold Fusion. (Of these four, only Cold Fusion has survived as a viable platform to the present day.)

Microsoft entered the fray with *Active Server Pages*, which combined server-side scripting capabilities with access to the wide variety of OLE and COM objects in the Microsoft arsenal, including ODBC data sources. Bundled with Microsoft's free Internet Information Server (IIS), ASP quickly gained popularity among Visual Basic programmers who appreciated the VB-like syntax and structure of ASP scripts. Unfortunately, that syntax and structure are ill-suited to modern web applications. ASP pages contain references to obscurely named COM objects intermixed with HTML formatting. Unlike object-oriented languages, such as Java or C++, the language used within ASP pages is flat, linear, and strictly procedural.

In Figure 9.3, there are two "script blocks" embedded within the page. The first block, which appears before the start of HTML markup, sets up the page context by creating a database connection, opening it with appropriate credentials, creating a result set, associating it with the connection, and populating it with the results of the database query. The second block is inserted in the HTML table; it contains procedural code that outputs table rows with cells containing values from columns in the result set.

Like PHP, the structure of ASP is simple: blocks delimited with the `<%` and `%>` character sequences contain script code to be executed by the server when it generates a response, while text found outside such blocks is treated as "raw" HTML. As with PHP, the page is divided between discrete blocks of code and HTML. (Note the presence of page directives in ASP, e.g., `<% @LANGUAGE = VBScript %>`.)

The fact that ASP is bundled with the Microsoft IIS web server makes it an attractive option for installations that employ Microsoft solutions. ASP is popular enough to have been ported to other

```
<% @LANGUAGE = VBScript %>
<%
  Set conn = Server.CreateObject("ADODB.Connection")
  conn.open("Data Source=mydata;User ID=myname;Password=*****")
  Set results = Server.CreateObject("ADODB.RecordSet")
  Set results.ActiveConnection = conn
  query = "SELECT X, Y, Z FROM TABLE1 WHERE X > 23"
  results.Open query
%>
<html>
<head><title>Active Server Page Example</title></head>
<body id="c09-body-0003" bgcolor="#ffffff">
  <table>
    <tr>
      <td align="center">X</td>
      <td align="center">Y</td>
      <td align="center">Z</td>
    </tr>
    <%
      While Not results.EOF
        Response.Write "<tr>"
        Response.Write "<td>" & results("X") & "</td>"
        Response.Write "<td>" & results("Y") & "</td>"
        Response.Write "<td>" & results("Z") & "</td>"
        Response.Write "</tr>"
      Wend
    %>
  </table>
</body>
</html>
```

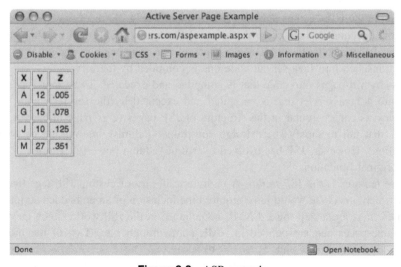

Figure 9.3 ASP example

platforms besides Microsoft's IIS. This bodes well for the future of ASP, given the security holes and other problems associated with IIS. As with Cold Fusion, its benefits are mostly in the area of speeding up the deployment of relatively simple web applications.

Microsoft's *.NET* purports to be a "framework" that alleviates many of the limitations of ASP. In reality, it is ASP on steroids: a set of extensions to the existing ASP infrastructure that offer many of the convenience features found in the Java language, coupled with some advanced page components and the option to create pages using a variety of languages (e.g., VB.NET and C#). There is a lot of additional power provided in .NET, but there are still limitations in scalability, flexibility, and reusability of components. Many installations that tried .NET found that they needed to migrate to a more scalable platform.

One reason that Microsoft's web development approaches have continued to be successful, despite the problems associated with them, is their emphasis on GUI tools. These tools are integral to Microsoft's web application development strategy. Application design and development are accomplished almost exclusively through these tools. In that sense, Microsoft has a tremendous lead over competing web application development approaches. Some non-Microsoft approaches have GUI tools to support application development, but they appear to be an afterthought rather than a primary development interface. They are also not as robust as the tools produced by Microsoft, in part because advocates of these approaches tend to eschew GUI tools. Microsoft tools may make simple things simple, but customizing applications built with those tools ends up requiring low-level coding which often introduces bugs that are very difficult to track down and fix.

9.2.8 Java Server Pages

JSP was Sun's answer to Microsoft's ASP. As with PHP, JSP support was implemented through a pre-processor that turned page objects with embedded code blocks into servlet source code. For example, the sample JSP page in Figure 9.4 translates into servlet code similar to that shown in Figure 9.5.

The first line in Figure 9.4 is the page directive to import classes in the `java.io` package. The next line is a variable declaration. Java code blocks are delimited by the `<%` and `%>` character sequences. HTML outside of these delimiters is translated into `print` statements as shown in Figure 9.5. The entire page is translated into Java servlet code that is compiled by the server.

JSP converts hybrid pages into code that is compiled and executed. To be more specific, the code is translated into a Java servlet that is compiled and executed by the servlet engine. The vestiges of its hybrid origins can be found in the structure of JSP pages (e.g., page directives, declarations, and – in pages that fail to satisfy strict design constraints – clumsy intermixing of "scriptlets" and HTML formatting). However, JSP has evolved over time, adding powerful features that enable it to transcend its original limitations.

Among these features is the JSP *taglib*. A taglib is a library of custom JSP tags that can abstract functionality, which otherwise would have required the inclusion of an embedded scriptlet containing Java code. These tags are a step toward XML compliance in the JSP world, since they are specified using XML namespaces and are defined in XML configuration files. Two of the most commonly used tags are `<jsp:useBean>` and `<jsp:getProperty>`. The `<jsp:useBean>` tag allows page designers to embed a *JavaBean* (constructed and populated by the application and perhaps persisted in the session) within a JSP page. They can access, and possibly modify, properties within that

```
<%@ page import="java.io.*" %>
<%!  private CustomObject myObject; %>
<h1>My Heading</h1>
<%
  for(int i = 0; i < myObject.getCount(); i++) {
%>
    <p>Item #<%= i %> is '<%= myObject.getItem(i) %>'.</p>
<%
  }
>
```

Figure 9.4 Sample JSP page

```
package jsp._myapp ;
import java.io.* ;
import java.util.* ;
import javax.servlet.* ;
import javax.servlet.http.* ;
import javax.servlet.jsp.* ;
public class _mypage extends HttpJspBase {
  private CustomObject myObject;
  public void _jspService(HttpServletRequest req,
                          HttpServletResponse resp)
  {
    ServletConfig config = getServletConfig() ;
    ServletContext application = config.getServletContext() ;
    Object page = this ;
    PageContext pageContext =
                    JspFactory.getDefaultFactory().getPageContext(this,
                                     req, resp, null, true, 8192, true) ;
     JspWriter out = pageContext.getOut() ;
     HttpSession session = request.getSession(true) ;
     out.print("<h1>My Heading</h1>") ;
     for(int i = 0; i < myObject.getCount(); i++) {
       out.print("<p>Item #" + i + " is '" + myObject.getItem(i) +
                                                     "'.</p>") ;
     }
  }
}
```

Figure 9.5 The result of translating the JSP page in Figure 9.4 into servlet code

JavaBean using the `<jsp:getProperty>` and `<jsp:setProperty>` constructs. The JSP translation process, which takes place prior to compilation and execution, converts these constructs into Java code. For example:

```
<jsp:usebean id="myBean" class="mypackage.MyBean" scope="session"/>
...
<p>The value of the 'thing' property
    is '<jsp:getProperty name="myBean" property="thing"/>'.</p>
```

is translated into:

```
MyBean myBean = (MyBean) session.getAttribute("myBean") ;
out.print("<p>The value of the 'thing' property is '" +
                          myBean.getThing().toString() + "'.</p>" ;
```

Note the syntactic complexities associated with variable substitution in the JSP environment. To access a JavaBean property, the `<jsp:getProperty>` tag must be included. (The alternative – using the `<%= object.variable %>` syntax – is arguably worse.) In addition, despite the claims that these tags make JSP pages XML-compliant, variable substitutions may force violations of XML formatting requirements. Take, for example, the attempt in Figure 9.6 to use a JavaBean property to specify the src parameter for an `<img>` tag.

```
<img src="<jsp:getProperty name="myBean" property="imageURL"/>">
```

Figure 9.6 Using a JavaBean property with the < syntax

The text in bold is a `<jsp:getProperty>` tag embedded within an HTML `<img>` tag. Not only is this difficult to read, it violates XML formatting constraints (tags cannot be embedded within one another). A more friendly notation for parameter substitution is desirable, especially if JSPs are intended for manipulation by page designers.

Nested Angle Brackets

The syntactic ugliness associated with variable substitution is not limited to the JSP mechanism. It is present wherever < and > are used as parameter substitution delimiters. It even manifests itself in the more recent Ruby on Rails' `erb` template notation, as we see in Section 9.2.14.

The evolution of the JSP mechanism did not end here. JSP 2.0 added a number of new features, including an expression language for accessing scoped variables within the page and simplified mechanisms for building user-defined tags. Additionally, Sun offered up *JSP Model 2* (see Section 9.2.9), which is a set of guidelines for making the JSP mechanism work better in an MVC context. To that end, Sun provided the *Java Standard Tag Library* (see Section 9.2.10) to make JSPs more usable for developing streamlined view components.

9.2.9 JSP Model 2

JSP Model 2 (not to be confused with JSP 2.0) is Sun's attempt to wrap the JSP mechanism within the MVC paradigm. It is not so much a product offering (or even an API) as it is a set of guidelines, which go along with Sun's packaging of Java-based components and services under the umbrella of Java EE.

The general structure of a web application using the JSP Model 2 architecture is as follows:

1. User requests are directed to the *controller* servlet.
2. The controller servlet accesses and modifies the *model*, possibly delegating the processing to helper classes.
3. The controller servlet (or the appropriate subordinate task) selects and passes control to the appropriate JSP page responsible for presenting the *view*.
4. The view page is processed and returned to the requesting user.
5. The user interacts with the controller servlet (via the view) to enter and modify data, traverse through results, etc.

Data access and application logic should be contained within the controller servlet and its helper classes. The controller servlet (or the helper class) should select the appropriate JSP page and transfer control to that page object based on the request parameters and session information, which commonly includes user identity. Based on user identity, the controller servlet can retrieve user preferences, select JSP pages, and let selected pages personalize the response. Another common dynamic customization pattern is to use the referring URL to perform content co-branding. By examining the request, it is also possible to identify the browser, infer the type of the device making the request, and choose between different formatting options (HTML, XHTML MP, VoiceXML, etc.).

In addition to the guidelines associated with JSP Model 2, Sun provided a set of *blueprints* for building applications using the MVC paradigm. These blueprints were eventually renamed the *Core J2EE Patterns*. They are too numerous and complex to examine in detail here, but some of the more important patterns are described below:

- **Front Controller** is a module (often a servlet) acting as the central entry point into a web application, responsible for managing request processing, performing authentication and authorization services, and selecting the appropriate view.
- **Service-to-Worker** and **Dispatcher Views** are strategies for MVC applications where the front controller module defers processing to a *dispatcher*. The dispatcher can be part of the front controller, but normally it is a separate task, selected by the controller module based on the request context. In the *Dispatcher View* pattern, the dispatcher performs static processing to select the presentation view. In the *Service-to-Worker* pattern, the dispatcher's processing is more dynamic, translating logical task names into concrete module references, and allowing these modules to perform complex processing that determines the presentation view.
- **Intercepting Filter** allows for pluggable *filters* to be inserted into the "request pipeline" to perform pre- and post-processing of incoming requests and outgoing responses. These filters can perform common services required for all or most application tasks, including authentication and logging.

- **Value List Handler** is a mechanism for caching results from database queries, presenting discrete subsets of those results, and providing iterative traversal through the sequence of subsets.
- **Data Access Object (DAO)** is a centralized mechanism for abstracting and encapsulating access to complex data sources, including relational databases, LDAP directories, and CORBA business services. The DAO acts as an adapter, allowing the external interface to remain constant even when the structure of the underlying data source changes.

The structures and guidelines defined by JSP Model 2 form the foundation for a number of advanced frameworks (including *Struts*, which we cover in Section 9.2.11).

9.2.10   Java Standard Tag Library

Sun continued to provide enhancements to JSP as a development platform, including the ability to create your own JSP tags. The result was a proliferation of specialized custom tags written locally by development teams, which only caused more confusion. Sun provided neither standards nor guidance for organizing and structuring custom tags.

Finally, Sun came out with a specification for a *Java Standard Tag Library* (JSTL). It specifies the standard set of tags for iteration, conditional processing, database access, and many other formatting functions. Originally provided as an optional adjunct to JSP, JSTL and its associated expression language, was incorporated into the JSP specification with the advent of JSP 2.0.

JSTL tags fit into several categories:

- The core tags provide the standard functionality you would expect from a template approach: inclusion, iteration, and conditional processing.
- The XML tags provide similar functionality within the XML context, as well as XPath-like traversal of XML documents.
- The SQL tags offer the means to define a data source, submit a query, and iterate through the results.
- The formatting tags include internationalization and localization functions, as well as the means to format dates and numbers.

Figure 9.7 illustrates the use of JSTL tags to execute a database query and present the results of that query as an HTML table. The SQL tags (`<sql:setDataSource>` and `<sql:query>`) establish a database connection, return the results of a query, and assign them to a variable. The core tag `<c:forEach>` iterates through the query results, presenting each returned row as a row in an HTML table (`<tr>`), with the table cells (`<td>`) representing the values in each column. (Note the similarities with the Cold Fusion example in Figure 9.2.)

Parameter substitution comes from the *expression language* (often called *EL*) associated with JSTL, which provides access to variables defined (presumably by a controller servlet) in page, request, session, and application scopes. The notation for variables is Unix-like: `${scopeName.variableName}`. The dotted notation can be extended further where variables represent complex Java objects, including arrays, collections, and maps (e.g., `${session.myObject.myMemberVariable}`). Originally, the expression language worked only within JSTL tags. With the advent of JSP 2.0, EL expressions

```
<%@ taglib uri="http://java.sun.com/jstl/core" prefix="c" %>
<%@ taglib uri="http://java.sun.com/jstl/sql" prefix="sql" %>

<sql:setDataSource var="myDatabase" driver="com.mysql.jdbc.Driver"
  url="jdbc:mysql://localhost:3306/myschema scope="session" />

<sql:query var="contacts" dataSource="${myDatabase}">
  select name, address, phone
  from contacts
</sql:query>

<html>
<head><title>JSTL Example</title></head>
<body id="c09-body-0004" bgcolor="#ffffff">
  <table border="1" cellpadding="4">
    <tr>
      <td align="center"><b>Name</b></td>
      <td align="center"><b>Address</b></td>
      <td align="center"><b>Phone</b></td>
    </tr>
    <c:forEach var="contact" items="${contacts.rows}">
      <tr>
        <td align="center">${contact.name}</td>
        <td align="center">${contact.address}</td>
        <td align="center">${contact.phone}</td>
      </tr>
    </c:forEach>
  </table>
</body>
</html>
```

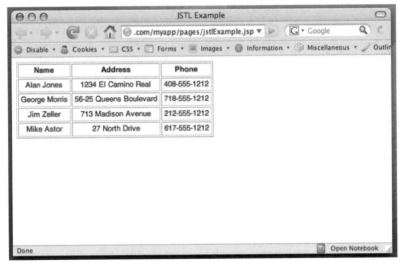

Figure 9.7 A JSP page using JSTL

are now valid anywhere in a page, not just inside of JSTL tags. Additionally, there are EL functions that support working with strings (substring, matching, replacement, upper and lower case).

When you hear developers express distaste for the JSP mechanism, they are more than likely referring to the tendency of JSPs to become bloated with embedded Java code (scriptlets) so complicated that the page becomes impossible to maintain. This is often an outgrowth of the "monolithic JSP" anti-pattern. Cluttered, scriptlet-ridden JSP pages are symptomatic of a failure to abide by the MVC paradigm. Controller logic and presentation formatting end up being intermingled, with predictably unmanageable results.

JSTL made it possible to write JSP pages without embedded Java code, removing much of the ugliness associated with early JSP implementations. It provides a viable view technology for the JSP Model 2 strategy, especially with an MVC framework, such as Struts. Although JSTL has the capacity to stand on its own as a complete web application solution using the SQL tags for database access, those tags are a violation of the MVC paradigm, in that they provide a service that belongs in the controller component, not in the view. JSTL is best employed as a pure view technology within the context of an MVC framework.

9.2.11   Struts

The *Struts* framework provides a robust infrastructure for JSP Model 2 application development. Developed within the open source Apache Jakarta project, it makes use of the *Model–View–Controller, Front Controller*, and *Service-to-Worker* patterns to provide a true framework for web application development.

A Struts application consists of the following components:

- **Controller**: The `org.apache.struts.action.ActionServlet` class that comes with Struts is flexible enough for most applications, though it is possible to extend this class if required. This servlet class represents the entry point for user requests.
- **Dispatcher**: The `org.apache.struts.action.RequestProcessor` class that comes with Struts is flexible enough for most applications, though it is possible to extend this class if required.
- **Request handlers (custom)**: These are application-specific classes, often called *actions*, that extend the `org.apache.struts.action.Action` class and override its `execute()` method to perform the processing required by the application.
- **View helpers (custom)**: These are JavaBeans that extend the abstract `org.apache.struts.action.ActionForm` class. They mediate between the model and the view, providing getter and setter methods for form fields and implementing custom validation if desired.
- **Views (custom)**: The Struts framework is platform-neutral with regard to views: they can be JSPs or Velocity templates, or can use any other mechanism that can access the servlet runtime context.

The main attraction of the Struts framework is that developers can make use of configurable application components (e.g., the controller servlet) that come with the Struts distribution, instead of having to implement these components themselves.

The whole application comes together through the XML configuration file, `struts-config.xml`, which is located in the application's WEB-INF directory. The application in Figure 9.8, deals with processing form submissions.

```
<struts-config>
   <controller processorClass="myapp.controller.MyRequestProcessor">
   <form-beans>
      <form-bean name="loginForm" type="myapp.view.LoginForm" />
         :
         :
   </form-beans>
   <action-mappings>
      <action path="/myapp/login" type="myapp.controller.LoginAction"
         name="loginForm" scope="request">
            <forward name="success" path="/myapp/success.jsp" />
            <forward name="failure" path="/myapp/failure.jsp" />
      </action>
         :
         :
   </action-mappings>
</struts-config>
```

Figure 9.8 Sample `struts-config.xml` file

The `<action-mappings>` section tells the dispatcher (`RequestProcessor`) which request handler (extending the `Action` class) should process an incoming request, based on the path portion of the request URL. The `<action>` element maps the action's "logical name" (the `/myapp/login` URL) to the name of the Java class implementing the request handler and establishes the scope of the action (the current request). The `<action>` element references the JavaBean associated with the form by its logical name, which is specified in the `<form-bean>` element.

In addition, `<forward>` elements (nested within `<action>` elements) map names (e.g., `success` and `failure`) to URL paths associated with views or other actions. The `execute()` method of the `Action` class returns an `ActionForward` object. The name associated with the returned `Action-Forward` object determines what the application does next.

Notice that there is no need to implement a new Java class for every action. It is possible to define just a few generic request handlers and control their behavior through the `<action>` configuration. Decisions about the generality of application-specific action classes, form beans, and other components are part of the application design.

Using a small set of extensible, reusable components, along with a well-organized structure tying those components together, Struts provides a viable platform for serious web application development. Add to this the Struts JSP taglibs that make it easier to format pages that make use of `ActionForm` beans, and you have a powerful framework. And, to top it all off, it is open source.

Still, this is not the be-all-and-end-all of web application frameworks. Struts has already been rewritten as Struts 2, and there is a newer framework that supports Sun's next-generation vision for presentation technology: Java Server Faces.

9.2.12 Java Server Faces

Although Microsoft's .NET framework received mixed reviews regarding its viability as a scalable web framework, there was one aspect of it that was universally appreciated – its UI components. Just as JSP was Sun's response to Microsoft's ASP, *Java Server Faces* (JSF) is Sun's response to .NET's UI functionality.

While JSTL provides a low-level approach to page layout, offering fine-grained controls for conditional processing and iteration over database query results, JSF provides a higher-level approach through coarser visual components. For example, in JSTL one might do what was demonstrated in Figure 9.7: use the JSTL <c:forEach> tag to iterate through rows retrieved from a database, presenting each one as a row in an HTML table (<tr>) with individual column values presented using the JSP Expression Language as HTML table cells (<td>). In JSF, the same result is achieved with the <h:dataTable> tag, which abstracts the notion of an HTML table populated by database query results:

```
<%@ taglib prefix="f" uri="http://java.sun.com/jsf/core" %>
<%@ taglib prefix="h" uri="http://java.sun.com/jsf/html" %>

<html>
<head><title>JSF Example</title></head>
<body id="c09-body-0002" bgcolor="#ffffff">
  <f:view>
    <h:dataTable value="#{bean1.contacts}" var="contact"
        styleClass="tab" headerClass="header" rowClasses="oddRow,evenRow">
      <h:column>
        <f:facet name="header">
          <h:outputText value="Name" />
        </f:facet>
        <h:outputText value="#{contact.name}" />
      </h:column>
      <h:column>
        <f:facet name="header">
          <h:outputText value="Address" />
        </f:facet>
        <h:outputText value="#{contact.address}" />
      </h:column>
      <h:column>
        <f:facet name="header">
          <h:outputText value="Phone" />
        </f:facet>
        <h:outputText value="#{contact.phone}" />
      </h:column>
    </h:dataTable>
  </f:view>
</body>
</html>
```

The Faces servlet translates these directives into HTML – or into some other target markup format. The idea is that the same directives could, if desired, support multiple presentation formats. This is where JSF is supposed to shine: JSF components abstract away the underlying HTML constructs, and can be used to render formats other than HTML. In practice, this capability is rarely employed. Unfortunately, there are few alternative JSF *renderkits* for non-HTML presentation and few applications seem to make use of this functionality.

Although JSF can make UI design less tedious, it has a number of disadvantages compared to more established approaches, such as Struts and JSP/JSTL:

- JSF pages are rendered by a separately configured Faces servlet, not by the JSP processor that comes with Java EE application servers. Although it is possible for JSP pages (with JSTL) to co-exist with JSF, this is difficult to achieve and even more difficult to manage.
- The JSF expression language is quite different from JSP EL. For one thing, it uses a different set of delimiters in its variable notation (#*variableName* rather than $*variableName*). JSF was originally developed in parallel with the JSTL EL, before either technology had been widely accepted and integrated into Java EE server standards. There was a perceived need for a distinctly different notation, which has compounded confusion and slowed the acceptance of JSF.
- While JSTL tags provide fine-grained control at the level of iteration, inclusion, and conditional processing, JSF components offer higher level functionality (e.g., a data grid or a login form). High-level components may accelerate initial development, but customizing them to fit the needs of a particular application (particularly when it comes to "look-and-feel" details) is difficult. This same problem has historically plagued Microsoft offerings – the "simple" things are very easy and can be done quickly, but customizing the look-and-feel or the underlying behaviors of the components is never easy and is often impossible without extensive recoding. Remember, this is what you were trying to avoid in the first place by using high-level components!
- The Struts framework already provides many advanced application services including validation. (This is becoming less of a disadvantage over time as JSF implementations are augmented to provide these services.)

The most common complaint about JSF is its complexity. Even though a component-based approach ought to be simpler than other approaches, there is a much higher learning curve associated with designing and developing JSF applications. The inconsistencies and collisions between JSP/JSTL and JSF notations and conventions do not help matters. Developers see Struts and JSF as an "either–or" decision, not as a set of complementary technologies whose capabilities can be cherry-picked to use the best of both.

Development on JSF began as JSTL and JSP 2.0 were just beginning to gain traction in the application development community. It went its own way rather than piggybacking on established approaches and, as a result, it remains incompatible. JSF provides its own controller servlet (`FacesServlet`) with its own XML configuration file (`faces-config.xml`) that mirrors the functionality of the Struts `ActionServlet` and the `struts-config.xml` file. It replicates the functionality of the `struts-html` JSP tags that work as an adjunct to JSTL tags in Struts/JSTL applications. Many developers see this as reinventing a wheel that already rolls quite well.

JSF advocates often compare JSF components not to JSP 2.0/JSTL but to the much older Struts tag libraries which have been supplanted by JSTL. While JSF compares favorably with those older tags, JSP 2.0 with EL and JSTL has evolved and matured, and a comparison between JSF and JSP 2.0 does not come out quite as well.

Perhaps the creators of JSF thought that justifiable disgust with early JSP specifications and implementations would lead developers to seek an escape to a different technology. However, the JSP mechanism is not going away and in its current incarnation it is still a viable and flexible presentation approach.

In the meantime, JSF continues to evolve. The latest specification, JSF 1.2, employs a *Unified Expression Language* (UEL) that converges at last with the JSP/JSTL expression language. A number of third-party UI component packages are available, both open source and commercial, including several that incorporate AJAX and DHTML functionality (e.g., *Ajax4Jsf* and *ICEFaces*). *Facelets* provides an alternative view handler for JSF that builds views from XHTML documents instead of JSPs. At the same time, new JSF-enabled frameworks such as JBoss Seam are beginning to garner interest among developers.

9.2.13   JBoss Seam

JBoss Seam is a relatively new framework that is gaining a bit of traction in the developer community. Developers who are interested in making use of JSF but have been scared off by its complexity and newness are looking at Seam as a way to write applications that connect JSF with EJB 3.0.

EJB Revival?

We have not touched on Enterprise Java Beans (EJB) in this book. While EJB has always been a strategic aspect of the Java EE architecture, it gained a reputation over the years as being inordinately complex and overkill for most applications. A number of evangelists for simpler approaches to application development (including Bruce Tate and Rod Johnson) have eschewed EJB entirely, suggesting that the vast majority of projects do not require EJB's features. Our discussion of application development approaches concurs with that notion, and focuses on approaches that do not rely on EJB.

However, EJB 3.0 is a milestone in that it simplified many of the complexities long associated with EJB technology. Taking a page from "simpler-is-better" frameworks, such as Spring and Hibernate, EJB 3.0 employs a simplified persistence model that focuses on Plain Old Java Objects (POJOs) as its persistent entities, rather than on the more complex objects required by earlier versions of EJB.

Seam is still the new kid on the block. Its biggest hurdle in gaining mass acceptance may be its origins. It was developed by JBoss, a company known for its open-source Java EE container. In the minds of many developers, there is a concern that Seam has been optimized to work with the JBoss application server and that it may be tricky to get it work with other Java EE servers. JBoss has stated a commitment to keep Seam container-agnostic, but the concern is still there.

Even though both JSF and EJB 3.0 are still relatively new technologies, Seam is a framework to keep an eye on. As JSF and EJB 3.0 gain traction, Seam may become the framework of choice to make use of those technologies. Seam 2.0 attempts to extend Seam's reach by removing its dependencies on specific front-end and back-end technologies, namely JSF and EJB 3.0, and integrating support for AJAX, Hibernate, Groovy, and Facelets.

9.2.14   Rapid application development: Ruby on Rails

"With flexibility comes complexity." While not universally valid, this axiom generally holds true for software development and for web application development in particular. Perhaps the most obvious example of this is Java EE – arguably the leading platform for scalable web-based enterprise applications. The Servlet API, coupled with Java Server Pages, JSTL and now JSF, provide a foundation for the web tier. The Java core libraries and extensions (including JNDI, EJB, and JavaMail) provide a solid base of functionality in other areas.

However, this range of functionality comes at a price:

- The learning curve for Java EE developers is very steep.
- The range of options for application frameworks – Struts, Spring, Hibernate, Velocity, JSTL, JSF, and so on – is mind-boggling, and daunting even to experienced developers.
- The number of separate components that need to be developed for a complete web application can also be quite daunting.
- The mechanisms for creating, configuring, and deploying applications are tedious.
- Sun provides specifications (and sometimes reference implementations) for the Java EE APIs, but production-worthy implementations of these APIs are left to commercial and open-source software providers. Despite standardization, each comes with its own set of idiosyncrasies that hinder development of interoperable applications.

All of the above factors limit the speed at which web applications based on Java EE can be developed and deployed, making them less attractive for businesses.

These issues caused some measure of disenchantment with Java EE in the web application development community at large. Bruce Tate (see Section 9.5) wrote an award-winning book called *Better, Faster, Lighter Java*, in which he extolled the virtues of lighter-weight non-EJB approaches such as Spring and Hibernate. At some point, his bitterness about Java became so extreme that he proclaimed the inevitable imminent death of Java in another book, *Beyond Java*. He notes that rather than moving in the direction of eliminating Java EE complexity, Java is guilty of "adding new features rapidly instead of simplifying what's already out there."

As a successor to Java, Tate points to *Ruby on Rails* as a web application framework for the future. It is often referred to as just *Rails*, since Ruby is simply the name of the programming language used in the Rails framework. It is a true open-source, full-stack MVC framework for developing and deploying web applications.

Ruby on Rails was developed by David Heinemeier Hansson, a Danish developer, in 2004. He saw reusable functionality in an existing web application written in Ruby, including template processing functionality and the abstraction of database access. He combined those common facets into what grew into a fully fledged web application framework. The initial beta version was released in July 2004 and the 1.0 version was made available by the end of 2005.

Rails has sophisticated template-processing functionality, providing support for template objects in HTML (.rhtml), XML (.rxml), and JavaScript (.rjs). (Note: In Rails 2.0, one of many major changes was that the suffixes were changed to .html.erb, .xml.erb, and .js.rjs.) It also has its own built-in, transaction-safe, object-relational mapping (ORM) service based on the *Active Record* paradigm advocated by Fowler (2002). Fowler describes this paradigm as "an object that wraps a row in a database table or view, encapsulates the database access, and adds domain logic on that data."

One area where Rails definitely comes out ahead of other frameworks is in its usage of *"convention over configuration."* If standard conventions are adhered to when designing and developing an application, very little configuration information needs to be constructed manually. What's more, this practice is encouraged by development tools that automatically generate application skeletons that conform to these conventions. This includes directory structures for application source files separated into discrete categories: models, views, controllers, and helpers. (Not too surprisingly, the first three of these categories just happen to conform to the name of an architectural paradigm we've been advocating for most of this chapter.)

Ruby on Rails shines when it comes to *rapid application development* and deployment. A basic Rails application that follows standard application development conventions is self-generating (at least the application skeleton), self-configuring, self-testing, and (with an additional package) self-deploying. Rails makes extensive use of *scaffolding* to automate the process of building a database-driven application skeleton with full Create–Read–Update–Delete (CRUD) functionality. It also offers tight integration with DHTML and AJAX toolkits, such as Prototype.

This is not to say that Ruby on Rails is the be-all-and-end-all of web application frameworks. It still falls short in a number of areas:

- **IDE and debugging support**: As we mentioned earlier, advanced IDE support for code written in loosely typed languages, such as Ruby, is difficult. Debugging support is on the weak side when compared to other established frameworks, but Ruby does provide a sophisticated command-line Read–Eval–Print Loop (*REPL*) tool called `irb` that facilitates interactive debugging.
- **Scalability**: A Rails application can be deployed locally on a developer desktop with incredible ease, but that only works in a limited single-user environment. Deploying that application to a production environment is another story. Rails has tried to piggyback on FastCGI to enable Rails applications to work with web servers like Apache, but with mixed success. *Mongrel* is a standalone HTTP server, written in Ruby, that is used by many Rails installations to achieve durability and scalability for Rails applications in a production environment. Apache can be configured to use Mongrel as a proxy for requests targeting Rails applications.
- **Parameter substitution notation in templates**: This is a lesson that ought to have been learned and relearned by now, but the problem keeps coming back even in newer frameworks. Basic template processing in Rails makes use of a notation that uses < and > as delimiters. Specifically, the *embedded Ruby* syntax calls for blocks that begin with <%= and end with %>. This is a throwback to the notations associated with PHP, ASP, and the original version of JSP, reviving the problems associated with those older notations.

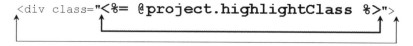

Figure 9.9   Parameter substitution using embedded Ruby syntax

The example in Figure 9.9 harks back to Figure 9.6, which shows a similar problem with embedded Java in JSPs. Java EE learned this lesson and the JSP EL uses $ { and } as delimiters.

It is a good bet that Ruby on Rails will outgrow these issues, but a new framework only gets one shot at Version 1.0; in subsequent releases, backward compatibility becomes an overwhelming concern. Still, Ruby on Rails is *the* up-and-coming web application framework. Apple recently started including Ruby on Rails as part of the Mac OS X Server 10.5 (Leopard) operating system.

Will the ascent of Rails lead to the oft-predicted death of Java? Maybe, but Java isn't going down without a fight. Following in the footsteps of Ruby on Rails, new approaches, such as *Grails* (which uses Java's *Groovy* scripting language), attempt to eschew the clumsy configuration mechanisms and complex interactions commonly associated with Java EE application development. Only time will tell whether Rails will mature to become a true enterprise framework, and whether alternatives, such as *Groovy on Grails*, will successfully challenge Ruby on Rails for the crown.

9.3 Summary

We have only touched on the most popular approaches and frameworks used in web application development. We have omitted discussion of approaches that are only of historical significance. We have not covered marginally popular frameworks that use XML as the foundation for their data models (e.g., Cocoon) or that use XSLT as the engine to transform data into appropriate presentation formats (e.g., XHTML, XHTML MP, SMIL, and VoiceXML).

Today, the best approach to building a durable, flexible, and extensible web application is to make use of the MVC paradigm, coupling a controller-driven framework with template-based views. The most viable approach that satisfies these requirements is the Struts framework, using JSTL as the view technology. In Chapter 10, we design a simple real-estate broker application using Struts and JSTL. In Chapter 11, we build the same application using Ruby on Rails so that we can compare the benefits and drawbacks of the two approaches.

Before we move on, let us spend some time on a side-by-side comparison of the web application development approaches (see Table 9.1). Even though we strive toward the MVC architecture, no existing framework (including Struts and Ruby on Rails) achieves all of its goals. In practice, we do not always get to choose the best platform for application development. With this in mind, it behooves us to summarize the capabilities – and limitations – of the most popular web application development approaches.

Table 9.1   Comparison of Web Application Development Approaches

Name Classification	Availability, Advantages, and Drawbacks
CGI Programmatic approach	**Availability:** Open standard implemented in all major web servers **Advantages:** • Portable across a wide variety of web server environments • Simple programming paradigm • Modules available to augment base language functionality **Drawbacks:** • HTML formatting is performed programmatically • Overhead of process creation and initialization for each request
FastCGI Programmatic approach	**Availability:** Open standard with custom implementations **Advantages:** • Portable across a wide variety of web server environments • Simple programming paradigm • Modules available to augment base language functionality • Less process creation overhead than standard CGI **Drawbacks:** • Requires more disciplined programming paradigm than standard CGI • Configuration issues in some server environments
Server Side Includes (SSI) Template approach	**Availability:** Open standard **Advantages:** • Simple syntax for external file inclusion • Allows inclusion of output from CGI scripts **Drawbacks:** • Security holes • Not enough power by today's standards (especially if CGI script inclusion is not enabled)
PHP Hybrid approach (though pages often referred to as template)	**Availability:** Open source **Advantages:** • Structural change from code focus to page focus • Modules available to augment base language functionality • Many popular web applications (MediaWiki, WordPress, phpBB) use it **Drawbacks:** • Abrupt intermingling of code and formatting • Scalability issues • Powerful but inflexible components

Table 9.1 *(continued)*

Name Classification	Availability, Advantages, and Drawbacks
Cold Fusion Template approach, evolved into hybrid approach	**Availability:** Proprietary (Adobe) **Advantages:** • Portable across wide variety of web servers (now only on Java EE) • First commercially successful template approach, with tags for conditional and iterative processing eliminating need for most embedded code • Rapid application development: quick way to get a web application up and running • Cold Fusion Components can be used as controller modules **Drawbacks:** • Original structure mixed program logic and data access within the page structure • Simpler than programmatic approaches, but still out of reach for most page designers • Proprietary
Velocity Template approach	**Availability:** Open source **Advantages:** • True template approach • Limits code infestation within templates to iteration and conditional processing constructs • Works well as a view technology within an MVC framework **Drawbacks:** • Limited utility: needs the support of a controller to provide data context
ASP and .NET Hybrid approach	**Availability:** Proprietary (Microsoft but ported to non-Microsoft environments) **Advantages:** • Direct access to COM and ActiveX objects and ODBC databases • UI components for rendering complex data structures • Strong GUI development tools • Rapid application development: quick way to get a web application up and running **Drawbacks:** • Abrupt intermixing of code and formatting • Scalability issues • Powerful but inflexible components • Too complex for page designers • Proprietary

(continued overleaf)

Table 9.1 *(continued)*

Name Classification	Availability, Advantages, and Drawbacks
Servlet API Programmatic approach	**Availability:** Proprietary specification (Sun); open source and commercial implementations **Advantages:** • Open specification with developer community involvement • Power and extensibility of Java language **Drawbacks:** • HTML formatting performed programmatically
Java Server Pages (JSP) Hybrid approach (often mistakenly called a template approach)	**Availability:** Proprietary specification (Sun); open source and commercial implementations **Advantages:** • Open specification with developer community involvement • Open source and commercial implementations (usually coupled with a servlet engine) • Powerful built-in tags complemented by custom taglibs for extensibility **Drawbacks:** • Lends itself to the "Monolithic JSP" anti-pattern
JSP Model 2 Framework specification without implementation	**Availability:** Open **Advantages:** • Encourages MVC approach • Provides architectural guidance • Many implementations (open source ones are the most popular) **Drawbacks:** • Not an actual framework offering (a manifesto for better programming practices) • JSP limitations remain
JSTL Template approach	**Availability:** Proprietary specification (Sun); open source and commercial implementations **Advantages:** • Template-like tags • JSPs can be written without embedded Java code • Simplified variable substitution with JSP Expression Language • Complete view technology solution, when coupled with MVC approach **Drawbacks:** • Tightly coupled with the JSP mechanism • Component capabilities limited by low-level constructs

Table 9.1 *(continued)*

Name Classification	Availability, Advantages, and Drawbacks
Struts Framework	**Availability:** Open source **Advantages:** • Fully fledged MVC framework for Java EE • Dynamic dispatching, form validation, custom taglibs • Flexibility in selecting presentation views (JSP, Velocity templates, etc.) **Drawbacks:** • Careful design is required to reap full benefits • Not easy to configure (although front-end tools exist to make initial application setup simpler)

Java Server Faces (JSF)
 	
Framework with sophisticated template functionality
	Availability: Proprietary specification (Sun); open source and commercial implementations
	Advantages:
	• High-level page components
	• Open specification fostered by community participation
	Drawbacks:
	• Incompatibilities with JSTL and JSP
	  • Different notation for its own expression language
	  • Requiring its own specialized servlet to render faces-based pages
	• Complexity
	• Unfulfilled promise of flexible renderkits that allow one JSF page to produce layout for multiple target formats or markup languages
	• Not enough customizable third-party components
	• Lack of fine-grained granular controls

JBoss Seam Framework	**Availability:** Open source (but associated with a specific Java EE container) **Advantages:** • Connects JSF presentation components directly to EJB 3.0 server-side components • Simplified configuration to enable easy connectivity between JSF and EJB • Very useful notion of "conversation" scope to group information for related requests **Drawbacks:** • The sole provider offers its own Java EE server (how well does it work with other server software?) • Simplification at the expense of best practice?

(continued overleaf)

Table 9.1 *(continued)*

Name Classification	Availability, Advantages, and Drawbacks
Ruby on Rails Framework with advanced template functionality	**Availability:** Open source **Advantages:** • Fully fledged MVC-capable framework with template capabilities • Simplified structure and automated setup (which speed up application design and development) • Integrated support for DHTML and AJAX frameworks including templates for page layout and embedded JavaScript **Drawbacks:** • Suitable for prototyping and small-scale development, but not scalable for high-volume applications without additional web server support layers (e.g., Mongrel as Apache proxy) • Same mistakes as older frameworks (e.g., variable substitution notation in templates)

QUESTIONS AND EXERCISES

1. What is the difference between a programmatic approach and a template approach? Provide examples. Can we apply this classification to the MVC paradigm? Explain.

2. Give examples of a hybrid approach. Explain why they are described as "hybrid."

3. What are the advantages of the Model–View–Controller paradigm for web application development?

4. The Model–View–Controller paradigm provides separation of content from presentation, which means that the same model can be associated with many different views. Give reasons why applications might require multiple views.

5. What are the main advantages of the Struts framework? Describe the main components of a Struts application and their operation.

6. Where do XML and XSLT fit in with respect to the available approaches and frameworks?

7. What was the approach that you used last? Were you satisfied with it? Describe your main concerns with regard to this approach. Can you recommend improvements?

8. What are the tradeoffs between simplicity (ease of development and deployment, learning curve, etc.) and flexibility (scalability, customizability, and functionality) in considering application development approaches? What is gained or lost in striving to achieve maximum flexibility? When does an approach achieve maximum simplicity? Describe a middle-ground approach that is both simple and flexible.

9.4   Bibliography

Bayern, Shawn, 2002. *JSTL in Action*. Greenwich (CT): Manning Publications.

Bellinaso, Marco, 2006. *ASP.NET 2.0 Website Programming: Problem – Design – Solution*. Indianapolis (IN): Wrox Press/Wiley Publishing.

Birznieks, Gunther, Guelich, Scott and Gundavaram, Shishir, 2000. *CGI Programming with Perl*. Sebastopol (CA): O'Reilly & Associates.

Bosanac, Dejan, 2007. *Scripting in Java: Languages, Frameworks, and Patterns*. Boston (MA): Addison-Wesley/Pearson Education.

Eide-Goodman, Heow and Lecky-Thompson Edward, *et al*., 2004. *Professional PHP5 (Programmer to Programmer)*. Indianapolis (IN): Wrox Press/Wiley Publishing.

Fowler, Martin, 2002. *Patterns of Enterprise Application Architecture*. New York: Addison-Wesley.

Gantz, Shlomy and Camden, Raymond *et al*., 2003. *Cold Fusion MX Developer's Handbook*. Alameda (CA): Sybex.

Geary, David and Horstmann, Cay, 2007. *Core Java Server Faces*, 2nd Edition. Santa Clara (CA): Sun Microsystems Press/Prentice-Hall.

Hall, Marty and Brown, Larry, 2003. *Core Servlets and Java Server Pages, Volume I: Core Technologies*, 2nd Edition. Santa Clara (CA): Sun Microsystems Press/Prentice-Hall.

Halloway, Stuart and Gehtland, Justin, 2007. *Rails for Java Developers*. Raleigh (NC): Pragmatic Bookshelf.

Holmes, James, 2006. *Struts: The Complete Reference*, 2nd Edition. Emeryville (CA): Osborne.

Hunter, Jason and Crawford, William, 2001. *Java Servlet Programming*, 2nd Edition. Sebastopol (CA): O'Reilly & Associates.

Johnson, Rod with Juergen Hoeller, 2004. *Expert One-on-One: J2EE Development Without EJB*. Indianapolis (IN): Wrox Press/Wiley Publishing.

Kurniawan, Budi, 2005. *Struts Design and Programming: A Tutorial*. Vancouver (BC): Brainy Software.

Tate, Bruce, 2002. *Bitter Java*. Greenwich (CT)Manning Publications.

Tate, Bruce, 2005. *Beyond Java*. Sebastopol (CA): O'Reilly Media.

Thomas, Dave, 2004. *Programming Ruby: The Pragmatic Programmer's Guide*, 2nd Edition. Raleigh (NC): Pragmatic Bookshelf.

Yuan, Michael Juntao, Orshalick, Jacob and Heute, Thomas, 2008. *Seam Framework: Experience the Evolution of Java EE*, 2nd Edition. Upper Saddle River (NJ): Prentice-Hall/Pearson Education.

CHAPTER 10

Web Application Primer 1: Struts and JSTL

> **IN THIS CHAPTER**
> - Case Study: Virtual Realty Listing Service (VRLS)
> - Application requirements
> - Technology choices
> - Overview of Struts
> - Structure of the VRLS application
> - Design decisions
> - Enhancements
>
> **OBJECTIVES**
> - Review the notion of a web application.
> - Use the VRLS case study to discuss the requirements gathering and application design processes.
> - Provide an overview of the Struts framework and examine the inner workings of a Struts application in the context of VRLS.
> - Explain the reasons behind application design decisions.
> - Propose enhancements to the VRLS application.

As we mentioned in Chapter 1, web applications are client–server applications that use a browser as their client program. However, web applications are not limited to the interactions between browsers and servers. Server-side application components can operate as "clients", interacting with back-end data sources such as databases, web services, and legacy systems. In *multi-tier* web applications, every set of adjacent tiers represents a pairing of a client and a server, and every intermediate tier may act as either a client or a server, depending on which of its neighbors it is interacting with. For example, just as the browser connects to the web server to make a request, the application component executing on the web server may connect to a business logic layer, acting as a client for that layer's services.

In the last few chapters, we have covered both client-side techniques and server-side frameworks that enable us to construct sophisticated web applications. In this chapter, we offer a primer for using this knowledge, by designing, developing, and deploying a sample web application that we call *Virtual Realty Listing Services*.

On the book's companion web site (www.webappbuilders.com), we offer this sample application for non-commercial tutorial purposes, in a package that includes source code, database schema, and configuration instructions. To get the most out of this chapter, we recommend that you install the application first, before working through the text. This will give you a better perspective on the look and feel of the application and its workflow. We also recommend that you refer to the source code and associated configuration files while reading this chapter.

10.1   Case Study: Virtual Realty Listing Services

Virtual Realty Listing Services (VRLS) is a fictitious on-line, real-estate company that supports *multiple listing services*, a cooperative venture that is common in the real-estate industry. Many bricks-and-mortar, real-estate brokers share listings for properties they want to sell or lease, in an attempt to attract customers who want to buy or rent these properties. If a customer goes to one broker and buys or rents a property associated with another, the two brokers split the commission. This way, there is a greater chance for all brokers to sell or rent their properties.

An on-line version of this service would link the web sites of several real-estate brokerages to an aggregated database of shared property listings. Customers locate the VRLS application through links from their real-estate broker, on-line search, print advertisements, or word-of-mouth. Through this application, they can access property listings from many different brokers. They can browse the available listings freely but need to register in order to see details about particular properties. When customers register, they remain associated with the broker whose site referred them to the VRLS registration page. The referring brokers are called *affiliates* or *partners*.

In the scenario in Figure 10.1, Jane starts her house search by visiting the Why-Kurt realty web site. While browsing through that site, she comes across a link to the VRLS application and follows it. Upon her initial arrival at the site hosting the VRLS application, her affiliation is identified based on the referring site (found in the HTTP request's `Referer` header) and she is presented with the welcome page co-branded to the look and feel of Why-Kurt. Jane uses the VRLS application to search for shared listings but does not follows links to property details and remains an anonymous user. Consequently, her affiliation with Why-Kurt is preserved only for the duration of the browser session.

Meanwhile, John visits the Decade23 web site and follows a link to the VRLS application from there. His affiliation is recognized and he is presented with the welcome page co-branded to the look

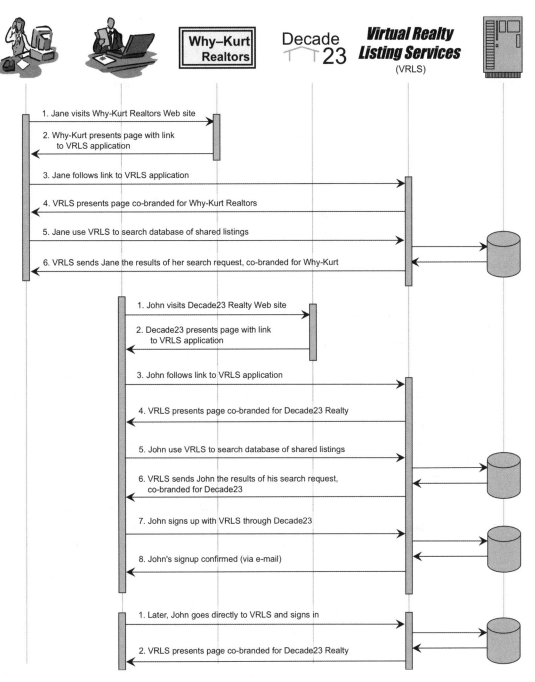

Figure 10.1 Search and access scenario.

and feel of Decade23. Just as Jane did, John searches for his dream house and finds a listing that looks interesting. He attempts to retrieve detailed information about the listing, which results in an invitation to login or register in order to proceed. When John registers, his temporary affiliation with the referring site Decade23 becomes permanent and is stored in his profile. John receives an e-mail message with his assigned password and logs in. From that point on, whenever he signs in, he is presented with pages co-branded to the look and feel of Decade23.

10.2   Application Requirements

Ideally, the prospective business customers of this proposed application would provide detailed requirements from the start. Anyone who has worked on real-world projects knows that this rarely happens. More often, application developers get a loosely defined set of objectives, which have yet to be detailed and clarified, to serve as the foundation for building the application. Nonetheless, it is important to clarify and refine requirements carefully and methodically.

With that in mind, let us assume that through a process of interviews with business users, use case scenarios, and business process analyses, we have come up with the following simplified set of application requirements:

1. There are four classes of user: *customers, anonymous visitors, partners,* and *administrators.*
2. There should be a mechanism for associating partner brokers with individual requests to the VRLS application. This identification can be implicit (e.g., identifying the partner using the referring URL) or explicit (e.g., identifying the partner via a query string parameter found in its links to the VRLS site). When unregistered visitors arrive from a partner site, they see partner-specific branding (e.g., a toolbar and company logo) that is applied across all pages served by the VRLS application.
3. Mechanisms should exist for login by registered customers and for new customer signup.
4. When existing customers log in, they should see co-branded pages, according to their partner affiliation. Partner identification for existing customers prior to login is on a "best-effort" basis. If it is not possible to determine the partner, the application should present a default view.
5. Customers should be able to create a personal profile at registration time and modify it in the future. Profile information should include a login name and password, name, address, phone number, e-mail address, and the identity of the partner. Customers should not be able to modify their system-assigned unique user ids, their login names, or their partner affiliation, but should be able to modify all other profile parameters.
6. After signing up, customers should receive a confirmation notice via e-mail. Their profile should not be "activated" until they visit the application again and confirm their receipt of the e-mail.
7. Customers should be able to search the available listings for properties that satisfy their search criteria, which could include the type of property, number of bedrooms, etc. Search results should include summary information about each listing that satisfies the search criteria.
8. Authenticated customers should be able to retrieve details about a particular property. Anonymous visitors attempting to view property details should be redirected to the login page, where they can follow a link to the signup page or identify themselves if they have already registered.
9. The details page should contain images and additional information about the property, including links for further inquiries.

So far, we have discussed requirements for the customer interface. However, an administrative interface for maintaining the application and its underlying data is just as important as the interface exposed to the outside world. This is something often forgotten in the course of establishing requirements and building applications. The administrative interface is frequently added as an afterthought when the application is already in production, once the client realizes that mechanisms are needed to update content without tedious manual intervention by programmers or database administrators.

Let us provide a brief summary of administrative requirements for this application:

- **Customer administration:** select customer, reset customer password, change customer status (active, suspended, etc.), remove customer;
- **Partner administration:** add new partner, specify custom markup (logos, background colors, etc.), specify partner selection rules, remove partner;
- **Listing administration:** add a new listing, modify listing (change summary and detail information, add or remove image), remove listing;
- **Authentication and authorization:** access to the administrative interface should be internal and restricted to IP addresses within the company firewall.

10.3   Technology Choices

In this chapter, we aim to provide a practical demonstration of application design principles. To that end, we want to employ an application development framework that represents state-of-the-art programming practices and paradigms. We therefore implement the VRLS application using *Struts*, the popular open source Model–View–Controller (MVC) application framework, and Sun's *Java Standard Tag Library* (JSTL) for pages that render the view components. This chapter is not a tutorial on Struts or JSTL. The focus is on applying the principles of web application architecture that are the subject of this book. These principles are transferable to other frameworks and approaches.

Struts is a stable MVC-based framework that is used successfully in different production environments on a variety of server platforms. The *action-mapping* abstraction feature is one of Struts' biggest selling points. Even in the simplest Struts application, the use of action mapping makes it possible to keep the exposed URLs unchanged even when the underlying pages (e.g., JSP templates) change or move. This remains true even when switching to a different view component architecture (e.g., Velocity templates).

The Struts framework provides tag libraries that offer dynamic application functions (e.g., conditional and iterative processing). In particular, the Struts HTML tag library (`struts-html`) provides a bridge between HTML forms and Struts `ActionForm` classes. However, these tag libraries have been superseded by JSTL, which makes JSP development more accessible to page designers. It is now an integrated component of Java Platform, Enterprise Edition (Java EE), employing consistent tags and an "expression language" that is much simpler than embedded Java scriptlets. While `struts-html` tags are not part of JSTL, the `struts-html` tag library now supports the expression language used in core JSTL tags. We employ the `struts-html` tag library along with JSTL in implementing our application.

We develop and deploy our application using Java SE 5 and J2EE 1.4 (a stable version of the Java EE platform that includes Servlet API 2.4 and JSP 2.0). We use the Apache Tomcat 5.5 server, which supports J2EE 1.4. Tomcat is a widely accepted application server that conforms to the Java EE specification.

> **Why Tomcat 5.5?**
>
> J2EE 1.4 was superseded by Java EE 5 in 2006. There are newer application servers that support Java EE 5, including Apache Tomcat 6.0, and Sun's own application server, which is based on the open-source server GlassFish. We chose to use Tomcat 5.5 (thus sticking to J2EE 1.4) because it was the stable version of Tomcat when we developed our sample application. The application also compiles, deploys, and executes properly in a Java EE 5 environment.

We use the MySQL relational database management system to support persistence. MySQL is a popular open source database server. MySQL has evolved significantly and now supports referential integrity and other advanced features. MySQL has a free "community version" of their database management system in addition to its commercial product line. For our application, we used MySQL Community Server 5.0. Like most other DBMSs, it has proprietary SQL extensions, which we chose to avoid.

Both our database schema and our persistence functionality employ the lowest common denominator of RDBMS capabilities, which enables the application to function with an RDBMS that does not support referential integrity (e.g., Hypersonic). Re-factoring the application to take advantage of advanced RDBMS features would involve reworking parts of the schema to employ referential integrity and stored procedures, which can greatly improve performance.

These choices ensure that our application is easily portable to other Java EE servers (e.g., WebLogic, WebSphere, or JBoss) and other database management systems (e.g., Oracle, Sybase, or PostgresSQL). The application is designed to run on any operating system that supports Java (e.g., Windows, Linux, or Mac OS X).

10.4   Overview of Struts

Although it is not our intention to provide a tutorial on Struts, we review the main organizing principles of a Struts application.

In an MVC application, incoming requests are directed to the **Controller** module, which serves as a "traffic cop" that determines, based on the request context, which task should be performed next. These tasks are mapped to application use cases. The components that perform these tasks may be part of the core Controller module or distinct processing components in their own right. They include functions that access and manipulate the **Model**, based on the current state and input parameters associated with the request. When the selected task is complete, the Controller determines whether it is necessary to perform another task, or to generate a response offering a specific presentation (the **View**) to the requestor. The presentation sent to the user may provide links back to the Controller to perform additional tasks.

In a Struts application, MVC components are organized as follows:

- The **Model** comprises a set of JavaBeans. In complex applications, a separate business layer (e.g., EJBs) may communicate with back-end data sources to provide access to the Model. Strategies utilizing the Data Access Object (DAO) design pattern are common for simpler applications.

- The **View** components are implemented as JSPs, although the Struts framework supports other alternatives (e.g., Velocity templates). In addition, there are *View Helper* classes (subclasses of `org.apache.struts.action.ActionForm`), which are implemented as JavaBeans used to support interaction with HTML forms.
- The **Controller** is implemented by the `ActionServlet` class, which is provided with the Struts distribution. A configuration file (`struts-config.xml`) contains *action mappings* that tell the `ActionServlet` to direct requests to application-specific components, called `Actions`, that implement individual processing tasks.

Each action mapping specifies a URL *path* (defined relative to the application context root) and a *type*, which is the name of the Java class (a subclass of `org.apache.struts.action.Action`) to be executed when requests directed at this URL path are processed by the `ActionServlet`.

Action mappings also specify a set of *forward* – symbolic names representing the set of possible processing outcomes. Forward are mapped either to URL paths (defined relative to the application context root) or to other `Actions`. Note that it is possible to define global forward that may be used for any `Action`.

When a request reaches the application, the Controller servlet examines its URL to select the appropriate action mapping and determines which `Action` class should be executed. In the course of processing, the `Action` class selects one of the defined forward by name. Consequently, it passes the context-relative URL to the constructor of the `ActionForward` class and returns the resulting object. The Controller servlet then routes processing to this URL, either by forwarding the request or by performing a redirect (depending on the value of the optional *redirect* attribute in the action mapping).

A fragment of a sample `struts-config.xml` file is displayed in Figure 10.2. The `<form-beans>` block contains the `<form-bean>` definitions, which associate `ActionForm` implementation classes with distinct names. The `<action-mappings>` block contains the `<action>` definitions, which associate URL paths with a custom `Action` class through the *type* parameter, and (optionally) with an `ActionForm` (a `<form-bean>`) through the *name* parameter.

An `<action>` block can include multiple `<forward>` definitions, specifying options available to the `Action` class for subsequent processing. Global names available across multiple actions are defined in the `<global-forward>` block.

`ActionForms` can be defined in "request" or "session" scope. Request-scoped `ActionForms` exist for the lifetime of a single request, while session-scoped `ActionForms` persist across multiple requests for the duration of an HTTP session.

Notice that not every `<action>` definition references a `<form-bean>`. For example, the `<action>` with the path of `/authcheck` does not refer to an `ActionForm` because it does not need one. Similarly, not every `<action>` specifies a set of `<forward>` definitions: the `<action>` with the path of `/home` unconditionally forward to a specific JSP.

Figure 10.3 provides an example of a custom `Action` class that extends `org.apache.struts.action.Action`. In the example, we override the `execute()` method, defining it to log out authenticated users and to direct anonymous users to the login page. The HTTP session is accessed by invoking `request.getSession()`. An attribute named `customer` is obtained from the session by invoking `session.getAttribute("customer")`. If the value of this attribute is null (i.e., if it has not been set), the user is not logged in, and is directed to the login page. If the attribute is set, the user

```
<?xml version="1.0" encoding="ISO-8859-1" ?>
<!DOCTYPE struts-config PUBLIC
  "-//Apache Software Foundation//DTD Struts Configuration 1.2//EN"
  "http://jakarta.apache.org/struts/dtds/struts-config_1_2.dtd">
<struts-config>
  <form-beans>
    <form-bean name="customerProfileForm"
               type="biz.vrls.struts.form.CustomerProfileForm" />
    ...
  </form-beans>

  <global-forwards>
    <forward name="notauthorized" path="/authcheck" />
    ...
  </global-forwards>

  <action-mappings>
    <action path="/home" forward="/pages/main.jsp?name=home" />
    <action path="/profile"
            type="biz.vrls.struts.action.CustomerProfileAction"
            name="customerProfileForm" scope="request" input="failure"
            validate="true">
            <forward name="success"
                     path="/pages/main.jsp?name=profileConfirm" />
            <forward name="failure"
                     path="/pages/main.jsp?name=profile" />
    </action>
    <action path="/authcheck"
            type="biz.vrls.struts.action.CustomerAuthCheckAction">
            <forward name="logout"
                     path="/pages/main.jsp?name=logout" />
            <forward name="login"
                     path="/action/login" redirect="true" />
    </action>
    ...
  </action-mappings>
<struts-config>
```

Figure 10.2   Fragment of a `struts-config.xml` file.

is logged in, so the attribute is removed, and the user is directed to the logout page. These alternative outcomes are implemented by passing either `login` or `logout` to the `mapping.findForward()` method and returning the result of its execution.

The presence of an input attribute (as in the `/profile` action) tells the controller that it should route initial requests to the view component specified by this attribute. This view component is responsible for the display of an HTML form used for data entry. The form fields must be defined in the subclass of `org.apache.struts.action.ActionForm` specified by the action's *name* attribute.

The data entered by the user in the displayed form is validated if the action's `validate` attribute is set to "true" and if the custom `ActionForm` class has a `validate()` method

```
public class CustomerAuthCheckAction extends Action {
  public ActionForward execute(ActionMapping mapping, ActionForm form,
              HttpServletRequest request, HttpServletResponse response) {

    HttpSession session = request.getSession();
    if (session.getAttribute("customer") == null) {
      return (mapping.findForward("login"));
    } else {
      session.removeAttribute("customer");
      return (mapping.findForward("logout"));
    }
  }
}
```

Figure 10.3 Example of an `Action` class.

containing application-specific logic for verifying data entered by the user. This method returns an `ActionErrors` object, which is a collection of `ActionMessage` objects representing errors encountered in the course of validation. Note that the `validate()` method is not invoked when an `ActionForm` object is created. Since the HTML form is likely to be presented initially with empty fields for the user to fill in, the `validate()` method would produce errors for empty fields that are "required".

If the returned `ActionErrors` object is empty, the validation is considered successful. If it is not empty, validation fails, indicating to the controller that it should redisplay the view component for corrections. Error messages can be defined in a properties file. The name of this file is defined by the "application" parameter associated with the Struts Controller servlet in the application's `web.xml` file.

`ActionForm` classes allow for the inclusion of an optional `reset()` method that can be implemented to provide initial values for the data entry form. This method would be invoked before the `ActionForm`'s attributes are populated from the HTML form variables or database entries.

10.5 Structure of the VRLS Application

Our application follows the general structure of a Struts application:

- The **Controller** is a custom subclass of the Struts `ActionServlet` class, which performs additional application-specific tasks, including partner identification.
- The **View** makes use of JSPs that do not embed Java code. Instead, they use JSTL tag libraries and the version of the Struts HTML tag library that supports the JSTL Expression Language. The pages that utilize form submission (e.g., login, profile, and search pages) are associated with corresponding form beans (subclasses of `ActionForm`).
- The **Model** is a small set of JavaBeans persisted in a relational database. The bean classes implement the `CustomerProfile`, `Listing`, and `Partner` interfaces.

In this section, we describe how our sample application is configured, and how the Controller, View, and Model components are organized.

10.5.1   Configuration

Struts applications are organized and packaged like any other Java EE application. They contain a WEB-INF directory that includes both executable code and configuration files. This directory includes a web.xml file, which is the means of configuring the application within the server environment. Figure 10.4 shows how our application is configured in the web.xml file. A custom servlet filter and its associated mappings are defined first, followed by the definition for the Struts ActionServlet and its mappings. Other components of the web.xml file not shown in Figure 10.4 include the "welcome file list", which defines the hierarchy of pages that the application should present if the context root is accessed, and the jsp-config block, which defines the JSP tag libraries. The complete web.xml

```
<?xml version="1.0" encoding="ISO-8859-1"?>
<web-app xmlns="http://java.sun.com/xml/ns/j2ee"
  xmlns:xsi="http://www.w3.org/2001/XMLSchema-instance"
  xsi:schemaLocation="http://java.sun.com/xml/ns/j2ee/web-app_2_4.xsd"
  version="2.4">
<web-app>
  <filter>
    <filter-name>VrlsFilterServlet</filter-name>
    <filter-class>biz.vrls.servlet.VrlsServletFilter</filter-class>
  </filter>
  <filter-mapping>
    <filter-name>VrlsFilterServlet</filter-name>
    <url-pattern>/*</url-pattern>
  </filter-mapping>
  <servlet>
    <servlet-name>action</servlet-name>
    <servlet-class>org.jakarta.struts.action.ActionServlet</servlet-class>
    <init-param>
      <param-name>application</param-name>
      <param-value>ApplicationResources</param-value>
    </init-param>
    <init-param>
      <param-name>config</param-name>
      <param-value>/WEB-INF/struts-config.xml</param-value>
    </init-param>
    ...
    <load-on-startup>2</load-on-startup>
  </servlet>
  <servlet-mapping>
    <servlet-name>action</servlet-name>
    <url-pattern>/action/*</url-pattern>
  </servlet-mapping>
  ...
</web-app>
```

Figure 10.4   Fragment of the web.xml configuration file for the VRLS application.

file is included with our source code distribution. The `WEB-INF` directory in a Struts application also contains the `struts-config.xml` configuration file, which was discussed in Section 10.4.

We chose to use the URL format of `/action/name` for defining actions (as specified in the `<url-pattern>` directive), so that the URL structure does not expose too much information about the underlying implementation. There is no dependency on suffixes such as `*.do` or `*.jsp`. When next-generation controller and view components (or even entirely new frameworks) come along, URLs such as `http://server/context/action/home` will be more reusable than URLs such as `http://server/context/home.do`.

- Table 10.1 summarizes the contents of the `struts-config.xml` file (a fragment of which is in Figure 10.2). For each mapping, this table displays the URL specified in the `<forward>` element and the URL of the target page for that element. The `<forward>` elements mostly specify URLs that point to a single JSP page, `/pages/main.jsp`, with a query string parameter that provides the name of the target page. For example, a path of `/pages/main.jsp?name=home` results in displaying `/pages/partnerName/home.jsp`, where `partnerName` is the name of the active partner (which can be found in a session attribute).

Since portions of the application are restricted to registered customers, we need a mechanism for identifying and authenticating customers when they access the application. We use forms-based authentication rather than HTTP authentication, because it provides more control and flexibility. Applications can use custom HTML forms to collect user credentials, and persist them as necessary. In our application, user credentials are stored in a relational database as part of the customer's profile. For additional security, the passwords are encrypted as one-way hashes.

Authentication Roles

There are alternative approaches that may make HTTP authentication more attractive for some applications. In version 2.2 and later of the Java Servlet API, the *web.xml* file can contain `<security-constraint>` elements. A `<security-constraint>` element may contain `<web-resource-collection>` elements, each defining a resource as a basic unit of authentication, and an `<auth-constraint>` element defining who has access to a resource. A `<web-resource-collection>` element defines a resource by specifying its name and the URL patterns that are associated with it. An `<auth-constraint>` element may contain any number of `<role-name>` elements specifying which roles (e.g., `enduser` or `administrator`) should have access to the defined resource.

The mechanism for specifying the roles and associating them with users is specific to the application container. For example, Tomcat comes with built-in support for specifying user names, passwords, and role membership via realms, which can be configured either in an XML file (`"tomcat-users.xml"`) or in a relational database.

Since our application requirements necessitated the flexibility of forms-based authentication, we did not pursue this option for implementing authentication. Additionally, we did not want to introduce dependencies on a particular application container (i.e., Tomcat). This option is worth considering if you have complex authorization requirements and you are already committed to using a particular application container.

Table 10.1   Action Mapping Summary for the VRLS Application

Action URL Purpose		Details
`/action/home` Presents home page	**Action:** **Form:** **JavaBean:** **Forward:**	Unconditional Struts forward *None* *None* `/pages/main.jsp?name=home` (`/pages/`*partnerName*`/home.jsp`)
`/action/authcheck` Route to the login or logout page, depending on current user state	**Action:** **Form:** **JavaBean:** **Forward:**	`biz.vrls.struts.action.CustomerAuthcheckAction` *None* *None* On login: `/action/login` On logout: `/pages/main.jsp?name=logout` (`/pages/`*partnerName*`/logout.jsp`)

`/action/login`
Identify and
authenticate users
	Action:
	Form:
	JavaBean:
	
	Forward:
		`biz.vrls.struts.action.CustomerLoginAction`
		`biz.vrls.struts.form.CustomerLoginForm`
		`biz.vrls.customer.CustomerProfile` (for user name and
		password)
		On failure (input): `pages/main.jsp?name=login`
		                    (`/pages/`*partnerName*`/login.jsp`)
		On success: invoke the `reroute()` method from the
		`BaseAction` class to return user to the activity being performed
		prior to login

(`/action/profile`)
Sign up
unauthenticated user
or modify profile of
logged-in user
	Action:
	Form:
	JavaBean:
	Forward:
		`biz.vrls.struts.action.CustomerProfileAction`
		`biz.vrls.struts.form.CustomerProfileForm`
		`biz.vrls.customer.CustomerProfile`
		On failure (input): `/pages/main.jsp?name=profile`
		(`/pages/`*partnerName*`/profile.jsp`)
		On success: `/pages/main.jsp?name=profileConfirm`
		(`/pages/`*partnerName*`/profileConfirm.jsp`)

`/action/search`
Browse for listings
satisfying search
criteria
	Action:
	Form:
	JavaBean:
	Forward:
		`biz.vrls.struts.action.CustomerSearchAction`
		`biz.vrls.struts.form.CustomerSearchForm`
		None
		On none (input or no results returned):
		`/pages/main.jsp?name=search`
		(`/pages/`*partnerName*`/search.jsp`)
		On many (more than 1 result returned): `/action/results`
		On one (1 result returned):`/action/details`
		(go directly to details page for result)

Table 10.1   (*continued*)

Action URL Purpose		Details
`/action/results` Display search results, with links to details page for each listing	**Action:** **Form:** **JavaBean:** **Forward:**	Unconditional Struts forward *None* `biz.vrls.listing.Listing` (actually `List<Listing>`) `/pages/main.jsp?name=results` (`/pages/`*partnerName*`/results.jsp`)

`/action/details`
Display listing details
(only for authenticated
users)
	Action:
	Form:
	JavaBean:
	Forward:
		`biz.vrls.struts.action.CustomerSearchDetailsAction`
		None
		`biz.vrls.listing.Listing`
		`/pages/main.jsp?name=details`
		(`/pages/`*partnerName*`/details.jsp`)

`/action/contact`
Allow user to send
e-mail to realtor
	Action:
	Form:
	JavaBean:
	Forward:
		`biz.vrls.struts.action.CustomerContactAction`
		`biz.vrls.struts.form.CustomerContactForm`
		`biz.vrls.customer.CustomerProfile` (for e-mail address)
		On failure (input): `/pages/main.jsp?name=contact`
		(`/pages/`*partnerName*`/Contact.jsp`)
		On failure (input): `/pages/main.jsp?name=emailConfirm`
		(`/pages/`*partnerName*`/emailConfirm.jsp`)

10.5.2   Controller components

The `org.jakarta.struts.action.ActionServlet` class is responsible for the initial processing and routing of requests. The `process()` method of this class locates the proper subclass of `org.jakarta.struts.action.Action`, based on the mappings defined in the `struts-config.xml` file, and passes control to that `Action`'s `execute()` method.

Figure 10.5 shows the class hierarchy of our custom `Action` classes, which are subclasses of our abstract `biz.vrls.struts.action.VrlsBaseAction` class (see Figure 10.6), which extends `org.apache.struts.action.Action`. This is considered good practice, because it allows you to put common code into one base `Action` class that your other custom `Action` classes can extend. `VrlsBaseAction` overrides the `Action` class's `execute()` method to perform common processing functions and then invoke an abstract method, `performAction()`. It is this method that must be overridden in our custom `Action` classes.

No Custom Controller This Time

In the original version of this application (developed for the first edition of this book), we defined a custom `ActionServlet` class that extended the `org.jakarta.struts.action.ActionServlet` class. We did this to ensure that certain session attributes were properly set every time an `Action` was executed, without having to include redundant code to perform those functions in every `Action` class.

> Starting with the version 2.4 of the Servlet API, this is better accomplished by including a custom `Filter` class that is configured to run before any `Action` code is executed. While the use of a custom base Action class is still considered a good development strategy for a Struts application, usage of a custom `Controller` class that extends `org.jakarta.struts.action.ActionServlet` should be reserved for complex situations when a `Filter` would not suffice.

Let us move on to a brief discussion of individual tasks and their action mappings, expanding the information in Table 10.1. Remember that the classes are subclasses of `biz.vrls.struts.action.VrlsBaseAction`.

/action/home

This is the entry page for the site, displaying a personalized welcome message. It also displays a navigation bar (included on all application pages) that links to other important application functions.

The `struts-config.xml` file maps the `/action/home` URL to the home page (`/pages/main.jsp?name=home`), which ultimately embeds `/pages/partnerName/home.jsp`.

/action/authcheck

This page is invoked when the customer selects "log in" or "log out" from the navigation bar. If the customer is already logged in, it returns the "logout" forward (`/pages/main.jsp?name=logout`),

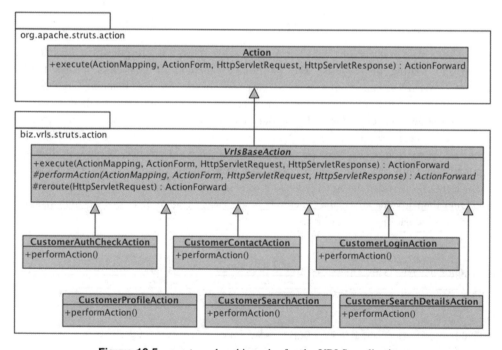

Figure 10.5   `Action` class hierarchy for the VRLS application.

```
package biz.vrls.struts.action;

import java.io.*;
import javax.servlet.*;
import javax.servlet.http.*;

import org.apache.struts.action.* ;
import org.apache.struts.actions.*;

import biz.vrls.partner.*;
import biz.vrls.services.*;

public abstract class VrlsBaseAction extends Action {
  public final ActionForward execute(ActionMapping p_mapping,
            ActionForm p_form, HttpServletRequest p_request,
            HttpServletResponse p_response) throws Exception {
    // Perform common housekeeping tasks here...
    return performAction(p_mapping, p_form, p_request, p_response);
  }

  protected abstract ActionForward performAction(
            ActionMapping p_mapping, ActionForm p_form,
            HttpServletRequest p_request, HttpServletResponse p_response)
                              throws IOException, ServletException;
}
```

Figure 10.6   Simplified code for `VrlsBaseAction` class.

which is mapped to the logout page (`/pages/partnerName/logout.jsp`). If the customer is not logged in, it returns the "login" forward (`/action/login`) and performs the login action.

The `CustomerAuthCheckAction` class is designed as a mediator between the `login` and `logout` actions. If the customer is logged in, its `performAction()` method invalidates the session and returns the `ActionForward` associated with the name `logout`, which is mapped to the page containing the logout notification. If the customer is not logged in, the `performAction()` method returns the `ActionForward` associated with the name `login`.

/action/login

This page is invoked either by `CustomerAuthCheckAction` or by actions not supported for anonymous users. For input (the failure forward, `/pages/main.jsp?name=login`), it displays the login page (`/pages/partnerName/login.jsp`) where the user enters user id and password for authentication. It validates and checks the credentials against the user database. On authentication failure, it redisplays the login page with error messages.

Once the user is authenticated:

- It constructs a `CustomerProfile` object from data recorded in the user database.
- It maintains the `CustomerProfile` object until logout.
- It forward to the home page (when invoked by `CustomerAuthCheckAction`) or to the original target (for actions not supported for anonymous users).

The `CustomerLoginAction` class uses the `CustomerLoginForm` form bean referenced on the `login.jsp` page to support entering the user name and password. The input attribute of the action, which specifies the initial data entry, is set to `failure` to treat the initial data entry the same way as a failed login (the only difference is error messages, which are absent for the first try). The login page is presented when the action is first invoked and again as long as the entered credentials do not match those of a registered user.

This action is performed when an anonymous user follows a link to `/action/login` or attempts to access a restricted application function. In the second situation, the application creates a session attribute to store the attempted URL. We define a method in the `VrlsBaseAction` class (called `reroute()`) that is invoked once the authentication credentials match. If the session attribute containing the stored URL exists, the method generates an HTTP response that redirects the user to the URL for the original restricted task. If the session attribute for the stored URL does not exist, the user is redirected to the application's home page.

/action/profile

This page is invoked when a customer selects "sign up" or "profile" from navigation bar. For input (the failure forward, `/pages/main.jsp?name=profile`), it displays the profile page (`/pages/`*partnerName*`/profile.jsp`), which allows unregistered visitors to sign up by entering a new customer profile into a blank form and allows registered customers to modify their profile in a form pre-populated with the appropriate `CustomerProfile` data.

The `CustomerProfileAction` class serves a dual purpose: to allow new users to enter profile information so that they can become registered customers, and to allow registered customers to modify their profiles. The profile page contains conditional logic that causes it to present itself differently for each of these situations. The input attribute of the action is set to `failure`, which routes to the profile page when the action is first invoked and repeats this routing until the entered information passes validation. At that point, the action's `performAction()` method returns the `ActionForward` associated with the name `success` (`/pages/main.jsp?name=profileConfirm`), which results in a confirmation page (`/pages/`*partnerName*`/profileConfirm.jsp`).

/action/search

This page is invoked when customers select "search" from the navigation bar. It provides a data entry form for search criteria in the `CustomerSearchAction` class. The input attribute of the action is set to `failure`, which routes to the search page (`/pages/`*partnerName*`/search.jsp`) when the action is first invoked.

- If no results are found, the action's `perform Action()` method returns the `ActionForward` associated with the name `none` (`/pages/main.jsp?name=search`), which redisplays the input page (`/pages/`*partnerName*`/search.jsp`).
- If the query produces multiple results, the action's `performAction()` method returns the `Action-Forward` associated with the name `many`, `/action/results`.
- If the query produces a single result, the action's `performAction()` method returns the `Action-Forward` associated with the name `one`, it routes directly to `/action/details`, bypassing the results page.

/action/details

This page is displayed when customers follow a link from the results page (results.jsp), and also when a search produces a single result. It displays details about a particular listing, identified by a request parameter. Anonymous visitors may not go to the details page.

The CustomerSearchDetailsAction class is responsible for displaying details about a particular property listing. It may be referenced explicitly or through the "search" action. The action's performAction() method returns the ActionForward associated with the name success (/pages/main.jsp?name=details) if the user is a signed-in, registered customer and if the listingId parameter corresponds to a valid listing and loads /pages/*partnerName*/ details.jsp. In the case of failure (/pages/main.jsp?name=error), it loads the error page (/pages/*partnerName*/error.jsp).

If the user is not signed in, the action's performAction() method returns the global Action-Forward associated with the name notauthorized (/action/login).

/action/images

The ImageDisplayAction class ensures that protected images associated with real estate listings are displayed only to authenticated users. Unregistered users should not be able to access an image URL, even if it was sent to them by a registered user.

It is referenced in <img> tags found in details.jsp to display images for a particular listing to registered users. It displays an image containing an error message to anonymous users.

/action/contact

This is invoked when customers select "contact us" from the navigation bar or the listing details page. It provides an input form for sending messages to realtors. Once the form is filled in, an e-mail is sent to the partner's e-mail contact address.

The CustomerContactAction class allows users to contact the broker to express interest in a particular listing or to request further information about the broker. The input attribute of the action is set to failure (/pages/main.jsp?name=contact), which routes to the contact page (/pages/*partnerName*/contact.jsp) when the action is first invoked and redisplays the contact page on failed validation (e.g., if the e-mail address entered in the form is improperly formatted).

If the user is an authenticated customer, the e-mail address field on the form is pre-populated from the CustomerProfile. If the user was looking at details for a particular listing, the subject field is pre-populated with a reference to the listing's ID. Once a valid address has been submitted, the action's performAction() method sends an e-mail to the referring partner's contact e-mail address and routes to the success forward (/pages/main.jsp?name=emailConfirm) which displays a confirmation page (/pages/*partnerName*/emailConfirm.jsp).

10.5.3   View components

The view components for our application are JSPs. JSPs interact with ActionForm objects, which are View Helpers that manage data transfer between controller and view components. Figure 10.7 shows the class hierarchy of our ActionForm classes.

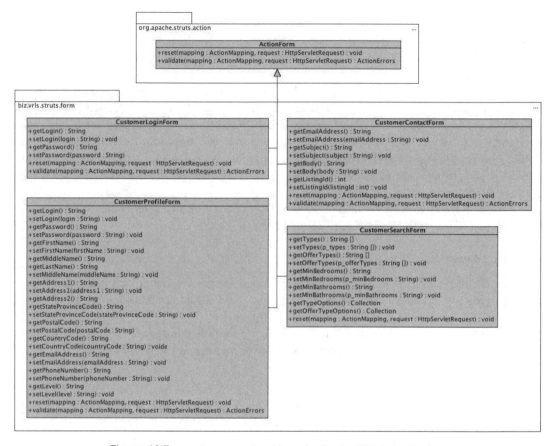

Figure 10.7 ActionForm class hierarchy for the VRLS application.

We need to present a number of different pages throughout the application. The home page, search results page, and listing details page are designed to display information, while the login, profile, search, and contact pages are interactive forms.

We also need to present partner-specific versions of these pages, with each set of pages having the "look and feel" of the partner's own branded web site. Design alternatives for supporting partner-specific presentations vary greatly. They range from the sharing of all page templates, to maintaining separate sets of page templates for each partner. Sharing templates between partners limits the degree of customization to style sheets (and possibly custom images such as corporate logos). We made the choice to maintain separate sets of templates in order to achieve the greatest flexibility and to enable partners to create and upload their own templates.

These pages have a lot in common: they reference the same JSP taglibs, display similar navigation bars, and have the same general look and feel. Clearly, something needs to be done to reduce redundancy.

Our first step in this direction is to create an include.jsp file (Figure 10.8), which is included in all other pages. This page defines tag libraries and initializes shared variables, which define

```
<%@ taglib uri="/WEB-INF/c.tld" prefix="c" %>
<%@ taglib uri="/WEB-INF/struts-html-el.tld" prefix="html" %>

<c:url var="url_home" scope="session" value="/action/home" />
<c:url var="url_authcheck" scope="session" value="/action/authcheck" />
<c:url var="url_profile" scope="session" value="/action/profile" />
<c:url var="url_search" scope="session" value="/action/search" />
<c:url var="url_results" scope="session" value="/action/results" />
<c:url var="url_details" scope="session" value="/action/details" />
<c:url var="url_contact" scope="session" value="/action/contact" />
<c:set var="partner_images" scope="session"
       value="${pageContext.request.contextPath}/pages/
              ${sessionScope.partner.code}/images" />
```

Figure 10.8 Shared `include.jsp` file.

commonly referenced URLs and paths used for the navigation bar and other shared page components. In `include.jsp`, the variables whose names begin with `url_` are set to the URL paths of various application functions. The variable named `partner_images` is set to the URL path to the directory containing partner-supplied images. For a partner named `XYZ`, the resulting path would be `/vrls/pages/xyz/images`, where `/vrls` is the web application context path stored in `${pageContext.request.contextPath}`.

To support co-branding, our original intent was to create a set of "root" pages, each of which would embed its corresponding custom page from a partner-specific directory. The application determines which partner is active when a user first arrives at the site. At that point, it places the appropriate `Partner` object in the session. Incoming requests reference the attributes of the `Partner` object (e.g., name, code) to present content appropriate for that partner. For example, `/pages/home.jsp` would embed `/pages/${sessionScope.partner.code}/home.jsp`. Note that the initial partner selection may be revised and the `Partner` object replaced on login.

However, as we discovered in the course of implementing this strategy, the only practical difference between the root pages was the name of the custom page to be embedded. Consequently, we re-factored our design to use *one* common root page, `main.jsp` (Figure 10.9), which determined the custom page that should be embedded via the query string parameter, `name`. For example, a request to `/pages/main.jsp?name=profile` would embed `/pages/xyz/profile.jsp`, assuming `"xyz"` was the code associated with the active partner.

Using JSTL's `<c:import>` tag, `main.jsp` selects and embeds a partner-specific page based on session information and request parameters, i.e., `${sessionScope.partner.code}/${param.name}.jsp`. It also references two CSS style sheets, one common and one partner-specific, found in the `/css` directory (`/css/common.css` and `/css/${sessionScope.partner.code}.css`).

Every custom page should include a navigation bar, but apart from that, we leave it up to each partner to design their page templates as they see fit. The navigation bar should include the following links:

- `/action/home` for the home page;
- `/action/authcheck` for the authorization action that routes to the login or logout page;
- `/action/profile` for the profile data entry action that routes to the profile page for new customer profile entry and existing customer profile modification;

```
<%@ include file="include.jsp" %>
<c:url var="jsCommon" scope="request" value="/js/common.js" />
<c:url var="cssCommon" scope="request" value="/css/common.css" />
<c:url var="cssPartner" scope="request"
       value="/css/${sessionScope.partner.code}.css" />
<html>
<head>
<meta http-equiv="Content-Type" content="text/html; charset=iso-8859-1">
<title>
<c:out value="${sessionScope.partner.name} - ${param.name}" />
</title>
<script type="text/javascript" href="${requestScope.jsCommon}"></script>
<link rel="stylesheet" type="text/css" href="${requestScope.cssCommon}" />
<link rel="stylesheet" type="text/css" href="${requestScope.cssPartner}" />
</head>
<c:import url="${sessionScope.partner.code}/${param.name}.jsp" />
</html>
```

Figure 10.9 Shared `main.jsp` file.

- `/action/search` for the page containing the search form;
- `/action/contact` for the customer contact page.

It does not make sense for the action that displays search results, `/action/results`, to be included in the navigation bar, since it should only be accessible through the search page. By convention, each page should not include a link to itself in the navigation bar (which is one reason why a common include page or tag for the navigation bar was not implemented).

The labels associated with links in the navigation bar are intended to be obvious: "home" for the home page, "login" for the login page, "profile" for the profile page, etc. However, these labels should depend on the visitor's "state" – logged-in or logged-out. When dealing with an anonymous visitor (someone who has not logged in), it is appropriate for the authentication link to have a label of "login" and the profile link to have the label "sign up". Conversely, for an authenticated customer (someone who has logged in), the authentication link should have the label "logout" and the profile link should have the label "profile."

Thus, the set of links in the navigation bar is static, but the set of labels is not. As you can see in Figure 10.8, the `include.jsp` page defines the set of links using the JSTL `<c:url>` tag as a set of session attributes. This tag is intelligent enough to create a context-relative link, and to append appropriate parameters to support URL rewriting when cookie support is not available from the browser.

The link labels are established in the `VrlsServletFilter` class. A custom object, an instance of the `biz.vrls.util.AppTextLabels` class, is stored as a session attribute with the name `navbar`. This class implements the `java.util.Map` interface and maintains two sets of label mappings: one for the logged-in state, and another for the anonymous state. The labels are retrieved from the `ApplicationResources.properties` file, where built-in Struts classes look for error message mappings and other localized application properties. Labels that are supposed to have different values depending on the customer state are defined twice, once using a generic name (e.g., `app.navbar.profile`)

```
app.navbar.home=home
app.navbar.authcheck=log in
app.navbar.authcheck.auth=log out
app.navbar.profile=sign up
app.navbar.profile.auth=profile
app.navbar.search=search
app.navbar.contact=contact us
```

Figure 10.10 Label definitions for the navigation bar.

and again with the suffix .auth for authenticated customers (e.g., app.navbar.profile.auth), as shown in Figure 10.10.

From these specifications, the AppTextLabels class builds and maintains two Maps, one for the authenticated state and one for the anonymous state. The isLoggedIn() method in the biz.vrls.utils.SessionUtils class is invoked to determine which set of label mappings should be displayed.

Now we are ready to move on to the discussion of default templates provided as part of the application.

home.jsp

This acts as a welcome page, personalized to display the customer name. It contains the navigation bar to link to other important application functions. This simple page displays static information and does not contain a form for interactive data entry.

login.jsp

This is a simple form for authenticating users by user name and password. It contains the navigation bar to link to other important application functions.

The struts-config.xml file associates the CustomerLoginForm class with the /login action, which uses the login.jsp page for input. A fragment of the page's code is shown in Figure 10.11.

The CustomerLoginForm bean does *not* directly correspond to a model component, but refers indirectly to the CustomerProfile object. The CustomerLoginForm's validate() method is invoked on form submission. The page is redisplayed on validation failure. Validation error messages, if any, are displayed through the <html:errors/> tag.

Note that in our sample application, we send these credentials "in the clear" (over a non-secure connection). We do this to simplify the installation procedure for the demonstration application. In a real-world application, the login action should always operate over a secure connection, especially if sensitive personal information is included in the transmission.

profile.jsp

The structure of this page is similar to login.jsp and CustomerLoginForm. It is used to enter personal information as part of user registration and for modifying existing customer profiles. It contains a navigation bar to link to other important application functions.

```
<html:form action="/login" focus="username">
<html:errors />
   <table>
      <tr>
         <td colspan="2" valign="top" align="left">
         </td>
      </tr>
      <tr>
         <td class="label">User ID:</td>
         <td class="input">
            <html:text property="username" />
         </td>
      </tr>
      <tr>
         <td class="label">Password:</td>
         <td class="input">
            <html:password property="password" />
         </td>
      </tr>
      <tr>
         <td class="buttons" colspan="2">
            <html:submit value="Login" />
            <html:reset value="Clear form" />
         </td>
      </tr>
   </table>
</html:form>
```

Figure 10.11   Template fragment for `login.jsp`

The `CustomerProfileForm` *does* directly correspond to the `CustomerProfile` object, but does not include direct getters and setters for its attributes.

The `struts-config.xml` file associates the `CustomerProfileForm` class with the `/profile` action, which uses the `profile.jsp` page for input. Remember that the label text associated with the link to this action depends on whether or not the visitor is signed in.

profileConfirm.jsp

The structure of this page is similar to `home.jsp`. It is displayed upon `success` of the `/profile` action and confirms successful entry of personal information. It contains a navigation bar to link to other important application functions. This page is displayed after successful entry or update of a user's profile.

search.jsp

The structure of this page is similar to `login.jsp` and `CustomerLoginForm`. It is used to enter search criteria for the property listings database. It contains a navigation bar to link to other important application functions.

The `struts-config.xml` file associates the `CustomerSearchForm` class with the `/search` action, which uses the `search.jsp` page for input.

results.jsp

This page is designed to display search results by iterating over a List of biz.vrls.listing. Listing objects, which are placed in the session as the result of the /search action (implemented by CustomerSearchAction). It contains a navigation bar to link to other important application functions.

The results displayed are based on the search criteria entered on the search.jsp page. Each displayed listing provides a link to the /details action, which is implemented by SearchDetailsAction, for individual results.

details.jsp

This page is designed to display details about individual properties. It contains a navigation bar to link to other important application functions.

It queries an instance of biz.vrls.listing.Listing placed in the session by the SearchDetailsAction class to display attributes of a particular property. It can only be seen by authenticated users.

contact.jsp

This page is designed as a mechanism for customers to contact brokers with general questions or queries about specific listings. The structure is similar to that of profile.jsp, CustomerProfile-Form, and profileConfirm.jsp. It contains a navigation bar to link to other important application functions.

The e-mail address is pre-populated for authenticated users. Anonymous visitors can enter their e-mail address manually. If reached from a link on the listing details page, the subject is pre-populated with a specific listing ID. emailConfirm.jsp serves as a confirmation page analogous to profile-Confirm.jsp.

The struts-config.xml file associates the CustomerContactForm class with the /contact action, which uses the contact.jsp page for input. The CustomerContactForm bean does not directly correspond to a model component.

10.5.4   Model components

The hierarchy of our model classes is shown in Figure 10.12. It includes JavaBean classes that implement interfaces associated with the three main objects in our application: CustomerProfile, Partner, and Listing. In turn, each of these interfaces extends Identifiable, Describable, and Logged. Classes that implement the latter set of interfaces have to contain "ID" fields, description fields, and fields tracking the creation date and last modification date of the object.

CustomerProfile

The CustomerProfile bean is designed to store information about a customer. Much of this information comes from user input provided during the signup process. When a visitor clicks the "sign up" link in the navigation bar, it routes to /action/profile and displays the profile.jsp page. In the struts-config.xml file, /action/profile is associated with the CustomerProfileForm bean.

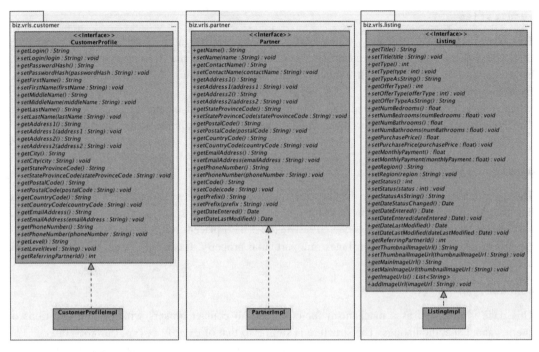

Figure 10.12   Model class hierarchy.

It may seem reasonable to use the same class for both the model and the form bean, but it is not a good idea. If the `CustomerProfile` class were used as the form bean, hostile users could figure out the names of bean properties that are not exposed to the outside world and construct HTTP requests that reset these properties and jeopardize the integrity of our application. In a way, `CustomerProfileForm` acts as a "firewall" for `CustomerProfile` – users do not have direct access to the setter and getter methods on the `CustomerProfile` class. Without this separation, we would be relying on "security through obscurity", which is a very dangerous practice.

Partner

The `Partner` bean stores partner-specific information, including the partner id and URL prefix that are necessary for inferring partner affiliation for new visitors.

Our design supports persistence, implemented through auxiliary service classes – `DataAccess Service` and `DomainService` (see Section 10.6.1). On successful login, an instance of `Customer- Profile` is populated from the database and stored in the session. This caches customer information for the duration of the session. A modification to one or more attributes of the `CustomerProfile` instance causes a "write through" to the database to maintain data integrity.

The `Partner` bean is populated from the database when a new session is established. The `VrlsServletFilter` has a method (`determinePartner()`) that figures out partner affiliation. This association may be modified on login if the initial inference about partner identity was incorrect. Modifications are handled the same way as with the `CustomerProfile` bean.

Listing

The `Listing` bean is designed to store details about individual real estate properties. Strictly speaking, it is not necessary to store the `Listing` bean in the session because of its transient nature. We do it to simplify processing in the `details.jsp` page, which refers to this session attribute to determine which listing should be displayed. We also make use of it in the `contact.jsp` page: if this attribute exists and is non-null, its ID is included in the subject of the e-mail to be sent to the partner.

Database schema

Figure 10.13 is a simplified version of the entity–relationship (ER) diagram for our application's database schema, omitting lookup tables for states, countries, and regions. The slight variances between different DBMSs are one good reason for using an *object–relational mapping (ORM)* package, such as Hibernate, to define an application's database schema so that it correlates directly to the Java classes associated with the data model.

10.6   Design Decisions

In the course of building this application, we made some critical design decisions. Here we discuss the rationale behind these decisions. In some cases, we also present alternatives and opportunities for improvement.

10.6.1   Abstracting functionality into service classes

In designing this application, we abstracted various functions into service classes in the `biz.vrls.services` package:

- `DataAccessService` is a high-level service class that encapsulates the acquisition of database connections and the execution of SQL queries and update statements.
- `DomainService` employs the Data Access Object (DAO) design pattern and provides methods to retrieve and persist the model components (`CustomerProfile`, `Partner`, `Listing`) associated with the application.
- `EmailService` obtains a `javax.mail.Session` through the web server's JNDI lookup facilities and uses it to process e-mail.

All these service classes exploit the *Singleton* pattern, which ensures that only one instance of a class is present in a system. In Java, this pattern is implemented by providing a static method, `getInstance()`, that is the only way to access an instance of the class. There are no public constructors for the class; the `getInstance()` method always returns a reference to the single instance, which is created using a *private* constructor. Applications use methods found in service classes by calling the static `getInstance()` method and invoking instance methods on the returned object:

```
Listing listing = DomainService.getInstance().retrieveListingById(1234);
```

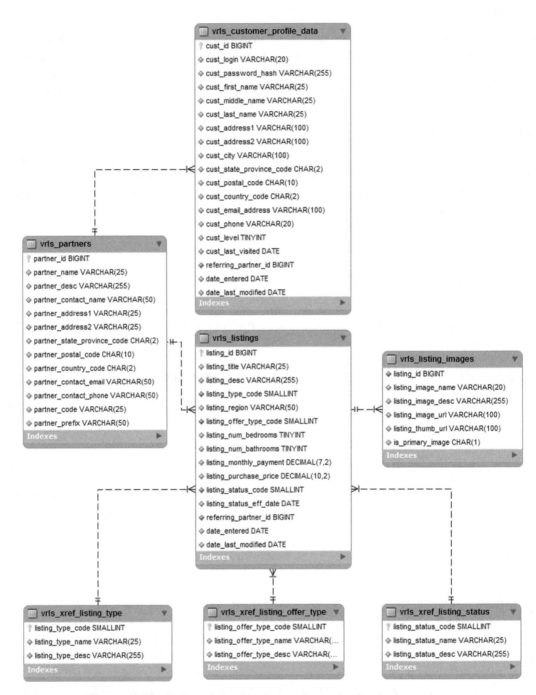

Figure 10.13   Entity–relationship diagram for application database schema.

Benefits

- *Code simplification:* For domain objects, retrieval or persistence is accomplished through a single method call within the `DomainService` class. For other database functions, queries can be executed directly via methods in the `DataAccessService` class. A `RowSet` (a disconnected implementation of the `java.sql.ResultSet` interface that can be cached) is returned for processing by the calling class. Developers do not need to know the details of how persistence and retrieval are implemented.
- *Flexibility:* The model components are designed explicitly around interfaces rather than concrete implementation classes and the return values for the methods in these classes are also interfaces. This makes the application independent of specific implementations of the model components.
- *Extensibility:* Since the code for persistence and retrieval functions is in one place, instead of being scattered throughout the application, it is simpler to maintain. Any or all of the service classes can be replaced with a new version that performs its operations differently. This opens the door for future versions that make use of more sophisticated persistence mechanisms, for example, based on Hibernate, Enterprise Java Beans (EJB), or Java Persistence Architecture (JPA).

Alternatives or improvements

- We could have defined our services as interfaces, and used the *Factory* pattern to create instances of classes that implement that interface. The particular implementation classes to be used can be specified in a properties file, providing flexibility in configuring the application at deployment time. Mock implementations of the service classes can be plugged in, to facilitate testing "outside the container" (i.e., independent of the application server and the database). This technique is called *dependency injection*. It is showcased in frameworks such as Spring, but the mechanisms and strategies of dependency injection are relatively easy to understand and implement without relying on an external framework.
- We could have added smart caching functionality to the `DomainService` class (see Section 10.7.4).

10.6.2   Including embedded pages to support co-branding

The VRLS application supports co-branding based on the referring partner. This means that if a visitor comes to the VRLS application through a particular partner broker's web site, the pages have a look and feel that conforms to the layout of that site. Partner affiliation for authenticated users is retrieved from their profiles.

The strategy was laid out in detail in Section 10.5.3:

- A single root JSP page, `/pages/main.jsp`, contains instructions for including common JavaScript files and CSS style sheets.
- URLs referencing the root page include a query string containing the `name` parameter, which is used in conjunction with the active partner code (which is stored in a session attribute) to construct the complete URL of the appropriate partner-specific JSP page.

For example, a visitor who comes to the site through a partner whose code is `partner1`, attempting to access the URL `http://host/context/action/home`, is routed to `http://host/context/`

pages/main.jsp?name=home, which embeds http://*host*/*context*/pages/partner1/home. jsp. Since the root page acts as a "wrapper" for the embedded page, the latter is assumed to contain only HTML body content (i.e., not the head part of the HTML document).

Benefits

- *Simplicity*: Individual partner pages are simpler and redundancy is minimized because these pages do not need to embed common resources defined in the root page.
- *Extensibility*: The addition of new partners does not require any modification to the application. It is simply a matter of adding a partner to the database, creating a directory to hold the partner's JSPs and images, and creating or uploading those JSPs and images.

Alternatives or improvements

- We could have eliminated virtually all the HTML in the root page and had it simply embed an entire page; however, this would mean that all inclusion and common functions would need to be replicated in every custom page.
- We could have created one set of common JSP pages and put placeholders in them to facilitate co-branding customization. The placeholders could have been used to change a small set of common elements such as the URL for the logo image, using substitution parameters provided in a partner configuration file or in attributes of the Partner object. This approach would work if we were willing to accept limited customization capability. For example, if we were to add a logo attribute to the Partner class and set it to the URL of a company's logo (e.g., http://partner1.com/images/logo.gif), it could be referenced as follows:

```
<img src="${sessionScope.partner.logo}" />
```

- Another possibility would have been to use *Tiles*, which is a framework that partners with Struts to provide JSP template functionality. The Tiles framework lets you create JSP templates that define the general page layout as a set of components (known as *tiles*). Other JSPs can use this layout, specifying external resources that should be used to fill in the template components. These external resources are referenced through the <tiles:insert> tag, which is functionally similar to a JSP include tag. When used in conjunction with Struts, both Tiles layouts and the associated URL paths can be configured directly in an XML file.

10.6.3 Creating and modifying customer profiles in one task

Two discrete tasks in this application were combined into one: the creation of a new customer profile by an anonymous user (during signup) and the modification of an existing customer profile by a registered user. While these tasks are similar, they are not the same. For example, the signup process allows users to select a login identifier, but the modification process does not allow them to change the identifier they selected during signup.

We could have chosen to treat each function as its own task, with its own `Action` class and its own view and view helper components (JSP pages and `ActionForm` classes). Instead, we chose to concentrate on what these two functions have in common, and create one `Action` class and one set of view components.

The `CustomerProfileAction` class determines whether the user is logged in. If so, it considers this a task that modifies an existing profile. Otherwise, it considers it a task to create a new one. If the task is to modify an existing profile, the HTML form is populated with the current profile values and conditional logic within the JSP page presents the login name as a fixed text field rather than a form input field. If the task is to create a new profile, the form is displayed in an unpopulated state, including a form input field for a user-selected login name.

The main benefit of this is that it *minimizes redundancy*. If we had created separate tasks and separate sets of view components, there would have been substantial duplication, e.g., two form pages with mostly redundant fields and two `ActionForm` beans. Too much duplication complicates maintenance. Our approach emphasizes what the two processes have in common rather than focusing on what makes them different. In doing so, we reduce the number of different objects.

As an alternative, we could have created separate `Action` classes, `ActionForm` beans, and JSP pages for each of these functions. Whether this is a good idea depends on how much difference there is between the views and processing for each task. Other applications may have requirements that cross this threshold.

10.7 Suggested Enhancements

No application is ever complete. Even if you successfully build an application that fulfills all the specified requirements, you can be sure that these requirements will change after the application is deployed – if not before!

This application is no exception. Since it was designed as a tutorial, some of the requirements were deliberately not implemented or were implemented only partially. The suggestions described in this section describe enhancements over and above the original requirements, as well as steps necessary to implement those unimplemented and partially implemented requirements.

10.7.1 Adding an administrative interface

Although we strongly emphasized that an application is not complete without an administrative interface, we did not make the implementation of the administrative interface available for download. The application package includes SQL queries for adding partners and listings to the database, but no mechanism (other than manual execution of SQL queries) for updating the database to add partners or listings.

The administrative interface should have its own authentication scheme. In other words, the mechanism used to identify and authenticate administrators must be separate from the one used to identify and authenticate customers. If you want an interface that employs one fixed administrative password shared by all administrators, you can include that (preferably encrypted) in the application resources file. It would be more thorough (and more secure) to provide a database table (similar to `VRLS_CUSTOMER_PROFILE_DATA`) used for administrator authentication.

Ideally, the administrative interface should be treated as a separate application. If it is designed as a Java EE application, it should be installed with a distinct servlet context that is not associated with the main application. It would naturally require its own set of actions and view components.

In Chapter 11, we implement the VRLS application's administrative interface using Ruby on Rails.

10.7.2   Enhancing the signup process through e-mail authentication

One of the requirements associated with this application was the ability for new users to sign up and create customer profiles. Our implementation allows users to enter all the information needed to populate a `CustomerProfile` object, including their chosen login name and password. The signup page includes a form field into which new users can enter their password of choice. They can then proceed to the login page to provide their login name and password.

However, application requirements dictate that a new user should *not* be allowed to use the application until the e-mail address has been verified. We want to confirm that entered e-mail addresses really do belong to the people signing up. If we do not confirm this, someone could enter another person's e-mail address and subject them to unwanted spam from our application.

One common way of fulfilling this requirement is to prevent a user from specifying their own password at signup time. Once the profile entry form has passed validation, the application presents a landing page informing the user that their entry is being processed, and that they should expect a confirmation e-mail to be delivered shortly. In the background, the application sends an e-mail that contains a random password automatically generated by the application. The user, upon receiving the e-mail, returns to the application and enters their chosen login name and the generated password. Once authenticated, the user can change the password to one of their own choosing, using the application's profile modification functionality.

This is a more secure method of enrolling new users than the one we have built into the application. In its current state, the application allows someone to enter an invalid e-mail address or someone else's valid e-mail address with impunity. Requiring that new users enter a valid e-mail address where they receive a message containing the initial password they need to log in provides basic assurances of their identity. This is how we could implement a little more secure process:

1. Remove the password field and the password confirmation field from the signup page. These fields are still needed when modifying profiles for existing customers, so the `profile.jsp` page must be modified appropriately to support this.
2. After successful form validation (but before routing to the profile confirmation page), the application should record the user's profile information with a dynamically generated random password. The `EmailService` class should then send an e-mail to the provided address, containing the random password generated by the application.
3. The profile confirmation page (`profileConfirm.jsp`) should tell new users that they should expect a confirmation e-mail containing their password.
4. The application must be modified so that the user is not considered "logged in" after entering this new profile.

As an alternative, the application could allow users to specify their own passwords at signup time while still ensuring that e-mail addresses are properly verified. At signup time, the application would store profile information temporarily in a staging area (e.g., another database table). The profile would be inactive. There would still be a confirmation e-mail sent, but instead of a generated password, it would contain a URL. The query string of this URL would contain a unique key of sufficient complexity that it would identify the user's unverified profile information in the temporary staging area. A request for this unique URL would indicate to the application that the user had received the e-mail and clicked on the link. The application would then retrieve the staged profile and activate it by storing it in the customer profile table. This approach would require an additional `Action` class that would perform this "profile activation" function. The URL sent to a new user at signup would be associated with this `Action` class in the `struts-config.xml` file. It would include a query string parameter that uniquely identified the user.

More about Profile Passwords

A more secure way to perform customer profile modification would be to require entry of the current password, making it a pre-condition for the processing of changes. Thus, three password fields (all initially blank) would be required on the form for profile modification: one for the current password, one for the desired new password, and one for confirmation of the desired new password. If the value in the current password field is incorrect, the form should fail validation. Changes to the password should only be processed when the current password is entered correctly and when both new password fields are filled in and match each other. If the new password fields are both blank, the password should not be changed, but other changes should be processed.

10.7.3 Improving partner recognition through a persistent cookie

One of the problems with the current design is that customers returning to the application may not have their partner affiliations recognized until after they log in. Some approaches to partner identification make this process easier (e.g., using a sub-domain strategy to always identify the partner for requests to `http://rrr.vrls.biz` as `rrr`). Using the referring URL for partner identification is more problematic, especially on subsequent visits when the customer comes directly to the site and there is no referring URL.

Saving a persistent cookie to identify the partner would partially alleviate this problem. This could be accomplished by having the `VrlsServletFilter` include a `Set-Cookie` header in its responses to successful authentication requests. This cookie should identify the application's domain and set a value of, for example, `partnerCode=abc`, and an expiration date far in the future. Subsequent requests from the same browser on the same computer would include a `Cookie` header providing this name–value pair. The `VrlsServletFilter`'s `determinePartner()` method should be enhanced so that it looks first for this cookie before trying to determine the partner via the `Referer` header.

Other information could be persisted in this cookie, including the customer's login name and password, which would cause the customer to be identified and logged in automatically. Best practices dictate that we not do this without giving customers the opportunity to enable or disable this feature explicitly. Some web applications compromise by persisting only the login name, which means that upon returning to the site the user needs to enter the password. However, even pre-populating the user name should be done only with the user's explicit consent. It is surprising that even web sites that need to be conscious of security issues, especially financial institutions, often fail to abide by this recommendation.

10.7.4　Adding caching functionality to the `DomainService` Class

Many different kinds of caching can be used in a web application. Here we discuss object caching, using the `DomainService` class. Methods that store and retrieve instances of `CustomerProfile`, `Partner`, and `Listing` make a database call every time, which may be very costly.

It is relatively simple to cache all retrieved objects in a `Map` that is maintained as an instance variable in the `DomainService` class. The key associated with an entry in the `Map` is the identifying field used to retrieve the object, and the value is the object itself. Java SE 5 introduced *autoboxing* and generics, enabling us to define this `Map` as `Map<Integer, CustomObject>`, assuming that the id field is an integer (`int`). Each retrieval method in the `DomainService` class could be modified as in Figure 10.14.

Similarly, the persistence methods should update the `Map` whenever objects are modified by the application. It should be noted that the underlying data source could be modified independently of the application (e.g., through direct database updates). A decision must be made as to whether the application should tolerate this discontinuity or provide a mechanism for clearing the cache to allow updated objects to be refreshed from the database.

To make this caching mechanism work, the following tasks must be performed:

- Modify the retrieval methods in the `DomainService` class (see Figure 10.14).
- Modify the persistence methods to update the `Map` when persisting new or modified objects.
- Provide public methods that can be invoked to clear object caches (individually or collectively). The administrative interface should provide a mechanism to invoke these methods directly, so that the cache can be cleared on request when necessary.

```
private final Map<Integer, CustomObject> m_customObjectCacheMap =
                              new HashMap<Integer, CustomObject>();

public CustomObject retrieveCustomObjectById(int p_id) {
  if (m_customObjectCacheMap.containsKey(id)) {
    return m_customObjectCacheMap.get(id);
  }
  else {
    CustomObject customObj = null;
    // perform database retrieval functions from original method
    ...
    if (customObj != null) {
      m_customObjectCacheMap.put(id, customObj);
    }
    return customObj;
  }
}
```

Figure 10.14　Object caching.

The caching mechanism should maintain a fixed maximum size for the cache, and should expire the least recently used entries when it becomes full. It is a good idea to set a maximum age beyond which cache entries are automatically expired. The *Apache Commons* project provides a custom `Map` class, `org.apache.commons.collections.map.LRUMap`, which implements this algorithm and could serve as the foundation for a custom cache implementation. *JBoss Cache* (formerly EHCache) is a configurable open source implementation that could also serve this purpose.

Free Cache!

Many ORM packages, such as Hibernate, provide caching functionality of their own, which, if you take advantage of it, renders this technique superfluous. See Section 10.7.8 for more information on using ORM packages.

10.7.5 Paging through cached search results

The result set returned from a search query can be quite large. Rather than displaying the entire result set on one page, the number of results per page should have a predefined limit, and the application should provide a mechanism for customers to page through the discrete result subsets. Sun refers to this as the *Value List Handler* pattern (one of the Core Java EE Patterns). In the past, it has been referred to as the *Paged List* or *Page-by-Page Iterator* pattern.

We have already laid the groundwork for implementing this pattern. Query execution methods in the `DataAccessService` class return a `CachedRowSet`, which is a disconnected cacheable implementation of the `RowSet` interface extending the `ResultSet` interface. Normally, `ResultSet` objects produced by database queries are tied to the database `Connection`. In other words, they are destroyed with the `Connection` and, since well-behaved applications close the `Connection` as part of their task cleanup, the `ResultSet` cannot "live" across multiple HTTP requests. `CachedRowSets` are "disconnected" (not tied to the `Connection`). They can be used across requests, provided they are stored in the HTTP session. Fortunately, the application already does this.

To implement this pattern in our application, the following tasks must be performed:

- Provide a mechanism for defining the number of results per page. Using a property in the `ApplicationResources.properties` file makes this parameter configurable.
- Modify the `SearchResultsAction` class to acknowledge a request parameter, `page`, which indicates the number of the page that should be displayed (defaulting to 1). Use this parameter to calculate the sequence numbers of the first and last results that should appear on the page. Store these values as attributes named `begin` and `end` in the page scope. In addition, set two Boolean attributes named `atBegin` and `atEnd` that indicate whether this is the first or last page in the result set and store them in the page scope as well.
- Modify the `<c:forEach>` tag on the `results.jsp` page so that it displays only the specified range of results. This is accomplished by adding these attributes:

```
begin="${pageScope.begin}"
end="${pageScope.end}"
```

- Add links to the page to allow forward and backward traversal to the next or previous page (e.g., `http://host/context/action/results?page=${request.page+1}`). Place these links within conditional constructs (e.g., `<c:if>` or `<c:choose>` tags) so that the next page link does not appear if this is the last page and the previous page link does not appear if this is the first page.

The Cost of Sessions

Since the overuse of HTTP session objects can be prohibitively expensive in environments with very large numbers of concurrent users, storing these objects in a server-wide cache (either homegrown or using functionality provided by the application server) is a better alternative than storing these objects in the session. Many application servers provide mechanisms for constructing and accessing server-wide caches (including the previously mentioned JBoss Cache). All that needs to be retained in the HTTP session is the key to retrieve the desired object from the cache. Under certain circumstances, the session ID itself can be used as the cache key (or as a component of that key).

10.7.6   Using XML and XSLT for view presentation

A forward-looking approach to presenting application views is to use XML and XSLT. An incremental approach to adding XSLT functionality would be to convert the existing HTML templates to XHTML. Once they are in an XML-compliant format, they can be used as an XML source to which XSLT transformations can be applied. These XSLT transformations would serve as a post-processing step that performs final customizations on presented views. This approach is the least intrusive but the most costly in terms of performance.

A more robust alternative is to construct the model as an XML document and use XSLT style sheets to transform the model into an appropriate view. The beauty of this approach is its inherent flexibility. The application can choose a target format (e.g., HTML, SMIL, VoiceXML) based on the type of device or program making the request. It can then select a specific presentation by choosing a custom XSLT style sheet appropriate for that target format. This technique fully realizes the promise of MVC: the model is completely decoupled from the view, and the number of views that can be made available is limited only by the number of style sheets that developers can construct. (Note: Even this is not a true upper limit, since XSLT style sheets can be constructed dynamically from embedded fragments, greatly increasing the number of possible combinations.)

This approach has two shortcomings that have impeded its acceptance in the web application development community: the sluggish performance associated with XSLT transformations and the overall complexity historically associated with XML and XSLT processing. XSLT performance has improved dramatically through mechanisms that allow the compilation and caching of style sheets. There is need for improvement, but performance is no longer the impediment to XSLT acceptance that it once was.

The complexity of both XML and XSLT processing has been reduced significantly. Early adopters of XML and XSLT had to deal with cumbersome configuration issues and inconsistent APIs. Now virtually all commercial frameworks and server products provide native support for XML processing and native support for XSLT is not far behind.

JSTL's XML tags represent possibly the most radical simplification in XML and XSLT processing. These tags provide not only the ability to parse XML documents into a Document Object Model (DOM) tree, but also the ability to perform direct XSLT transformation on a constructed or imported XML document. Let us assume that the controller component has constructed an XML document and dropped it into a session, and that this or another component has imported or constructed an appropriate XSLT style sheet and dropped *it* into the session as well. Then, the controller could route processing to a JSP page as follows:

```
<%@ taglib prefix="x" uri="http://java.sun.com/jstl/xml" %>
<x:transform xml="${sessionScope.xmlDocument}"
             xslt="${sessionScope.styleSheet}" />
```

XSLT (covered in Chapter 5) is a powerful mechanism for transforming XML documents into human-readable presentations, but it is rather complex. It was hoped that web designers would ultimately be the ones who created XSLT style sheets. Unfortunately, most designers have not taken it upon themselves to learn XSLT. Given its complexity, this is not surprising.

Yet another alternative is to build a DOM tree using the JSTL <x:parse> tag and access individual elements (or sets of elements) using the <x:out>, <x:set>, and <x:forEach> tags. The select attribute in each of these tags can be set to an XPath expression that may return an individual element or (with the <x:forEach> tag) a node set. Using this approach, the results.jsp page could be rewritten as in Figure 10.15.

In this fragment, a variable called listings is constructed as an XML DOM tree from the listingsAsXml session attribute using the <x:parse> tag. (In a properly segmented MVC application, the controller would have built this XML document and stored it in the session.) The <x:forEach> tag selects each element matching the XPath expression /listings/listing and processes it, displaying the values of elements found within it.

As you can see, there are a number of options available for using XML, XSLT, and XPath functionality to make the selection and generation of application views more dynamic and flexible.

```
<x:parse var="listings" xml="${sessionScope.listingsAsXml}" />
<x:forEach select="$listings/listings/listing">
  <x:set var="listingId" select="id" />
  <c:url value="/action/details" var="detailURL" scope="page">
    <c:param name="listingId" value="${listingId}" />
  </c:url>
  <span class="listingTitle">
    <html:link href="${pageScope.detailURL}">
      <x:out select="title" />
    </html:link>
  </span>
  <br/>Property Type: <x:out select="typeAsString" />
  <br/>Offer Type: <x:out select="offerTypeAsString" />
  <br/>Region: <x:out select="region" />
  <hr/>
</x:forEach>
```

Figure 10.15 Example of parsing XML documents using the JSTL <x:parse> tag.

10.7.7   Tracking user behavior

Keeping track of user actions and recording them for later analysis is another capability that is important for our application. For example, when customers visit the search page and enter criteria for browsing the listing database, their entries could be recorded. When a customer views the details of a particular listing, this fact also could be saved (in a log or in a database table) for future reference.

This recorded data could be used by our application, and other applications, to perform a number of tasks:

- Sending targeted e-mails based on tracked behaviors about the availability of specific kinds of real-estate properties.
- Reminding customers who have not logged in for an extended time about the application. Such reminder e-mails are especially useful for subscription web sites, which always want to notify inactive customers that their subscription or free trial has lapsed or is about to lapse.
- Personalizing customer home pages by showing thumbnails of new property listings that satisfy their past search criteria.
- Keeping anonymous statistics about the popularity of individual listings based on the results of searches and detailed views.

To accomplish this, the `Action` classes need to be modified to record information about tracked events. The least intrusive approach would be to record these events into a log file. Each log entry would need to contain all the relevant information, including timestamps, customer ids, listing ids, etc. The format of log records should be standardized so that those records could be browsed and searched later. Our `LoggingService` class simplifies the process of writing records to a log.

A more methodical approach would record tracked events in a database. This means creating tables that contain records of well-defined events that need to be tracked, e.g., "customer login", "listing view", "customer search". The main advantage of this approach is that it is much easier to perform analysis by querying a database than by parsing log entries from a text file.

10.7.8   Using an object-relational mapping tool

For this application, we manually created the Java classes associated with the data model and the underlying database schema into which the data is persisted. In more complex applications with more elaborate data models, this would be a daunting task. There are GUI-based tools that facilitate database design, which can produce DDL statements for a variety of DBMSs and code skeletons for major languages including Java. However, the preferred approach today is the use of *object–relational mapping (ORM)* packages, such as *Hibernate*.

Hibernate uses *mapping files* that define objects in the data model to produce both Java code and DBMS-specific DDL. It can also be used to generate DDL from existing Java classes or, conversely, Java code from an existing database schema. The goal is to correlate database tables directly with Java classes. Where a class definition includes aggregations of or associations with other classes, this is reflected in the mapping files, so that Hibernate understands the composition of complex objects and can retrieve or update related data accordingly.

More importantly, Hibernate circumvents the need to use the JDBC data layer, giving developers higher-level abstractions to work with for data persistence. The Hibernate "session" is used to manage persistence and control transactions. Queries can be written in SQL, in Hibernate's own object-oriented query language (HQL), or using dynamically generated Hibernate criteria. The results returned from Hibernate queries are not in the form of JDBC `ResultSets` or `CachedRowSets`, they are `Lists` of Java objects. For example, assuming the appropriate Hibernate mappings, queries selecting data from the CUSTOMER table would return a `List` of `Customer` objects (`List<Customer>`).

Other ORM packages (e.g., *iBatis*) exist, but Hibernate has taken the lead in adoption. The most recent version of Hibernate fully supports the Java Persistence API (JPA) introduced in Java SE 5.0. Whether you choose to employ Hibernate or some other ORM package would depend on your environment and your application requirements. There is a learning curve associated with adopting Hibernate instead of JDBC and the injection of an additional layer for persistence can introduce issues that lead to a variety of problems. Still, for sufficiently complex applications with elaborate data requirements, an ORM package can dramatically improve both developer productivity and application reliability in the long term.

10.7.9 Adding DHTML and AJAX for an enhanced user experience

Finally, the application's user interface can be greatly enhanced through judicious use of DHTML and AJAX functionality.

Validation of most information entered in HTML forms requires a time-consuming request–response "roundtrip" to the server. The most prominent example is the customer profile entry page. AJAX-facilitated remote validation (as described in Chapter 8) can eliminate this lag by invoking a custom JavaScript handler (`onblur` or `onchange`) as form fields are modified. This handler can perform local client-side validation where appropriate. For example, it can ensure that both entered password fields match, check minimum and maximum lengths for user names, and verify the e-mail address format. It can also submit AJAX requests to validate that entered information matches data that can only be found on the server (e.g., confirming that the entered value for the current password matches the one stored in the database or verifying that the domain specified in the entered e-mail address corresponds to a real Internet domain).

The user experience could be enhanced by using AJAX to present individual listing details. Clicking a link on the results page currently submits a foreground request for a new page that contains details about the individual listing that was selected. Instead, the link could trigger an AJAX request that would fetch the listing details and populate a hidden page element. Once the listing details have been fetched, the hidden page element could be made visible in various ways ranging from the mundane (simply making the element appear on top of other page elements) to the dramatic (fading in the element or having it grow from a pinpoint size to fill the available screen space). A "close" button would be needed that would return the listing details page element to its original non-visible state.

The operative word here is "judicious". You could have the entire application reside on a single JSP page, with AJAX requests and DHTML functions causing every aspect of the application's functionality to appear and disappear magically as needed. This would qualify as an example of going overboard. Consider whether adding AJAX or DHTML really enhances the user experience, or whether introduction of that functionality just serves to make the application flashy, sacrificing usability in the process.

10.8   Summary

Our goal in this chapter was to walk through the process of designing and implementing a web application. We reviewed application requirements, made technology selections, and discussed the implementation. We explained our design decisions, including the use of service classes that implement the Data Access Object (DAO) pattern and the use of embedded JSPs to support presentation co-branding.

We chose the Java EE platform (specifically J2EE 1.4) as the foundation of our application. Of the available options, Java EE solutions provide the most flexibility, reliability, and scalability. The list of modern, open-source Java EE servers includes JBoss, Glassfish, and Tomcat. Since we did not need the full set of Java EE features (such as EJB support), we chose Tomcat as our Java EE server solution. Tomcat has been around longer than the other Java EE servers and continues to be well-supported by the Apache community.

Within the Java EE world, we chose Struts, which is an established, well-supported, and stable framework that provides the functionality required by our application. We used Struts 1.3, the most recent release in the Struts 1.x line. Struts 2.0 is a new offering that represents a complete overhaul of the Struts architecture to provide a more event-driven modular approach. While it is gaining support in the community, Struts 1.x is still the more popular choice.

For the presentation layer, we employed Java Server Pages (JSP) using the Java Standard Tag Library (JSTL) along with the Struts HTML tags. JSP and JSTL are core components of Java EE and Tomcat provides built-in support for both. The Struts tag library, like the Struts framework itself, is an additional component requiring separate download and installation. JSTL and Struts tags provide a more granular level of functionality than, for example, Java Server Faces (JSF). While JSF provides high-level components (e.g., for rendering database query results as an HTML table), JSTL offers fine-grained tags that support iteration and conditional processing (Section 9.2.12). We found JSTL's approach to be powerful and flexible in controlling presentations.

For data persistence, we chose MySQL, a popular open-source relational database management system. When we first implemented this application, MySQL was the most readily available open source RDBMS on the market that provided sufficient functionality to fulfill our application requirements. Today, there are other good, open-source RDBMS options, many of which would suffice for this application.

We provided source code for a complete working application as a starting point for our readers. The enhancements suggested in Section 10.7 provide readers with the opportunity to build on this implementation. In Chapter 11, we consider an alternative approach for implementing one of these enhancements, the administrative interface, using Ruby on Rails.

QUESTIONS AND EXERCISES

1. Install and deploy the sample application. Follow the instructions found on the web site, at http://www. webappbuilders.com/package/readme.html. (You need to register and sign in to download the application package.)

2. What changes need to be made to the `DataAccessService` class to allow the application to work in environments that do not support JNDI-lookup for JDBC `DataSources`? How could this be done in a

way that would still provide runtime configuration options (i.e., without hard-coding database connectivity parameters)?

3. In Section 10.5.3, we mention that we did not implement a custom tag or an includable page to display the navigation bar, because the links presented on the navigation bar would be different on every page (i.e., a page should not present a link to itself). Remember that a parameter in the request URL identifies the current page. Thus, it is possible to build a reusable mechanism for presenting the navigation bar that uses conditional processing to skip the label and link associated with the current page. Implement this functionality using either an included JSP page or a custom tag, and modify embedded pages to refer to it.

4. Formulate a plan for building the administrative interface described in Section 10.7.1. Include a separate database table containing credentials for application administrators.

5. Modify the application to provide the enhancements described in Section 10.7.2. What changes need to be made to the `profile.jsp` page to support this? What other components need to be modified to enable the new functionality?

6. Enhance the application to use a persistent cookie for partner identification as described in Section 10.7.3. Include the functionality that would also enable automatic login if customers indicate this as a preference in their profiles. What changes must be made to the `profile.jsp` page? What other components need to be modified to enable this functionality?

7. Modify the application to provide the enhancements described in Section 10.7.4, providing caching functionality within the service classes. Include the functionality that would clear the cache on request. Which part of the application should expose this function?

8. Enhance the application to provide a mechanism for paging through large result sets using discrete subsets, as described in Section 10.7.5,

9. What difficulties are likely to arise in maintaining an application that makes use of the "less intrusive" XML support strategy described in the opening part of Section 10.7.6?

10. Modify the application to implement the model as an XML document and use XSLT style sheets to transform the model into an appropriate view, as described in Section 10.7.6. What are the maintainability and performance improvements over the original approach, and over the less intrusive alternative described earlier in that section? What issues does this approach solve?

11. Describe the advantages and disadvantages associated with using an ORM package such as Hibernate.

12. The second example offered in Section 10.7.9 (using AJAX to display listing details) makes an unintentional but significant modification to application behavior that violates the requirements. What can be done to remedy this problem so that the application operates as originally intended? (Hint: See Requirement 8.)

10.9   Bibliography

Bayern, Shawn, 2002. *JSTL in Action*. Greenwich (CT): Manning Publications.

Brittain, Jason and Darwin, Ian, 2007. *Tomcat: The Definitive Guide*. Sebastopol (CA): O'Reilly Media.

Chopra, Vivek *et al.*, 2004. *Professional Apache Tomcat* 5. Wrox Press.

Elliott, James 2004. *Hibernate: A Developer's Notebook*. Sebastopol (CA): O'Reilly Media.

Goodwill, James, and Hightower, Rick, 2004. *Professional Jakarta Struts*. Indianapolis (IN): Wrox Press/Wiley Publishing, Inc.

Heffelfinger, David, 2007. *Java EE 5 Development Using GlassFish Application Server*. Birmingham, UK: Packt.

McGovern, James *et al.*, 2003. *Java 2 Enterprise Edition 1.4 Bible*. Indianapolis (IN): Wiley Publishing, Inc.

Siggelkow, Bill, 2005. *Jakarta Struts Cookbook*. Sebastopol (CA): O'Reilly Media.

CHAPTER 11

Web Application Primer 2: Ruby on Rails

IN THIS CHAPTER

- Comparison of Ruby on Rails with Java EE approaches
- Application requirements
- Administrative interface as a Rails application
- Benefits and drawbacks of using Rails
- Whither Enterprise Java?

OBJECTIVES

- Introduce Ruby on Rails as an alternative to Java EE with Struts/JSTL for web application development.
- Define the requirements for the VRLS administrative interface application to be implemented using Rails.
- Demonstrate the advantages of Rails' rapid application development features (including automated scaffolding).
- Illustrate customization options by improving default page layouts using lookup tables.
- Add pagination, validation, and authentication functionality to the application.
- Show how Rails makes use of inheritance in both application code and reusable page layouts.
- Consider the benefits and drawbacks of using Rails for rapid application development.
- Discuss Rails' readiness as an enterprise application platform.
- Examine Java EE responses to the challenges presented by Rails.

In Chapter 10, we built a VRLS application, implemented as a Java EE application using Struts and JSTL. We also made a strong suggestion that it was not complete without an administrative interface. Without such an interface, seemingly trivial administrative tasks such as adding new listings, resetting customer passwords, and configuring settings for participating realtors would all require intervention by developers or database administrators. In the end, we left the development of this interface using Java EE and Struts as an exercise for our readers.

In this chapter, we implement that administrative interface using Ruby on Rails. We describe the process of designing, developing, and deploying the VRLS administrative interface as a Rails application. In essence, we are reversing the case study by implementing the administrative interface and leaving the core application as an exercise for the readers. For reasons that we hope to make clear as you read this chapter, the administrative interface is better suited as a case study for Ruby on Rails development than the core VRLS application.

Like the previous chapter, this is an illustration of application development principles for Ruby on Rails applications rather than an in-depth tutorial. In the course of our discussion, we draw comparisons between Ruby on Rails and the more traditional approach based on Java EE, Struts, and JSTL.

11.1   Comparing Rails with Java EE

We chose Ruby on Rails because, as we were working on this edition of the book, Rails was the up-and-coming rapid application development framework of choice. There has been a lot of on-line buzz about Rails, and its advocates have done much to publicize and evangelize it on blogs, in journals, and at conferences. Our goal was to learn Rails and contrast its strategy with the more formal enterprise development approach associated with Java EE.

11.1.1   Similarities

The Rails framework has much in common with Java EE, in general, and with Struts in particular.

Like Struts, Rails is an MVC framework. Rails applications are structured as Model, View, and Controller components making it hard *not* to use the MVC paradigm. Struts uses a `struts-config.xml` file to configure the "actions" that an application can perform. Rails uses an `app/controllers/`*`application_name`*`_controller.rb` file for the same purpose. In Rails, default routing strategies can be overridden in the `config/routes.rb` file.

Struts applications use `Action` classes as controllers, `ActionForm` beans and Plain Old Java Objects (POJOs) to support the data model, and JSPs for the view components. Similarly, Rails employs controller classes that inherit from a common `ActionController::Base` class, data model classes that are as simple to construct as POJOs, and templates for HTML views and dynamic JavaScript components.

The Rails framework supports direct access to relational databases. The object–relational mapping (ORM) features associated with external packages, such as Hibernate, are built into Rails as part of its `ActiveRecord` functionality, which conforms to the original *Active Record* design pattern described in (Fowler 2002). Similarly, starting with Java EE 5, the Java Persistence API (JPA) incorporates the ORM functionality associated with Hibernate. Some Java EE 5 containers, such as JBoss, use Hibernate as their underlying implementation of JPA.

Included within Rails are built-in mechanisms for testing and deployment of applications. *Rake* is a multi-purpose tool (much like Ant in the Java world) that performs a variety of tasks, including the execution of unit tests, management of database schemas, and the packaging and deployment of applications using *Capistrano*, a package written in Ruby that manages remote application deployments. Java EE's deployment strategies employ standardized application packaging formats (WAR and EAR files). Although integrated tools for building, deploying, and testing applications are absent from both the Java EE specification and the Struts framework, Ant and JUnit are open source tools that support these functions and are widely used and easy to install.

11.1.2 Differences

Although Ruby on Rails provides many of the same benefits and features associated with Java EE and Struts, there are important differences between the approaches.

Ruby is a loosely-typed interpreted language, while Java is a strictly-typed compiled language. It may boil down to a matter of personal taste and programming style, but Rails advocates claim that the looser structure associated with Ruby makes for a faster and more robust development process.

Rails provides integrated support for AJAX, with built-in tags that employ the Prototype/ Scriptaculous toolkit. For Java EE applications, there are many alternatives for AJAX integration. The field is cluttered with numerous options, from DWR to Google Web Toolkit, none of which has emerged as a standard and none of which is seamlessly integrated into Java EE and Struts.

Perhaps the most critical of all differences is Rails' use of *scaffolding*. Setting up a basic application skeleton is the normal first step in the Rails application development process. The `rails` command creates the underlying directory structure for a complete Rails application and the `generate` script builds skeletons for the controller, model, and view classes. Although add-on packages, such as *EasyStruts*, attempt to provide similar services for Struts applications, scaffolding is an integral part of the Rails framework.

11.2 Application Requirements

In the previous chapter, we outlined the requirements associated with the administrative interface:

- **Customer administration:** select customer, reset customer password, change customer status (active, suspended, etc.), remove customer;
- **Partner administration:** add new partner, specify custom markup (logos, background colors, etc.), specify partner selection rules, remove partner;
- **Listing administration:** add a new listing, modify listing (change summary and detail information, add or remove image), remove listing;

- **Authentication and authorization:** access to the administrative interface should be restricted to designated administrators with proper credentials and restricted to IP addresses within the company firewall.

11.3 Building the Administrative Interface as a Rails Application

In this section, we go through the process of building and deploying a Rails application implementing our VRLS administrative interface.

11.3.1 Downloading and installing Ruby and Rails

Rails is available for all major computing platforms and operating systems. The Ruby on Rails wiki contains pointers to instructions for installing Rails on a wide variety of platforms (`http://wiki.rubyonrails.org/rails/pages/GettingStartedWithRails`). Make sure that you obtain an installation package for the most recent version of Rails, which was version 2.0.2 as we were writing this chapter.

11.3.2 Building an application skeleton

Before we get started on the administrative interface, let's implement a simple "Hello world" application.

To establish a proper environment for Rails development, it is recommended that you create a directory specifically for Rails projects. In our example, we assume an environment with a command shell (Unix, Linux, or Mac OS X). We create a `rails_apps` directory under the home directory. In that directory, we run the `rails` command to initiate the automated creation of a Rails project (see Figure 11.1).

The argument `example` passed to the `rails` command is both the name of the application and the name of the directory that is created to contain it. The listing in Figure 11.1 shows only some of the output produced by the `rails` command. The critical directories created under `~/rails_apps/example` are listed in Table 11.1.

After running this command, we run the `script/server` command in the `example` directory to start the Mongrel Web server, which is included with the Rails installation. Once the server is running,

```
$ mkdir ~/rails_apps
$ cd ~/rails_apps
$ rails example
    create
    create  app/controllers
    create  app/helpers
    create  app/models
    create  app/views/layouts
    ...
```

Figure 11.1 Output from executing the `rails example` command.

Table 11.1 Directories and Files Created by the `rails` Command

Directory	Contents
`app/`	Subdirectories for model, view, controller, and helper components
`config/`	Configuration files in Ruby and YAML format
`log/`	Server log files (including distinct production, development, and test logs)
`public/`	Static web resources including images, JavaScript files, and the default `index.html` welcome page.
`script/`	Ruby scripts for generating skeletons, running the server, displaying an interactive console, etc.
`test/`	Subdirectories for unit tests, functional tests, mock objects, etc.
`tmp/`	Temporary directory used by server for session data, sockets, process IDs, and caching

we open the `http://localhost:3000/` URL in the browser. Note that we must execute `script/*` and other commands from the project's root directory (in this case, `~/rails_apps/example`). Once we confirm that the server is running, we can stop it for now by typing CTRL-C.

Now we can create basic controller components by executing the `script/generate` command:

```
$ script/generate controller ExampleApp
      exists  app/controllers/
      exists  app/helpers/
      create  app/views/example_app
      exists  test/functional/
      create  app/controllers/example_app_controller.rb
      create  test/functional/example_app_controller_test.rb
      create  app/helpers/example_app_helper.rb
```

A Case of Case Sensitivity

Rails is smart enough to realize that some operating systems use case-sensitive file names, where `AbC.txt` is a different file from `abc.txt`, while others treat those two names as references to the same file. To make Rails interoperable across these different operating systems, the internal names associated with classes may use camel-case notation (e.g., `ExampleAppController`), but notice that the generated file names use the convention of lower-case plus underlining (e.g., `example_app_controller.rb`).

The stubs and skeletons are all in place, but the application doesn't do anything yet. To get it to perform a simple "Hello World" function, we need to edit some files and restart the server.

In the `app/controllers` directory, `example_app_controller.rb` is a Ruby class file specifying the `ExampleAppController` class which inherits from `ApplicationController` (a class defined in `application.rb`). We can edit `example_app_controller.rb` to add "action paths" to

Figure 11.2 Browser error when `example_app/hello.html.erb` does not exist.

the application. For the sake of simplicity and tradition, we add a "Hello World" function with the URL path `example_app/hello`:

```
class ExampleAppController < ApplicationController
  def hello
  end
end
```

The inserted lines in this file identify the `example_app/hello` path to the application, which will route processing to the default view component for that path. Remember that Rails emphasizes "convention over configuration," and the convention is that the URL path `example_app/hello` routes to the default view component found at `app/views/example_app/hello.html.erb`. We have to create this file because it is not built by the scaffolding script when invoked with the `script/generate controller` option. If we restart the server without creating that file, we see the error in Figure 11.2 when we try to access `http://localhost:3000/example_app/hello`.

Let's create this file as a simple HTML page that says "Hello, World!":

```
<!DOCTYPE html PUBLIC "-//W3C//DTD XHTML 1.0 Strict//EN"
    "DTD/xhtml1-strict.dtd">
<html>
<head>
  <title>Our First Rails Application</title>
</head>
<body>
  <h1>Hello, world!</h1>
</body>
</html>
```

After refreshing the browser window, we see the output shown in Figure 11.3.

Mongrel and its Pedigree

Mongrel is a web server written in Ruby with C extensions. Rails uses Mongrel as its default underlying web server. You can still opt for the older options (WEBrick and LightTPD with FastCGI) through arguments

Figure 11.3   Browser display after creating `example_app/hello.html.erb`.

passed to `script/server`, but Mongrel is increasingly the web server of choice. It runs faster than its predecessors and is easier to configure.

Mongrel, WEBrick, and LightTPD are lightweight HTTP servers that do not scale well for use in a real-world production environment. For this reason, it is recommended that Apache be used as a front-end to whatever server Rails is actually running on. Apache Web Server 2.2 supports simple configuration directives (using the `mod_proxy_balancer` module) to load-balance requests routed to Mongrel servers running Rails applications. Apache can take care of static resources and makes Rails more configurable and scalable than older solutions.

Now we can begin building the real functionality we want in our VRLS application.

11.3.3   Creating a new project and configuring the database

First, we create a new Rails application for the VRLS administrative interface. We execute the `rails` command from the `rails_apps` directory, specifying a particular database adapter, namely the one for MySQL:

```
$ cd ~/rails_apps
$ rails -d mysql vrlsadmin
...
```

Before Rails 2.0, MySQL was the default database platform. With Rails 2.0, SQLite version 3 has become the new default. SQLite is an even lighter database system than MySQL, advertising itself as "a self-contained, serverless, zero-configuration, transactional SQL database engine." If we do not specify a database adapter using the `-d adapter` option, Rails constructs the `config/database.yml` file based on the default SQLite adapter.

For our new application, the `config/database.yml` file is tailored for use with MySQL, using the standard default names for development (`vrlsadmin_development`), test (`vrlsadmin_test`), and production (`vrlsadmin_production`) databases. Since we already have a production database, called `vrls`, that was created for the core VRLS application, we need to edit the `config/database.yml` file (Figure 11.4) to enter the proper database names and credentials.

In conjunction with this step, we have to create the `vrls_dev` and `vrls_test` databases in MySQL. Note that the `vrls` database was created when we built the core VRLS application. We also have to

```
# MySQL - Version 5.0 is recommended.
  ...
development:  adapter: mysql  encoding: utf8  database: vrls_dev
  username: root  password: your-mysql-root-password
  socket: /tmp/mysql.lock

# Warning: The database defined as 'test' will be erased and
# re-generated from your development database when you run 'rake'.
# Do not set this db to the same as development or production.
test:
  adapter: mysql  encoding: utf8  database: vrls_test
  username: root  password: your-mysql-root-password
  socket: /tmp/mysql.lock

production:
  adapter: mysql  encoding: utf8  database: vrls
  username: root  password: your-mysql-root-password
  socket: /tmp/mysql.lock
```

Figure 11.4   Modified `config/database.yml` file.

run the SQL scripts provided with the VRLS application to define and populate the `vrls_dev` and `vrls_test` databases, mirroring the `vrls` database.

How Does Rails Know Which Database to Use?

It all depends on how you start the server.

```
$ script/server [ -e development|test|production ]
```

By default the `script/server` command uses the development environment. This means that the server uses the development database and reads its environment settings not only from the global file `config/environment.rb` but also from `config/environments/development.rb`. In production mode, Rails uses the production database defined in `config/database.yml` and the production settings found in `config/environments/production.rb`.

Rails configures appropriate default settings in the `config/environments/*.rb` files (e.g., the debugger is enabled in development but not in other environments), but you can edit these files to customize the settings.

11.3.4   Scaffolding for the model, view, and controller classes

The next step is to take advantage of Rails' scaffolding to build model, view, and controller classes. Because we are working with an existing database schema, the usefulness of the data model scaffolding features is limited. We need to override a significant amount of information in the generated model classes and edit some default Rails configuration settings.

Rails defaults correlate model classes with table names, making use of a feature known as *pluralization*. It is assumed that the names of model classes are singular (because each instance of a class refers to a single object of a specific type), while the table name is plural (because it contains a collection of items of the specified type). Thus, `Listing` is the name of a class (contained in a file called `listing.rb`) that corresponds to a database table called `listings`.

Unfortunately, the main VRLS application already defines a table for listings called `vrls_listings`. Additionally, its primary key column is called `listing_id`, rather than the default primary key column name (`id`) that Rails expects. To address this situation, we have to override the default setting for database table name pluralization. The following line must be added at the bottom of the global `config/environment.rb` file:

```
ActiveRecord::Base.pluralize_table_names = false
```

Next, we have to generate default files for the model, view, and controller classes and modify these classes to override defaults. We can create the files for the `Listing` class by executing a different flavor of the `script/generate` command (see Figure 11.5).

Among the files produced by this command is `app/models/listing.rb`, which contains the definition for the `Listing` class. We edit this file to add directives that override the defaults and explicitly define the table name and the primary key column name (Figure 11.6).

We now have a fully functional Rails application for performing create–read–update–delete (CRUD) functions against the `vrls_listings` table. Once we have run the database creation and population scripts for the `vrls_dev` database, we can start the server using the `script/server` command. Once the server is up and running, visiting `http://localhost:3000/listings` would produce a "listing of Listings" (see Figure 11.7) based on the content of the `app/views/entity/index.html.erb` file.

We can see the listings stored in the `vrls_listings` table. We can click the "Show", "Edit", and "Destroy" links for individual listings, or the "New listing" link at the bottom of the page, to see some of the other pages that Rails scaffolding has built for us:

- The "Show" links point to `http://localhost:3000/listings/`*id*, which displays attributes of the selected listing as static text (see Figure 11.8).

```
$ script/generate scaffold Listing listing_id:integer \
   listing_title:string listing_desc:text listing_type_code:integer \
   listing_region:integer listing_offer_type_code:integer \
   listing_num_bedrooms:integer listing_num_bathrooms:integer \
   listing_monthly_payment:integer listing_purchase_price:integer \
   referring_partner_id:integer listing_status_code:integer \
   listing_status_eff_date:date date_entered:date date_last_modified:date
...
```

Figure 11.5 The `script/generate scaffold` command.

```
class Listing < ActiveRecord::Base
  set_table_name "vrls_listings"
  set_primary_key "listing_id"
end
```

Figure 11.6 Modified contents of `app/models/listing.rb`.

Listing	Listing title	Listing desc	Listing type code	Listing region	Listing offer type code	Listing num bedrooms	Listing num bathrooms	Listing monthly payment	Listing purchase price	Referring partner	Listing status code	Listing status eff date	Date entered	Date last modified			
1	Big White House	Roomy white house with many bedrooms and office space	1	Capital District	2	10	3	10000.0	5000000.0	7777	1	2008-04-21	2008-04-21	2008-04-21	Show	Edit	Destroy
2	Plush Indian Palace	Large palatial estate with beautiful interior and exterior	1	Subcontinent	1	3	1	10000.0	5000000.0	7777	1	2008-04-21	2008-04-21	2008-04-21	Show	Edit	Destroy
3	Love Shack	It's a little old place where we can get together	1	Athens	1	1	1	100.0	50000.0	7777	1	2008-04-21	2008-04-21	2008-04-21	Show	Edit	Destroy

New listing

Figure 11.7   Displaying `http://localhost:3000/listings`.

Figure 11.8   Displaying `http://localhost:3000/listings/1`.

Figure 11.9 Displaying `http://localhost:3000/listings/1/edit`.

- The "Edit" links point to `http://localhost:3000/listings/id/edit`, which displays a form page with fields containing attributes of the selected listing (see Figure 11.9). We can edit the form fields and press the Update button at the bottom of this page to save the modified listing.
- The "Destroy" links invoke a JavaScript function, which prompts us for confirmation of deleting the listing. Upon confirmation, the entry is deleted and the page is re-rendered.
- The "New listing" link at the bottom of the page points to `http://localhost:3000/listings/-new`. It takes us to a similar form page with blank fields, making it possible to fill in the blanks and create a new listing.

No Trailing Slash

There is a good reason why URLs generated by Rails do not have trailing slashes. While these URLs may appear to reference directories (because they lack a file name suffix such as `.html`), they are actually RESTful URLs that reference discrete web resources (see Section 5.3.2).

Table 11.2 illustrates the default URL mapping scheme, using the word "entity" (and its plural, "entities") for a hypothetical class named `Entity`.

Table 11.2   URL Mapping Scheme for the `Entity` Class

URL	Maps to	Purpose
`http://host/entities`	`app/views/entity/index.html.erb`	Display all entities
`http://host/entities/`*id*	`app/views/entity/show.html.erb`	Display a particular entity
`http://host/entities/`*id*`/edit`	`app/views/entity/edit.html.erb`	Edit that entity
`http://host/entities/new`	`app/views/entity/new.html.erb`	Enter a new entity

To complete the application, we have to generate scaffolding for the remaining tables or objects, update the model classes to support foreign keys and form validation, customize the view components, build additional functionality based on our requirements, and add authentication and authorization.

Scaffolding in Rails 2.0

If you are familiar with Rails 1.x scaffolding commands, the example we provided may look strange to you. Many of the scaffolding features changed radically with the advent of Rails 2.0. The proper way to generate scaffolding now is to execute the `script/generate scaffold` command, supplying it with a class name and the names and data types of fields associated with that class.

```
$ script/generate scaffold Listing listing_id:integer \
    listing_title:text listing_desc:text ...
```

You would think that, since we are working from a pre-existing database schema, Rails would be smart enough to make use of database metadata and would not need explicit field definitions. Unfortunately, this is not the case. Because our table names do not conform to Rails naming conventions, we have to alter our model file to specify the real table name and primary key column name as shown in Figure 11.6. When the *set_table_name* directive is employed, Rails has no way of inferring the table name as the basis for defining fields for models.

Sadly, this is true even if we were to preemptively create a "draft" model class that includes a *set_table_name* directive and then run the *script/generate scaffold* command. Although this functionality would certainly make Rails scaffolding more robust with respect to legacy database schemas, the developers of Rails have indicated that they do not consider this to be a bug and would not change the codebase to enable this functionality.[1]

This attitude toward scaffolding in Rails 2.0 has raised concerns among developers about the direction in which Rails is moving.[2] Some defenders of the new scaffolding approach try to diminish the importance of scaffolding as a prominent feature of Rails, even though it is a feature (if not the feature) that attracted many developers to Rails in the first place. Hopefully the Rails community will recognize how important scaffolding really is and will ensure that it is made as robust as possible in the future.

11.3.5   Enhancing the application

While the application pages we discussed are functional, they have only bare-bones functionality. Rails has automatically built and configured controller classes with an organized routing infrastructure not unlike Struts. It has created model classes and rudimentary view components.

Still, a simple default CRUD application is hardly production-worthy. In its current state, the application presents data that may have to be hidden (e.g., the primary key ID values for objects). It presents numeric codes instead of their corresponding lookup values (e.g., in displaying a listing, the referring partner's ID is displayed rather than their name). The layout of the pages is raw and primitive.

Completing the data model

First, we need to add scaffolding for the other domain objects that are administered by this interface. This includes customers, partners, and images that accompany real-estate listings. We also need to add model classes for auxiliary objects used for lookups and cross-references: listing status (active, inactive, etc.), listing type (house, townhouse, apartment, etc.), and listing offer type (buy, rent, etc.). Since the last three only require model definitions, we use the `script/generate model` command.

Once the additional scaffolding is in place, we can visit the pages for displaying and editing customers and partners. (See the URL scheme described in Table 11.2 for details.) Next, we need to edit the model definitions in `/app/models`: to insert `set_table_name` and `set_primary_key` directives, and to establish foreign key relationships. Since we already set the table name and primary key column in `app/models/listing.rb`, only the relationships to other tables need to be established:

```
class Listing < ActiveRecord::Base
  set_table_name &vrls_listings"
  set_primary_key &listing_id"
  belongs_to :partner, :foreign_key => "referring_partner_id"
end
```

We need to specify the foreign key column explicitly, because our database schema does not abide by Rails' naming conventions for primary and foreign key columns. The other model definition files will require corresponding modifications.

Customizing views and using lookup tables

Next, we can customize view components, for both aesthetics and usability. By default, the `app/views/*/index.html.erb` components display all the columns for each entity. The application employs a master–detail pattern, in which the list page displays only columns needed for identification of an item, allowing the user to "drill down" to details on another page. With this in mind, we remove all but a few columns from this view. This means editing the `app/views/*/index.html.erb` files to remove the `<td>` and `<th>` tags that define those columns in the table's body and header. We can also make changes to CSS directives to enhance the layout and edit the column labels (see Figure 11.10).

The `app/views/*/show.html.erb` pages display details about an individual entity. Unfortunately, these details are displayed in their "raw" state – without accounting for lookup tables that translate codes into readable text. For example, the `referring_partner_id` field is displayed as a number, referring to the primary key found in the `vrls_partners` table. Obviously it would be considerate to our users to display names of partners instead of "id" numbers.

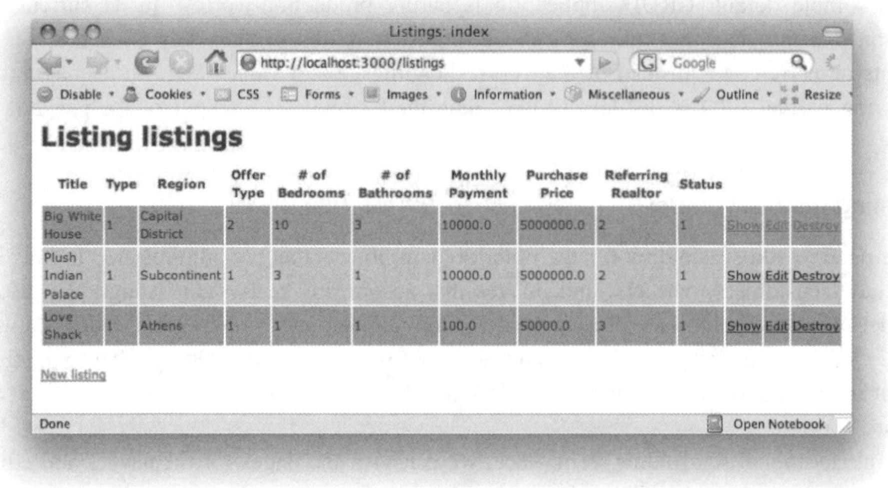

Figure 11.10 Enhanced display using modified `app/views/listing/index.html.erb`.

Fortunately, it's not complicated to add this lookup into the page. Inspecting the `app/views/listings/show.html.erb` file, we notice that each field in the object defined by the variable `@listing` is displayed on the page via an `h` tag:

```
<%=h @listing.referring_partner_id %>
```

This tag simply presents the HTML-escaped value of the field. Hence, we see the numeric partner id. To present the name of the partner instead, we change this line to the following:

```
<%=h
Partner.find_by_partner_id(@listing.referring_partner_id).partner_name %>
```

This line is a tribute to just how effective Rails can be. It executes the `find_by_partner_id()` method of the `Partner` class, passing the value of the listing's `referring_partner_id` field as an argument, extracts the `partner_name` field from the retrieved `Partner` object, and displays the name instead of the numeric id value.

Where'd That Method Come From?

There's just one problem: the `Partner` class does have a `find` method, which it inherited from the `ActiveRecord::Base` class and which can take arguments in the form of generic selection criteria:

```
Partner.find(:first, :conditions =>
  {:partner_id => @listing.referring_partner_id})
```

but we didn't define a `find_by_partner_id` method ... did we?

Fortunately, Rails' `ActiveRecord` classes use a feature called *dynamic finders*. In the Ruby language, all classes inherit a method called `method_missing`, which is invoked whenever an object receives a message referring to a method name it does not know about. In the `ActiveRecord::Base` class (and its subclasses), this method is overridden to react to unknown method names that begin with `find_by`, by translating them dynamically into calls to the `find` method as described above. This means you don't need to go to the trouble of tediously writing a long list of custom finder methods.

We can make corresponding changes to the code for displaying the `referring_partner_id` field in `app/views/listings/show.html.erb`, and for the `listing_status`, `listing_type`, and `listing_offer_type` fields as well. We should also change the labels displayed with each field from the database column name to something more meaningful. These changes are reflected in Figure 11.11.

We can make corresponding changes in the `app/views/listings/index.html.erb` file (assuming fields that we want to change are still displayed on this page after the previous step). The remaining `app/views/*/index.html.erb` and `app/views/*/show.html.erb` files can be modified similarly.

The page for editing real estate listings, which displays an HTML form consisting of editable text boxes, poses a different problem. We could inject the correct value for the partner's name into its corresponding text box, but allowing free-form text editing on a field defined by a lookup value is not a great idea. We need a dropdown, using HTML `<select>` and `<option>` tags that correlate the partner IDs with their names. Changing the selected item in the dropdown and clicking the `Update` button should result in saving the listing with the newly selected partner ID.

Figure 11.11   Display of `http://localhost:3000/listings/1` after customization.

Rails can enable this lookup with a single line of code. In the `app/views/listings/edit.html.erb` file, the HTML form is defined via a `form_for` tag:

```
<% form_for(@listing) do |f| %>
```

Each field in the object defined by the variable `@listing` is displayed on the page via an `f.text_field` or `f.text_area` tag, for example:

```
<%= f.text_field :referring_partner_id %>
```

This tag presents an `<input type="text">` form field containing the current value of the referring partner's numeric ID. To present a dropdown displaying partners by name, with the current partner as the selected item, we can change this line to the following:

```
<%= collection_select("listing", "referring_partner_id",
    Partner.find(:all), "partner_id", "partner_name") %>
```

This code associates the `referring_partner_id` field in the `listing` object with the selected item in the HTML dropdown element generated by this tag. The items in the dropdown element will be populated from a list of all the partners registered in the database, with item values set to the numeric IDs and labels set to partner names. In the rendered edit page, the `collection_select` tag is expanded:

```
<select id="listing_referring_partner_id"
        name="listing[referring_partner_id]">
  <option value="1">Default</option>
  <option value="2" selected="selected">Leon</option>
  <option value="3">Rich</option>
</select>
```

When the Update button in the form is clicked, the listing is saved in the database with the `referring_partner_id` field set to the selected value.

We can change the number of rows displayed in the `<textarea>` element associated with the `listing_desc` description field:

```
<%= f.text_area :listing_desc, :rows => 2 %>
```

We can also change the way date fields are presented for editing in this form by adding an argument specifying the ordering of month, day, and year:

```
<%= f.date_select :listing_status_eff_date,
        :order => [:month, :day, :year] %>
```

Finally, we can change the labels associated with each field to make them more user-friendly. The results of our efforts can be seen in Figure 11.12. Once again, we can make corresponding changes in the other `app/views/*/edit.html.erb` files. Similar changes can be made to the `app/views/*/new.html.erb` files, which contain the forms for creating new entities.

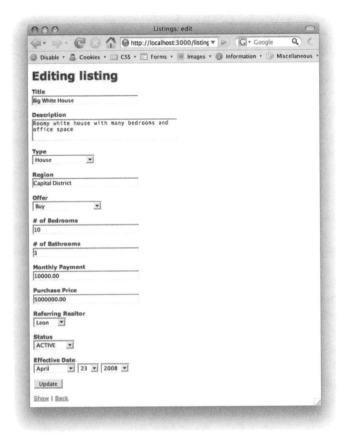

Figure 11.12 Display of `http://localhost:3000/listings/1/edit` after customization.

Form validation

Form validation in Rails can be accomplished by adding simple directives to the underlying model class. For example, let's assume that the form for creating or updating customers should validate that the customer's login name is unique and that it is between 5 and 12 characters long. It should prompt the user to enter the password twice and verify that the entered values match. It should also confirm that a valid phone number has been entered in the appropriate form field and that other required fields contain sensible values.

The validation functionality can be implemented by adding declarative directives to the `app/models/customer.rb` file:

```
class Customer < ActiveRecord::Base
  set_table_name "vrls_customer_profile_data"
  set_primary_key "cust_id"
  belongs_to :partner, :foreign_key => "referring_partner_id"
  validates_length_of :cust_login, :within => 5..12,
```

```
      :too_short => "- Login name must be at least 5 characters long.",
      :too_long => "- Login name must be no more than 12 characters long."
    validates_uniqueness_of :cust_login,
      :message => "- That login is already in use. Choose another."
    validates_confirmation_of :cust_password_hash,
      :message => "- The passwords must match exactly."
    validates_format_of :cust_phone,
      :with => /^[2-9][0-9]{2}-[2-9][0-9]{2}-[0-9]{4}$/,
      :message => "- Phone number must be in 999-999-9999 format."
    validates_presence_of :cust_address1,
      :message => "- Address field 1 must not be blank."
end
```

The directives indicate the kinds of validation each field requires:

- If the user-provided value for the login name (`cust_login` field) is not between 5 and 12 characters long, the `validates_length_of` directive flags this as an error.
- If the entered login name already exists in the database, the `validates_uniqueness_of` directive flags that as an error.
- The `validates_confirmation_of` directive checks that the password values entered in the `cust_password_hash` and `cust_password_hash_confirmation` fields are the same, and flags it as an error if they are not.
- The entered phone number is checked against the regular expression in the `validates_format_of` directive, which enforces the "999-999-9999" format (with additional restrictions on the digits in certain positions).
- Finally, the `cust_address1` field must not be blank, so the `validates_presence_of` directive makes sure that it isn't.

For each of these error conditions, a custom error message is defined. When the form is submitted, the validation checks are performed and, if any of them fail, the form is presented back to the user with a list of errors at the top of the page (Figure 11.13).

The Rails framework supports a number of other declarative validation directives, including:

- `validates_acceptance_of` (e.g., "By checking this box, I accept this license agreement");
- `validates_inclusion_of` (confirms that the value of a form field comes from a defined list);
- `validates_numericality_of` (confirms that the value of a form field is numeric).

Developers can extend validation processing by adding their own validation directives or by overriding the `validate()` method. Rails provides built-in support for the Prototype and Scriptaculous toolkits, but the automated generation of server-side validation code is not accompanied by the corresponding client-side validation code (DHTML and AJAX). A third-party plug-in, *ActiveScaffold*, can be used to generate View components that incorporate both server-side and client-side validation functionality (and also provide a much nicer page layout), but it is not a standard component of Ruby on Rails.

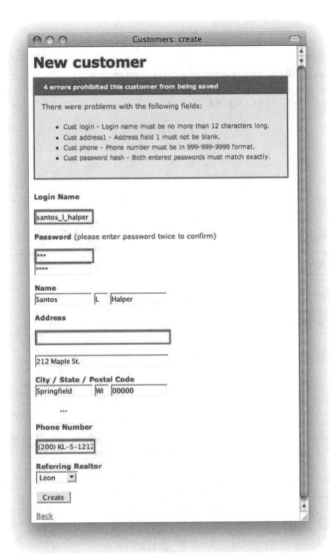

Figure 11.13 New customer form page with validation errors highlighted.

Pagination

In Rails, it is relatively easy to tailor views to support pagination. First, we update the controller class to tell it to use pagination:

```
class ListingsController < ApplicationController
  # GET /listings
  # GET /listings.xml
  def index
```

```
    @listings = Listing.find(:all)
    respond_to do |format|
      format.html {
        @listings = Listing.paginate :per_page => 2,
            :page => params[:page],
            :order => 'listing_id'
      }
      format.xml { render :xml => @listings }
    end
  end
  ...
end
```

Since our listings table only has three listings, we set the value of the :per_page argument to 2 so that the results span two pages. Next, we add pagination to the view, near the bottom of the page:

```
<%= will_paginate @listings %>
```

We also add the following line at the very bottom of our config/environment.rb file:

```
require "will_paginate"
```

We then restart the server. The result is shown in Figure 11.14.

"Relatively Easy" is Relative

When we said that adding pagination was "relatively easy", we didn't tell the whole story ...

We left out the fact that the original pagination functionality available in Rails 1.x was removed in Rails 2.0. The Rails 1.x pagination examples in print and on-line tutorials no longer work in Rails 2.0.

After a bit of research, we found that installation of a new plug-in, called will_paginate, was the key to getting pagination working in Rails 2.0. This installation was not a simple task. It should have been enough to run script/install plug-in, but attempting to contact the download server consistently produced a 404 Page Not Found error. Further research indicated that the plug-in should be downloaded not through script/install plug-in but through the gem command.

Confused? Frustrated? We certainly were. A commonly used web application feature was simply removed from the new version of Rails without regard for developers who were actively using it. The alternatives for Rails 2.0 were difficult to find and, although will_paginate was purported to be both simpler and more powerful, documentation on it is sparse and no less difficult to find.

Reusable layout components

Rails provides mechanisms for building page layouts from reusable components. By default, the scaffolding commands build an html.erb layout file in app/views/layouts for each controller class. Using the principle of "convention over configuration", a controller is automatically associated with an appropriately named layout. For example, the controller for the Listing object (app/controllers/listings_controller.rb) is associated with the preconfigured layout found

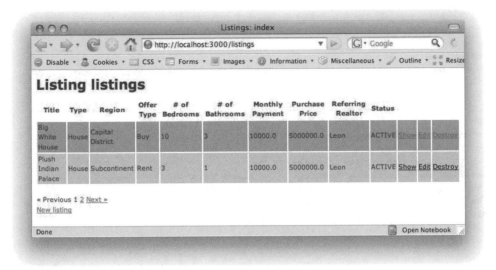

Figure 11.14 Browser display with pagination.

in `app/views/layouts/listing.html.erb`, so all the views presented by that controller (i.e., `app/views/listings/*.html.erb`) are wrapped by that layout.

Figure 11.15 shows the content of the generated `app/views/layouts/listing.html.erb` file. The `<%= yield %>` tag (on the third line from the bottom) represents the position within the page layout where the view content is injected. This layout is used by all views associated with listings. It can be customized, as shown in Figure 11.16.

The change adds a banner and a menu to the layout as shown in Figure 11.17. The `link_to` tags reference the `listings_path`, `partners_path`, and `customers_path` variables, all of which were automatically set up during scaffolding, as links to the respective index pages associated with each class (e.g., `http://localhost:3000/listings/`).

```
<!DOCTYPE html PUBLIC "-//W3C//DTD XHTML 1.0 Transitional//EN"
 &http://www.w3.org/TR/xhtml1/DTD/xhtml1-transitional.dtd">
<html xmlns="http://www.w3.org/1999/xhtml" xml:lang="en" lang="en">
<head>
  <meta http-equiv="content-type" content="text/html;charset=UTF-8" />
  <title>Listings: <%= controller.action_name %></title>
  <%= stylesheet_link_tag 'scaffold' %>
</head>
<body>
  <p style="color: green"><%= flash[:notice] %></p>
  <%= yield %>
</body>
</html>
```

Figure 11.15 Content of generated `app/views/layouts/listing.html.erb`.

```
<!DOCTYPE html PUBLIC "-//W3C//DTD XHTML 1.0 Transitional//EN"
      "http://www.w3.org/TR/xhtml1/DTD/xhtml1-transitional.dtd">
<html xmlns="http://www.w3.org/1999/xhtml" xml:lang="en" lang="en">
<head>
  <meta http-equiv="content-type" content="text/html;charset=UTF-8" />
  <title>Listings: <%= controller.action_name %></title>
  <%= stylesheet_link_tag 'scaffold' %>
</head>
<body>
 <div class="banner"><%= image_tag "logo.gif" %></div>
 <div class="menu">
    <b>VRLS Administrative Interface:</b>
   <%= link_to "Administer Listings", listings_path %>
   <%= link_to "Administer Partners", partners_path %>
   <%= link_to "Administer Customers", customers_path %>
 </div>
 <p style="color: green"><%= flash[:notice] %></p>
  <%= yield %>
</body>
</html>
```

Figure 11.16   Content of modified `app/views/layouts/listing.html.erb`.

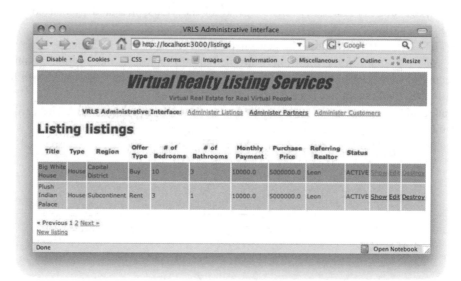

Figure 11.17   Browser display for listings page with modified layout.

The banner and menu could be refactored into a reusable *partial view*, which could be included in each of the common layouts. The changes to Figure 11.15 could be replaced by the following line in each of the `app/views/layouts/*.html.erb` files:

```
<%= render :partial => '/banner_menu' %>
```

This directive references a partial view file named app/views/_banner_menu.html.erb, which would contain the banner and menu <div> tags. Here we are simply embedding a static page fragment, but the directive can include parameters to render its content dynamically (e.g., the way the list of items in the main VRLS application's menu bar changes depending on which page is being viewed).

Another approach would be to create one common layout that would be used by all views associated with the same controller. To do this, we would create one common layout file (e.g., app/views/layouts/common.html.erb), then add a single line to all of the app/controllers/*.rb files to reference this common layout:

```
class ListingsController < ApplicationController
  layout "common"
  ...
end
```

Authentication and authorization

We've seen how Rails makes good use of inheritance in a number of areas (e.g., page layouts). Here we look at how Rails' use of inheritance simplifies the process of user authentication.

Because all our controller classes extend the ApplicationController class defined in app/controllers/application.rb, changes we make to that class are inherited by all controllers. Rails controllers can make use of filters, so we define a before filter that every controller executes before it performs its processing. The before_filter defined in the base ApplicationController class references a protected method, authenticate, which we add to that class:

```
class ApplicationController < ActionController::Base
  before_filter :authenticate
  ...
  protected
  def authenticate
    authenticate_or_request_with_http_basic do |username, password|
      # code here performs authentication based on username/password
      username == "admin" && password == "admin"
    end
  end
end
```

The authenticate method is executed before a request is processed. Basic HTTP authentication is invoked using the authenticate_or_request_with_http_basic method which is new to Rails 2.0. The server sends a response with a 401 (Unauthorized) status code, causing the browser to prompt the user for credentials. If the method returns true for the supplied credentials, the user is authenticated and processing can continue. If not, authentication fails, and the browser displays the "Access denied" message.

This example performs very trivial authentication – it employs a single line of code that tests whether or not the supplied user name and password are both "admin". That line should be replaced by something more practical, such as a query against a `vrls_administrators` table that only returns true if it finds a row where both the user name and password columns match the entered values:

```
VrlsAdministrator.find_by_username_and_password(username, password)
```

Moreover, basic HTTP authentication could be replaced with more flexible forms-based authentication. The `acts_as_authenticated` plug-in can also be used to provide more sophisticated authentication functionality. The point of this example is not to prescribe specific methods for performing user authentication, but to demonstrate how a simple change to a single class can enable authentication for our entire application.

Authorization would need to be performed at the server level. Mongrel is not capable of restricting access by IP address, but if we add an Apache server front end to our Rails application, it becomes a simple matter to configure the server to restrict the application to a range of IP addresses.

Replacing the Rails home page

We mentioned earlier that the default home page displayed by Rails could easily be modified by editing the application's `public/index.html` file. Because that page is just a static HTML file, though, it would not be protected from access by unauthenticated users. The home page URL (`http://localhost:3000/`) can be protected by associating it with a controller that extends the `ApplicationController` class, which was modified in the previous section to enforce user authentication. Here are the steps that accomplish this task:

1. Run the `script/generate controller HomePage index` command. It builds the `app/controllers/home_page_controller.rb` file (containing the `HomePageController` class) and the `app/views/home_page/index.html.erb` file.
2. Edit the `config/routes.rb` file to add the following line, which maps the null path (`''`) to the `HomePageController` class.

```
map.connect '', :controller => 'home_page'
```

3. Edit the `app/views/home_page/index.html.erb` file to provide a customized presentation for the application's home page.
4. Delete the `public/index.html` file.
5. Restart the server.

That's it. If we visit `http://localhost:3000/`, we should see the new home page after entering the proper credentials.

Summary

Let's review what we have accomplished:

1. We downloaded and installed Ruby on Rails and built an example application.
2. We executed Rails' scaffolding commands to build the skeletal infrastructure for the VRLS administrative interface.

3. We fleshed out the application by running additional scaffolding for all the model components.
4. We customized views to enhance application usability, including the use of lookup tables to display human-readable translations of id numbers.
5. We added form validation, pagination, flexible layouts, authentication, and a custom home page.

There are still a number of features not included in the application, but this should provide a good sense of what building a Rails application is all about.

Compared to the Java EE and Struts approach, Rails enabled us to get things done a lot faster. We were up and running quickly, in much less time than it took to get a Struts application off the ground. Some functionality was dramatically easier to implement in Rails. Validation of form fields, pagination of query results, referencing lookup tables to populate dropdown selection lists, reusable page layout components, and trivial user authentication were all remarkably simple to introduce into the application.

Although all of these features were available with Java EE and Struts, Rails made it significantly easier to include them in the application. Adding declarative validation directives to Model classes is simpler than using the Struts Validator API. Likewise, lookups for populating dropdown selection lists can be accomplished using JSTL tags, but Rails' mechanisms are even easier. The Tiles framework provides layout management functionality for Struts applications, but Rails' approach is, again, simpler. Other functions including pagination and authentication require more coding in Java EE and Struts than they do in Rails.

On the other hand, once we have a basic working application, the effort required to customize it, both in terms of front-end presentation and back-end server-side functionality, is similar. Rails' scaffolding builds a complete CRUD application "out of the box", but customizing that application to fit specific requirements is just as much work with Rails as it is with Java EE and Struts.

11.4 Benefits and Drawbacks of Using Rails

Truth be told, we did not get the opportunity to exercise the full array of features associated with Ruby on Rails while building our application. We did not examine Rails' generation of fixtures for unit tests, its database migration capabilities, or its application deployment functionality. Nonetheless, the experience of building this application in Rails gives us a solid perspective for evaluating the benefits and drawbacks of this framework.

11.4.1 How rapid *is* rapid application development?

Rails' use of scaffolding is supposed to be one of its most prominent features. Setting up Rails application projects through automated scaffolding represents a welcome change from the tedious manual effort employed in setting up Java EE projects. Eclipse and other *Integrated Development Environment* (IDE) tools have taken some of the pain out of creating new Java EE applications, but *smart* scaffolding that builds enough structure to run a simple application "out of the box" is preferable. When there is an excessive amount of boilerplate code that needs to be written, coupled with an intimidating number of configuration files that need to be customized, it becomes difficult to get something running quickly. Developers are naturally frustrated at the current state of affairs in application development, where tedious initial efforts to set up application projects do not produce immediately visible results. Overcoming this impediment is an important goal for any new web development framework.

Is Rails really any faster or better than using an IDE like Eclipse to generate scaffolding? Ultimately, yes, because Rails builds a functional, well-organized, MVC-based CRUD application that is modifiable and extensible. As we've seen, modifying and extending that application was an easier task than it would be with a Java EE application. Ruby's status as a loosely-typed language (compared to the strict typing inherent in Java) worked to our advantage in effecting genuinely rapid development. Dynamic finders are another useful feature that eliminated a significant amount of repetitive boilerplate code. Integrated support for JavaScript and AJAX toolkits made it easier to incorporate Web 2.0 functionality into an application.

On the flip side, it is difficult for IDEs to provide the same level of support for a loosely-typed language, such as Ruby, that they do for more strictly-typed languages, such as C++ and Java. Good IDEs attempt to catch potential problems (e.g., type mismatches in code) at the earliest opportunity. They scan through the application codebase to find problems, prompting developers to correct them before building the application. With a loosely-typed language, the whole notion of "type mismatches" goes out the window, so many programming errors are not as likely to be caught early on in the process. Still, there is a good deal of support for Rails developers. TextMate, a Mac OS X editor, was one of the first programs to provide integrated support for Rails and has gained traction among developers. Aptana's RadRails is one of many new IDEs available and established IDEs, such as Eclipse and Idea, are adding Rails support. Ruby provides an interactive command-line debugger, *irb*, which helps to monitor and debug Rails applications.

Overall, we had a positive experience with using Rails. In spite of the learning curve associated with a new framework and various limitations we encountered during development (see Section 11.4.3), Rails significantly increased our speed of application development.

11.4.2 Database support

Rails' built-in support for relational databases is impressive. Scaffolding can generate a workable database schema and `ActiveRecord` functionality employs a proven design pattern for object–relational mapping out of the box.

At the same time, this support has limitations, especially with respect to enterprise applications with complex database schemas. One such limitation is the lack of support for composite primary keys. It is common for schemas, especially for tables that support many-to-many relationships, to have primary keys that are composed of multiple columns. Third-party plug-ins exist to add a measure of support for composite primary keys, but integrated support as part of the standard Rails distribution is not available.

11.4.3 Limitations of scaffolding

As we mentioned earlier, you get the biggest benefit from Rails' scaffolding functionality if you are starting from scratch, building a brand new Rails application without an existing database schema. Using Rails with a legacy schema requires a lot more manual intervention. Fortunately, there is a page on the Ruby on Rails wiki site[1] devoted to using legacy schemas. It is disappointing that scaffolding is only of limited value with legacy schemas. It is even more disappointing that the developers of the

Rails framework do not see enhancing scaffolding for applications using legacy schemas as important. Since many of the trial applications built by organizations that are evaluating Rails connect to legacy schemas, it would behoove those developing and enhancing Rails to pay attention to this issue and provide better support for that scenario.

A schema generated by scaffolding is not likely to be production-worthy. Database administrators (DBAs) would need to get involved to optimize both the schema and the queries used to interact with it. Though Rails has made significant strides in automating the design and configuration of databases, it has not eliminated the need for formal schema design and DBA support.

Despite all of this, it should be said that even though significant manual intervention was required to get this application going with our existing database schema, the amount of work was significantly less than what would have been required for, say, a Struts application.

11.4.4 Scalability

Although Rails applications can run on a standalone Mongrel web server, for real-world production applications need to use an external proxy through a more robust web server. Earlier versions of Rails supported FastCGI under Apache. This mode of operation has been deprecated in favor of using Apache Web Server 2.2 with the `mod_proxy_balancer` module to delegate Rails requests to an array of Mongrel servers. This is workable but no less complicated than configuring Java EE deployments.

11.4.5 Performance and clustering

It's not clear how well Rails performs in comparison to Java EE applications running in a clustered environment. Solutions exist that provide support for clustering (including persistent sessions), but they are still in the experimental stage. Employing such solutions is tricky and prone to problems.

Rails' performance is definitely reasonable enough for small-scale intranet applications with a limited number of concurrent users, but high-volume production applications will not fare well with Rails.

11.4.6 Version 2.0 issues

New frameworks are often quite exciting to work with during their pre-Version 1.0 days. During that phase of development, new things are tried, new paradigms are developed, and powerful new functionality evolves. During this phase, it is acceptable to make changes that eschew backward compatibility. After all, that's what beta software is all about: you should *expect* things to change radically. No one in their right mind would build dependencies on pre-1.0 code that they know is likely to change.

Once the kinks are worked out, Version 1.0 is released and the situation becomes very different. People start building dependencies on the framework, expecting some degree of stability. For this reason, releases that follow Version 1.0 need to be backward compatible. If they are not and if existing applications require significant rework to allow them to execute using the new version, framework developers run the risk of alienating developers who have used the framework, deployed applications built with it, and evangelized it to others.

The problem is that the kinks are rarely "all worked out" with the release of Version 1.0. Issues are discovered that result in design changes that alter how the framework works and backward compatibility suffers.

Version 2.0 of Rails introduced a number of changes, including new suffixes for template names (changing from .rhtml and .rjs to .html.erb and .js.rjs), radically modified syntax for executing standard scaffolding functions, and deprecation of both dynamic scaffolding and pagination functions. Needless to say, a lot of confusion has arisen in the Rails development community over these changes. Things that used to work no longer do. On-line tutorials that were clear and informative for Version 1.x caused chaos for people using Version 2.0. Some people have said that the benefits associated with the original version of Rails are being eroded as new releases provide improved techniques that are incompatible with the original techniques. How agile *is* Rails if migrating a Rails 1.x application to Rails 2.0 is going to be as much of a pain as building a Java EE application from scratch?

It is one thing for a framework to be successful and popular in its initial release. It is quite another thing for it to remain successful and popular after it has gone through a major restructuring in a subsequent release. Java has not been immune to this phenomenon and Sun has been guilty of making changes that break old code. Microsoft claims to ensure backward compatibility across multiple releases of multiple software products, but we've all experienced the exceptions to that rule. Nonetheless, established software vendors with a grounded user base have much less to lose from this phenomenon than the creators of a fledgling framework who want to expand their audience, not alienate it.

11.4.7   Is Rails web-designer-friendly?

An important factor to be considered in examining any new framework is the degree to which web designers can exercise autonomous control over presentation layout, without requiring assistance from developers. We have discussed the limitations associated with frameworks that require designers to call upon developers to make simple modifications to page layouts.

Rails responds to that concern by providing a new set of tags and widgets that perform complex operations. For example, we have seen the collection_select tag, which constructs an HTML <select> element containing a list of <option> elements defined by a database table lookup. There are also *asset helper tags*, such as image_tag and javascript_include_tag. However, parameter substitution in embedded page content uses the <%=...%> notation known to cause the kind of problems we see in Figure 11.18. As we mentioned in Chapter 9, this notation violates XML formatting constraints, is hard to read, and is extremely cumbersome for web designers. Many of Rails' custom tags seem to exist for the express purpose of circumventing this problem (e.g., image_tag, stylesheet_link_tag). Rails would do well to follow the lead of JSP 2.0 and use an expression language that expresses parameter substitution values in a format not delimited by < and > characters (e.g., ${object.attribute}).

The tags and widgets in Rails may appear to reduce the amount of work for designers, but having to learn a whole new set of constructs for controlling page presentation may be a step backward. Designers already know HTML and CSS. More experienced designers have a decent command of JavaScript, understanding at a bare minimum the injection of <script> tags that reference external JavaScript files and the invocation of JavaScript functions within the page. It makes sense to provide

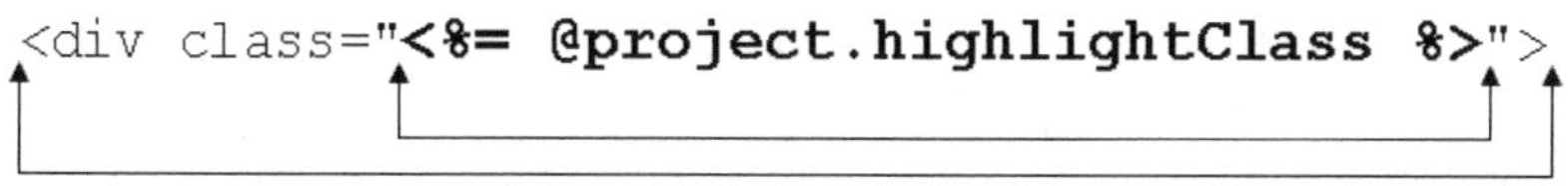

Figure 11.18 Nested < . . . > tags.

a small set of simple constructs that perform more generalized iterative and conditional processing on top of the standard presentation languages with which designers are already familiar. (This is the approach taken by JSTL.)

Providing a large set of new custom tags each of which performs a narrowly defined task, reminds us of a custom API for View components. While developers may be comfortable sifting through volumes of documentation to use complex APIs, designers are not. They are already familiar with HTML, CSS, and JavaScript. They should not be required to learn a whole new set of custom tags.

This problem is by no means unique to Rails – PHP and JSF are also culprits, which makes it worse because similarly purposed custom tags in PHP, JSF, and Rails each have radically different formats and syntaxes. Knowledge accrued from learning specialized tags for one framework is not transferable when learning those for another framework. This is the very situation we have been trying to avoid in the world of competing, proprietary application frameworks.

A common argument is that providing a small set of generalized tags (the JSTL approach) is too "low level", resulting in minimal productivity gains for designers. On the other hand, problems with complex framework-specific APIs may be far worse. The custom tags generate fixed blocks of HTML over which designers have little or no control. Designers must learn these new custom APIs as adjuncts (or replacements) for their existing HTML knowledge, with each framework having its own distinct vocabulary. The road we ought to be going down lies somewhere between these two extremes.

11.5   Whither Enterprise Java?

Does the advent of Rails represent the death knell for Java? This may be a popular sentiment in the blogosphere, but nothing could be further from the truth. Java, as both a programming language and a web development platform, still has plenty of life left in it.

For one thing, there is Java EE 5. Compared to its forerunners in the Enterprise Java world, Java EE 5 is leaner and far less complicated. The new specification for Enterprise Java Beans, EJB 3.0, has eliminated a significant amount of the baggage associated with earlier versions. EJB 3.0 allows both session and entity beans to be Plain Old Java Objects (POJOs), rather than requiring them to conform to arcane interface requirements. The Java Persistence API (JPA) incorporates Hibernate-style ORM functionality that can be used with or without EJB, giving developers even more flexibility. Use of annotations greatly reduces the need for manual editing of configuration files (although they do create a tighter coupling between Java code and deployment descriptors that can inhibit code reuse).

In addition, there is *Groovy on Grails*. Groovy is a scripting language with Java-like syntax that produces JVM-compatible bytecode. Though Java purists may scoff at the looseness and informality of the language, its advocates have found it a welcome enhancement to the Java platform. Grails, unsurprisingly, is a Rails-like framework that uses Groovy as its underlying programming language, mimicking many of Rails' most prominently promoted features. This gives Grails a number of advantages comparable to Rails, while also providing access to the power of Enterprise Java services (such as JNDI, JDBC, and JMS). Some view Grails as just a stepping stone, producing prototypes that can be gradually transformed into full-blown production applications. Grails applications need not be viewed in such a limited way: Grails *is* a complete Java EE MVC framework and compiled Groovy code performs comparably to compiled Java code in production. Both Groovy and Grails have generated a lot of excitement in the Java development community and both have gained a lot of traction.

Additionally, there is *JRuby on Rails*, which uses an integrated Java implementation of the Ruby interpreter within the Rails framework. It is intended to give developers the flexibility of Ruby combined with the power of Java.

There will be a place both for simpler frameworks that offer rapid application development and for more complex frameworks that offer scalability, clustering, and advanced transactional processing. In the long run, neither approach is ideal. The complex frameworks require too much initial effort, and the simple frameworks get you only so far, rapidly yielding a working application but not one that's production-worthy. The key is enabling initial development of an application in a simpler framework, coupled with the ability to migrate this application iteratively to a more sophisticated environment.

11.6   Summary

In conclusion, the Rails experience was for the most part a positive one. Development velocity increased dramatically and the process of enhancing the application constructed automatically from scaffolding commands was far less tedious (and far less intimidating) than an equivalent process in a Java EE and Struts environment.

On the other hand, there are a number of concerns about Rails' viability in the real world of large-scale enterprise applications. Even an environment where requests are routed through an Apache server using the `mod_proxy_balancer` module connected to an array of Mongrel servers has serious scalability limitations. Our administrative application is a prime example of a low-volume intranet application that is conducive to a Rails implementation. However, performance-critical, high-volume applications may still require the robustness of Java EE or another enterprise framework.

There are also concerns about the limited benefits derived from using scaffolding when working with legacy applications and databases. Future versions of Rails need to account for the way Rails is often introduced into new environments – with prototype applications that connect to legacy schemas as a proof-of-concept. Providing support for that kind of application will be critical to Rails' success in the long run.

A charge often leveled at Microsoft is that .NET makes simple things simple, at the expense of making complex things extremely difficult or even impossible. Based on the limitations that were discussed in this chapter, we have to question whether Rails is just as guilty of this. Rails is a young framework that has experienced explosive growth in a very short time. We hope that future versions will transcend current limitations.

QUESTIONS AND EXERCISES

1. Install and deploy the sample Rails application. Follow the instructions found on the book's web site, at `http://www.webappbuilders.com/package/railsapp/readme.html`.

2. Customize the administrative interface by modifying the view components (the `app/views/model_name/*.html.erb` files), beyond the modifications already suggested in this chapter. How easy or difficult was this process? What could be done to improve it? How difficult would it be for a web designer to make the changes you made?

3. Build the original VRLS application as a Rails application. Work from the ground up, without the benefit of an existing database, and make use of Rails' database scaffolding features. Use default names wherever possible.

4. Enhance the pages that list entities (the `app/views/model_name/index.html.erb` files) to add search functionality enabling administrators to find entities based on user-specified criteria. (Hint: The `paginate` method can take an optional `:conditions` parameter. See the webcast at `http://railscasts.com/episodes/51` for more information.)

5. Try adding an `xml` suffix to a URL for displaying an individual object (e.g., http://localhost:3000/listings/3.xml) and visit that URL in your browser. Where can you override this behavior?

6. As a developer, what advantages have you found in using the Rails approach? What drawbacks?

7. Assuming that Rails represents the current generation of web application frameworks, what could the next generation of frameworks do to improve on the current generation?

11.7   Bibliography

Bini, Ola, 2007. *Practical JRuby on Rails Web 2.0 Projects*. New York: APress/Springer-Verlag.

Halloway, Stuart and Gehtland, Justin, 2007. *Rails for Java Developers*. Raleigh (NC): Pragmatic Bookshelf.

Holzner, Steve, 2006. *Beginning Ruby on Rails (Wrox Beginning Guides)*. Indianapolis (IN): Wrox Press/Wiley Publishing.

Orsini, Rob, 2007. *Rails Cookbook*. Sebastopol (CA): O'Reilly Media.

Rocher, Graeme, 2006. *The Definitive Guide to Grails*. New York: APress/Springer-Verlag.

11.8   Web Links

Bates, Ryan, 2007. *Railscasts: `will_paginate`*. Available at `http://railscasts.com/episodes/51`.

Fowler, Martin, 2002. *Patterns of Enterprise Application Architecture*. New York: Addison-Wesley.

Harms, Steven G., 2008. *Scaffolding has changed in Rails 2.0: Has it become un-Agile?*. Available at `http://stevengharms.com/scaffolding-has-changed-in-rails-20-has-it-become-un-agile`.

Ruby on Rails wiki. *How to Use Legacy Schemas*. Available at `http://wiki.rubyonrails.org/rails/pages/howtouselegacyschemas`.

11.9   Endnotes

1. http://wiki.rubyonrails.org/rails/pages/howtouselegacyschemas
2. http://stevengharms.com/scaffolding-has-changed-in-rails-20-has-it-become-un-agile

CHAPTER **12**

Search Technologies

IN THIS CHAPTER

- Web search
- Search applications
- Search engine optimization

OBJECTIVES

- Introduce and illustrate basic search algorithms.
- Examine common enhancements to search algorithms.
- Discuss Google's Page Rank and other web search techniques.
- Analyze web spider architecture and principles of operation.
- Analyze the architecture of modern search applications.
- Examine techniques used in search engine optimization, including "Black Hat" techniques.

People use the web for many different reasons: to shop, to be entertained, to read news, and to perform research. As the exponential growth of the web continues, new on-line resources are constantly appearing, while old resources move, change and sometimes disappear. Search engines have become the primary means for finding relevant information. It is not enough for web site owners simply to offer content and applications that people want; they must make sure that global search engines find their offerings and attract visitors to their sites.

The importance of search technology is not limited to the global search engines like Google, Yahoo, and Ask.com. It is just as critical for local applications that provide search functionality for a single site or a set of related sites. The global search engines make use of proprietary search technologies, which are not available to the general application development community. The most popular of the publicly available technologies are *Fast, Google Enterprise* (which includes a limited subset of Google's proprietary search functionality), *Lucene* (which is a popular, open-source search library written in Java), and *Solr* (which is an open-source enterprise server based on Lucene).

In this chapter, we cover a variety of topics related to search technology:

- We open the chapter with a discussion of algorithms for indexing and searching plain text documents. Our objective is to provide our readers with insights into the inner workings of the search engine. We also aim to give readers enough information to make good design decisions when building their own search applications.
- Next, we concentrate on challenges and solutions that are specific to two kinds of search application – global applications for searching the entire web and applications that enable site search. In the course of discussing web search, we provide an overview of Google's Page Rank algorithm. In the course of discussing local search applications, we provide a brief summary of Lucene.
- We conclude the chapter by discussing how site owners can use their insights into the inner workings of search engines to make their pages easier to find. The set of measures that allows a site to maximize search engine traffic is called *Search Engine Optimization* (SEO).

What Is (and Isn't) a Search Engine?

The term "search engine" is overloaded – it can refer both to the technologies behind full text search and to applications and services that index and search content across many unrelated sites. To avoid ambiguity, we apply the term "search engine" only to applications that provide search capability across the entire web.

12.1 Overview of Algorithms

This section provides an overview of the main principles underlying search technologies. We start with the vanilla algorithm based on the vector space representation of documents and queries, and discuss the most common simplifications and enhancements. The objective is to provide readers with insights into the inner workings of open source and commercial search technologies. Such insights are invaluable, both in building local search applications and in devising SEO strategies.

12.1.1 Historical perspective

The history of search technologies predates the Internet. It goes back to the 1960s, when Gerald Salton and his team of Cornell scientists created Salton's Magic Information Retriever of Text (SMART). SMART pioneered the *vector-space* model and other critical innovations, which influenced future evolution of search technologies, including the relevance feedback algorithm (personalized reweighting of query terms based on the user history of queries and selections). Later developments in search technologies included *Latent Semantic Indexing* (*LSI*), which was patented in 1988 by

S. Deerwester, *et al*. LSI is based on conceptual grouping of documents and the terms contained in these documents. An example of term grouping is a word cluster that contains the words "train" and "plane". A search for "train" would yield documents containing either of the terms.

The first Internet search engines (such as Archie and WAIS) used straightforward implementations of the vector space models. Their followers (such as AltaVista and Excite) all built their own heuristics that augmented the same basic algorithms. These proprietary heuristics were behind the search experiences of the 1990s; it was common to get no intersection between top search results for queries posted to different search engines. Google was first to systematically take advantage of the additional information hidden in the hyperlinked nature of web resources.

12.1.2   Basic vector-space algorithm

Before we get to modern search technologies, let us discuss the vanilla search algorithm, which you can implement simply and quickly. It can be used to build and support your own search engine, which provides a good feel for search engine behavior. This comes in handy when using open source and commercial search engines.

We start by building an index for three short documents (see Figure 12.1). We are not attempting to implement *semantic search* (search based on the *meaning* of queries). In this simple algorithm, we disregard both the sentence structure and any meaning that spans multiple words. We implement keyword search and ignore words that might otherwise be considered to be search modifiers (e.g., "not" or "and"). This means that we can discard "this", "their", "is", "not", "and", "or", "of", and other so-called *stop words* that do not have meaning out of context (see Figure 12.2). For sophisticated algorithms, the criteria for designating stop words can be much more stringent and they depend on the language in which the stop words are written.[1]

Our next step is to remove punctuation marks and to reduce words to their root form or stem (see Figure 12.3). This process is called *stemming*. It is commonly implemented as a combination of suffix and prefix reduction rules (e.g., from "students" to "student" and from "technologies" to "technology") and table lookups for irregular stem transformations (e.g., "swam" to "swim"). The

---

Document 1
Search technologies have been around for over forty years. Over this time, their user base expanded first from scientists and technologists to information professionals, and finally from information professionals to pretty much everyone.

Document 2
Math and physics students are familiar with the challenge of finding the unambiguous "right answer". The same is not true for information retrieval. Finding the "right document" may be as much art as science.

Document 3
Many serial killers do not suffer from psychosis and appear to be quite normal. Search for such serial killers can take years, even with the latest police technologies, and the results are often shocking.

Figure 12.1   Documents to be indexed.

Document 1

Search technologies ~~have been~~ around ~~for over~~ forty years. ~~Over this~~ time, ~~their~~ user base expanded first ~~from~~ scientists ~~and~~ technologists ~~to~~ information professionals, ~~and~~ finally ~~from~~ information professionals ~~to~~ pretty much everyone.

Document 2

Math ~~and~~ physics students ~~are~~ familiar ~~with the~~ challenge ~~of~~ finding ~~the~~ unambiguous "right answer". ~~The same is not true for~~ information retrieval. Finding ~~the~~ "right document" ~~may be as~~ much art ~~as~~ science.

Document 3

Many serial killers ~~do not~~ suffer ~~from~~ psychosis ~~and~~ appear ~~to be quite~~ normal. Search ~~for such~~ serial killers ~~can~~ take years, ~~even with the~~ latest police technologies, ~~and the~~ results ~~are often~~ shocking.

Figure 12.2 Documents with stop words identified for removal.

Document 1

search technology around forty year~~s~~ time user base expand~~ed~~ first science technology information professional~~s~~ final~~ly~~ information professional~~s~~ pretty much everyone

Document 2

math physics student~~s~~ familiar challenge find~~ing~~ unambiguous right answer information retrieval find~~ing~~ right document much art science

Document 3

many serial killer~~s~~ psychosis appear normal search serial killer~~s~~ take year~~s~~ latest police technology result~~s~~ shock~~ing~~

Figure 12.3 Documents with stemming changes identified.

---

same rules that are applied when indexing documents need to be applied when processing search requests. Modern commercial search engines use more sophisticated techniques – from *lemmatization* (varying transformation and reduction rules for different parts of speech) to *stochastic algorithms*, which are based on trainable probabilistic models. Since we want to keep it simple, we stick to stemming.

Should "science" and "scientist" both be reduced to the same stem? If they are, it helps to reduce complexity but also adds "noise" to search results. We err on the side of simplicity.

Now that we have removed stop words and performed stemming, it is time to construct the vector space of terms, which is the core of our index. We start by building the dictionary; adding a new word when it first occurs in one of the documents. In Figure 12.4, the numbers in brackets indicate references to entries in the dictionary with *italics* indicating repeat word occurrences:

Now we have the dictionary of stemmed words that occur in the three documents in our repository (Figure 12.5). Note that the words are referenced by the order of their occurrence in the documents. This way, references do not have to change when adding new documents.

We can represent a document as a 40-dimensional vector (one dimension per unique word in our dictionary). The values in the <dictionary reference>:<number of occurrences> format represent the number of each word's occurrences in respective documents (Figure 12.6).

```
Document 1
search[1] technology[2] around[3] forty[4] year[5] time[6] user[7] base[8] expand[9]
first[10] science[11] technology[2] information[12] professional[13] final[14]
information[12] professional[13] pretty[15] much[16] everyone[17]

Document 2
math[18] physics[19] student[20] familiar[21] challenge[22] find[23]
unambiguous[24] right[25] answer[26] information[12] retrieval[27] find[23]
right[25] document[28] much[16] art[29] science[11]

Document 3
many[30] serial[31] killer[32] psychosis[33] appear[34] normal[35] search[1]
serial[31] killer[32] take[36] year[5] latest[37] police[38] technology[2]
result[39] shock[40]
```

Figure 12.4   Documents with unique words identified.

```
[1] search [2] technology [3] around
[4] forty [5] year [6] time
[7] user [8] base [9] expand
[10] first [11] science [12] information
[14] final [15] pretty [16] much
[17] everyone [18] math [19] physics
[20] student [21] familiar [22] challenge
[23] find [24] unambiguous [25] right
[26] answer [27] retrieval [28] document
[29] art [30] many [31] serial
[32] killer [33] psychosis [34] appear
[35] normal [36] take [37] latest
[38] police [39] result [40] shock
```

Figure 12.5   Search dictionary.

```
doc1(1:1, 2:2, 3:1, 4:1, 5:1, 6:1, 7:1, 8:1, 9:1, 10:1, 11:1, 12:2, 13:2, 14:1,
     15:1, 16:1, 17:1, 18:0, 19:0, 20:0, 21:0, 22:0, 23:0, 24:0, 25:0, 26:0, 27:0,
     28:0, 29:0, 30:0, 31:0, 32:0, 33:0, 34:0, 35:0, 36:0, 37:0, 38:0, 39:0, 40:0)

doc2(1:0, 2:0, 3:0, 4:0, 5:0, 6:0, 7:0, 8:0, 9:0, 10:0, 11:1, 12:1, 13:0, 14:0,
     15:0, 16:1, 17:0, 18:1, 19:1, 20:1, 21:1, 22:1, 23:2, 24:1, 25:2, 26:1, 27:1,
     28:1, 29:1, 30:0, 31:0, 32:0, 33:0, 34:0, 35:0, 36:0, 37:0, 38:0, 39:0, 40:0)

doc3(1:1, 2:1, 3:0, 4:0, 5:1, 6:0, 7:0, 8:0, 9:0, 10:0, 11:0, 12:0, 13:0, 14:0,
     15:0, 16:0, 17:0, 18:0, 19:0, 20:0, 21:0, 22:0, 23:0, 24:0, 25:0, 26:0, 27:0,
     28:0, 29:0, 30:1, 31:2, 32:2, 33:1, 34:1, 35:1, 36:1, 37:1, 38:1, 39:1, 40:1)
```

Figure 12.6   Representation of documents as 40-dimensional vectors.

Now that we have the vector space, which consists of the three documents, we can use it to find the most relevant documents for any free-form query. The idea is simple; represent a query as a vector in our document space, compute the distance between the query vector and the document vectors, and rank documents in reverse order of their distance from the query vector. We do not discuss vector operations here. There are well-known algorithms as well as commercial and open source libraries that support these computations.

Example

Let us consider the following sample query:

```
the promise of search technologies
```

As when building the document space, we start by eliminating the stop words and stemming. This leaves us with the following query:

```
the promise of search technology
```

Notice that "search" and "technology" are present in the dictionary and "promise" is not. If we were adding a document to the vector space, we would have added the word "promise" to the dictionary. Strictly speaking, we would have had to update document vectors. In practice, this can be avoided if we establish the convention that missing vector arguments are always set to "0". This way, existing vectors would not need to change – newly added words could not have occurred in these documents, otherwise these words would already be in the dictionary.

A query vector is only a transient addition to the vector space (for the duration of the query). Hence, there is no reason to account for words that do not occur in the dictionary. After dropping the word "promise", the surviving terms are:

```
search technology
```

The following vector represents this query:

```
doc-q(1:1, 2:1)
```

According do our convention, this is equivalent to:

```
doc-q(1:1, 2:1, 3:0, 4:0, 5:0, 6:0, 7:0, 8:0, 9:0, 10:0, 11:0, 12:0, 13:0,
    14:0, 15:0, 16:0, 17:0, 18:0, 19:0, 20:0, 21:0, 22:0, 23:0, 24:0, 25:0,
    26:0, 27:0, 28:0, 29:0, 30:0, 31:0, 32:0, 33:0, 34:0, 35:0, 36:0, 37:0,
    38:0, 39:0, 40:0)
```

Now it remains to compute distances between the query vector and document vectors accounting for dimensions present in the query vector. The shortest distance means the best match. The result is unexpected and counterintuitive – we find that the shortest distance is between **doc-q** and **doc3** instead of **doc-q** and doc1, and doc2 is not even in the running.

Enhancement 1: weighting for multiple occurrences

Clearly, this is not a good result. Intuitively, more occurrences of the query terms in the document should make it a better match. We can achieve this by introducing a heuristic multiplier (e.g., 1000) to the vector representation of query terms:

```
doc-q(1:1000, 2:1000)
```

Now the results are intuitive – the multiplier is large enough to ensure documents with multiple occurrences of query terms get precedence. We find that the shortest distance is between **doc-q** and **doc1**, the second shortest is between **doc-q** and **doc3**, and the longest is between **doc-q** and **doc2**.

Enhancement 2: weighting for phrases

This is better but not good enough – the third document relates to using police technologies to search for serial killers. It is not relevant to the spirit of our query while the second document belongs to the same domain as the first and is semantically relevant. However, the words "search" and "technology" occur in the third document, but not in the second, which uses terms "information retrieval".

We need to find a simple way to give more weight to phrases as opposed to individual terms and create connections between phrases that are semantically similar. The simplest path is to add a human processing step – analyze the document domain, define common phrases, and establish connections between them.

In our example, we define the following phrases:

```
search technology
police technology
information professional
information retrieval
```

We establish a connection between "search technology" and "information retrieval" so that these phrases are synonymous within our vector space. We have to update the dictionary to accommodate our multi-word terms (see Figure 12.7). Our document vectors are different as well (see Figure 12.8).

The query vector also changes to account for the occurrence of the phrase:

```
doc-q(1:1000, 2:1000, 42:1000)
```

Note that we are applying the heuristic multiple introduced in Enhancement 1 to both word and phrase terms.

Before we try our query again, let us consider the relative impact of word and phrase matches. The distance between query and document vectors should reflect the higher selective power of phrase matches. A simple solution is to assign a higher weight to the occurrence of a phrase by introducing a heuristic multiple. For example, we can say that an occurrence of a phrase is equivalent to 10 occurrences of an independent term. (The number 10 is arbitrary – a proper setting would require much experimentation and analysis.) Resulting document vectors are shown in Figure 12.9.

Computing the distances from the query vector to document vectors, the best match is for document 1 and the second best match is for document 2.

```
[1] search [2] technology [3] around
[4] forty [5] year [6] time
[7] user [8] base [9] expand
[10] first [11] science [12] information
[14] final [15] pretty [16] much
[17] everyone [18] math [19] physics
[20] student [21] familiar [22] challenge
[23] find [24] unambiguous [25] right
[26] answer [27] retrieval [28] document
[29] art [30] many [31] serial
[32] killer [33] psychosis [34] appear
[35] normal [36] take [37] latest
[38] police [39] result [40] shock
[41] search technology/information retrieval
[42] police technology
[43] information professional
```

Figure 12.7   Search dictionary with synonymous phrases.

```
doc1(1:1, 2:2, 3:1, 4:1, 5:1, 6:1, 7:1, 8:1, 9:1, 10:1, 11:1, 12:2, 13:2, 14:1, 15:1,
  16:1, 17:1, 18:0, 19:0, 20:0, 21:0, 22:0, 23:0, 24:0, 25:0, 26:0, 27:0, 28:0, 29:0,
  30:0, 31:0, 32:0, 33:0, 34:0, 35:0, 36:0, 37:0, 38:0, 39:0, 40:0, 41:1, 42:0, 43:2)

doc2(1:0, 2:0, 3:0, 4:0, 5:0, 6:0, 7:0, 8:0, 9:0, 10:0, 11:1, 12:1, 13:0, 14:0, 15:0,
  16:1, 17:0, 18:1, 19:1, 20:1, 21:1, 22:1, 23:2, 24:1, 25:2, 26:1, 27:1, 28:1, 29:1,
  30:0, 31:0, 32:0, 33:0, 34:0, 35:0, 36:0, 37:0, 38:0, 39:0, 40:0, 41:1, 42:0, 43:0)

doc3(1:1, 2:1, 3:0, 4:0, 5:1, 6:0, 7:0, 8:0, 9:0, 10:0, 11:0, 12:0, 13:0, 14:0, 15:0,
  16:0, 17:0, 18:0, 19:0, 20:0, 21:0, 22:0, 23:0, 24:0, 25:0, 26:0, 27:0, 28:0, 29:0,
  30:1, 31:2, 32:2, 33:1, 34:1, 35:1, 36:1, 37:1, 38:1, 39:1, 40:1, 41:0, 42:1, 43:0)
```

Figure 12.8   Vector space with synonymous phrases.

```
doc1(1:1, 2:2, 3:1, 4:1, 5:1, 6:1, 7:1, 8:1, 9:1, 10:1, 11:1, 12:2, 13:2, 14:1, 15:1,
  16:1, 17:1, 18:0, 19:0, 20:0, 21:0, 22:0, 23:0, 24:0, 25:0, 26:0, 27:0, 28:0, 29:0,
  30:0, 31:0, 32:0, 33:0, 34:0, 35:0, 36:0, 37:0, 38:0, 39:0, 40:0, 41:10,42:0, 43:20)

doc2(1:0, 2:0, 3:0, 4:0, 5:0, 6:0, 7:0, 8:0, 9:0, 10:0, 11:1, 12:1, 13:0, 14:0, 15:0,
  16:1, 17:0, 18:1, 19:1, 20:1, 21:1, 22:1, 23:2, 24:1, 25:2, 26:1, 27:1, 28:1, 29:1,
  30:0, 31:0, 32:0, 33:0, 34:0, 35:0, 36:0, 37:0, 38:0, 39:0, 40:0, 41:10,42:0, 43:0)

doc3(1:1, 2:1, 3:0, 4:0, 5:1, 6:0, 7:0, 8:0, 9:0, 10:0, 11:0, 12:0, 13:0, 14:0, 15:0,
  16:0, 17:0, 18:0, 19:0, 20:0, 21:0, 22:0, 23:0, 24:0, 25:0, 26:0, 27:0, 28:0, 29:0,
  30:1, 31:2, 32:2, 33:1, 34:1, 35:1, 36:1, 37:1, 38:1, 39:1, 40:1, 41:0, 42:10,43:0)
```

Figure 12.9   Vector space with heuristic multiple for phrases.

12.1.3   Common enhancements

The enhancements we discussed in the previous section require much analysis and tuning to be effective. More sophisticated algorithms use a wide range of techniques to automate this analysis.

The goal of the first enhancement (a heuristic multiple for query terms) is to ensure that the query vector is "closer" to document vectors representing a higher number of repeated occurrences of terms found in the query. Instead of selecting an arbitrary "large enough" multiple (e.g., "1000"), we can set it to the maximum number of occurrences of a single dictionary term in any document. Since the multiple is used to compute the query vector in the context of a particular collection of documents, the magnitude of any of its projections would never be lower than that of a document vector within the same collection. This ensures the desired property of rewarding the largest number of occurrences of the query terms in indexed documents.

The goal for the second enhancement is to reward phrases more than individual terms. The manual process works but it requires laborious analysis and selection of term pairs that occur in the documents. A common approach is to add pairs of terms occurring in the collection to the dictionary automatically. The problem is the high number of incidental noise pairs. A common way to cut down on such incidental pairs is to define a threshold for the number of occurrences of such word pairs (usually at least three occurrences). This would not have worked in our document collection because it is too small.

Even with these two enhancements, our algorithm only takes into account the *term frequency* (the number of term occurrences in individual documents); it does not account for the *inverse document frequency* (IDF). IDF is the number of documents in the collection in which a term occurs. A higher term frequency is a positive bias. Higher IDF should have the opposite effect. The more documents contain the same term, the lower its selective power.

Consider a collection of documents dedicated to mammals. The term "monkey" refers to a broader classification than "baboon", which is a specific species. Consequently, "monkey" should occur in more documents and have a higher IDF than the term "baboon", and "baboon" should have the higher selective power. For a query "baboon monkey", a document about baboons should be rated higher than documents about other monkeys (no matter how many times the term "monkey" occurs in these documents).

We can account for IDF when computing distances between query and document vectors. Computations for individual terms are not affected. However, the contribution of these computations in calculating distances between vectors is not the same. It is determined by the IDF term weighting and has an inverse dependency on the IDF.

IDF term weighting is heuristic in nature, but it works so well that it has led to many attempts at theoretical explanations, none of which have been entirely successful. The most common formula for computing IDF term weights, which is experimentally proven to produce good results, calculates a term weight as the logarithm of the ratio of the number of documents in the collection to the number of documents containing the term.

12.1.4   Word clustering

The two generally accepted measures of quality of search results are *precision* and *recall*. Precision is defined as the ratio of the number of *relevant* documents retrieved during a search to the total number of documents retrieved during that search. It measures the amount of "noise" in the results. A precision score of "0.0" means that the results are all noise. Conversely, a score of "1.0" means that all results are relevant.

Recall is defined as the ratio of the number of relevant documents retrieved during a search to the total number of relevant documents that exist in the collection. It measures the *completeness* of search results. A recall score of "1.0" means that every relevant document in the collection was found.

Enhancements that were discussed earlier in this chapter aimed at increasing both precision and recall. In this section, we discuss word clustering techniques that are specifically designed to improve document recall, even at the cost of precision.

In the example in Section 12.1.2, we manually mapped "search technology" to "information retrieval" because we considered these phrases to be semantically related. There exist statistical methods that make it possible to discover such semantic relationships. These methods are based on the assumption that two terms or phrases are semantically similar if they co-occur with the same set of common words. For example, "car" and "automobile" are likely to occur within the same context. We can successfully apply these methods to discover semantic relationships between terms that occur in real-world document collections.

Details of the statistical methods for discovering semantic relevance are out of scope for this book. Our sample document space is too small to apply these methods but we can illustrate their effect by constructing word clusters by hand. The hand-constructed clusters are too inclusive (include words that are not always closely related) because we have too few terms to choose from. Consider the following word clusters for our example:

```
[1]  search/retrieval/find
[2]  technology/science/math/physics
[3]  year/time
[4]  information/document
[5]  first/final/latest
[6]  user/student/professional
[7]  unambiguous/right
[8]  answer/result
[9]  much/many
[10] psychosis/shock
[11] police/killer
[12] around [13] forty [14] base
[15] expand [16] pretty [17] everyone
[18] familiar [19] challenge [20] art
[21] serial [22] appear [23] normal
[24] take
```

Now, our documents will have the following form (compare with Figure 12.4):

```
Document 1
search[1] technology[2] around[12] forty[13] year[3] time[3] user[6]
base[14] expand[15] first[5] science[2] technology[2] information[4]
professional[6] final[5] information[4] professional[6] pretty[16]
much[9] everyone[17]
```

Document 2
```
math[2] physics[2] student[6] familiar[18] challenge[19] find[1]
unambiguous[7] right[7] answer[8] information[4] retrieval[1] find[1]
right[7] document[4] much[9] art[20] science[2]
```

Document 3
```
many[9] serial[21] killer[11] psychosis[10] appear[22] normal[23] search[1]
serial[21] killer[11] take[24] year[3] latest[5] police[11] technology[2]
result[8] shock[10]
```

We can rewrite them in the form of document vectors:

```
doc1(1:1, 2:2, 3:2, 4:2, 5:2, 6:3, 7:0, 8:0, 9:1, 10:0, 11:0, 12:1, 13:1,
     14:1, 15:1, 16:1, 17:1, 18:0, 19:0, 20:0, 21:0, 22:0, 23:0, 24:0)

doc2(1:3, 2:3, 3:0, 4:2, 5:0, 6:1, 7:3, 8:1, 9:1, 10:0, 11:0, 12:0, 13:0,
     14:0, 15:0, 16:0, 17:0, 18:1, 19:1, 20:1, 21:0, 22:0, 23:0, 24:0)

doc3(1:1, 2:1, 3:1, 4:0, 5:1, 6:0, 7:0, 8:1, 9:1, 10:2, 11:3, 12:0, 13:0,
     14:0, 15:0, 16:0, 17:0, 18:0, 19:0, 20:0, 21:2, 22:1, 23:1, 24:1)
```

As before, we can reduce the query "the promise of search technology" to "search technology". As discussed in Section 12.1.3, we set our query term multiple to 3 (the maximum number of occurrences of a single term in any of our documents). Now we have the query vector:

```
doc-q(1:3, 2:3)
```

Documents 1 and 2 remain the best hits but document 1 now has a higher ranking. This is an interesting result, which is well justified by the meaning of the documents. Word clustering does not capture document semantics directly. However, constructing word clusters based on the statistical analysis of word context does introduce the element of semantics. Consequently, we can find documents that otherwise would not be included in the results. Using information retrieval terminology, this improves the *recall rate*. These improvements may come at the cost of precision.

12.1.5 Custom biases

Throughout this section, we have used simple solutions to illustrate general ideas behind search technologies. Real-life commercial and open-source implementations use more sophisticated algorithms than the ones discussed here. In addition, such implementations use complex heuristics to implement proprietary enhancements, take advantage of additional information (e.g., classifications and output of data mining tools), and impose *custom biases* on search results.

A common example of a custom bias is publishing time for news items. When searching news, the more recent item is usually more relevant. Finding the right balance between relevancy and publishing time is very tricky. Combining these and other biases is commonly relegated to custom heuristics.

A simpler approach to searching for news is to use a basic keyword search and prioritize hits based on publishing time. This works if the hit list is relatively constrained. Algorithms that we have discussed in this section implement so-called "implied OR", where the hit list includes documents containing all or some of the terms in the query. This does not work well with time sorting because marginally relevant documents may end up at the top. For example, you may search for "General Motors" and the top hit is the most recent news item about a visit to Turkey by General Petraeus. In practice, time sorting is combined with "implied AND," which can be implemented as the intersection of hit lists for individual terms of the query.

12.2   Searching the Web

This section covers search engines, which are built to support web-wide search, and the unique issues associated with their design and operation. It is critical that web application architects have a clear understanding of the design principles behind web search engines. Insights into search engine operation are necessary for constructing successful strategies for search engine optimization (SEO). As we discuss in Section 12.4, SEO strategies cannot be an afterthought and have to be considered at the early stages of web site design.

Searching the web is very different from searching limited collections of static documents. There are differences both in scale and in the nature of the web resources to be indexed and searched. The scale associated with web search is in the billions – both billions of documents and billions of queries. This translates into serious software engineering challenges in indexing, searching, and retrieving content.

12.2.1   Google page ranking

In web searches, lower precision results are almost never useful. In practice, only the top $10-20$ matches are of interest to users. Consequently, recall takes a back seat to precision and some of the popular indexing techniques, such as stemming and word clustering, cannot be used successfully in their original form.

Stemming and word clustering are useful tools in reducing the scale of the vector space and improving recall, but they reduce precision dramatically. With this in mind, search engines often resort to techniques more sophisticated than stemming. Word clustering can still add significant value to the quality of search. What we need is a way to compensate for the imprecise nature of word clustering while retaining its benefits.

Fortunately, the hyperlinked nature of the web holds an opportunity to account for the popularity of pages. Google's rise to fame closely relates to the notion of *page rank*. A page rank is calculated by adding the ranks of pages that reference it divided by the number of links on these pages:[2]

```
PR(A) = (1-d)+d (PR(T_1)/C(T_1) +... + PR(T_n)/C(T_n))
```

Here, A is the page in question, T_1 through T_n are documents that reference A, PR is the page rank, $C(T_i)$ is the total number of links to outside resources on page T_i, and d is a heuristic damping factor, which was set to 0.85. Google designed the page rank to form a probability distribution, which means that the ranks of all pages add to 1. It is relatively simple to write an iterative algorithm for computing the page rank.

The idea of page rank is to reward frequently referenced pages by presenting them higher in the search results. A similar but simpler idea was used in the past to rank research papers by the number of citations. With the Google page rank, the value of a reference is directly proportional to the rank of the referring page and inversely proportional to the number of references on that page. Google managed to achieve excellent results by combining page ranks with results of traditional queries based on full text content and page metadata.

The algorithms used by real-world search engines are more complex than the vanilla search algorithms we've discussed so far. In the case of page-rank computations, they need to detect circular references and other deceptive ways of convincing search engines to assign higher ranks than the pages actually warrant. (This kind of cheating is known as *rank spoofing*.) The same goes for content indexing – both in using heuristics to assign different weights to marked up text depending on the markup tags and in detecting and ignoring various forms of hidden content (e.g., white text on a white background).

12.2.2   Web spiders

Because web sites are always changing, it is a challenge for search engines to notice and process new and updated web pages. The process of automatically following links embedded within HTML and XML pages and retrieving and indexing HTML, XML, Microsoft Word, Adobe PDF and other documents is called *web spidering*. Programs designed for this task are called *web spiders* (also referred to as *web crawlers* and *robots*).

Web spiders start from a set of *seed* URLs and from there traverse the web without human intervention. Like browsers, web spiders submit HTTP requests and process HTTP responses, but unlike browsers, they do not render the pages and retrieve secondary content (such as, images or CSS style sheets). Spiders parse the bodies of HTTP responses, indexing the content and looking for embedded links. They resolve relative links (see Section 7.3) and execute JavaScript code embedded within pages to construct dynamic links. Spiders follow these links and continue the process recursively on subsequent pages that they encounter.

Web spidering serves many purposes. The purpose that concerns us here is the way search engines use spidering to populate and maintain web-wide databases of HTML, XML, Microsoft Word and other documents. Single-site search applications may use a spider to maintain their content databases, but this goal can more easily be achieved by tying index generation and update processes to publishing and content management systems. In other words, the publication of a new or updated page via a site's content management system can trigger an update to the index.

Other applications of spiders include their internal use by web sites to maintain link integrity and to validate hosted HTML pages. On the less benign side, spammers use spiders to harvest e-mail addresses, telephone numbers, and other personal information from web pages.

Spiders employed by search engines face unique and very difficult challenges because of the incredible volume and the extraordinary rate of change that characterize the web document space. The high volume makes it necessary for the spider to prioritize page retrievals because it can retrieve only a limited number of web pages within a fixed period. Dynamic page generation, which is controlled by complex combinations of URL parameters, exacerbates the problem further, forcing spiders to decide between relevant and irrelevant combinations of these parameters. (A combination is relevant if it produces unique content instead of rearranging the same content on the page or applying a different style sheet.)

The high rate of change makes the prioritization problem even more difficult. By the time the spider finishes traversing a site, some of its pages may already have been updated or deleted. Spiders that do not take into account the frequency of updates would make it impossible for their search engines to maintain any reasonable measure of the freshness of content. Such spiders may end up revisiting unchanged pages and failing to update pages that change frequently. Note that it is much more important for search engines to learn about page deletion than incremental updates. An incremental update to page content may have minimal impact because the old content used for indexing was close enough not to matter for search results. Clearly, it is not good practice for content sites to reuse the same URLs for very different content. We come back to this discussion in Section 12.4.

Spider behavior is controlled by a number of *policies*:

- The *selection* policy controls page retrieval. Popular selection policies include breadth-first and top-page-rank-first. Page rank is a great measure of page importance but it is not always available to the spider. Real search engines use hybrid selection policies that they keep proprietary.
- The *re-visit* policy controls the frequency of page retrievals. Advanced re-visit policies take into account the page rank, the frequency of change, the trustworthiness of a site's declarations about its change frequency (Section 12.4.1), and the extent of change. For search engines, it is important not only how often pages change but also how much they change, because small incremental changes may not have any impact on search results.

Figure 12.10 is a simplified illustration of spider operation. The Spider Client module starts off by submitting requests to designated seed URLs. It filters responses by their MIME types (`text/plain`, `text/html`, `application/xml`, `application/msword`, and other common types). HTML and XML documents that require additional processing to complete their transformation and assembly are forwarded to the Page Normalizer. The remaining XML, HTML, plain text, Microsoft Word, Adobe PDF, and other documents are passed directly to the Markup Stripper, which extracts the text and saves it in the content database.

The Page Normalizer populates IFRAMES, applies XSLT style sheets and executes JavaScript functions involved in constructing dynamic URLs. After completing the processing, the Page Normalizer

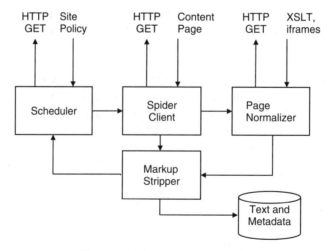

Figure 12.10 Spider architecture.

forward normalized documents to the Markup Stripper. In addition to extracting and saving text, the Markup Stripper parses HTML and XML documents to retrieve resolved URLs and pass them on to the Scheduler for later processing. The Markup Stripper also may apply heuristics that assign higher weight to the page title and headings, by repeating them multiple times in the text version.

The Scheduler is a multi-threaded program that manages URL queues and communicates with Spider Clients. It implements the selection and re-visit policies established by the search engine. It retrieves site policies from the `robots.txt` files (Section 12.4.1), which may contain important information about URLs to ignore, location of site maps, etc. Scheduler is responsible for detecting circular references. It may maintain information about site misbehavior and use it in de-prioritizing requests to that site. Spider Clients submit requests initially to seed URLs and later to URLs provided by the Scheduler.

Commercial and open-source implementations may differ from the outline described in this section but the main components and their interaction have to be fairly close to perform their intended function. We return to this discussion in Section 12.4.

12.2.3 Summary

The main benefit provided by search engines is in helping users to find the most relevant content and applications. At the same time, the content sites seek to use search engines as a means of attracting users. In practice, there is not always a symbiotic relationship between web sites and search engines. Some web site owners employ tricks that cause their sites to get better positioning in search results than they merit, sometimes to the point of getting their pages to show up inappropriately in completely unrelated searches. Most sites, however, are not that duplicitous. They simply want to find legitimate ways to make their pages visible to the search engines. We cover these mechanisms in Section 12.4.

12.3 Site Search Applications

In the previous section, we discussed the challenges associated with implementing search engines, which provide search capability across the web. In this section, we concentrate on local search applications that provide search capability within a single site or a related set of sites.

The usability of a web site depends on how easy it is to locate the right function or content. Site navigation is the subject of many books on front-end design and information architecture. However, you can only accomplish so much by optimizing traversal of a complex site. Such sites need search applications that provide users with a friendly way to find the pages they are looking for. Search technology is the heart of such applications but these applications require other critical components as well.

At a minimum, they have to ensure that newly published pages are indexed and become available through the search interface. It is the responsibility of the search application to capture publishing events and pass new or updated pages associated with these events to the indexer. Many search technologies are packaged with pre-processing components, which are responsible for extracting text from documents in Microsoft Word, Adobe PDF, HTML, and other popular formats. If the pre-processing components are not available with search technologies, they become the responsibility of search applications. It is common for text-extraction modules to implement markup-based awards. For example, a word occurring in the title of an HTML document may be inserted into the generated text several times, depending on the configuration.

Modern search applications are not limited to full text search. Google's concept of "OneBox," which was first introduced to retrieve stock quotes in concert with full-text queries, is based on a thin layer of query analysis fronting a wide variety of related applications, from full-text search technologies to custom company name search and quote retrieval applications. Properly designed OneBox applications can deliver very rewarding user experiences, but they can be complex and present unique challenges to application designers.

We start this section with an overview of the general architecture of search applications, followed by a discussion of Lucene, an open-source search technology that is used by major commercial web sites. We conclude this section with a discussion of OneBox implementations.

12.3.1   General architecture

It is common for search applications to maintain separate indexes for different types of content and for different sources of information describing the same content (Section 12.1.1). Examples of different types of content include text, pictures, and video, where indexes for pictures and video are constructed from associated captions, descriptions, or video scripts. For an example of different sources, consider scientific articles, which can be indexed separately based on their full text, abstracts, and editorial keywords. Advanced search applications that execute queries against multiple sources are responsible for their own logic in combining the results of these queries.

In Figure 12.11, HTTP requests initiated by users through their browsers arrive at the Query Processor hosted at the application server. This module is responsible for analyzing the requests and generating full-text queries for text, images and video. The Document Query Manager is responsible for executing the text query against two different indexes (full content and article abstracts) and combining the results. The logic for combining the results is application-specific. It may compensate for articles that only have their abstracts on-line or, conversely, articles that do not have abstracts. It may reinforce query results for articles that come out on top for both queries.

The Query Processor is also responsible for executing queries for images and video. Having received the results of queries for text, images and video, the Query Processor combines them into a single results page. Loading the results page may trigger AJAX requests to additional applications that make use of the original query. In Figure 12.11, the Query Processor applications are responsible for selecting the most relevant publicly traded companies based on information in the query, finding their ticker symbols and retrieving their latest available stock quotes. We revisit the method of passing query information to multiple applications in Section 12.3.3.

If this system were implemented using Java servlets, given the single-threaded nature of servlet execution flows, the HTTP response carrying the results page would take at least as much time as the all individual search queries combined plus additional processing time.

The alternative architecture in Figure 12.12 addresses this problem by deferring search queries for images and video. Here, the Query Processor formats results returned by the Document Query Manager and adds JavaScript code, which can initiate AJAX requests for the remaining queries (images and video). When the results page is rendered (the `onload` condition), the AJAX requests are submitted to the query processing servlet, which is dedicated to processing queries and search results for images and video. The side-benefit is the limited impact on user experience if searches for images or video are slow or failing. Users are able to access search results for text documents without delays or timeouts.

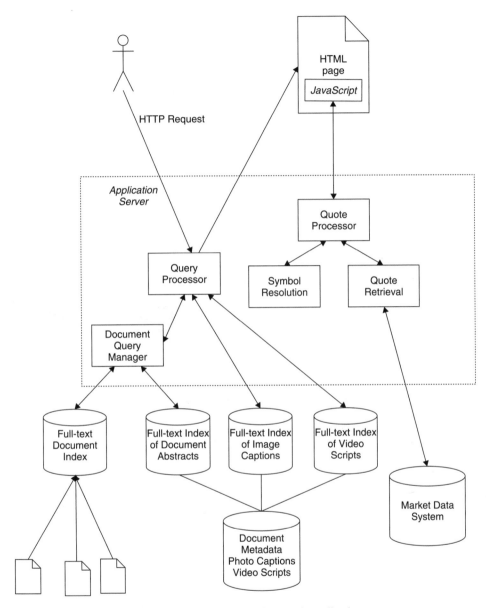

Figure 12.11   Structure of a search application.

12.3.2 Lucene

Lucene is a scalable Java library of search components, which enables the construction of custom full-text indexing, search, and retrieval applications. It is not a ready-built technology; you should not make the common mistake of confusing reference applications with out-of-the-box solutions. Lucene

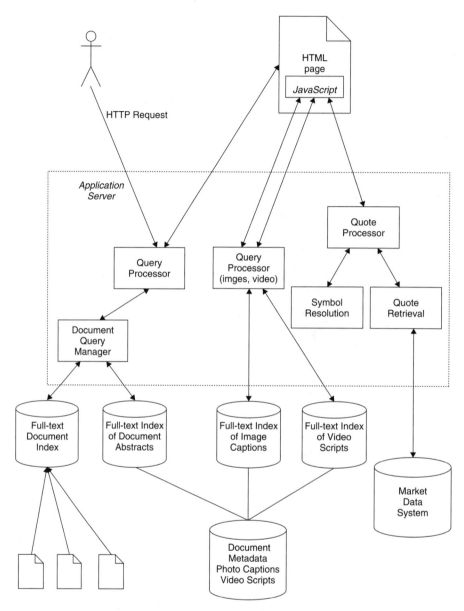

Figure 12.12 Alternative structure of a search application.

is being developed as part of the Apache project.[3] It was first released in 2000 and has become the most popular alternative to commercial search technologies.

Lucene index construction classes, just like the technologies that were discussed in Section 12.1, require that all documents be in plain text format. Lucene does not come with a toolbox for extracting text from Adobe PDF files, Microsoft Word documents, or even HTML and XML files. Fortunately,

```
// Extract text
StringWriter writer = new StringWriter();
wordDoc.writeAllText(writer);
String text = writer.toString();
  ...
// Create a new Lucene Document (org.apache.lucene.document.Document)
// and add extracted text
Document doc = new Document();
doc.add(Field.UnStored("body", text));
```

Figure 12.13 Creating indexable Lucene documents for Microsoft Word files.

such tools are available from other open-source libraries. For example, the PDFBox[4] library includes the `org.pdfbox.searchengine.lucene` package, which is designed to work with Lucene. It contains the `LucenePDFDocument` class, which hides the complexities of extracting text from PDF documents. A simple PDF document can be converted to an indexable Lucene document object with a single statement:

```
Document doc = LucenePDFDocument.getDocument(new File("./mysample.pdf"));
```

Text extraction from Microsoft Office documents is supported by the Apache POI project.[5] The POI project provides Java APIs for manipulating file formats based upon Microsoft's OLE 2 Compound Document format. It makes it possible to read and write Microsoft Office files (e.g., Word documents and Excel spreadsheets) using Java. However, we don't need the full power of POI to manipulate these files. All we need to enable Lucene indexing is to extract the plain text content and add it to a Lucene document. That is easily accomplished through the `writeAllText()` method of the POI `WordDocument` class (see Figure 12.13).

In this code snippet, `wordDoc` is a `WordDocument` object. The `writeAllText()` method outputs extracted text to a `StringWriter`, which stores the accumulated text in a `StringBuffer`. We retrieve the text by invoking the `toString()` method of `StringWriter`. Once we have the text, we create a Lucene `Document` object and assign the extracted text to the `body` of this object.

There are great many open-source solutions for extracting text from HTML and XML documents. HTML documents may present a bit of a challenge because a significant number of them are not well-formed XML documents (see Section 5.1.1). The JTidy parser[6] is a good choice for retrieving plain text from malformed HTML and XML documents. It is a port of the W3C's Tidy utility, which has been through a decade of development first at W3C and later by a group of enthusiasts at Sourceforge. It is invoked through the `parseDom()` method of the `Tidy` class, which infers and returns the DOM tree, which corresponds to the closest well-formed analog of the original document. It is a simple task to retrieve text contained within individual elements of a well-formed document, potentially giving special treatment to text within <title>, <meta> and other tags.

The code snippet in Figure 12.14 illustrates the process of extracting the body of the document and adding it to a Lucene document object. We create an instance of the `Tidy` class and invoke its `parseDom()` method, which returns a DOM `Document` object. Note that the `stream` argument of the `parseDOM()` method is an `InputStream` object associated with the HTML document. The

```
// Extract text
org.w3c.dom.Document domDoc = (new Tidy()).parseDOM(stream, null);
String text = getText(domDoc);
// implement getText() to use DOM methods to traverse the DOM tree and retrieve text
  ...
// Create a new Lucene Document and add extracted text
Document doc = new Document();
doc.add(Field.UnStored("body", text));
```

Figure 12.14   Creating indexable Lucene documents for HTML files.

```
Directory dir = FSDirectory.getDirectory("/var/docs/index/", true);
IndexWriter writer = new IndexWriter(dir, analyzer, true);
Document doc = new Document();
// add text to the document - see examples above
...
writer.addDocument(doc);
```

Figure 12.15   Creating a Lucene index.

Document object is passed to the getText() function, which traverses the DOM tree and retrieves the text. (The implementation of getText() is not shown.) In the last two lines of the code snippet, we create a Lucene Document object and assign the extracted text to the body of this object. Our examples so far have assumed that we are only populating the body attribute. Lucene makes it possible to create multiple attributes and index them independently, which enables a flexible query mechanism.

Lucene uses Analyzer classes to process Document objects created from Microsoft Word, Adobe PDF, HTML, and other kinds of document, as illustrated in Figures 12.13 and 12.14. The Lucene distribution includes extensions of the Analyzer class that take care of language-specific tokenization, processing stop words, and stemming (see Section 12.1.2). Many applications further extend these classes to implement the logic described in Section 12.1.3 as well as custom logic for application domains. Custom Analyzer classes may take advantage of text structure, affording special treatment to the document title, authors, etc. Such analyzers can be particularly effective if paired with custom text extraction and parsing components.

The code snippet in Figure 12.15 illustrates how to create a Lucene index. The first step is to create a Lucene Directory object, which is required by the constructor for the IndexWriter class. The next step is to create an IndexWriter, passing Directory and Analyzer objects to the constructor. Once an IndexWriter object is created, we can use it to add Document objects to the Lucene index.

Lucene's DefaultSimilarity class implements a sophisticated scoring algorithm that is based on vector-space concepts and accounts for term frequency. Lucene's scoring algorithm allows for the so-called "boosting factors", which are designed to combine scores from querying different fields associated with the same documents. Of course, that is only possible if these fields are processed separately at the text extraction and analysis stages and indexed individually. Default boost factors are set to 1.0 and few applications go so far as to change the defaults. Different values may be well

```
Directory dir = FSDirectory.getDirectory("/var/docs/index/", true);
IndexSearcher searcher = new IndexSearcher(dir);
Query query = QueryParser.parse("car AND truck","body", new SimpleAnalyzer());
Hits hits = searcher.search(query);
  ...
Document doc = hits.doc(1);
```

Figure 12.16   Querying a Lucene index.

justified based on application logic, but changing the settings requires deep understanding of scoring algorithms and quite a bit of experimentation and tuning.

A simple code snippet illustrating the querying of a Lucene index is shown in Figure 12.16. Just as with the `IndexWriter` class, the constructor for the `IndexSearcher` class takes as its argument a `Directory` object. For `IndexSearcher`, the `Directory` object must be associated with an existing Lucene index. Here, `body` is the name of an indexed attribute and `car AND truck` is a query expression that is split into terms by the analyzer. In the example, the result is a `Query` object with two required clauses. The result of the query is a `Hits` object. Its `doc()` method takes an integer indicating the rank order of a document in the result set and returns this document.

Lucene is a powerful library that makes it possible to build applications with different levels of customization. For simple applications, it can be used effectively even without a deep understanding of search concepts. At the same time, Lucene provides powerful opportunities for developers who need to implement sophisticated search applications based on custom logic.

12.3.3   OneBox applications

Google uses the term "OneBox" to describe execution patterns where the same search query (and sometimes the results of its processing) are passed on to multiple applications and the results of their execution are combined into a single presentation. Figures 12.11 and 12.12 illustrate a search application that combines the results of querying text, images, and video with stock quotes. The results page is constructed in stages. Initially, it includes search results for text documents, images, and video (only text documents in Figure 12.11), as well as JavaScript components that fire AJAX requests for stock quotes (plus images and video in Figure 12.12). To fulfill requests for stock quotes, it is necessary first to match the original query against the database of company names and descriptions to find the company ticker, and second to submit the quote request for that ticker. Other examples of OneBox functionality may vary from weather reports to targeted advertising. Note that while AJAX is a convenient mechanism for implementing OneBox applications, it is not required. In Figure 12.11, OneBox functionality for querying text, images, and video is supported by server-side applications.

AJAX requests invoke the `stockQuote` web application, which implements the Quote Processor, Symbol Resolution, and Quote Retrieval modules in Figures 12.11 and 12.12. The application uses keywords in the query string to find the best match with company names or descriptions, identify the company ticker, and retrieve the stock quote. If there is no match or the quote is not available, the application returns the 400 status code and the AJAX call does not make any changes to the results page. If the quote is retrieved successfully, the application returns the HTML fragment containing the

```
function getQuote(keyword) {
  new Ajax.Updater("quote",
              "http://www.financestuff.com/search/stockQuote?kw=" + keyword,
    { method : "get" }
  );
}

window.onload = function() {
  getQuote("general+motors");
}
```

Figure 12.17 OneBox quote retrieval using the Prototype toolkit.

```
<div class="module" style="display:none" id="quote_block">
  <div class="moduleBody" style="margin:0;">
   <div class="stockQuote" id="quote"
    style="width:700px; border:1px solid #ccc; height:100px; margin-bottom:0;">
   </div>
  </div>
</div>
```

Figure 12.18 HTML fragment that enables OneBox quote retrieval.

quote, and the `Ajax.Updater` function (part of the Prototype toolkit – see Section 8.5.2) inserts this fragment into the quote's `<div>` tag.

AJAX requests that invoke `stockQuote` are submitted by the JavaScript function `getQuote` (Figure 12.17), which is triggered when the search results page is loaded into the browser. A fragment of the results page is presented in Figure 12.18. Note that the URL, which is passed as an argument to the `getQuote` function, contains the original query ("general motors"). The Query Processor generates both the results page and this URL. The query string portion of the URL would be different for different queries.

A user would initially see the results page without the quote, which could be added by the AJAX call. As with AJAX requests to query images and video, the side-benefit of deferring quote requests to the browser is the minimal impact on the user experience. If the quote is not available, the users can still access search results pages without delays or timeouts.

Solutions for finding company matches and resolving tickers are application-specific. They vary between full-text queries for company descriptions and rule-based approaches. Rules may be based on exact matches (e.g., "match the query consisting of the word 'apple' to the ticker for Apple Inc.") or term occurrences (e.g., "match the query containing words 'Chicago' and 'exchange' to Chicago Mercantile Exchange Holdings"). Rule-based algorithms commonly use rule hierarchies to aid conflict resolution. Maintaining ticker resolution rules can be a challenge. Manual rule maintenance is rarely practical due to the scope (hundreds of thousands of tickers) and frequent updates to company names and ticker symbols. Rule generation algorithms are complex and out of scope for our discussion.

Examples of OneBox functionality are not limited to stock quotes. Other popular examples include additional searches (article archives, discussion boards, and blogs), custom applications (e.g., weather summaries for queries containing geographic terms), and context-based advertising. The latter may be as simple as passing keywords to an ad server or a variation on using the original query to select a pre-defined ad channel.

The concept behind OneBox functionality is simple. It involves passing input from a single form to multiple applications or application chains. The example of an application chain that was discussed in this section is composed of the filter application and the responder application. The filter application takes the original input, tries to match it to a publicly traded company, and figures out the company ticker if the match exists. The responder application uses the ticker to retrieve the stock quote and other company information, format it, and send it back to the browser.

OneBox applications may be architected to execute on the server in response to a single HTTP request. As we discussed in this section, such a solution may have negative performance implications. It requires very careful error handling to avoid lengthy timeouts and broken pages if one or more of the OneBox applications are unavailable. A more popular and easier to implement solution is based on a single master application that formats and returns the main search results. The results page may include JavaScript calls that are executed when the page is loaded into the browser. These calls initiate AJAX requests that pass the information available to the master application to other one-pass applications. As we discussed, this solution has the benefit of making the main body of information available to users while additional information is being retrieved. Apart from performance advantages, this solution is more resilient when some of the applications are not available.

12.4 Search Engine Optimization

Search Engine Optimization (SEO) refers to the measures web sites can implement to advance their chances of discovery through search engines. Individual web sites (or clusters of closely related sites) implement SEO measures to increase their search engine rankings. The higher a site's ranking, the earlier it appears in search results, making it more likely for users to visit it. SEO measures may be generalized, they may target specific subject areas or industries, or they may be designed for specialized search engines (e.g., those that specialize in images and video).

The most successful SEO strategies stem from insights into the operation of search engines and the algorithms used by technologies they employ. They are derived from an understanding of search and spidering technologies, and from insights into the habits of search engine users. Common SEO measures include:

- Simplification of URL structure, with a preference toward short URLs and the elimination of query string parameters that affect page content.
- Site maps explicitly listing URLs that refer to unique content together with information about last modification times and update frequencies.
- Elimination of circular references that impede search engines from spidering the entire site.
- Hosting content that is unique to the site and avoiding multiple URLs referencing the same content.
- Making the site appealing to users to attract link-backs from other sites.

There are other techniques that can improve a site's ranking, including paid searches, "link-back" deals, and other "unnatural" means of attracting traffic. These measures represent business strategies rather than technological ones, so they are not covered in this book.

There are also more shady tactics for improving a site's ranking. These tactics, often called *"Black Hat" SEO* or *spamdexing*, include the use of "link farms" that exist solely to mislead search engines, as well as various techniques for stuffing invisible search keywords into pages (e.g., white text on a white background or inserting inappropriate keywords within HTML metadata). Such tactics obviously detract from the user experience and they eventually backfire on those who use them. When discovered, search engines blacklist sites that employ such practices and either downgrade page rankings for these sites or remove them from their indexes outright.

In this section, we discuss the means available to web sites for communicating information about the URL structure, content location, its expected change frequency, and other related information to search engines. We discuss the structure of the `robots.txt` file, which is the primary mechanism for this communication, as well as sitemap formats. We provide brief coverage of "Black Hat" tactics along with reasons not to use them. We conclude the section with a discussion of broad SEO strategies.

12.4.1 Robots.txt

Search engines and web sites that serve quality content have the common goal of directing users to what they are looking for. It stands to reason for both sides to establish a communication mechanism. Such a communication mechanism is the `robots.txt` file.[7] This file was introduced to establish a convention advising web spiders against accessing all or parts of a publicly accessible web site. The `robots.txt` file has to be located in the document root directory (see Section 6.1.2). Spiders are not supposed to apply specifications found in a domain's document root directory to its sub-domains (unless they happen to share the same root directory).

The examples in Figure 12.19 illustrate the use of `User-agent` and `Disallow` instructions to limit spider access. There is no enforcement mechanism associated with `robots.txt` instructions.

```
// Allow all spiders access to all directories
User-agent: *
Disallow:

// Disallow all access for all spiders
User-agent: *
Disallow: /

// Disallow access to three directories for all spiders
User-agent: *
Disallow: /images/
Disallow: /css/
Disallow: /mpeg/

// Disallow access to a specific file for all spiders
User-agent: *
Disallow: /keepalive.txt

// Disallow access to two directories for a specific spider
User-agent: SpiderX
Disallow: /images/
Disallow: /css/
```

Figure 12.19 Sample `robots.txt` configurations.

It is based on the honor system and mutual interest on the part of search engines and web site owners.

User-agent instructions define the applicability of Disallow instructions to all or only certain spiders (SpiderX in the last example). Notice that it is possible to use multiple Disallow instructions and that a Disallow instruction referencing a specific file does not impose any limitations on other files within the same directory (all directory paths are defined relative the document root). You may encounter examples of using the Disallow instruction with the "*" instead of a directory path. In this context, "*" is equivalent to "/". This is a non-standard extension and some spiders may not honor it. However, it is legal according to the proposed extended specification.

Individual HTML pages may use <meta> tags to instruct spiders to forego indexing the page or following links that occur on the page (see Figure 12.20). The first example in Figure 12.20 instructs spiders to ignore the links and forego indexing the content. The second example instructs spiders to follow the links but forego the indexing and the third example instructs spiders to do the reverse – index the file but forego following the links. Instructions in the last example have no effect because they prescribe the default behavior.

Spiders process meta tag instructions through Markup Stripper modules (see Section 12.2.2), which are responsible for retrieving the links as well as page content. Note that page exclusions in the robots.txt file have precedence because spiders do not parse excluded files.

Figure 12.21 illustrates extensions to the robots.txt specification, which are supported by spider programs used by the most popular search engines. The Allow directive specifies exceptions for disallowed directories. In the first example, all spiders are advised to ignore the /images/ directory and its subdirectories except for /images/captions/, which contains text files.

Instructions in the second and third examples disallow access to the /images/ directory and all of its subdirectories. The second example uses the Crawl-delay instruction, which is supported by most major spiders, to impose a 10-second time interval between successive requests from the same spider. The third example uses the Request-rate instruction, which is part of the proposed extended specification, to indicate one request every 10 seconds; it is roughly equivalent to the Crawl-delay setting in the second example. Visit-time also is a part of the proposed extended specification. In the example, it restricts the permissible time for spider requests to the period from 1:00 a.m. to 6:00 a.m.

```
// Disallow both indexing and link following
<meta name="robots" content="noindex,nofollow" />

// Disallow indexing but allow link following
<meta name="robots" content="noindex,follow" />

// Allow indexing but disallow link following
<meta name="robots" content="index,nofollow" />

// Allow indexing and link following
<meta name="robots" content="index,follow" />
```

Figure 12.20 Meta tag instructions for spiders.

```
// Disallow access to /images/ directory (except /images/captions/) for all spiders
User-agent: *
Disallow: /images/
Allow: /images/captions/

// Disallow access to /images/ directory and impose delay for all spiders
User-agent: *
Disallow: /images/
Crawl-delay: 10

// Disallow access to /images/ directory and impose limits on request rate
// and visit times
User-agent: *
Disallow: /images/
Request-rate: 1/10
Visit-time: 0100-0600
```

Figure 12.21   Common `robots.txt` extensions.

12.4.2   Sitemaps

Figure 12.22 illustrates the use of the `Sitemap` instruction. Sitemaps are XML files that are designed to provide detailed information about the location and freshness of site content to spiders. They are supported by all major search engines, including Google, Yahoo!, Ask.com, and Microsoft. Sitemaps afford fine-grained controls for web sites to inform search engines about resources they want spidered. Some of these resources may not be reachable through any of the seed pages known to the search engines.

The first instruction in Figure 12.22 references a sitemap located at `http://www.zyxnews.com/test/sitemap.xml`. Note that the location of the sitemap imposes limitations on URLs that it can reference. A sitemap located in the `http://www.zyxnews.com/test/` directory cannot reference URLs that do not have the `http://www.zyxnews.com/test/` prefix. The second instruction references a compressed file. Use of compression is recommended for large files to reduce bandwidth requirements. `Sitemap` instructions are not spider-specific and are not tied to `User-agent` instructions. They may appear anywhere within the `robots.txt` file.

Figure 12.23 is the sample sitemap for the fictitious zyxnews.com site on April 7, 2008. The first item corresponds to a developing story. The format for the last-modification date allows you to omit the time portion, but we want it for the developing story. The change frequency for the story is set to `always`, which describes a document that cannot be counted on to remain the same between any two

```
// Sitemap location
Sitemap: http://www.zyxnews.com/test/sitemap.xml

// Sitemap location (compressed file)
Sitemap: http://www.zyxnews.com/sitemap.xml.zip
```

Figure 12.22   Sitemap instructions in `robots.txt`.

```
<?xml version="1.0" encoding="UTF-8"?>
<urlset xmlns="http://www.sitemaps.org/schemas/sitemap/0.9">
  <url>
    <loc>http://www.zyxnews.com/article/id0739843920080407</loc>
    <lastmod>2008-04-07T03:44Z</lastmod>
    <changefreq>always</changefreq>
    <priority>0.8</priority>
  </url>
  <url>
    <loc>http://www.zyxnews.com/article/id1251326120080406</loc>
    <lastmod>2008-04-06</lastmod>
    <changefreq>hourly</changefreq>
    <priority>0.4</priority>
  </url>
  <url>
    <loc> http://www.zyxnews.com/article/id3796453620080301</loc>
    <lastmod>2008-03-01</lastmod>
    <changefreq>weekly</changefreq>
    <priority>0.2</priority>
  </url>
  <url>
    <loc> http://www.zyxnews.com/article/id8325673420070505</loc>
    <lastmod>2007-05-05</lastmod>
    <changefreq>yearly</changefreq>
    <priority>0.1</priority>
  </url>
</urlset>
```

Figure 12.23   Sample sitemap.

accesses. The priority, which is a value between 0.0 and 1.0, is relative to other items on the same site. It does not affect the relative importance of items on the zyxnews.com site compared to other sites. It is in the interest of the zyxnews.com site to assign higher priority to items that are likely to be of more interest to web users.

The second item in Figure 12.23 corresponds to a story from the day before. It may still change because of unexpected new developments or corrections. Still, hourly checks are more than enough and the priority is about half that for the developing story. The third and fourth items correspond to news stories that are one and 11 months old respectively. The older the story, the less likely it is to change. Consequently, the sitemap assigns older stories lower relative priorities and change frequencies. Note that search engines consider change frequencies defined in sitemaps as hints. They take them into account but use their own algorithms to set crawl frequencies. Note that setting change frequency values in the sitemaps much higher than the actual rate of changes may have the negative effect of search engines deciding to ignore these settings for your site in the future.

Sitemap files can grow prohibitively large, which is even more of a problem if they require frequent updates. Fortunately, the Sitemap specification supports the referencing of multiple sitemap files in a sitemap index file (see Figure 12.24). It is common practice to maintain separate sitemaps for different areas of the site, as well as for items with different change frequencies. A sitemap index file can only reference sitemaps on the same domain. Its format is very similar to the format of sitemap files.

```
<?xml version="1.0" encoding="utf-8"?>
<sitemapindex xmlns="http://www.sitemaps.org/schemas/sitemap/0.9">
  <sitemap>
    <loc>http://www.zyxnews.com/sitemap_local_news_current.xml.zip</loc>
    <lastmod>2008-04-07T03:44Z</lastmod>
  </sitemap>
  <sitemap>
    <loc>http://www.zyxnews.com/sitemap_local_news_recent.xml.zip</loc>
    <lastmod>2008-04-06</lastmod>
  </sitemap>
  <sitemap>
    <loc>http://www.zyxnews.com/sitemap_local_news_archive.xml.zip</loc>
    <lastmod>2008-03-15</lastmod>
  </sitemap>
  <sitemap>
    <loc>http://www.zyxnews.com/sitemap_world_news_current.xml.zip</loc>
    <lastmod>2008-04-07T21:39Z</lastmod>
  </sitemap>
  <sitemap>
    <loc>http://www.zyxnews.com/sitemap_world_news_recent.xml.zip</loc>
    <lastmod>2008-04-06</lastmod>
  </sitemap>
  <sitemap>
    <loc>http://www.zyxnews.com/sitemap_world_news_archive.xml.zip</loc>
    <lastmod>2008-03-15</lastmod>
  </sitemap>
</sitemapindex>
```

Figure 12.24   Sample sitemap index file.

Figure 12.24 illustrates the strategy of splitting sitemaps by purpose and by frequency of update. There are two groups of sitemaps – one for local and one for international news. Each of the groups is, in turn, split into three sitemaps. The first sitemap in every group references articles that have been published over the last 24 hours. The second sitemap references articles that have been published over the last 30 days excluding articles that were published on the current date. Finally, the third sitemap references archived articles that were published more than 30 days ago.

Figures 12.25 and 12.26 demonstrate sample sitemaps referencing current and recent articles. The sitemap referencing current articles (Figure 12.25) is updated when a new article is published or when there is a change to an existing article, in order to add an entry or update the modification date. On every update, entries that are older than 24 hours are purged. The site map referencing recent articles (Figure 12.26) is updated once a day, at midnight. At that time, references to articles from the previous day are added and references to articles that were published more than 30 days previously are purged.

Notice that the same article (the second item in Figure 12.25 and the first item in Figure 12.26) is referenced in both sitemaps; in Figure 12.26, its modification frequency is shown as `daily` instead of `always`. The reason is to avoid frequent modifications to the potentially much larger sitemap referencing 30 days' worth of recent articles. As you can see, with this strategy an article may temporarily be referenced by two sitemaps but it is always referenced by at least one.

```
<?xml version="1.0" encoding="UTF-8"?>
<urlset xmlns="http://www.sitemaps.org/schemas/sitemap/0.9">
  <url>
    <loc>http://www.zyxnews.com/article/id0739843920080407</loc>
    <lastmod>2008-04-07T03:44Z</lastmod>
    <changefreq>always</changefreq>
    <priority>0.8</priority>
  </url>
  <url>
    <loc>http://www.zyxnews.com/article/id1251326120080406</loc>
    <lastmod>2008-04-06T23:48Z</lastmod>
    <changefreq>always</changefreq>
    <priority>0.8</priority>
  </url>
</urlset>
```

Figure 12.25   Sample sitemap file for current local news (`sitemap_local_news_current.xml`).

```
<?xml version="1.0" encoding="UTF-8"?>
<urlset xmlns="http://www.sitemaps.org/schemas/sitemap/0.9">
  <url>
    <loc>http://www.zyxnews.com/article/id1251326120080406</loc>
    <lastmod>2008-04-06</lastmod>
    <changefreq>daily</changefreq>
    <priority>0.4</priority>
  </url>
  <url>
    <loc> http://www.zyxnews.com/article/id3796453620080311</loc>
    <lastmod>2008-03-11</lastmod>
    <changefreq>daily</changefreq>
    <priority>0.4</priority>
  </url>
</urlset>
```

Figure 12.26   Sample sitemap file for recent local news (`sitemap_local_news_ recent.xml`).

We have described one possible strategy for splitting references into different sitemaps. Strategies vary between sites, depending on the nature of the content, its volume, and frequency of modification. However, the main principles for designing an efficient sitemap strategy remain:

- Separate references into different sitemaps by modification frequency.
- If necessary, reduce sizes of individual sitemaps through separating references by subject or similar criteria.
- Avoid referencing the same page from different sitemaps using the same modification frequency.
- Ensure that every page is referenced by at least one sitemap at any time.

12.4.3 Sitemap extensions

The sitemap protocol supports proprietary extensions. The most popular and commonly used extension is Google News (see Figure 12.27). As you can see, a Google News sitemap references a second namespace and associates it with the `news` prefix. Figure 12.27 is the evolution of the example in Figure 12.25, which makes use of Google's proprietary news tags. Publication date is required and reflects the time of the latest article update. Note the slight but important difference – the publication date is supposed to reflect the time and date of the release. It may not be the same as the timestamp associated with the file containing the article in Figure 12.25. For news, the publication date is more important because it reflects the newest version of the story and ignores file distribution delays.

The `<keywords>` element contains comma-separated keywords that describe the content of the article. The `<stock_ticker>` element contains the comma-separated list of stock tickers for companies, mutual funds and other tradable entities that constitute the main subject of the article. Not every ticker mentioned in the article has to appear within the `<stock_ticker>` element.

12.4.4 Site and URL structure

We have discussed two critical components associated with increasing search engine traffic: defining proper exclusions in the `robots.txt` files and providing explicit content references through the sitemap mechanism. However, making content available to spiders is just one side of the coin. It is also important that they find just one copy of the content. If there are multiple copies of the content

```xml
<?xml version="1.0" encoding="UTF-8"?>
<urlset xmlns=http://www.sitemaps.org/schemas/sitemap/0.9
        xmlns:news=http://www.google.com/schemas/sitemap-news/0.9>
  <url>
    <loc>http://www.zyxnews.com/article/id0739843920080407</loc>
    <lastmod>2008-04-07T03:44Z</lastmod>
    <changefreq>always</changefreq>
    <priority>0.8</priority>
    <news:news>
      <news:publication_date>2008-04-07T03:44:00Z</news:publication_date>
      <news:keywords>Business, Mergers, Acquisitions</news:keywords>
      <news:stock_tickers>MSFT, GOOG, YHOO</news:stock_tickers>
    </news/news>
  </url>
  <url>
    <loc>http://www.zyxnews.com/article/id1251326120080406</loc>
    <news:news>
      <news:publication_date>2008-04-07T03:44:00Z</news:publication_date>
      <news:keywords>Business, Revenue, Projections</news:keywords>
      <news:stock_tickers>INT, AMD</news:stock_tickers>
    </news/news>
  </url>
</urlset>
```

Figure 12.27 Google News sitemap extension.

available from different URLs, users might find more than one version of the content and third-party web sites might link to these different URLs. As you may recall, the page rank depends on the number of links pointing to the page (Section 12.2.1). The more different paths to the same content spiders can find, the worse the page rank dilution is going to be. In other words, different paths on the same site to the same content would be competing with each other for the page rank and neither may come out on top in most searches.

There are legitimate scenarios when a site may want to provide multiple paths to the same page. One such situation arises when a news article appears on multiple channels (e.g., political news and business news) and the site uses different templates to display news articles that come through different channels, where different templates would yield links that differ in their URL paths.

Maintaining multiple paths to the same content may not be a problem for a site that designs and implements a consistent SEO strategy. Here are highlights of a sample policy that satisfies these requirements:

- Select a dedicated path for your articles. Ideally, this path would not depend on a news channel and use a generic template without ads and extraneous information in iframes.
- Avoid assigning different URLs to versions of the same article with small incremental differences.
- Disallow all article paths (except for the dedicated path above) in the `robots.txt` specification.
- Create pages composed of links to current and archived articles and make sure they are reachable from the home page and other landing pages.
- Generate and set up update processes for sitemaps pointing to current and archived articles, and reference these sitemaps in the sitemap index file.
- Reference the sitemap index file from the `robots.txt` file. As an additional measure, it is advisable to submit the sitemap index file directly to search engines.
- As a precaution, include the `<meta name="robots" content="noindex,nofollow"/>` tag in channel-specific templates. This way, even if a spider happens on an article served from an alternate path, it knows to ignore it.

As we discussed earlier in the chapter, traversing dynamically generated pages is a challenge because of the endless variations of query string parameters, Sites that use query string parameters to select page content make it very difficult for search engines to decide which query string parameters should and should not be ignored. Making life difficult for search engines is contrary to the goal of making your pages easier to find. Struts and other application frameworks make it easy for application designers to include information about page content in the path portion of the URLs. That is a good practice: it promotes readable URLs and improves search engine traffic.

SEO-conscious site and application design keeps the size of the URLs to a minimum, avoids query string parameters to select page content, reuses URLs for small incremental changes to the content, and prevents search engines from indexing pages that represent the same content. Effective SEO measures cannot be an afterthought – they have to be an integral part of application design.

12.4.5 Black Hat SEO

"Black Hat" SEO tactics include the use of *link farms* to improve page ranks, the stuffing of irrelevant keywords into pages just because these keywords relate to popular queries, and *invisible text*. A link farm is a group of sites each of which is composed of pages that reference every other site in the group. Link farms are commonly created by automated programs in an effort to increase the page ranks of hosted pages (see Section 12.2.1). Invisible text techniques are designed to include text in a page that is invisible to the human eye but is still "visible" to spiders. They are used to hide both irrelevant keywords "stuffed" into the promoted pages and links that serve the sole purpose of connecting different sites in the farm. Invisible text was originally implemented by using a font with the same color as the page background, but spiders learned very quickly to recognize this. An advanced variation of this technique uses colors for the fonts and page background that are different but indistinguishable to the human eye.

A more sophisticated tactic, known as *doorway pages*, employs pages that can be seen by spiders but are not seen by visitors to the site. The idea is to create dynamic pages stuffed with links and keywords and reference these pages through cross-links, site maps and other mechanisms to attract spiders. "Doorway" URLs reference applications that analyze incoming requests and produce keyword-stuffed pages in response to spider requests while generating 301 permanent redirects (Section 3.3.5) in response to browser requests. These redirects take users to pages containing the "real" content that webmasters using this tactic want them to view. Browsers and proxies that cache 301 redirects would bypass these doorway URLs for follow-up requests.

The attraction of this tactic is that the content pages served to real users do not contain bogus links or keywords, hidden text, or other obvious attributes of "Black Hat" deceptions. An advanced implementation of doorway pages would coordinate keywords that are stuffed into pages served to spiders, with corresponding content pages served to real users. Some implementations go even further to take advantage of particular spider algorithms. Such implementations produce custom pages for individual spiders. Search engines are on the lookout for doorway pages and routinely blacklist sites that use this tactic. Doorway pages can drive traffic in the short term but they invariably create problems for sites that make use of this technique in the long run.

There are many creative variations on the tactics we describe here, but webmasters need to ask themselves whether it is really worth it. Given the amount of work required, and the risks associated with using these tactics, their time and effort would be better spent making use of legitimate SEO methods.

12.5 Summary

We have dedicated a significant part of this chapter to discussing simple full-text indexing and retrieval algorithms. We also discussed spidering algorithms and the architecture of spider applications. While readers may never get the opportunity to design and implement such algorithms on their own, an understanding of the principles behind open source and commercial full-text indexing and search technologies is useful in building effective local search applications. In addition, an understanding of both full-text indexing and spider behavior is beneficial to site owners in designing successful SEO strategies.

Lucene is the most popular open source library and is used by many sites to index local content. It would be very difficult to build and tune effective Lucene applications without a good understanding of underlying technologies. Many commercial tools are just as demanding, though some sacrifice flexibility for simplicity.

SEO techniques are rarely effective in isolation. It is preferable to avoid multiple URLs referencing the same content. but if that is necessary, warning spiders away from alternate paths may compensate for the negative impact of the duplication. Still, even these steps are not fully effective because of link dilution. Link dilution occurs when third-party sites point to multiple URLs that reference the same content. This negatively affects page ranks and makes it less likely that these pages appear among the top hits in web searches. The solution lies in constructing holistic SEO strategies that strive to find the optimal balance in combining multiple measures. Web sites differ in their purpose and priorities, and no universal SEO strategy applies to all of them.

We provided brief coverage of "Black Hat" SEO tactics, which rely on unethical techniques to cause pages to rank higher in search results. They are considered unethical because they employ deception to lure users to content not directly related to their searches. Ethical concerns are reason enough to avoid these techniques, but there are also pragmatic considerations for not using them: the use of "Black Hat" tactics ultimately damages the credibility of sites that employ them. Search engines monitor sites for the use of such techniques and routinely lower ratings for the sites that engage in them or even drop these sites altogether. The ability to recognize the use of "Black Hat" tactics by unethical sites, however, is very useful to both webmasters and web application developers.

Recent advancements in searching are tied to metadata extraction technologies. Such technologies can classify and analyze text and extract metadata entities related to countries, cities, companies, commodities and complex concepts related to the content. Extracted metadata often makes it possible to increase the precision of full-text searches and to build creative OneBox applications.

As the nature of the web changes, links between sites will acquire sophistication and become more complex, and concepts of the semantic web will take hold. New technologies will emerge that aim to take advantage of the semantic web. These technologies are one of the topics that we cover in Chapter 13.

QUESTIONS AND EXERCISES

1. What is stemming? Why is it problematic for indexing web resources?

2. Take the first four sentences in this chapter and treat them as separate documents. Build a vector space using the basic vector-space algorithm described in Section 12.1.2. Try processing the query "web search". What is your document ranking? How would you improve this ranking?

3. What is word clustering? What impact does it have on recall and precision?

4. What changes do you need to make to the spider implementation in Figure 12.10 to retrieve and follow links from Microsoft Word documents?

5. What is the main idea behind OneBox applications? Compare the search applications in Figures 12.11 and Figure 12.12. What are the advantages and disadvantages of these architectures?

6. Name at least three applications that would be good candidates for OneBox implementations. What common features make these applications good candidates for such implementations?

7. Name at least five common measures that compose an SEO strategy.

8. What is page rank? What impact does it have on SEO strategies?

9. Propose a modification to the page-rank algorithm to counter the duplicate content problem. How would you design an SEO strategy to take advantage of your proposal?

10. What is the relationship between `robots.txt` files and sitemaps? Are these mechanisms redundant? Would you use one of them or both in your SEO strategy? Why?

11. What is the purpose of robot instructions in HTML `<meta>` tags? Would you plan to use these instructions in your SEO strategy? Would you use the instructions in `<meta>` tags if you already have a `robots.txt` file and sitemaps? Why?

12. Ethical considerations aside, explain why you would or would not choose to use "Black Hat" SEO tactics.

13. How would you go about discovering web sites that use "doorway pages"?

14. Implement a basic spider that can traverse the Internet, detect sites that use "doorway pages", and compile a report. Produce daily reports for a week and compare the results. Do the same for a month. How do you explain changes in the report?

12.6 Bibliography

Davis, Harold, 2006. *Search Engine Optimization: Building Traffic and Making Money with SEO*. Sebastopol (CA): O'Reilly Media.

Dornfest, Rael, Bausch, Paul, and Calishain, Tara, 2006. *Google Hacks: Tips & Tools for Finding and Using the World's Information*, 3rd Edition. Sebastopol (CA): O'Reilly Media.

Gospodnetic, Otis and Hatcher, Erik, 2004. *Lucene in Action*. Greenwich (CT): Manning Publications.

Hemenway, Kevin and Calishain, Tara, 2003. *Spidering Hacks: 100 Industrial-Strength Tips and Tools*. Sebastopol (CA): O'Reilly Media.

Ledford, Jerri, 2007. *SEO: Search Engine Optimization Bible*. Indianapolis (IN): Wiley Publishing.

Schrenk, Michael, 2007. *Webbots, Spiders, and Screen Scrapers: A Guide to Developing Internet Agents with PHP/CURL*. San Francisco: No Starch Press.

12.7 Web Links

English Stopwords. Available at http://www.ranks.nl/tools/stopwords.html.

Apache Lucene Project. Available at lucene.apache.org.

Apache POI Project. Available at poi.apache.org.

Brin, Sergey and Page, Lawrence, 2000. "The Anatomy of a Large-Scale Hypertextual Web Search Engine". Available at http://infolab.stanford.edu/pub/papers/google.pdf.

PDFBox, Java PDF Library. Available at www.pdfbox.org.

Web Robots Pages. Available at www.robotstxt.org.

12.8 Endnotes

1. http://www.ranks.nl/tools/stopwords.html
2. http://infolab.stanford.edu/pub/papers/google.pdf
3. http://lucene.apache.org
4. http://www.pdfbox.org
5. http://poi.apache.org
6. http://jtidy.sourcefoge.net/
7. http://www.robotstxt.org

CHAPTER 13

Trends and Directions

IN THIS CHAPTER

- XML query language
- RDF and the Semantic Web
- Future of web application frameworks
- Current trends

OBJECTIVES

- Examine new and emerging technologies.
- Review XML Query.
- Introduce the Semantic Web and provide an overview of the Resource Description Framework (RDF) and RDF applications.
- Speculate about the future of web application frameworks.
- Discuss current trends in web technology.

Rapid expansion of Internet technologies has come at the cost of technological incompatibilities and inconsistencies, which have put much strain on the web application development process. Today, after more than 15 years of exponential growth, Internet technologies are finally becoming stable and robust. We are seeing encouraging examples of technology convergence. XHTML has supplanted HTML, WML is being phased out and replaced with XHTML MP (see Section 5.2.2), and the relationship between XSL, XSLT, XSLFO, and other style sheet specifications has been clarified (see Section 5). The most recent specifications from the World Wide Web Consortium and other standards-setting bodies, including the Web Services Interoperability Organization (WS-I)[1] and the Organization for the

Advancement of Structured Information Standards (OASIS),[2] concentrate on achieving improvements to accepted and emerging technologies, as well as convergence between them, as opposed to dramatic new directions.

The first part of this chapter is devoted to the leading specification for querying XML documents, *XML Query*, followed by a discussion of the *semantic web*, which is a major effort on the part of W3C encompassing a suite of emerging technologies:

- ***Resource Description Framework (RDF)***, which is currently the leading specification for machine-understandable metadata;
- ***Composite Capabilities/Preference Profiles (CC/PP)***, which is a pioneering RDF application for serving content across multiple devices and formats;
- ***RDF Query***, a specification that makes it possible to query RDF models and further clarifies the distinction between RDF models and their XML representation.

In the final part of this chapter, we turn to the immediate concerns of evolving application frameworks based on existing technologies. We discuss the limitations of existing frameworks and propose solutions to transcend those limitations.

13.1   XML Query Language

As the scope and variety of XML applications have grown, so have the integration requirements associated with those applications and with them the necessity to query XML-structured information. The convergence and consolidation of XML specifications made it practical to define uniform query facilities for extracting data from both real and virtual XML documents, with the ultimate goal of accessing and querying XML information as a distributed database.

The challenge is that XML documents are very different from relational databases. Instead of tables where almost every column has a value, we have to deal with distributed hierarchies, and with optional elements that may or may not be present in a particular document. Relational query languages such as SQL are thus not suited for XML data.

The XML Query language, *XQuery*, has reached the status of an official recommendation by W3C. There are already numerous implementations based on the specification. XQuery borrows and extends concepts from XPath, which was designed primarily to express traversal patterns in XSLT style sheets (see Section 5.4.1). XQuery combines the notions of query and traversal. The traversal component serves to define the query context, which is determined by the current XML element and its location in the DOM tree. The query component serves to evaluate conditions along different axes (attribute, child, descendant, parent, self, and descendant-or-self) in the query context. Both components are involved in evaluating an expression.

For example, consider the XML document (sample.xml) from Figure 5.1. We have modified this example to support unique identifiers for individual books by adding the <isbn> element (Figure 13.1). We make use of the unique identifiers later in this section to demonstrate multi-document queries.

The XQuery expressions in Figure 13.2 are designed to select books written by Rich Rosen.

The first expression in Figure 13.2 uses full syntax to define traversal from the document root down to the author element. Notice that the expression is composed of slash-separated criteria for selecting

```
<?xml version="1.0" standalone="yes"?>
<!-- XML example for the XQuery section of the Web Architecture book -->
<!DOCTYPE books SYSTEM "books_plus_isbn.dtd">
<books status="In Print">
  <book>
    <title>Web Application Architecture</title>
    <subtitle>Principles, protocols and practices</subtitle>
    <author firstName="Leon" lastName="Shklar"/>
    <author firstName="Rich" lastName="Rosen"/>
    <isbn>047051860X</isbn>
    <info>
      <pages count="500"/>
      <price usd="55" gbp="27.50"/>
      <publication year="2008" source="&jw;"/>
    </info>
    <summary>An in-depth examination of the basic concepts and general
             principles associated with web application development.
    </summary>
  </book>
...
</books>
```

Figure 13.1 Modified `sample.xml` file.

```
document("sample.xml")/child::*/child::*/child::author
  [attribute::firstName = "Rich" and attribute::lastName = "Rosen"]

document("sample.xml")/*/*/
  author[@firstName = "Rich" and @lastName = "Rosen"]

document("sample.xml")/**/
  author[@firstName = "Rich" and @lastName = "Rosen"]

document("sample.xml")/books/book/
  author[@firstName = "Rich" and @lastName = "Rosen"]
```

Figure 13.2 Sample XQuery expressions.

traversal axes. Here, `child::` denotes the `child` axis, `child::*` means that any outgoing element edge should be investigated, and `child::author` limits the traversal paths to outgoing edges that lead to `<author>` elements. The predicate enclosed in square brackets establishes selection conditions, limiting acceptable `<author>` elements to those that have `firstName` and `lastName` attributes set to "Rich" and "Rosen" respectively.

The second expression in Figure 13.2 is identical to the first, except that it makes use of the abbreviated syntax, which includes the default selection of the element axis.

The third expression in Figure 13.2, while producing identical results for `sample.xml`, has somewhat different semantics – it results in evaluating all paths along the element axis that originate at the document root and lead to the `<author>` element, no matter the number of hops.

Finally, the fourth expression in Figure 13.2 contains very explicit instructions for the evaluation engine to only consider element edges through the <books> and <book> element nodes. It is easy to see that, in terms of performance, this expression is optimal for the evaluation engine, while the third expression is potentially the most expensive option.

Notice that the syntax and semantics of XQuery expressions are closely related to XPath – the simple, specialized query and traversal language that we discussed briefly in the context of XSLT (see Section 5.4.1). This is not a coincidence – XQuery designers made every effort to be consistent with existing XML specifications.

Of course, there has to be more to the XML query language than path expressions. The language has to provide ways to express complex conditions that involve multiple documents and path expressions, and to control the format of the result.

For example, suppose we want to analyze book sales logs that are collected daily in XML format (Figure 13.3). The sales log, which is stored in the file sales_log.xml, has a very simple format – the root element <records> contains the date attribute; every individual <record> element corresponds to a single sale and contains the single attribute of the ISBN reference. We need a report on the sales of books that reach at least 100 copies per day.

The query to generate a sales report from Figure 13.3 is shown in Figure 13.4. The for clause implements iteration through <book> elements in sample.xml. The $i variable is always bound to the current element in the set. The let clause defines the join and produces the binding between

```
<?xml version="1.0" standalone="yes"?>
<!-- XML example - sales log -->
<!DOCTYPE books SYSTEM "book_sales_daily_log.dtd">
<records date="12/12/2008">
  <record isbn="047051860X"/>
  <record isbn="..."/>
  ...
</records>
```

Figure 13.3   Daily sales log in XML format.

```
for $i in document("sample.xml")/*/book
  let $s := document("sales_log.xml")/*/record[@isbn = $i/isbn]
  where count ($s) > 99
  return
    <active-book>
      {
      $i/title,
      $i/isbn,
      <sales>{count($s)}</sales>
      }
    </active-book>
  sortby (sales) descending
```

Figure 13.4   XQuery statement for the sales log.

the `<book>` element and `<record>` elements in the `sales_log.xml` file. The `count($s) > 99` condition in the `where` clause eliminates all bindings that do not include at least 100 sales records.

The `return` clause, which determines output format, is executed once for every binding that was not eliminated by conditions in the `where` clause. It produces units of output that are sorted according to the `sortby` clause. For every execution of the `return` clause, the `$i` variable is bound to the current `<book>` element, which provides context for path expressions in the `return` clause (`$i/title` and `$i/isbn`).

XQuery is a very complex language. We have not even scratched the surface in our brief discussion. There are many different kinds of expressions that we have not covered, as well as the whole issue of XQuery types and their relationship to the XML Schema. Still, the examples should provide a flavor of the language expressions and query construction.

13.2 Semantic Web

The semantic web is a major effort on the part of the W3C to create the next generation Internet infrastructure, where information has a well-defined meaning, making it possible for people and programs to cooperate with each other. It is about interoperability and about creating a connection between information on the web and real-world objects.

Berners-Lee (2000) describes the semantic web as "a dream for the web [in which computers] become capable of analyzing all the data on the web – the content, links, and transactions between people and computers." In his vision, the "day-to-day mechanisms of trade, bureaucracy and our daily lives will be handled by machines talking to machines. The 'intelligent agents' people have touted for ages will finally materialize."

The challenge in realizing this vision is to make it possible for machines to *understand* interconnected data. The critical step is to associate data with meaning, and here the important role belongs to enabling technologies, the first and foremost of which is the Resource Description Framework (RDF), which we discuss in this section. In the long term, we expect that RDF, in conjunction with other standards such as RDF Schema, XML and XML Schema, Dublin Core, and the XML and RDF query languages, serve as the foundation for semantic web applications.

When RDF first came out a few years ago, people often thought of the semantic web as a collection of RDF applications. New RDF-based specifications, including the *DARPA Agent Markup Language (DAML)* and the *Ontology Inference Layer (OIL)*, strengthened the belief that RDF would be the foundation of the semantic web.

It is going to be some time until DAML and OIL applications become practical. As a result, more and more people are taking a wider view of the semantic web, including the possibility of using existing standards in conjunction with RDF models for building advanced web services. Applications that benefit from the use of machine-understandable metadata range from information retrieval to system integration.

Machine-understandable metadata is emerging as a new foundation for component-based approaches to application development. Web services represent an advance in the context of distributed component-based architecture. Whether applications make use of RDF or are trying to achieve similar goals by using XML, WSDL, UDDI, SOAP, or XSL, they create fertile ground for the future.

We discussed XML, XML Schema, web services, and other related specifications in Chapter 5. In this section, we cover RDF and RDF Schema, CC/PP (an RDF application that enables mobile devices to describe their capabilities), and the emerging RDF query language.

13.2.1   Resource Description Framework (RDF)

The next wave of technological advances may very well be powered by *machine-understandable metadata*. Metadata technologies are gaining momentum with the consolidation of the base standards and the emergence of robust metadata extraction technologies using text analysis. RDF is a standard that was designed to support *machine-understandable* metadata and to enable interoperability between metadata-based applications. Early applications of RDF address real problems in the areas of resource discovery, intelligent software agents, content rating, mobile devices, and privacy preferences. RDF is used to construct metadata models that may be understood by processing agents.

Strictly speaking, RDF is not an XML application, but XML is a common vehicle for encoding and transporting RDF models. Natively, RDF models are defined as sets of *triples*, and may be encoded using XML, *Notation 3* (also known as *N3*), and other representation mechanisms.

Dublin Core

The Dublin Core (DC) metadata standard predates RDF. It was proposed as an element set for describing a wide range of networked resources. DC's initial design goals were very ambitious and not all of them materialized. What emerged was a set of 15 elements, the semantics of which have been established through long and painful negotiations within an international, cross-disciplinary group that included librarians and computer scientists.

The DC elements cover such core notions as Title, Creator, Publisher, Date, Language, Format, and Identifier. Together with qualifiers, the nouns corresponding to these key concepts can be arranged into simple statements, which enable simple "pidgin-level" communications. DC elements are easy to use but are not up to the task of communicating complex concepts.

The emergence of RDF breathed new life into the DC specification. RDF provides the formal mechanism for describing DC concepts. More importantly, the DC specification provides the necessary "semantic grounding" for RDF models through atomic concepts that were designed for describing networked resources.

The most basic RDF concept is that of a resource, which is any entity represented with a URI. An RDF *triple* is the combination of a *subject*, an *object*, and a *property* (also called a *predicate*). Both subjects and properties are RDF resources, while objects may be either resources or *literals* (constants). The example in Figure 13.5 is the simplified RDF model for this book. The meaning of the model is obvious – it describes the book, by specifying creators (authors) and the publisher. RDF models are designed to be *machine-understandable* – their meaning may be interpreted and acted upon by computer programs that do not have any built-in knowledge of the matter (in this case, publishing).

The three triples in Figure 13.5 identify relationships between the book, two authors, and a publishing company. They establish that the two authors are the creators of the book and the company is its publisher. The book resource is the object of all three triples and is identified by its URI: http://purl.org/net/waabook. The resources associated with the authors are identified by

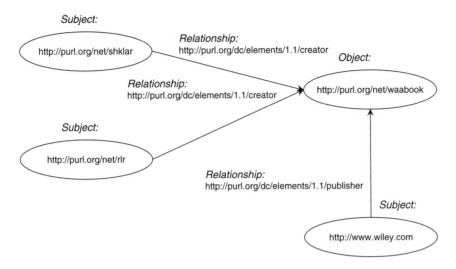

Figure 13.5 Sample RDF model.

```
@prefix dc: <http://purl.org/dc/elements/1.1/>
@prefix id: <http://purl.org/net/>
id:shklar  dc:creator id:waabook
id:rlr  dc:creator id:waabook
<http://www.wiley.com> dc:publisher id:waabook
```

Figure 13.6 N3 representation of the RDF model in Figure 13.5.

http://purl.org/net/shklar and http://purl.org/net/rlr. Each of these resources is a subject of the Creator property represented by http://purl.org/dc/elements/1.1/creator. The `Publisher` property is represented by http://purl.org/dc/elements/1.1/publisher, where the subject of the triple is the resource representing the John Wiley & Sons publishing company.

The N3 representation of this model is shown in Figure 13.6. N3 is designed to be a shorter and simpler alternative to the XML representation of RDF models. It provides for a more concise representation of the triples in Figure 13.5. Here, `dc:creator` is equivalent to `<http://purl.org/dc/elements/1.1/creator>` and `id:shklar` is equivalent to `<http://purl.org/net/shklar>`.

The XML representation of the model is shown in Figure 13.7. The DC vocabulary of atomic concepts is identified by its URI – http://purl.org/dc/elements/1.1/ – which was defined as a prefix in the N3 representation. The semantic grounding of RDF properties is achieved by mapping them to the DC concepts Creator and Publisher. The triples in Figure 13.5 all relate to the common object represented by the `<rdf:Description>` element. The `<dc:creator>` and `<dc:publisher>` elements represent RDF properties and the content of these elements represents the subjects of their respective triples.

By the nature of XML, the structure in Figure 13.7 is hierarchical, which creates the impedance mismatch problem for arbitrary RDF models. In the example, the hierarchical nature of XML works

```
<?xml version="1.0"?>
<rdf:RDF xmlns:rdf="http://www.w3.org/1999/02/22-rdf-syntax-ns#"
         xmlns:dc="http://purl.org/dc/elements/1.1/">
  <rdf:Description rdf:about="http://purl.org/net/shklar/waabook">
    <dc:creator>http://www.neurozen.com</dc:creator>
    <dc:creator>http://purl.org/net/shklar</dc:creator>
    <dc:publisher>http://www.wiley.com</dc:description>
  </rdf:Description>
</rdf:RDF>
```

Figure 13.7   XML representation of the RDF model in Figure 13.5.

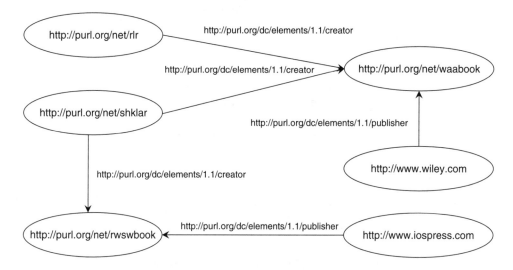

Figure 13.8   Extending the RDF model from Figure 13.5.

to our advantage, resulting in a very compact representation. It gets a lot more complicated for more advanced models.

The same resource may be the subject of more than one triple. In Figure 13.8, we show the modification of the original model with two additional triples that describe another book. One triple states that one of the authors of the original book is also an author for the new book. The other triple describing the new book states that the resource with the URI www.iospress.com is the subject of the `<dc:publisher>` property.

The N3 representation in Figure 13.9 is similar to the representation in Figure 13.6. Note that ", " is the shorthand notation that indicates multiple objects of the same property with the same subject. The new prefixes are added for illustration and are simply a matter of convenience.

The structure of the XML representation in Figure 13.10 is not very different from the XML document in Figure 13.7. However, you can recognize the early signs of trouble – the author resource identified with http://purl.org/net/shklar is referenced in two different places, which is not the case in the model (Figure 13.8). In XML representations of complex models, there may be numerous

```
@prefix dc:     <http://purl.org/dc/elements/1.1/>
@prefix id:     <http://purl.org/net/>
@prefix wiley:  <http://www.wiley.com>
@prefix ios:    <http://www.iospress.com>

id:shklar dc:creator    id:waabook, id:rwswbook
id:rlr    dc:creator    id:waabook
wiley:    dc:publisher id:waabook
ios:      dc:publisher id:rwswbook
```

Figure 13.9   N3 representation of the RDF model in Figure 13.8.

```
<?xml version="1.0"?>
<rdf:RDF xmlns:rdf="http://www.w3.org/1999/02/22-rdf-syntax-ns#"
         xmlns:dc="http://purl.org/dc/elements/1.1/">
  <rdf:Description rdf:about="http://purl.org/net/waabook">
      <dc:creator>http://www.neurozen.com</dc:creator>
      <dc:creator>http://purl.org/net/shklar</dc:creator>
      <dc:publisher>http://www.wiley.com</dc:description>
  </rdf:Description>
  <rdf:Description rdf:about="http://purl.org/net/rwswbook">
      <dc:creator>http://purl.org/net/shklar</dc:creator>
      <dc:publisher>http://www.iospress.com</dc:description>
  </rdf:Description>
</rdf:RDF>
```

Figure 13.10   XML representation of the RDF model in Figure 13.8.

references to the same resource, which is an indication of the impedance mismatch problem we mentioned earlier.

The hierarchical nature of XML makes it impractical to process XML representations of RDF models directly. Instead, RDF processors convert such representations to the N3 notation or use them as input for constructing RDF graphs. In other words, RDF is more than another XML application. It is a separate specification based on an entirely different, non-hierarchical model. RDF serves the purpose of expressing complex interrelationships between Internet resources. Its long-term goal is to enable automated reasoning in the space of resources, their properties, and relationships.

PURLs of Wisdom – Persistent URLs

You may have noticed that addresses of Dublin Core elements refer to purl.org. Remember, back in Chapter 3, we discussed that a Uniform Resource Identifier (URI) may be either a Uniform Resource Locator (URL) or a Uniform Resource Name (URN). By definition, URNs do not change when pages move.

URNs used to be a theoretical notion, but purl.org is an attempt to make it practical. The name of the site stands for "persistent URL". It is a free public service site that makes it possible to assign persistent names to Internet resources.

This is exactly what we did with the book resource, http://purl.org/net/waabook. At the moment, this URI maps to http://www.wiley.com/WileyCDA/WileyTitle/productCd-0471486566.html. If www.wiley.com is reorganized, all we need to do is change the mapping on the `purl.org` site and the URN will continue to work. As long as we distribute the URN and not the physical address of the page, and make sure that it stays current, the link will continue to work.

RDF Schema

The RDF Schema specification aims at constraining the model context by introducing the notion of *model validity*. This is quite different from the validity of XML documents – a valid XML document may represent an invalid RDF model. Remember, XML is just one of many representation vehicles for RDF documents.

RDF Schema enables the definition of new resources as specializations of the ones that already exist. This makes it possible to define new concepts by semantically grounding them to existing specifications. For example, we can take advantage of the Dublin Core `Creator` property and its meaning in defining two new properties, `firstAuthor` and `secondAuthor` (Figure 13.11).

The new properties are defined as specializations of the `dc:creator` property through `rdfs:subClassOf`, which is defined in the RDF Schema specification. The `rdfs:necessity` property, which is also defined in the RDF Schema specification, serves to express occurrence

```
<?xml version="1.0"?>
<rdf:RDF   xmlns:rdf="http://www.w3.org/1999/02/22-rdf-syntax-ns#"
           xmlns:rdfs="http://www.w3.org/2000/01/rdf-schema#"
           xmlns:dc="http://purl.org/dc/elements/1.1/">

<rdf:Property rdf:about="http://purl.org/net/shklar/rdfschema/sample/firstAuthor">
  <rdfs:subClassOf rdf:resource="http://purl.org/dc/elements/1.1/creator"/>
  <rdfs:necessity rdf:href="http://www.w3.org/TR/WD-RDF-Schema#ExactlyOne"/>
  <rdfs:label xml:lang="en-US">First Author</rdfs:label>
  <rdfs:comment xml:lang="en-US">
    The author whose name appears first on the book cover.
  </rdfs:comment>
  <rdfs:isDefinedBy rdf:resource="http://purl.org/net/shklar/rdfschema/sample/"/>
</rdf:Property>
<rdf:Property rdf:about="http://purl.org/net/shklar/rdfschema/sample/secondAuthor">
  <rdfs:subClassOf rdf:resource="http://purl.org/dc/elements/1.1/creator"/>
  <rdfs:necessity rdf:href="http://www.w3.org/TR/WD-RDF-Schema#ZeroOrOne"/>
  <rdfs:label xml:lang="en-US">Second Author</rdfs:label>
  <rdfs:comment xml:lang="en-US">
    The author whose name appears second on the book cover.
  </rdfs:comment>
  <rdfs:isDefinedBy rdf:resource="http://purl.org/net/shklar/rdfschema/sample/"/>
</rdf:Property>
</rdf:RDF>
```

Figure 13.11 Sample RDF schema.

```
<?xml version="1.0"?>
<rdf:RDF xmlns:rdf="http://www.w3.org/1999/02/22-rdf-syntax-ns#"
         xmlns:dc="http://purl.org/dc/elements/1.1/"
         xmlns:book="http://purl.org/net/shklar/rdfschema/sample/">

  <rdf:Description rdf:about="http://purl.org/net/waabook">
    <book:firstAuthor>http://purl.org/net/rlr</book:firstAuthor>
    <book:firstAuthor>http://purl.org/net/shklar</book:firstAuthor>
    <dc:publisher>http://www.wiley.com</dc:description>
  </rdf:Description>
  <rdf:Description rdf:about="http://purl.org/net/rwswbook">
    <book:secondAuthor>http://purl.org/net/shklar</book:secondAuthor>
  <dc:publisher>http://www.iospress.com</dc:description>
  </rdf:Description>
</rdf:RDF>
```

Figure 13.12   An invalid RDF model according to the schema in Figure 13.11.

constraints – a book always has at least one author, but may have two or more; only one author may appear in the particular position on the cover. Note that the order of triples representing the dc:creator property in Figure 13.7 and Figure 13.10 is arbitrary and not semantically meaningful.

Now that we have defined our new properties and specified the authoritative location of the new schema (rdfs:isDefinedBy), we can modify the model in Figure 13.10 to take advantage of the new specification (see Figure 13.12). As you see, we introduce the additional namespace book and use it to qualify the new properties. The XML document in Figure 13.12 is valid but the RDF model it represents is not – it violates the rdfs:necessity constraint imposed on the firstAuthor property in Figure 13.11. This required property must occur exactly once.

A valid version of the RDF model is shown in Figure 13.13. The firstAuthor property now occurs exactly once in each description, as mandated by the schema. The original model does not

```
<?xml version="1.0"?>
<rdf:RDF xmlns:rdf="http://www.w3.org/1999/02/22-rdf-syntax-ns#"
         xmlns:dc="http://purl.org/dc/elements/1.1/"
         xmlns:book="http://purl.org/net/shklar/rdfschema/sample/">

  <rdf:Description rdf:about="http://purl.org/net/waabook">
    <book:secondAuthor>http://purl.org/net/rlr</book:secondAuthor>
    <book:firstAuthor>http://purl.org/net/shklar</book:firstAuthor>
    <dc:publisher>http://www.wiley.com</dc:description>
  </rdf:Description>
  <rdf:Description rdf:about="http://purl.org/net/rwswbook">
    <book:firstAuthor>Unknown</book:firstAuthor>
    <book:secondAuthor>http://purl.org/net/shklar</book:secondAuthor>
    <dc:publisher>http://www.iospress.com</dc:description>
  </rdf:Description>
</rdf:RDF>
```

Figure 13.13   A valid version of the model according to the schema in Figure 13.11.

contain information about the first author of the second book, so we have to use a generic literal (Unknown) to comply with the schema. To repeat the obvious, RDF Schema is not an alternative to the XML Schema. Figure 13.12 and Figure 13.13 both represent valid XML documents, but the RDF model represented in Figure 13.12 is not valid. RDF Schema provides the same service for RDF models as the XML Schema does for XML documents – it enables specialized applications.

13.2.2   Composite Capabilities/Preference Profiles

One of the early applications of RDF is the *Composite Capabilities/Preference Profiles* (CC/PP) specification, which is a joint effort of W3C and the Wireless Access Protocol (WAP) Forum. The idea is quite simple – let the devices and user agents describe themselves and make those descriptions available to smart services that tailor their responses accordingly. User agents that run on different platforms may expect different content types (e.g., XML, XHTML, XHTML MP) and structures (e.g., different arrangement into tables and cards or different use of graphics).

The flexibility of RDF makes it possible to create self-describing device specifications based on their screen size, keyboard (if any), display characteristics, and other parameters. Devices are represented as composites of features, and properly constructed services do not need to be modified every time a new device comes out. Services can combine information about devices and user agents with information about connection bandwidth and use it dynamically to customize output.

Targeted transformations of specialized XML documents to XHTML and XHTML MP formats taking into account device and platform limitations, lend themselves to the application of XSLT technology. XSLT style sheets can be composed from parameterized feature-specific components. An efficient server can optimize style sheet construction by caching XSLT components as well as intermediate composites. For example, the server could cache device-specific style sheets based on device profiles and combine them with style sheet components that are determined by the operating system, user agent software, and connection bandwidth.

Figure 13.14 contains a CC/PP-compliant description of a device (the fictitious 123 from the XYZ Corporation). In this example, rdf, ccpp, and prf prefixes are bound to URIs for, respectively, RDF Syntax, CC/PP Structure, and the WAP Forum's User Agent Profile namespaces. The first element of the specification is the rdf:Description for our device; it contains only one specification component that describes the device hardware. The rdf:type element references the schema element that identifies the hardware platform; prf:CPU defines the default CPU; prf:Vendor defines the default manufacturer of the device; prf:Model defines the default model designation; prf:ScreenSize defines the default screen size; and prf:ImageCapable indicates default support for rendering images.

Figure 13.15 contains CC/PP-compliant descriptions of software for the same device. It includes a component that describes the device operating system (the hypothetical XYZ-OS, in prf:OSName). Acceptable content is limited to text/plain and text/vnd.wap.xhtml+xml (prf:CcppAccept). A second component describes the user agent as the version of Mozilla that supports tables (prf:BrowserName, prf:BrowserVersion, and prf:TablesCapable).

The semantic grounding of CC/PP concepts is based on existing specifications. For example, acceptable values for prf:CcppAccept are MIME types and acceptable values for prf:Vendor and prf:Model come from industry registries. This "by reference" approach to defining semantics is well-suited for the real world. There are a growing number of CC/PP specifications for wireless devices developed and maintained by equipment manufacturers.

```
<?xml version="1.0"?>
<rdf:RDF xmlns:rdf="http://www.w3.org/1999/02/22-rdf-syntax-ns#"
         xmlns:ccpp:="http://www.w3.org/2006/09/20-ccpp-schema#"
         xmlns:prf="http://www.wapforum.org/profiles/UAPROF/ccppschema-20010330#">
  <rdf:Description rdf:about="http://www.xyz-wireless.com/123Profile">
    <ccpp:component>
      <rdf:Description rdf:ID="HardwarePlatform">
        <rdf:type rdf:resource="http://www.wapforum.org/profiles/UAPROF/
                              ccppschema-20010330#HardwarePlatform"/>
        <prf:CPU>Dual: XYZ Special</prf:CPU>
        <prf:Vendor>XYZ Corp.</prf:Vendor>
        <prf:Model>123</prf:Model>
        <prf:Keyboard>PhoneKeypad</prf:Keyboard>
        <prf:ScreenSize>200x240</prf:ScreenSize>
        <prf:ImageCapable>No</prf:ImageCapable>
      </rdf:Description>
    </ccpp:component>
  </rdf:Description>
</rdf:RDF>
```

Figure 13.14 Sample device description.

Individual devices and user agents often differ from default configurations. For example, my personal version of the 123 device from the XYZ Corporation may have an optional screen and may be image capable. Fortunately, it is possible to incorporate default configurations by reference as in Figure 13.16.

The prf:Defaults element references the default profile from Figure 13.14, which is available from http://www.xyz-wireless.com/123Profile. Here, prf:ScreenSize and prf:ImageCapable override default properties of the device. The resulting profile is uploaded to the profile registry when the device first goes on-line or after the profile is modified. The server-side agent that controls the automated assembly of XSLT style sheets would interpret the profile. Ideally, this style sheet would produce markup that can take advantage of optional features added to the device.

CC/PP, in combination with XML and XSLT, enables applications that can serve content to a wide variety of desktop and wireless devices. Most importantly, properly constructed applications would require minimal or no modification to expand support to new and modified devices and software platforms.

13.2.3 RDF query language

With RDF and RDF-based specifications gaining recognition, the scope and variety of RDF applications have grown as well. This has created a need for uniform facilities for querying RDF models, with the ultimate goal of searching the web for semantic information. While XQuery can be used to extract information from XML representations of RDF models, there are two major problems with this approach:

- XQuery is designed to extract data from XML documents. Queries have to be expressed in terms of the XML graph, elements, and attributes. Trying to use XQuery to query XML representations of RDF models is just as painful as using SQL to query XML graphs stored in relational tables.

```
<?xml version="1.0"?>
<rdf:RDF xmlns:rdf="http://www.w3.org/1999/02/22-rdf-syntax-ns#"
         xmlns:cccp="http://www.w3.org/2006/09/20-ccpp-schema#"
         xmlns:prf=" http://www.wapforum.org/profiles/UAPROF/ccppschema-20010330#">
  <rdf:Description rdf:about="http://www.xyz-wireless.com/123Profile">
  <ccpp:component>
    <rdf:Description rdf:ID="SoftwarePlatform">
      <rdf:type rdf:resource="http://www.wapforum.org/profiles/UAPROF/
                              ccppschema-20010330#SoftwarePlatform"/>
      <prf:OSName>XYZ-OS</prf:OSName>
      <prf:CcppAccept>
        <rdf:Bag>
          <rdf:li>text/plain</rdf:li>
          <rdf:li>text/vnd.wap.xhtml+xml</rdf:li>
        </rdf:Bag>
      </prf:CcppAccept>
    </rdf:Description>
  </ccpp:component>
  <ccpp:component>
    <rdf:Description rdf:ID="BrowserUA">
      <rdf:type rdf:resource="http://www.wapforum.org/profiles/UAPROF/
                              ccppschema-20000405#BrowserUA"/>
      <prf:BrowserName>Mozilla</prf:BrowserName>
      <prf:BrowserVersion>Symbian</prf:BrowserVersion>
      <prf:TablesCapable>Yes</prf:TablesCapable>
    </rdf:Description>
  </ccpp:component>
  </rdf:Description>
</rdf:RDF>
```

Figure 13.15   Sample description of device software.

- XML is just one representation for RDF models. There is considerable overhead in applying XQuery to search RDF models represented as graphs or using the N3 notation.

The SPARQL query language is designed specifically to extract data from RDF models. Most SPARQL queries contain *triple patterns*, which differ from RDF triples in that each of the subject, predicate and object may be a variable. Triple patterns combine into a graph representing an RDF query. A *match* is a substitution for variables in the query with RDF terms resulting in a graph equivalent to a subgraph of a queried model.

Consider the RDF model presented in Figure 13.8. We construct the first SPARQL query in Figure 13.17a to retrieve books authored by <http://purl.org/net/shklar>. The WHERE clause contains a triple pattern with the variable ?book as the object. The pattern matches two triples in Figure 13.8 and the matching variable substitutions are shown in Figure 13.17b. The purpose of the second query in Figure 13.17 is to retrieve all authors and their books in the graph in Figure 13.8. The WHERE clause contains a triple pattern with the variables ?author and ?book as the subject and object, respectively. This query produces the variable substitutions for the three matching triples shown in Figure 13.17c.

```
<?xml version="1.0"?>
<rdf:RDF xmlns:rdf="http://www.w3.org/1999/02/22-rdf-syntax-ns#"
         xmlns:cccp="http://www.w3.org/2006/09/20-ccpp-schema#"
         xmlns:prf="http://www.wapforum.org/profiles/UAPROF/ccppschema-20010330#">
  <rdf:Description about="http://www.my-wireless-service.com/registry/123675894">
    <ccpp:component>
      <rdf:Description rdf:ID="HardwarePlatform">
        <rdf:type rdf:resource="http://www.wapforum.org/profiles/UAPROF/
                              ccppschema-20000405#HardwarePlatform"/>
        <prf:Defaults rdf:resource="http://www.xyz-wireless.com/123Profile" />
        <prf:ScreenSize>220x280</prf:ScreenSize>
        <prf:ImageCapable>Yes</prf:ImageCapable>
      </rdf:Description>
    </ccpp:component>
  </rdf:Description>
</rdf:RDF>
```

Figure 13.16 Individual hardware profile.

```
PREFIX dc:<http://purl.org/dc/elements/1.1/>
PREFIX id:<http://purl.org/net/>
SELECT ?book WHERE
{
   id:shklar dc:creator ?book.
}
SELECT ?author ?book WHERE
{
   ?author dc:creator ?book.
}
```

(a)

book
<http://purl.org/net/waabook>
<http://purl.org/net/rwswbook>

author	book
<http://purl.org/net/shklar>	<http://purl.org/net/waabook>
<http://purl.org/net/shklar>	<http://purl.org/net/rwswbook>
<http://purl.org/net/rlr>	<http://purl.org/net/waabook>

(b)   (c)

Figure 13.17 Querying the RDF model: a) two SPARQL queries, b) the result of the first query and c) the result of the second query.

The query in Figure 13.18a consists of two triple patterns. Within a graph pattern, a variable must have the same value no matter where it is used. In this example, only one book is an object of both the <http://purl.org/dc/elements/1.1/creator> predicate and the <http://purl.org/dc/elements/1.1/publisher> predicate, the subject of which is <http://www.wiley.com>. This query produces the variable substitutions for the three matching triples shown in Figure 13.18b. Notice that only two rows satisfy this query, as opposed to three

```
PREFIX dc: http://purl.org/dc/elements/1.1/
PREFIX id: <http://purl.org/net/>
PREFIX wiley: <http://www.wiley.com>
SELECT ?author ?book WHERE
{
   ?author dc:creator ?book.
   wiley:  dc:publisher ?book.
}
```

(a)

author	book
<http://purl.org/net/shklar>	<http://purl.org/net/waabook>
<http://purl.org/net/rlr>	<http://purl.org/net/waabook>

(b)

Figure 13.18   a) A multi-pattern SPARQL query and b) its result.

rows in Figure 13.17c. The row for the book published by <http://www.iospress.com> is not included because it does not satisfy the second pattern in the query in Figure 13.18a.

SPARQL is a sophisticated language that makes it possible to match subgraphs in an RDF graph using *triple patterns*, which are triples that may contain variables in place of concrete values. The variables act as "wildcards" that match terms in the RDF model. We discussed the SELECT query, which can be used to extract data from an RDF graph, returning it as a tabular result set. We have not discussed complex constructs of the language but, as with XQuery, the examples should provide a flavor of the language expressions and query construction.

13.3   Future of Web Application Frameworks

Although web application frameworks have come a long way during the course of the last few years, there are still outstanding issues with currently available frameworks that aggravate existing problems in web application development and deployment.

13.3.1   One more time: separate content from presentation

Foremost among the outstanding issues is the difficulty that arises when content and presentation are mixed. When this mixture occurs, collisions are bound to occur between web page designers and programmers responsible for the development and maintenance of a web application. We still do not have a framework that enforces module-level separation of responsibility. This means that input from both designers and programmers is required to create and modify web application modules. Depending on the framework, designers must provide input for code modules or programmers must provide input for page view modules. Even MVC-compliant frameworks, such as Struts, do not have all the answers. The view component in these frameworks is supposed to be the responsibility of page designers, but the technologies used (e.g., JSPs) are still too complex and open-ended for non-programmers to handle on their own.

The inefficiency that arises from this situation should not be underestimated. The current state of affairs dictates that designers first come up with a page layout based on creative input, which programmers then modify to embed programming constructs. In all probability, such a module becomes a hodgepodge of design elements and programming constructs that neither programmers nor designers have control over. Efforts employed by various frameworks to separate these elements within a module have not been entirely successful. In theory, designers could make direct changes to the module. In practice, a seemingly simple change in page layout made by a designer may require radical reworking of the module. Programmers must either embed the constructs they need all over again in the new layout or try to fit new and modified design elements into the existing module.

Since we have been bringing up the issue of separating content from presentation throughout the book, it is about time we proposed some solutions. A solution would require a two-pronged approach. First, the next generation of web application frameworks should enforce a cleaner separation between application code, representing the `Controller` in the MVC model, and "pages" representing the `View`. Application code should establish a page context that determines discrete display components that can be selected for presentation on the page. Second, the tools used to develop web applications, especially front-end design tools, need to catch up with the rest of the technology and support integration and cooperation with these frameworks.

As we suggested earlier, pages should be structured as templates that use markup languages such as XHTML, XHTML MP, VoiceXML, and SMIL. Style sheet technologies, such as CSS and XSLT should be used to provide flexible formatting. Page templates should be "owned" and maintained by page designers, who use display components available within the page context. Programmers should be responsible for making these components available to designers through standard uniform interfaces. The display components should support a simple limited set of programmatic constructs for dynamic content generation through iteration, conditional logic and external resource inclusion. The simplicity is important because it is designers, not programmers, who own and maintain the templates.

Designers should be the ones who decide how to present the results and they should be able to make these decisions without requiring programmer assistance. A clean separation between application code and presentation views is a necessary condition for this to happen.

Keeping Complex Processing Out of the Page

The page is not the appropriate container for complex business logic or, arguably, even for deciding which of several possible views should be presented. If such processing is required, its place is within the application code.

When an application module produces a discrete atomic result, it can be included in the page context as a display component that the designer can use in the presentation. For example, a processing component that determines the "state" of a transaction performed by the application (e.g., "completed" or "in progress") should set the value of a display component in the page context that reports this state. Designers can map different states to messages of their choosing (e.g., "This transaction is still in progress. Please wait.") and make use of this in the page layout. (Note that the actual messages are not in the realm of application code, so modifying them does not require a code change.)

On the other hand, when the difference between the possible results of such processing is dramatic enough, the application code should make a choice as to which page should present the results, rather than deferring the decision between coarse-grained presentation alternatives to the page itself. In other words, if the presentation to be employed when the state is "completed" is radically different from the one desired when the state is "in progress", it may not be advisable to expose the state to designers within the page context. Doing this would lead to several alternative presentations embedded in one page. Instead, the application code should choose between different templates. This way, each presentation is an individual template that is the designer's responsibility.

All the aforementioned suggestions are feasible but not enforced within existing frameworks. We hope to see that changed in the next generation of frameworks.

13.3.2 Use the right tools for the job

The second facet of the solution is to make the tools used by page designers functional within these new frameworks. Today, page designers rarely code HTML by hand; they make use of automated page design tools such as Adobe Dreamweaver, Microsoft Visual Studio, and the open source Eclipse IDE. In order for these tools to work properly within the kinds of framework described above, they would need to provide support for the dynamic constructs that can be embedded within a page.

For example, support for iterative constructs in these tools could be designed to allow creation of a `foreach` block where the substitution variables are populated with data dynamically generated by the tool, so that designers can get an idea of what the final result would look like. A more sophisticated approach would be to integrate the tool with the development environment, so that the tool has knowledge of what substitution variable names are available from the page context, and of their data types and likely sizes. Similar support could be provided for constructs used for conditional logic and inclusion of external resources.

Figure 13.19 shows a page fragment using JSTL tags for iterative and conditional processing. Designers need to see the results of their work as they progress, but attempting to preview the JSP fragment shown in Figure 13.19 would not work: browsers would ignore the JSP tags and display the substitution variables (e.g., `${transactiondata.order_number}`), as in Figure 13.20.

To achieve tighter integration between front-end design tools and back-end application frameworks, one solution is to introduce a browser preview function that understands the iterative and conditional constructs used in the underlying framework. At the very least, the design tools should mock up an appropriate page layout, based on heuristic estimates for each of the display components, presenting "dummy" data of the appropriate type and length so that the browser preview is meaningful to the designer.

Figure 13.21 is a mockup of a dialog box that could be used in a page design tool, to control presenting results from the `foreach` tag when the designer previews the page. Figure 13.22 shows how a browser with framework integration would preview the results. In a more integrated environment, the design tool might have access to application configuration information and derive the estimates without human intervention.

Advances in web application frameworks indicate that we are moving in the right direction. Smarter frameworks already provide intelligence in their iteration constructs (e.g., the `foreach` directives or tags in Velocity and JSTL) to make them *class agnostic*. In other words, they don't care what kind of object is returned from a data request, as long as it is an object that they can somehow iterate over (e.g., an array, `Enumeration`, `Iterator`, `Collection`, or `Vector`). This may enable more seamless

```
<table border="1" align="center">
  <tr>
    <td valign="bottom" align="center"><b>Order<br>Number</b></td>
    <td valign="bottom" align="center"><b>Customer<br>ID</b></td>
    <td valign="bottom" align="center"><b>Total<br>Amount</b></td>
    <td valign="bottom" align="center"><b>Completed?</b></td>
  </tr>
  <c:foreach var="transactiondata"
             items="${sessionScope.transactionResults}">
    <tr>
      <td align="left">${transactiondata.order_number}</td>
      <td align="left">${transactiondata.customer_id}</td>
      <td align="left">${transactiondata.total_amount}</td>
      <td align="center">
        <c:if test="${transactiondata.completed}">*</c:if>
      </td>
    </tr>
  </c:foreach>
</table>
```

Figure 13.19   Example of page fragment using JSTL `foreach` and `if` tags.

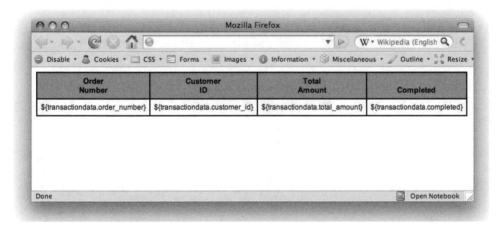

Figure 13.20   Browser preview of the page fragment without framework integration.

integration between front-end design tools and application frameworks. It would be nice to see these class-agnostic constructs extended to support tabular objects as well (e.g., RowSets, collections of JavaBeans, or Lists of Map objects).

13.3.3   Simplicity

The inordinate complexity of application development frameworks continues to be a problem in the web development world. Too often, we are willing to complicate simple tasks to achieve maximum flexibility when developing APIs and tools for other developers. This can make the tools difficult for

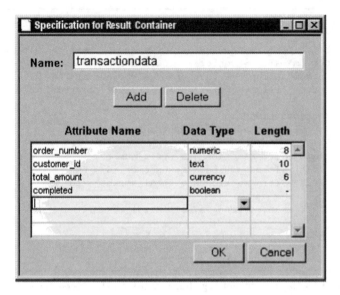

Figure 13.21   Dialog box for specifying content to be displayed by an iterative page construct.

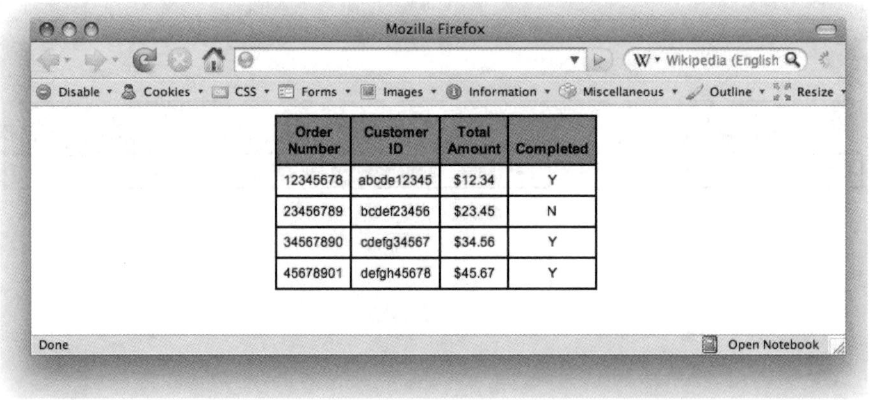

Figure 13.22   Browser preview of the page fragment with framework integration.

anyone to use – except perhaps for the developers themselves! There have even been on-line debates among developers about "civil disobedience" against overly complicated specifications that make it difficult to do simple things in a simple way.

Spring, Ruby on Rails, and other similar approaches have arisen and flourished in reaction to this complexity. To a large degree, they are a rebellion against the direction taken by Java Platform, Enterprise Edition (Java EE). These approaches have demonstrated that power and flexibility need not come at the price of inordinate complexity. They employ scaffolding (automated construction of application skeletons), greatly reducing the need for repetitive boilerplate code and the configuration nightmares of "XML hell". Java EE 5 has sought to address many of the concerns about unnecessary complexity in application development and deployment. Only time will tell which of these approaches, if any, wins out. Suffice to say that it is no longer reasonable to produce a framework whose power comes at the cost of increased complexity in the development process.

Part of the problem in the web application framework space is the difference in perspective between developers and the supposed target audience of the presentation-level tools, the page designers. Developers see it as "no big deal" to "simply" write a program or script, insert a code snippet, or compile and build a tool. This is why programmatic approaches appeal more to developers than to page designers. Unfortunately, the price for using programmatic approaches is that programmers must get involved in the maintenance of the view component. This means that programmers and not designers must implement even trivial design changes. Programmers who advocate these approaches don't seem to realize that they are making extra work for themselves in the long run.

Creative and business staff may sometimes have good reasons for requesting frequent changes to page layouts, but programmers see recurring requests to "tweak" page layouts as an intrusion on their time, which would be better spent developing applications. When the nature of the application development approach requires that programmers are the ones who make such changes, the application's flexibility and viability suffer. Page designers (or even site administrators) should be able to make these changes themselves, without programmer intervention.

Using programmers to perform trivial tasks is not only a misapplication of staff resources; it is also an inordinate waste of time for the entire organization. When programmers make changes to code, the code must go through an entire "build" cycle, where it is recompiled, unit tested, integration tested, packaged for deployment, deployed to a "test" environment for functional and regression testing, and finally deployed to the production environment. Changes made at the presentation level (or through an administrative interface) can bypass a good portion of this process. Designers can preview them locally, approve them, and deploy them to production.

One More Reason for Separating Content and Presentation

This brings us back to another reason why we do not want programmers creating markup as part of the application code.

Imagine an application that invokes the Weather Service we described earlier in the chapter. Suppose this application provides all the information obtained from the Weather Service in a page fragment that includes formatting:

```
<table border="1">
  <tr>
    <td align="right"><b>Temp:</b></td>
    <td align="left">28&deg; f</td>
  </tr>
  <tr>
    <td align="right"><b>Conditions:</b></td>
    <td align="left">Sunny</td>
  </tr>
  <tr>
```

```
        <td align="right"><b>Wind:</b></td>
        <td align="left">SE 5 MPH</td>
     </tr>
  </table>
```

If creative or business people were to decide that this formatting should be changed (e.g., the temperature should stand out by itself in large red text), this would require a change to the code rather than to the page template.

By inserting individual data items associated with the Weather Service into the page context as discrete display components, we bring the layout completely under the control of the page designers, allowing them to change it themselves.

For example, the following code uses discrete display components in the page context:

```
<table border="1">
  <tr>
     <td align="right"><b>Temp:</b></td>
     <td align="left">${weather.temp}&deg; ${weather.tempscale}</Td>
  </tr>
  <tr>
     <td align="right"><b>Conditions:</b></td>
     <td align="left">${weather.conditions}</td>
  </tr>
  <tr>
     <td align="right"><b>Wind:</b></td>
     <td align="left">${weather.winddirection}
               ${weather.windvelocity} ${weather.windvelocityunits}
     </td>
  </tr>
</table>
```

The following code is an alternative way to specify the same page fragment using discrete display components:

```
<table border="0">
  <tr>
     <td align="center" valign="center">
       <img src="/images/weather/${weather.conditions}.gif">
       <br><span class="small">${weather.conditions}</span>
     </td>
     <td align="center" class="bigred" bgcolor=#ffff99>
       ${weather.temp}&deg; ${weather.tempscale}
     </td>
  </tr>
  <tr>
     <td colspan="2" align="center">
```

```
        ${weather.winddirection}
        ${weather.windvelocity} ${weather.windvelocityunits}
    </td>
  </tr>
</table>
```

This page fragment could be rendered in the following way:

```
<table border="0">
  <tr>
    <td align="center" valign="center">
      <img src="/images/weather/Sunny.gif">
      <br><span class="small">Sunny</span>
    </td>
    <td align="center" class="bigred" bgcolor=#ffff99>
      28&deg; f
    </td>
  </tr>
  <tr>
    <td colspan="2" align="center">
      SE 5 MPH
    </td>
  </tr>
</table>
```

Designers want ready-made, user-friendly tools that do not require them to become programmers. Perhaps the root of this problem is in the question: "Why are people who don't care about simplicity, ease-of-use, and user-friendliness building interfaces and tools for people who do?"

Many people in the open-source community have a disdain for Microsoft and the products they offer. In fairness, Microsoft products have been successful in the marketplace, primarily because they were designed to keep simple things simple, (e.g., through user-friendly interfaces called "wizards"). The argument that these products can *only* do the simple things has some merit. Fortunately, this is not an "either–or" situation. Tools, APIs, and application development frameworks can be designed to make simple things simple for those who design, develop, deploy, and administer web applications, while still providing flexibility for those who need sophisticated functionality. It is not unlike the dichotomy between those who prefer command-line interfaces and those who prefer GUIs. There is no reason both cannot exist side by side, in the same environment, with the individual free to choose the mode in which they want to work.

It is easier to keep simple things simple in a web application when the framework is designed to support such simplicity. Even in the absence of such a framework, it is still the responsibility of web application architects to employ sound design practices, so that tasks that *ought to be* easy to perform actually are. They should rigorously analyze and document application requirements upfront, including use case analysis to determine the tasks likely to be performed. Web architects have to walk the thin line between excessive flexibility (and the resulting complexity) and supporting evolutionary changes without rebuilding the entire application. Proper utilization of these practices should ensure that the application is flexible, extensible, and viable.

Such goals can be accomplished within existing frameworks (e.g., Struts), but only by following solid application design and development practices. Existing frameworks do not *enforce* good design practices; the best of them simply *encourage* them. We hope that the next generation of frameworks will make it easier to follow these practices, so that web applications can be more flexible and can be developed more quickly.

13.4 Current Trends

In this section, we consider current trends and enabling technologies in web applications.

13.4.1 Everything old is new again

Those of us who have been around the software industry for a while have a first-hand perspective on its cyclic nature. Trends in software move back and forth like a pendulum. Years ago, hierarchical databases were the way to go, then relational databases appeared on the horizon and changed all that. More recently, the complexities and performance issues associated with relational databases have given way to renewed interest in simpler hierarchical approaches to data management (e.g., LDAP).

Analyzing the history and pre-history of web applications reveals similar patterns. Back in the days of mainframe systems, end-user applications used block mode terminals (e.g., IBM 3270) that employed request–response protocols. Entering data into fixed form fields locally and then pressing the ENTER key to transmit was seen as a limitation, so the next generation of client–server applications, which ran mostly on PCs, enabled live updates of data. The client–server technology would transmit information to the server as it was entered and live data updates produced on the server would be displayed simultaneously on the client.

These client–server applications had serious problems. They used non-standard protocols, and the client-side application components had to be bundled with proprietary protocol stacks, hence the label "fat clients." The lack of standardization in communication protocols also meant that deployment and maintenance of these applications was inordinately complex.

The web browser represented a return to interactive applications that used a request–response protocol, namely HTTP. The limitations of a simple request–response protocol were readily apparent from the very inception of the web. The lack of support for state maintenance in the original HTTP protocol led to the introduction of cookies. JavaScript was added into the mix as a programmatic mechanism for enabling dynamic page presentations.

HTTP is still the underlying technology supporting web transactions, but over time things have evolved significantly. Web interactions may once have had more in common with IBM 3270 terminal transactions but today, thanks largely to AJAX and Web 2.0 technologies, these interactions more closely resemble the immediacy associated with traditional client–server applications.

Frameworks such as Adobe's Flex and Microsoft's Silverlight take this a step further, embedding *Rich Internet Applications* directly into web pages. Java applets were an early attempt to provide similar functionality, but they achieved only limited success. It remains to be seen whether the Rich Internet Application frameworks will catch on as the next step in the evolution of web applications.

13.4.2   Social networking and community web sites

Social networking on the web has also experienced a pendulum swing of sorts. In the early days of the web, before e-commerce applications had taken hold, personal web pages were a significant aspect of on-line life. In those days, people manually built their own personal pages, "blogged" (before the word had even been concocted) by manually updating their pages, and linked to each other through link pages and "web rings". Today, millions of people seek to build an on-line presence of their own and most of them don't have the skill set to create or manage their own web pages. Web sites that support creation and management of personal web pages, automated services for blogging, and maintaining interconnections with others have taken off, in particular MySpace and Facebook. As more of these sites arise, the ability of users to manage and coordinate profiles on multiple social networking sites becomes critical, and we are already seeing significant development activity in this area. Privacy issues and concerns about parental controls help to ensure that there will be ongoing development effort in enhancing these web applications.

The semantic web that Tim Berners-Lee described was actually the second part of his dream for the future of the web. The first part of that dream was the collaboration between people that the web facilitates, with "shared knowledge" accessible to "groups of all sizes, interacting electronically with as much ease as they do now in person." He imagined the web "as something to which everyone [would have] immediate access, not just to browse, but to create." The social networking "community web sites", along with collaborative web applications, such as Wikipedia, and *collaborative tagging/social bookmarking* applications, such as de.licio.us and Digg, are helping to make that part of the dream a reality.

13.4.3   Cloud computing and "Weblications"

The term *cloud computing* refers to on-line services (sometimes called *weblications*) that offer functionality commonly provided by desktop applications. Application data files are managed by web users and stored on servers running web applications. Users connect to these applications remotely through desktop browsers, cellular phones, and other web-capable devices. Examples of cloud computing services include:

- photo- and video-sharing applications (e.g. Flickr and YouTube);
- web-based, customer-relationship management (CRM) solutions (e.g. Salesforce.com);
- financial applications, including on-line brokerage (e.g. eTrade), tax preparation (e.g. TurboTax), and payment-processing services (e.g. PayPal);
- web-based email services (e.g. Gmail);
- remote office-productivity software (e.g. Google Docs);
- other "software-as-a-service" (SaaS) applications, such as Adobe's "Create PDF" service.

The collaborative editing functionality provided by *blog* services and *wiki* applications, as well as the social networking sites such as MySpace and Facebook, are other examples of cloud computing.

What's in a Cloud?

The name "cloud computing" is a reference to the fact that, historically, an image of a cloud has been used to represent unknown external systems in network diagrams. Since the Internet can be thought of as a nebulous external network outside the boundaries of a local environment, the cloud has become a natural metaphor for representing the Internet.

One of the best-known examples of a commercial cloud computing service is *Google Docs*. It provides through a web browser functionality that is usually associated with office productivity software such as Microsoft Office (Word, Excel, and PowerPoint). Users can edit text documents, construct spreadsheets, and create presentations. The Google Docs user interface includes DHTML editing widgets, which provide functionality closely resembling a word processor, a spreadsheet, or a canvas. The files produced by Google Docs are stored on Google's servers and are only accessible by their creators and those to whom they grant access.

One element common to most cloud-computing services is user-identity management. Users want to manage access to the on-line content they have created. They may want to be the only ones who can view and edit that content, they may want to publish that content for all to see, or they may want to share it exclusively with family members, colleagues, and friends. An authentication mechanism is required to validate user identities. Such a mechanism implies the presence of a user registration process allowing people to sign up for access to the service. Users also need a mechanism to define and manage the list of other users that can access their content. An authorization mechanism that validates access permissions for authenticated users is also required.

Another feature found in many cloud-computing services is the ability to edit and configure user-supplied content. User-friendly mechanisms for uploading and editing content via a web client are critical. Laborious upload processes that do not provide users with immediate confirmation and instant gratification are not a recipe for success and should be avoided.

The DHTML editing widgets used in services such as Google Docs and Gmail are just one example of such a mechanism. Drag-and-drop functionality can be used to organize on-line address books and photo albums. More sophisticated photo-sharing services provide the ability to adjust, crop, and resize photos through their interfaces. These functions usually employ AJAX and DHTML, but sometimes they are implemented using Rich Internet Application (RIA) frameworks, such as Adobe Flex, or the Java Applet mechanism.

A common feature on social networking sites is the live status update (made popular by *Twitter*). Users can update their "status" (whatever they happen to be doing at the moment) from anywhere – including their cellular phones – so that their friends are informed instantaneously about their current activities wherever they are.

Live status updates and similar forms of real-time interactivity require that cloud-computing services be accessible via mobile devices (such as cellular phones, smart phones, and network-capable PDAs). To that end, well-designed services provide customized mobile versions of their web applications, with page layouts optimized for the smaller screens associated with mobile devices. The `User-Agent` header found in HTTP requests submitted to these services tells the application what kind of device is being used, allowing the application to tailor the presentation accordingly. Applications can employ separate CSS style sheets for mobile devices or create separate mobile-only versions of their web sites (e.g., m.google.com/). Some services even provide custom client applications that run only on specific devices (e.g., the iPhone).

13.5 Summary

Today, there is growing excitement behind the semantic web. Arguments against RDF are on the decrease and the RDF specification, which has seen relatively slow uptake, is gaining acceptance. The first RDF applications are already taking hold (e.g., CC/PP) and more are under development. The development of SPARQL is a major step in advancing real-world RDF applications.

In the future, web clients will be found in everything from medical monitoring devices to automobiles and household appliances. An ever-expanding variety of data will be collected and published by all sorts of currently unimaginable sensors and other devices. We will need the power and flexibility of the semantic web to make sense out of that brave new world. It is too early to say whether RDF will remain the main power behind the semantic web, but it is promising.

There is the growing realization in the web community that developers and designers are two distinctly separate groups with different needs. The next generation of web application development frameworks should address many of the pressing web application lifecycle problems that currently face developers and designers. These new frameworks will need to reduce dramatically the complexity associated with developing and deploying web applications. Frameworks such as Ruby on Rails have been successful in gaining traction in the web development community, precisely because they provide an environment in which application development is simplified without sacrificing power and flexibility.

The current generation of web applications, from blogs and wikis to social networking sites and cloud computing services, demonstrates the ever-changing nature of the web as a platform for software applications. A decade ago, few would have predicted the ascent of services such as Wikipedia, Facebook, YouTube, and Google Docs. As web technology continues to advance, the one thing we should expect is the unexpected.

QUESTIONS AND EXERCISES

1. What is RDF? What is the purpose of introducing the RDF specification?

2. What is the relationship between RDF and XML? Since an RDF model can be represented in XML, is it not enough to use XML Schema to impose constraints on the model? Why do we need an RDF Schema?

3. What is the relationship between RDF and Dublin Core?

4. What is the purpose of CC/PP? What is the relationship between CC/PP and RDF?

5. If your cell phone supports web browsing, can you find or define a CC/PP-compliant description for it?

6. Let us go back to the CarML markup language and XML documents, which resulted from the exercises in Chapter 5. Define an XQuery-compliant query to retrieve all red cars that have two doors and whose model year is no older than 2000.

7. Suppose that you have access not only to documents describing cars, but to the owner records as well (you can make assumptions about the structure of these records). Can you define a query to retrieve all red cars that have a six-cylinder engine and are owned by a person who is less than 25 years old?

8. What is the purpose of SPARQL? Why is it not enough to apply XQuery to RDF models represented in XML?

9. Consider the RDF model in Figure 13.8. Define a SPARQL query to retrieve books authored by both `<http://purl.org/net/shklar>` and `<http://purl.org/net/rlr>`.

10. What future advances in web application development approaches would you consider to be most important? Explain.

11. Imagine that you work for a company that publishes content on its web site. Page designers build web page layouts, which developers must translate into code embedded in server-side application components. Any change to a page layout (e.g., modifying the color scheme or the heading fonts and sizes or changing the displayed image containing the company logo) requires that developers update the application code. A full development cycle (including integration testing, quality assurance, and staging) must be performed before such changes can be incorporated in the production environment. What would you suggest to improve this process?

13.6   Bibliography

Alur, Deepak *et al.*, 2003. *Core J2EE Patterns*, *2nd Edition*. Palo Alto (CA): Sun Microsystems Press (Prentice-Hall).

Berners-Lee, Tim, 2000. *Weaving the Web: The Original Design and Ultimate Destiny of the World Wide Web*. New York: HarperBusiness.

Fensel, Dieter *et al.* (eds), 2005. *Spinning the Semantic Web: Bringing the World Wide Web to Its Full Potential*. Cambridge (MA): MIT Press.

Powers, Shelley, 2003. *Practical RDF*. Sebastopol (CA): O'Reilly Media.

Vossen, Gottfried and Hageman, Stephan, 2007. *Unleashing Web 2.0: From Concepts to Creativity*. Burlington (MA): Morgan Kaufmann.

Walmsley, Priscilla, 2007. *XQuery*. Sebastopol (CA): O'Reilly Media.

13.7   Web Links

Organization for the Advancement of Structured Information Standards. Available at www.oasis-open.org/.

Web Services Interoperability Organization. Available at www.ws-i.org/.

13.8   Endnotes

1. http://www.ws-i.org/
2. http://www.oasis-open.org/

CHAPTER **14**

Conclusions

The web has entered a new era in which continued exponential growth is tempered with a new-found sophistication and maturity. It is impossible to imagine a serious business that does not have at least a basic web presence, while larger commercial enterprises employ sophisticated web applications for online search and e-commerce functions. Newspaper and magazine publishers are tripping over each other to cannibalize their shrinking print businesses in favor of growing their online presence. Technological advances have given rise to a new breed of "online hangouts", which have become the centers of an ever-growing social networking community. The influence of Microsoft's software monopoly has become less pervasive, thanks to Google's advantages in online search, Apple's advances in the world of mobile entertainment, and the increasing availability of powerful software from the open-source community.

Modern interactive applications are becoming increasingly complex. Content sharing creates intricate interdependencies between web sites. The proliferation of application development approaches is staggering, with new web development frameworks arising on what seems like a daily basis.

This rapidly changing landscape makes it critically important for developers to go back to the basics and learn core Internet technologies. In complex environments, HTTP remains the common denominator that ties together .NET, Java EE, PHP, Rails, and other seemingly incompatible approaches. Learning the underpinnings of HTTP interactions helps developers to understand APIs based on first principles. They can then apply that understanding to APIs and frameworks that come along in the future. This is a far cry from what we have seen historically in the web development community, where developers who were not well grounded in the underlying principles had to learn each new API from scratch.

Without HTTP-level analysis, problem resolution in complex environments may take a very long time and consume extensive resources. Casually implemented redirects can cause intermittent problems that are very difficult to diagnose. Browser and proxy caching are examples of functionality that almost never work correctly out-of-the-box, especially across application frameworks. Often tuning the HTTP headers responsible for caching responses is what makes the difference in optimizing applications for load and performance.

Understanding server and browser architecture is another critical component in building and maintaining effective web applications. It is essential for managing server and browser processing of HTTP requests, including URL resolution, content caching, redirects, session management, and access control. Familiarity with browser architecture is key to building effective presentation components involving XHTML, CSS, and JavaScript.

The world of web application development is changing at breakneck speed. Even though Web 2.0 is more of a business label than a technology trend, its emergence has breathed new life into JavaScript, CSS, and other technologies that have been around since the early days of the web. Web 2.0 has facilitated the advance of interactive applications that promote information sharing and collaboration between users. These applications have evolved into an expanding variety of web-based communities including social networking sites, blogs, and wikis.

Social networking and other modern web applications demand dynamic interactivity in presenting web pages. Advances in CSS and JavaScript brought about Dynamic HTML and eventually AJAX. Though AJAX was simply a clever repurposing of existing technology, it produced a critical paradigm shift in web application design. It gave JavaScript a new lease on life, dismissing the skeptics that predicted its inevitable demise. The hacks and bad coding practices long associated with JavaScript have given way to a more disciplined approach to building structured user interfaces.

Rapid growth in the number and diversity of desktop and mobile browsers adds to the complexity, making it necessary to design applications that can adjust their presentation dynamically. XML and XSL provide powerful mechanisms for tailoring presentation to address browser limitations. Server applications can consult HTTP headers for incoming requests to select appropriate XML templates and XSL transformations.

The importance of XML goes far beyond flexible presentations. It has become the enabling technology for application protocols, data feeds, multimedia packaging, metadata representation, and much more. XML specifications, including XML Schema, XSL, XSL FO, SOAP Web Services, XPath, and XQuery further the objective of making XML a mainstream technology. Support for web services is now an integral part of many commercial products.

The future is getting more interesting and exciting all the time. Imagine all the possibilities that the semantic web can open for us. Just a few years ago, it seemed both distant and abstract. Now, machine-understandable metadata is winding its way into real-life applications.

The key technology long associated with the semantic web is RDF. Due to its complexity, RDF has been relatively slow to gain momentum. However, recent developments show the growing acceptance of this technology. The first RDF applications are already taking hold (e.g., CC/PP) and more are under development. The development of SPARQL is a major step in advancing real-world RDF applications.

It is too early to say whether RDF will be the main power behind the semantic web, but the chances are good that it will. We would not be surprised if, in the next edition of the book, RDF and RDF applications find their way out of Chapter 13 and into the main body of the book.

In the more immediate future, the challenge is in finding better ways to combine different technologies into a single solution. The best of durable, flexible, and extensible web applications make use of the widely accepted MVC paradigm, combining a controller-driven framework with template-based views. A robust and viable approach that satisfies these requirements is the Struts framework, using

JSTL tags to support views. JSTL tags represent a huge step toward making JSPs accessible to page designers. JSP 2.1 further raises the bar, advancing the Expression Language as part of the JSP syntax and opening the door for the declarative definition of custom tags.

Alternative approaches to page presentation exist, both open source (Velocity) and proprietary (Adobe ColdFusion and Microsoft ASP.NET). The more flexible approaches strive to fit into the MVC paradigm, serving as a possible View component architecture for Struts and other similar frameworks.

Struts, however, is not the be-all-and-end-all of enterprise application frameworks. Challengers to Struts's supremacy include JBoss Seam, which uses EJB 3.0 coupled with Java Server Faces (JSF). JSF has made inroads of its own, even though it continues to exhibit significant incompatibilities with the JSP and JSTL approach.

Until recently, each new specification of Java Platform, Enterprise Edition (Java EE) has offered increased flexibility and power, but always at the cost of making even the simplest applications difficult to build, configure, and deploy. Reaction to this increasing complexity has led a significant number of developers to seek alternatives to Java and Java EE.

Many of them are considering rapid application development approaches such as Ruby on Rails. They tout Rails's use of scaffolding to build application skeletons automatically and its use of "convention over configuration" through intelligent defaults and naming conventions to minimize the need to edit configuration files manually. Still, Rails is in its infancy, and has competitors of its own in the Java world (e.g., Groovy on Grails). Only time will tell which frameworks will flourish.

Of course, the focus of this book is web application architecture, so naturally we wanted to present case studies that walked through the process of designing, developing, and deploying web applications. We dedicated an entire chapter to a simple real-estate broker application using Struts and JSTL. We also implemented a similar application using Ruby on Rails, to compare the benefits and drawbacks of the two approaches.

Web applications today are living and breathing entities. They have to enable user interactions, support the publication of new content, and exhibit flexibility in morphing their look-and-feel in reaction to both external events and internal campaigns (not to mention keeping it fresh to prevent end-user boredom). This works best if developers do not need to get involved in normal operational changes (e.g., simple page layout modifications and adding or deleting database entries). If they do have to get involved, things slow down because the changes need to go through the software lifecycle process. Developers would spend time implementing, testing, and deploying these changes, drawing resources away from new development. Moreover, positions involving an excessive amount of routine work tend to scare off more experienced and skilled developers.

As web applications expand beyond the desktop, the challenges developers face are compounded. Mobile phones and PDAs are already connected to the web. Very soon, common appliances in our homes and offices will become web-enabled. We will need a rich web services infrastructure to support this explosion in the number and variety of web devices. Web-based home automation applications will become more prevalent and home servers will be needed to coordinate entertainment centers, microwave ovens, backyard sprinklers, and home-security systems. These applications will access public and commercial web services to retrieve movies, cooking instructions, weather updates, and security advisories. In the not-too-distant future, people with health issues could have nanobots running HTTP servers in their bloodstream, instantaneously transmitting information about their current condition to their doctors.

With this explosive growth comes great risk. As web servers and applications move out of IT centers and into the hands of individuals, security and reliability become even more critical. Designers and developers must be vigilant in building applications that limit the threat of web-borne viruses, worms, and other forms of attack. Likewise, systems need to be self-maintaining so that the software can be kept current, ensuring that both bug fixes and security updates are deployed as soon as possible.

The next generation of web application development frameworks should address many of the pressing problems faced by developers and designers of web applications. We hope this book has prepared you, not only to understand the current generation of web technology but also to play a part in the development of the next generation.

Leon Shklar and Rich Rosen
New York, October 31, 2008

Index